AF348491

Everything, Always, Everywhere

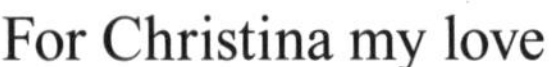

For Christina my love

Everything, Always, Everywhere
Rafaël Rozendaal

With contributions by
Marvin Jordan
Kodama Kanazawa
Christiane Paul
Margriet Schavemaker

Valiz, Amsterdam

TABLE OF CONTENTS

Into Time .us, 2012

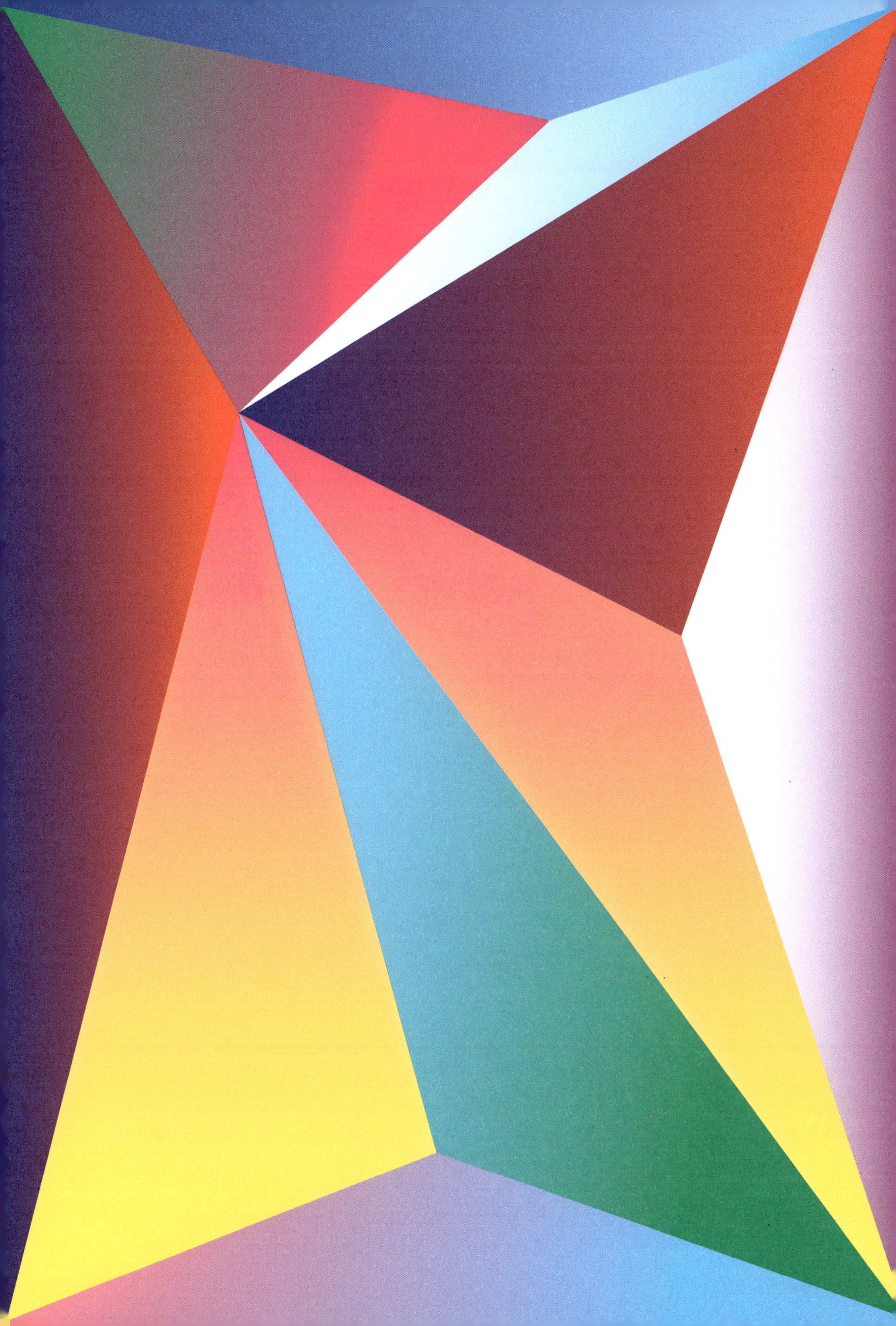

Into Time .us, 2012

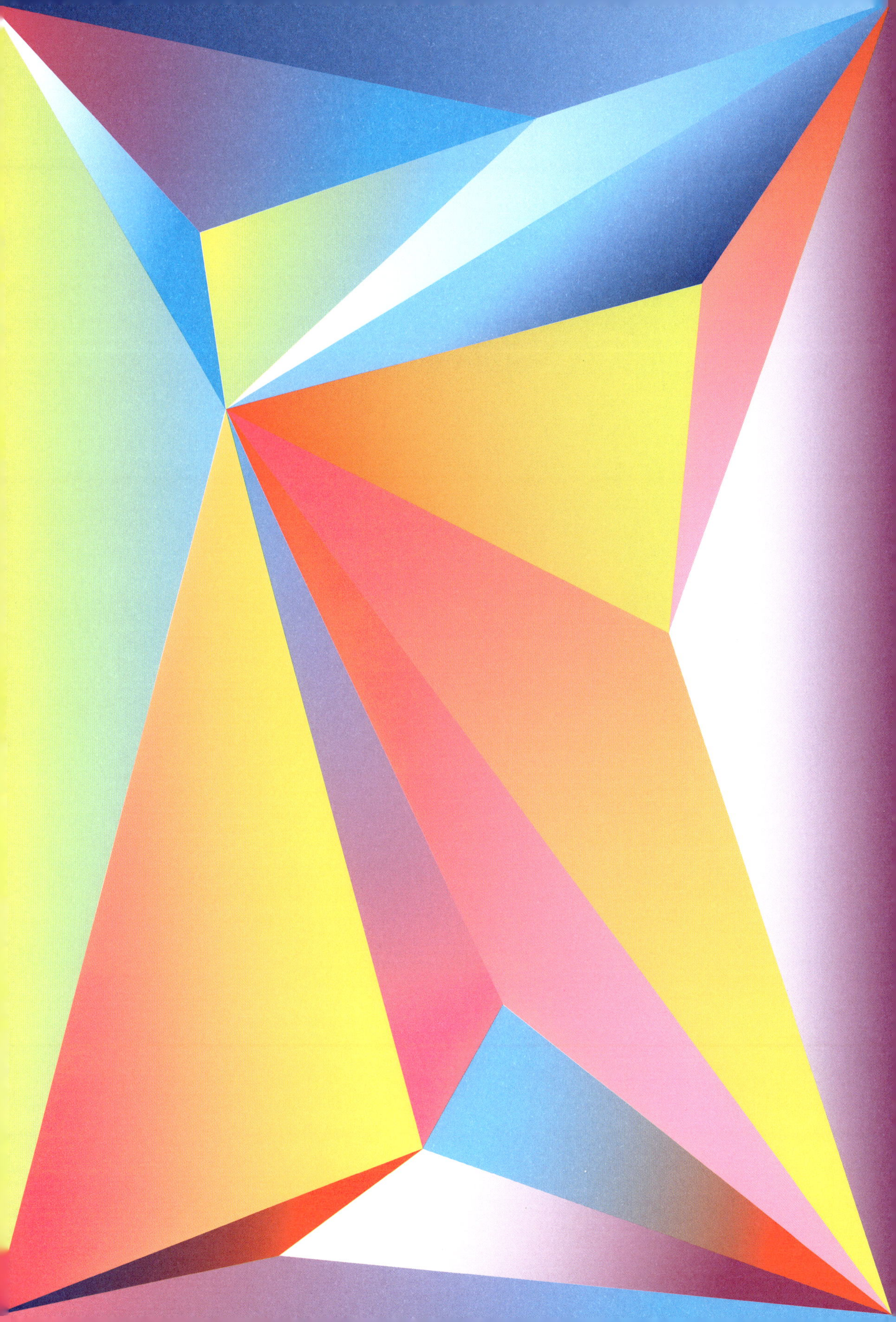

Into Time .us, 2012

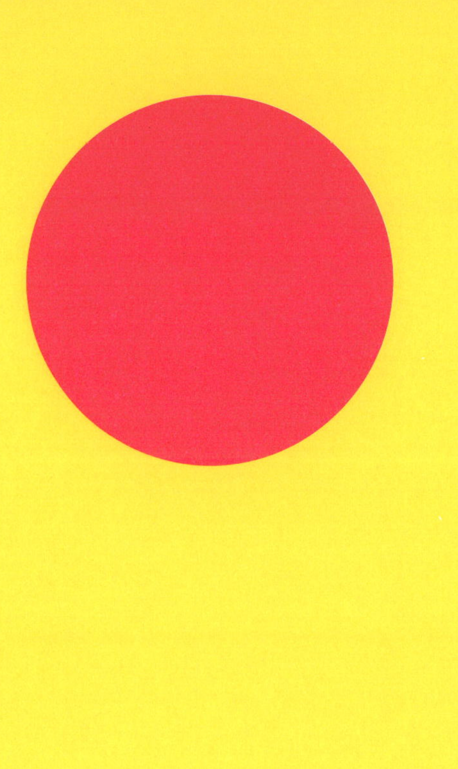

Never Nowhere .com, 2014

Never Nowhere .com, 2014

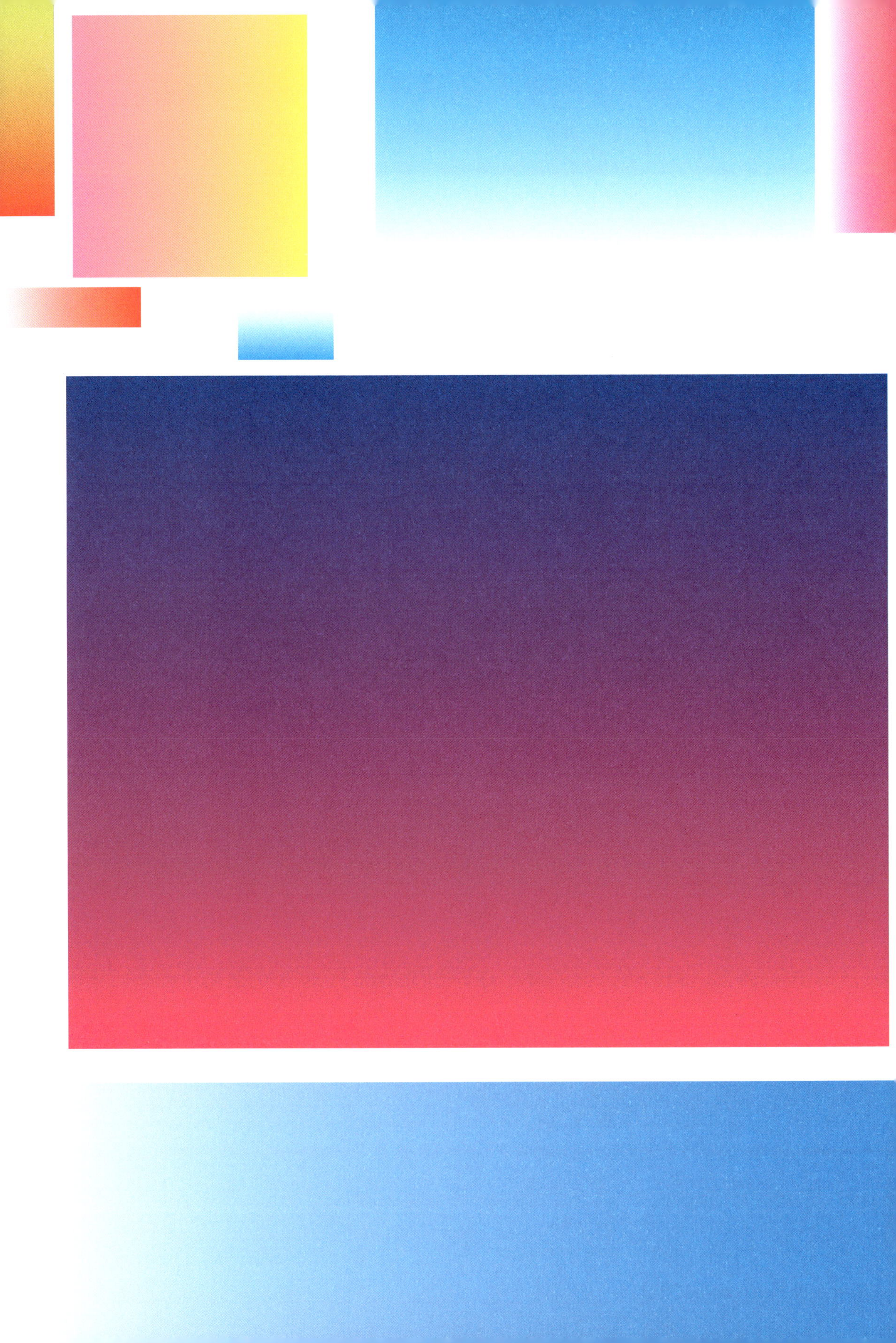

Random Fear .com, 2013

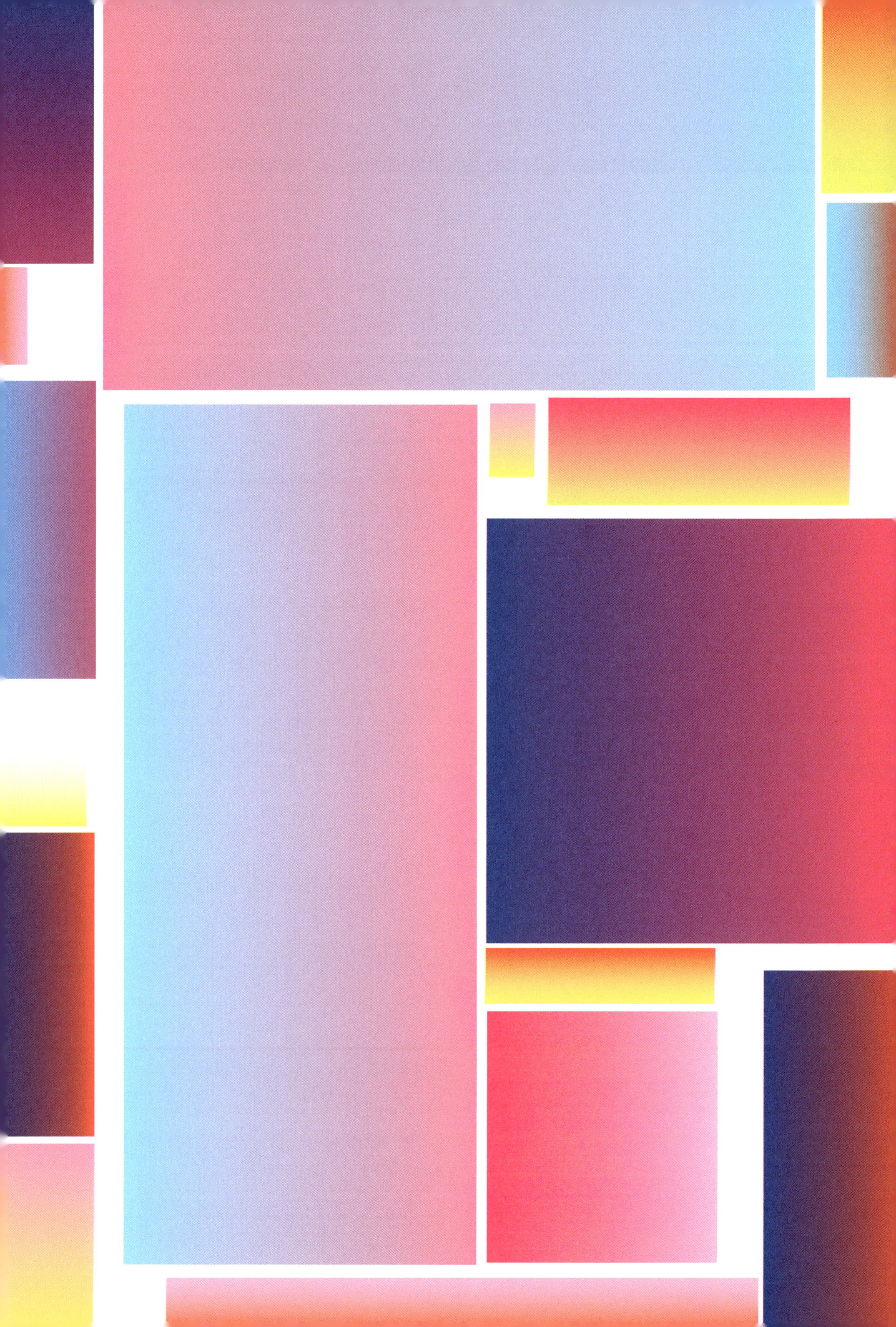

Random Fear .com, 2013

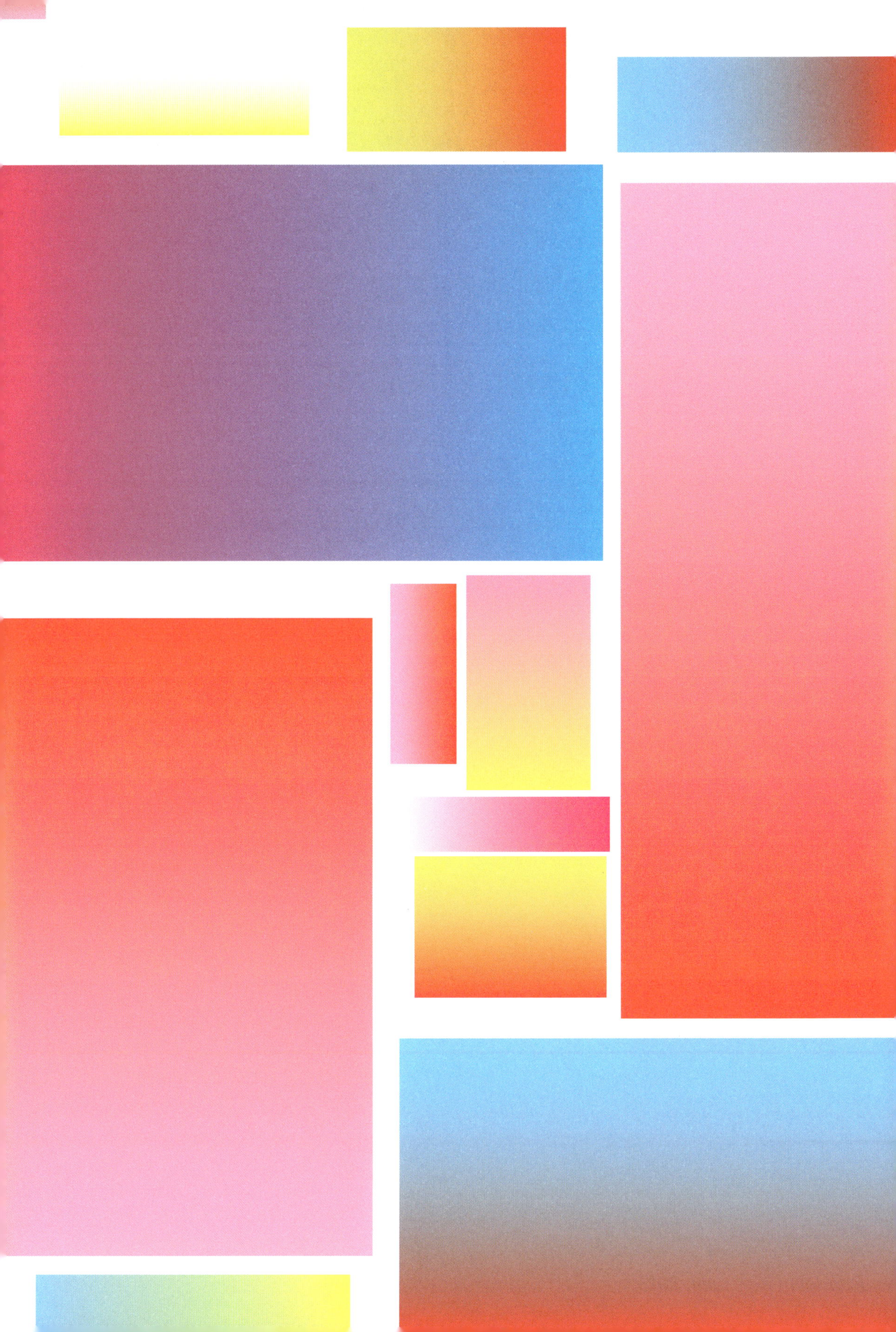

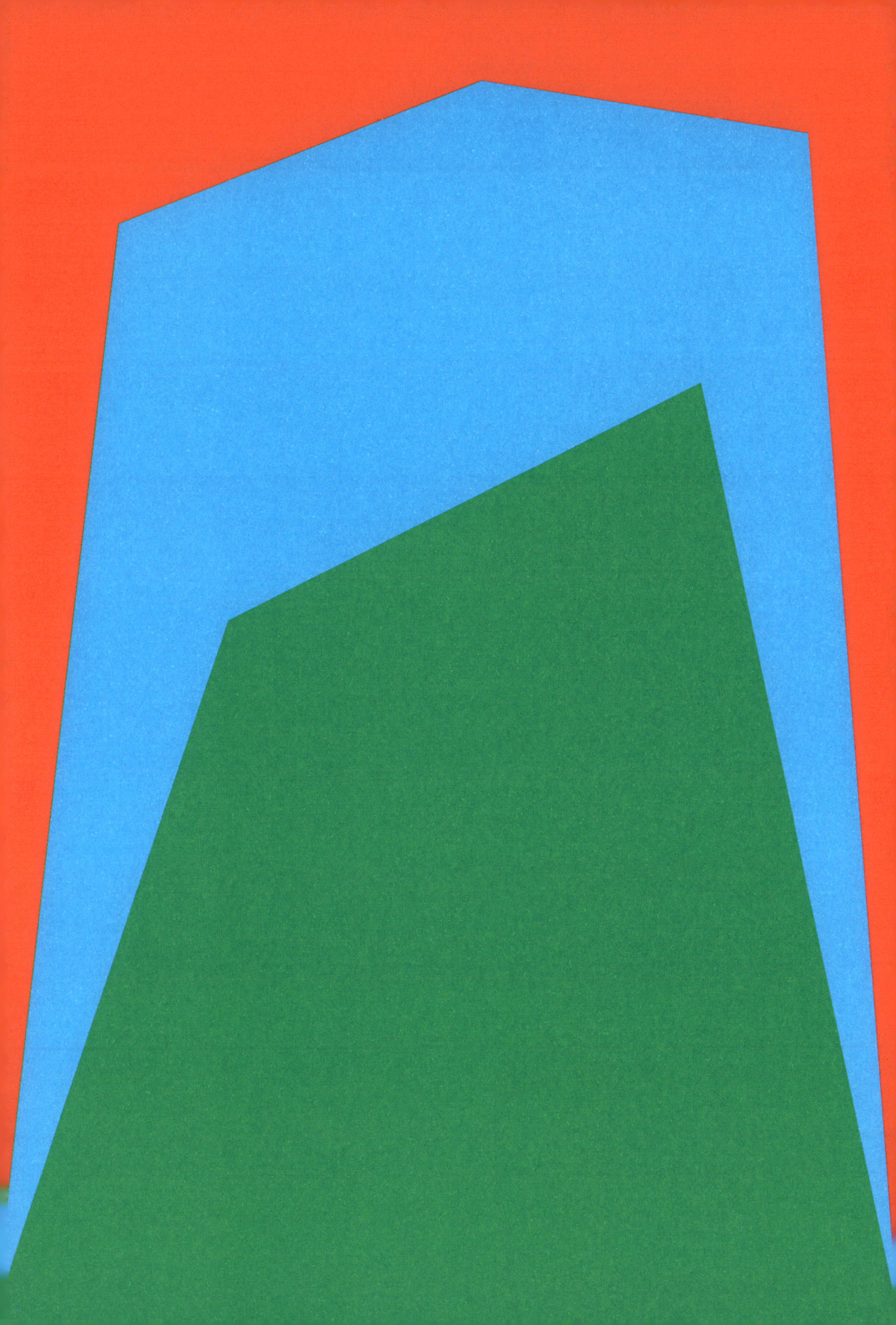

Falling Falling .com, 2011

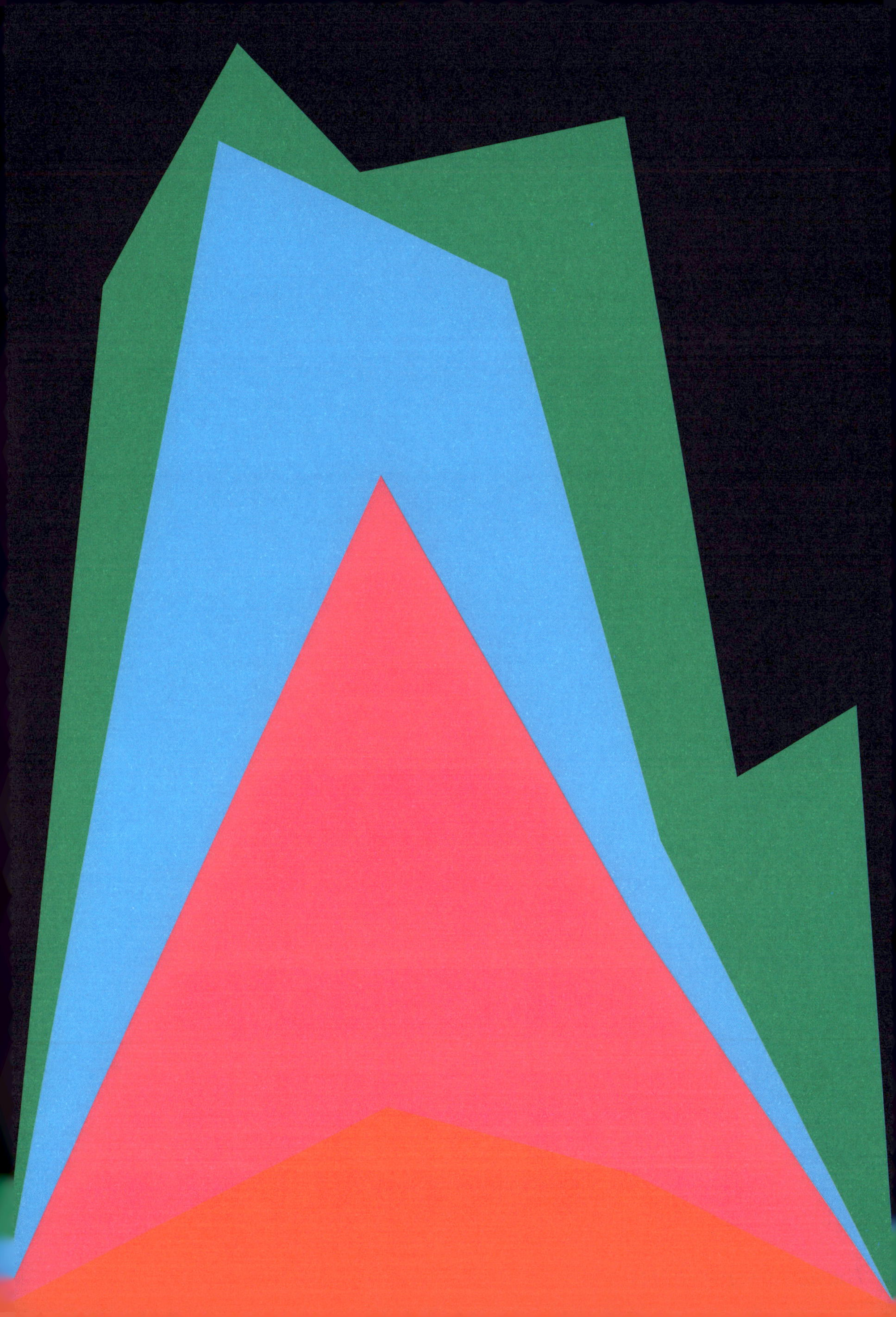

Falling Falling .com, 2011

Falling Falling .com, 2011

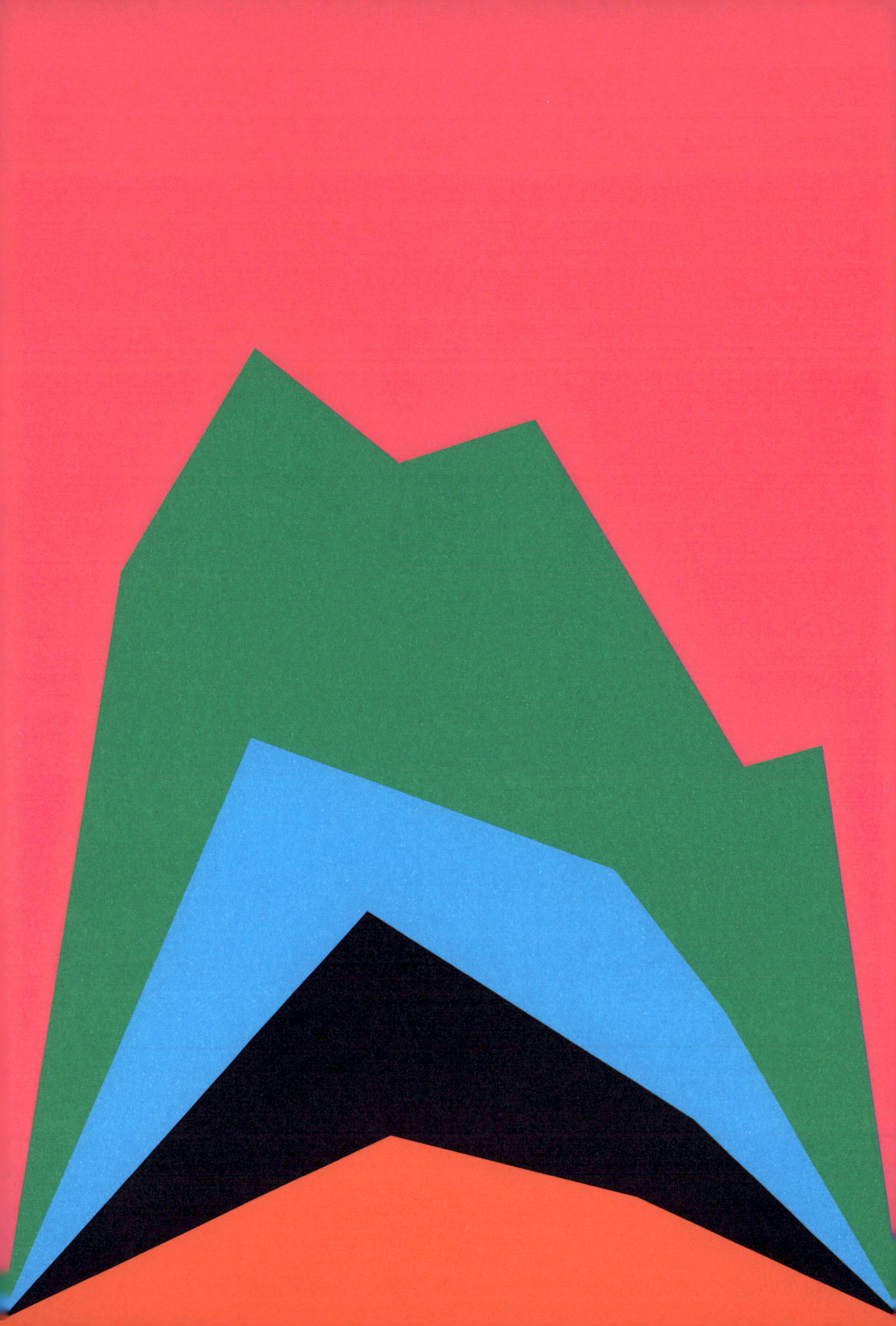

Falling Falling .com, 2011

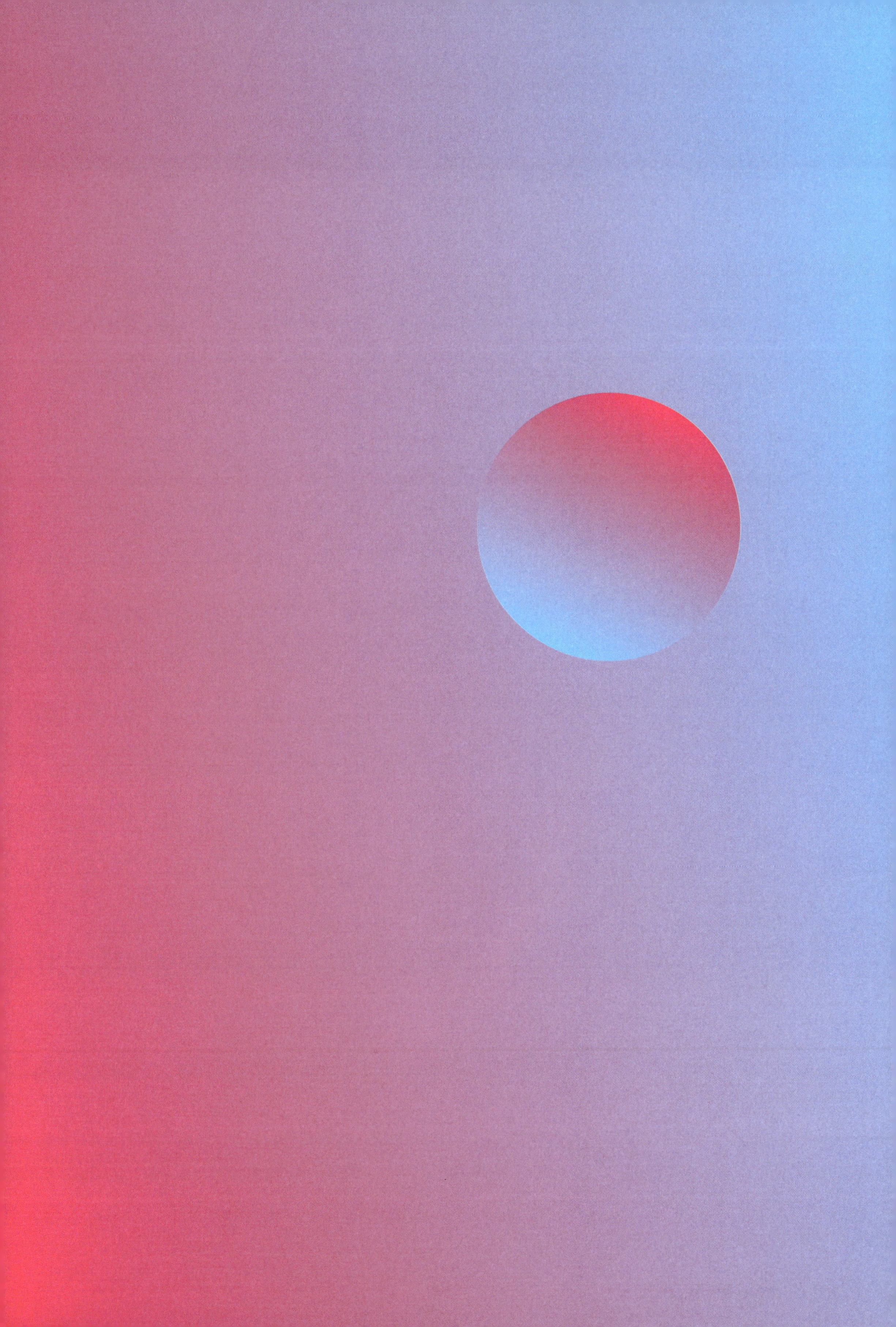

Float Bounce .com, 2016

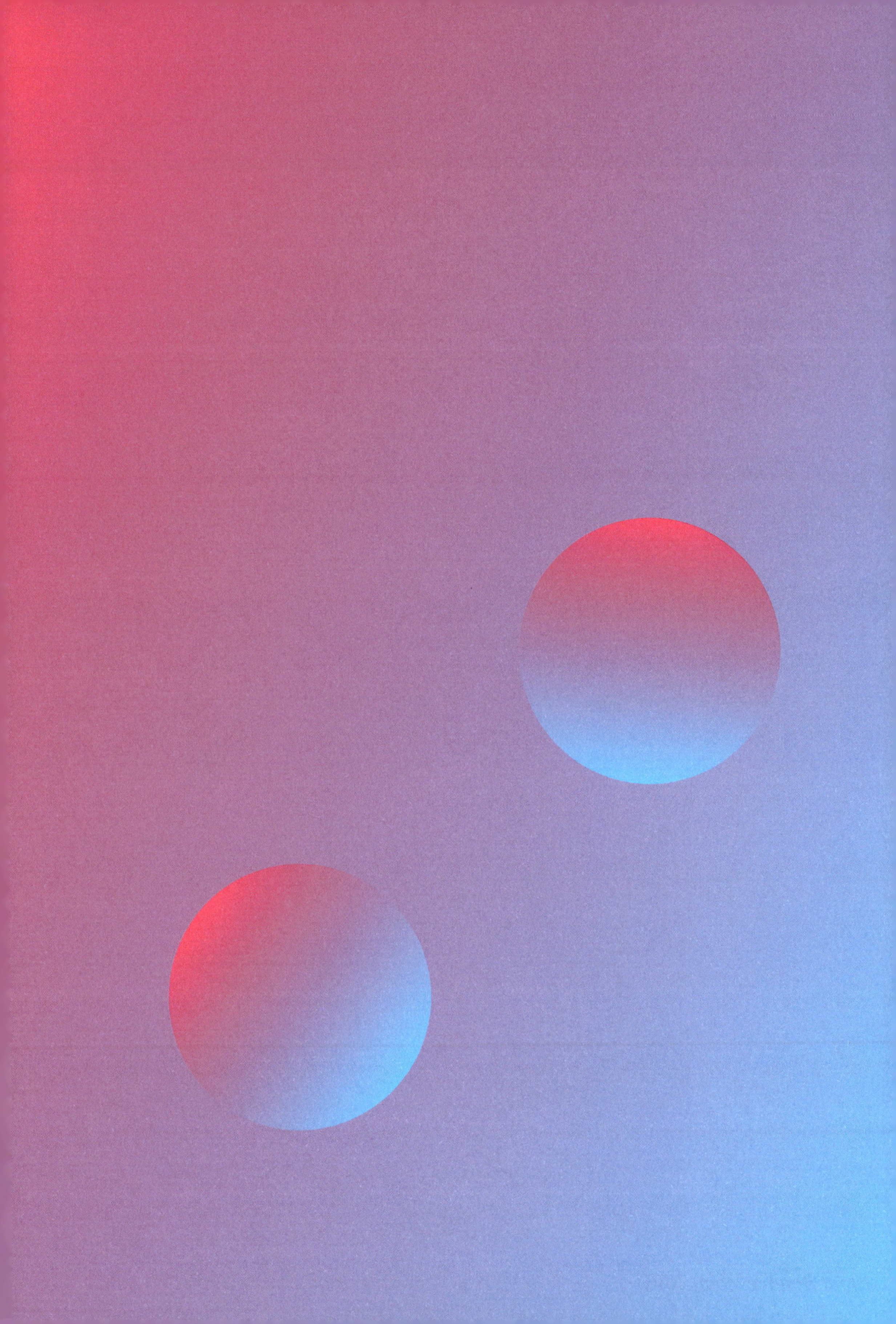

Float Bounce .com, 2016

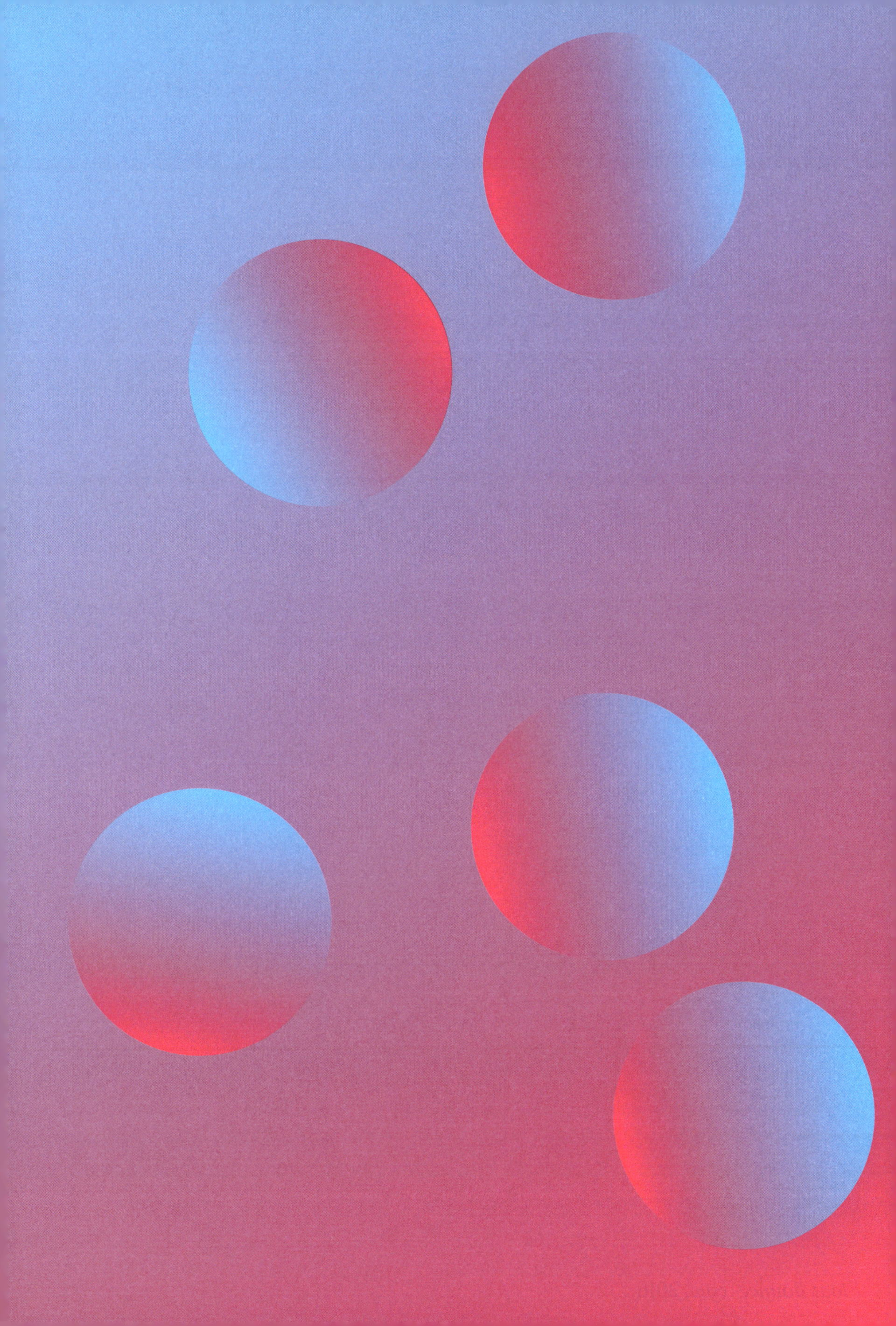

Float Bounce .com, 2016

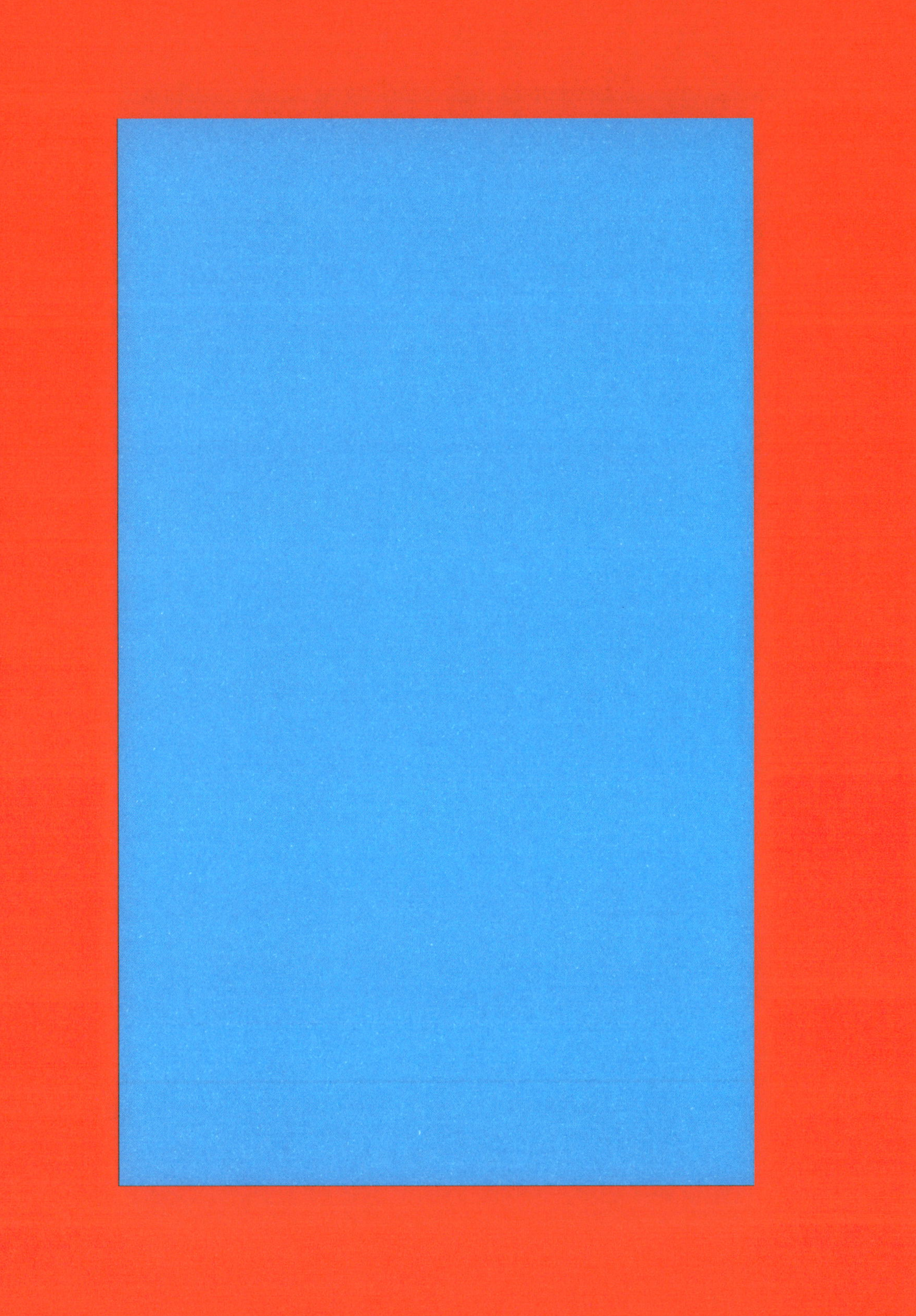

Hex Attack .com, 2013

Hex Attack .com, 2013

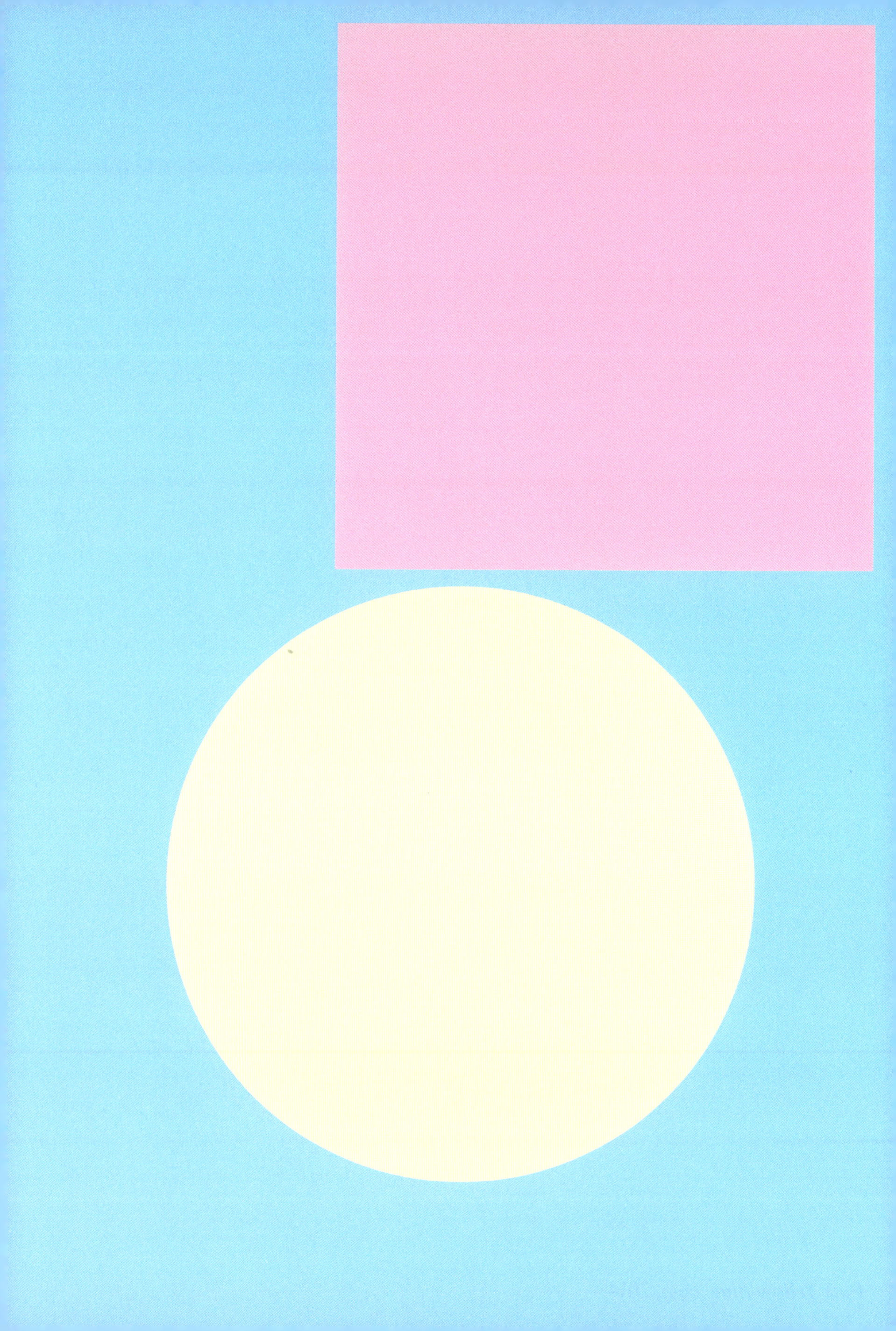

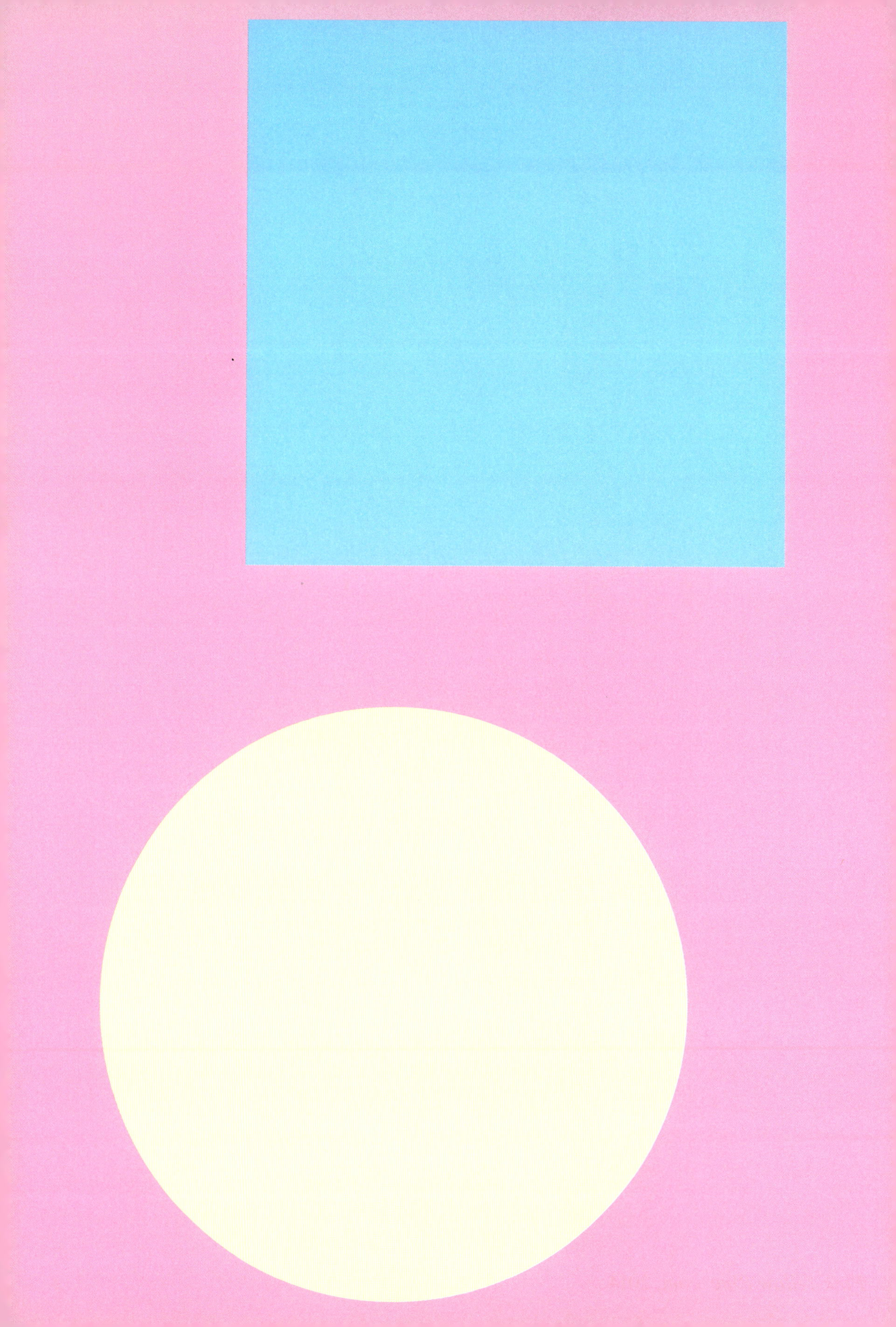

Pink Yellow Blue .com, 2014

Yes No If .com, 2014

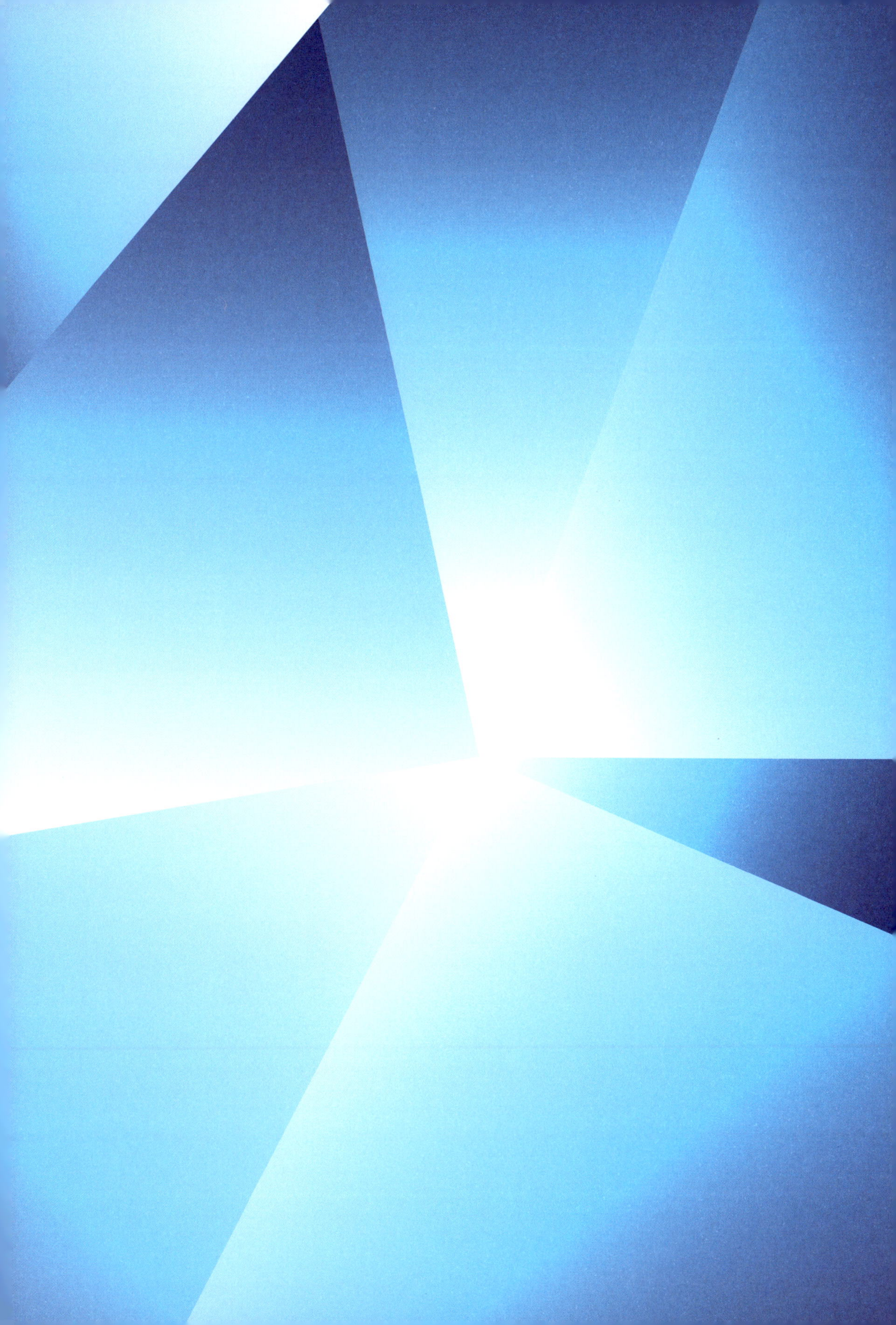

Yes No If .com, 2014

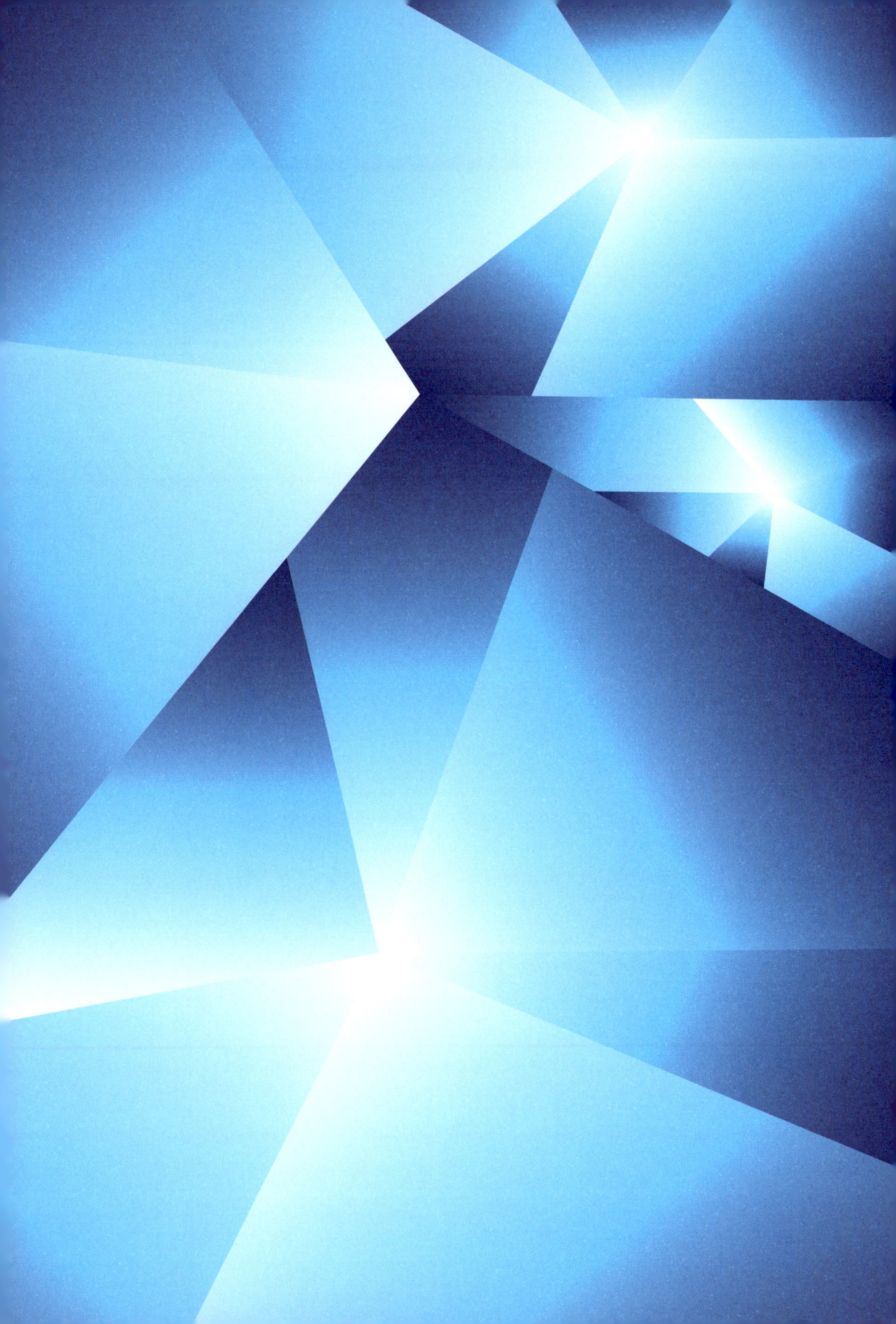

Yes No If .com, 2014

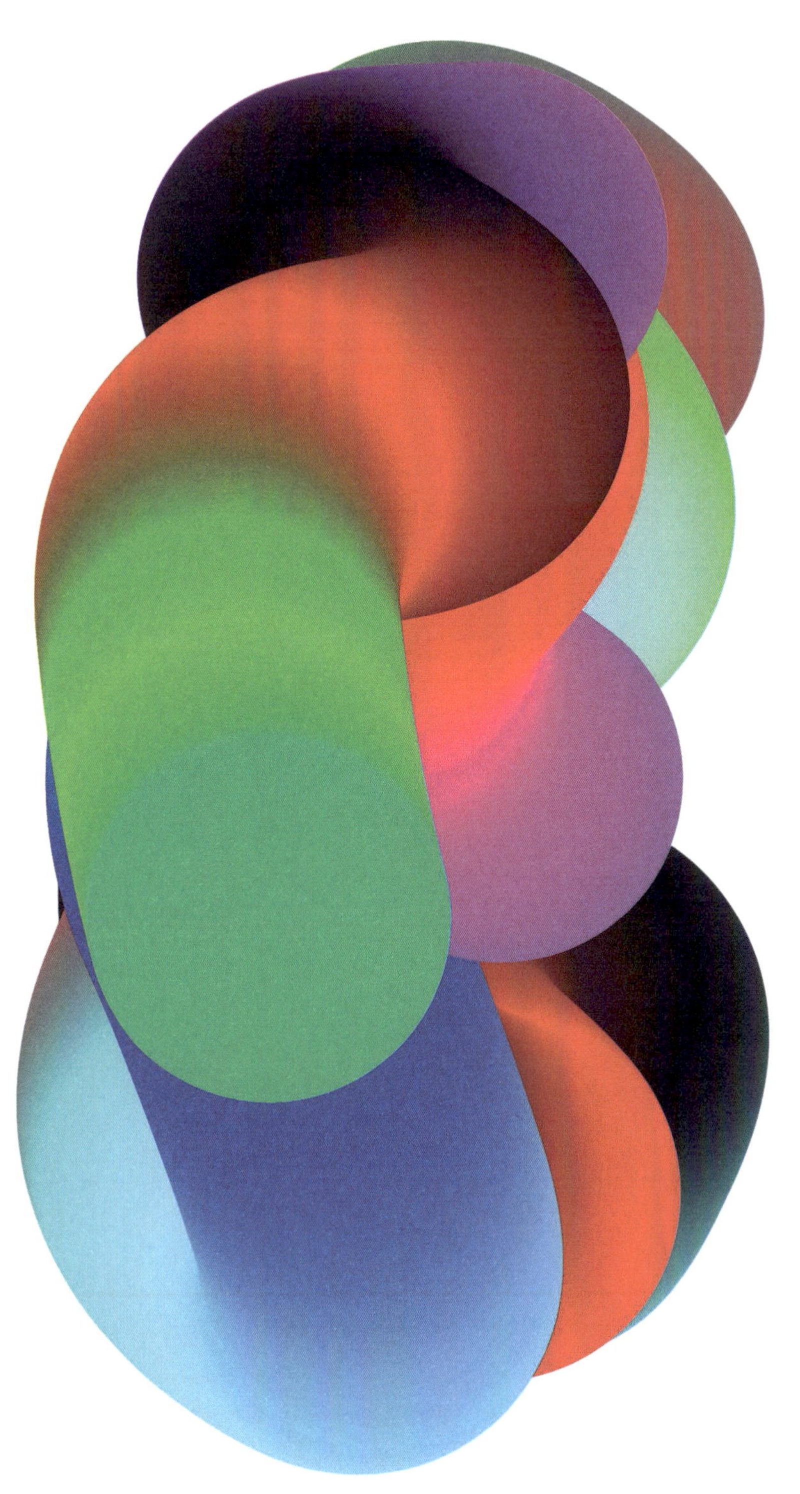

Ooze Move .com, 2014

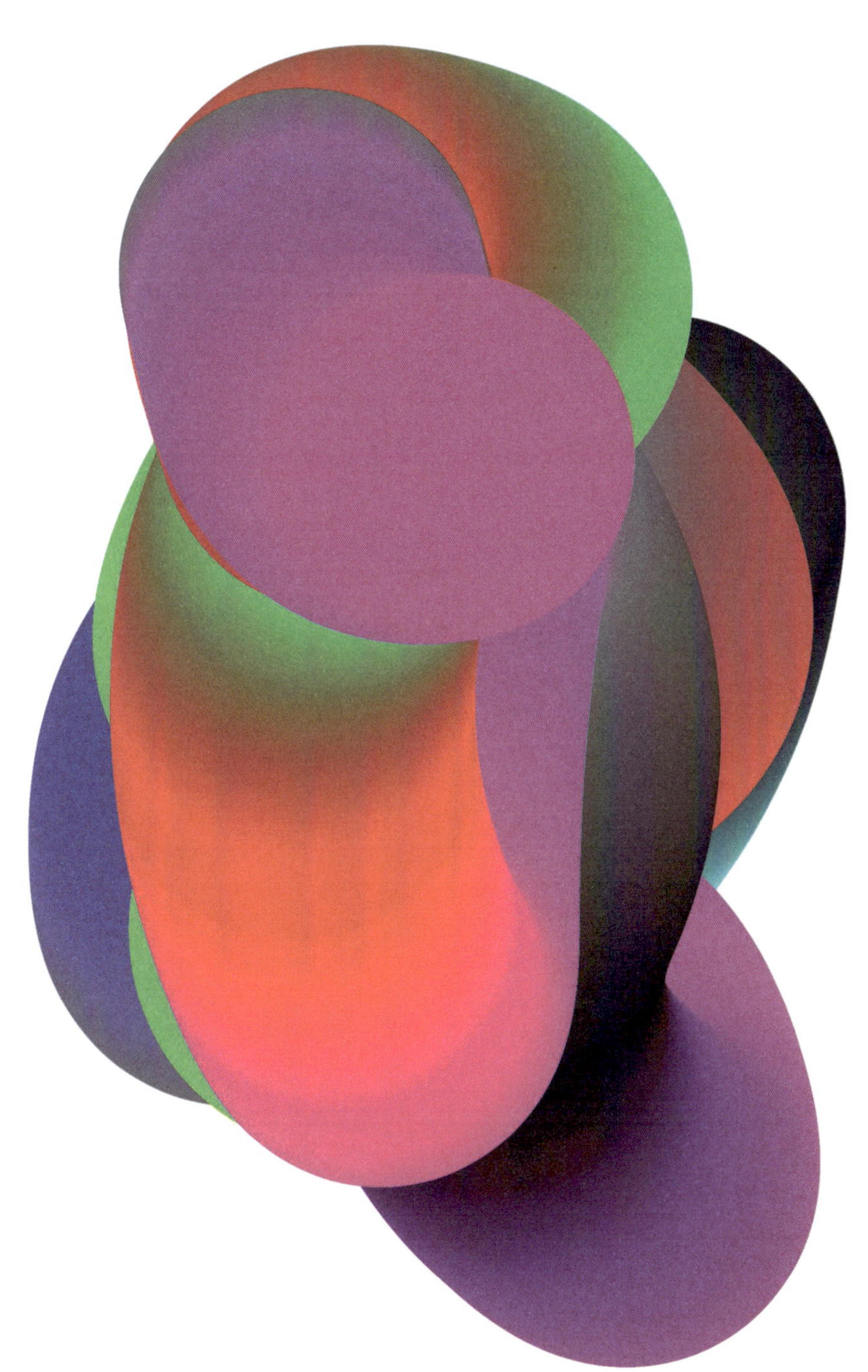

Ooze Move .com, 2014

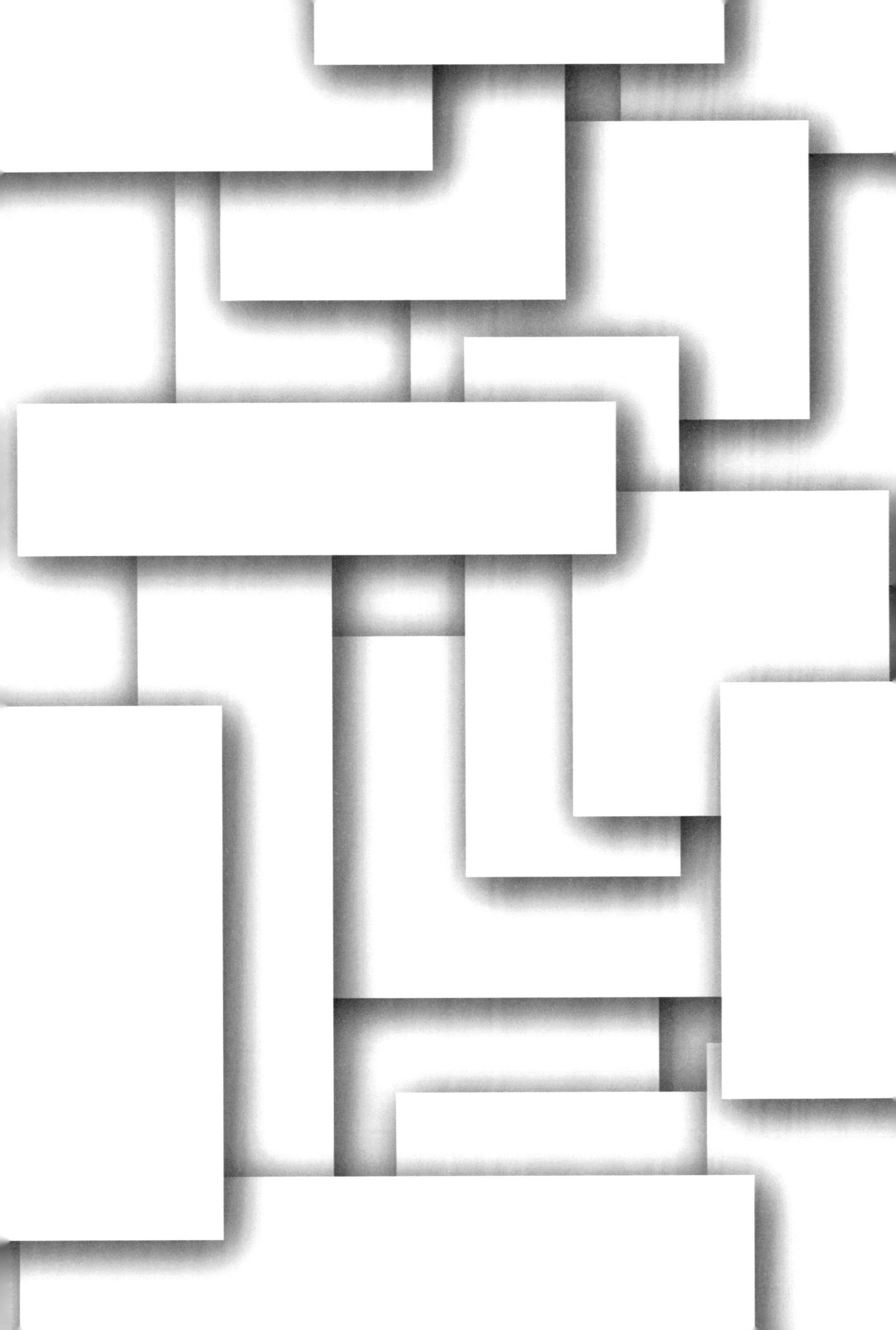

Blank Windows .com, 2016

Blank Windows .com, 2016

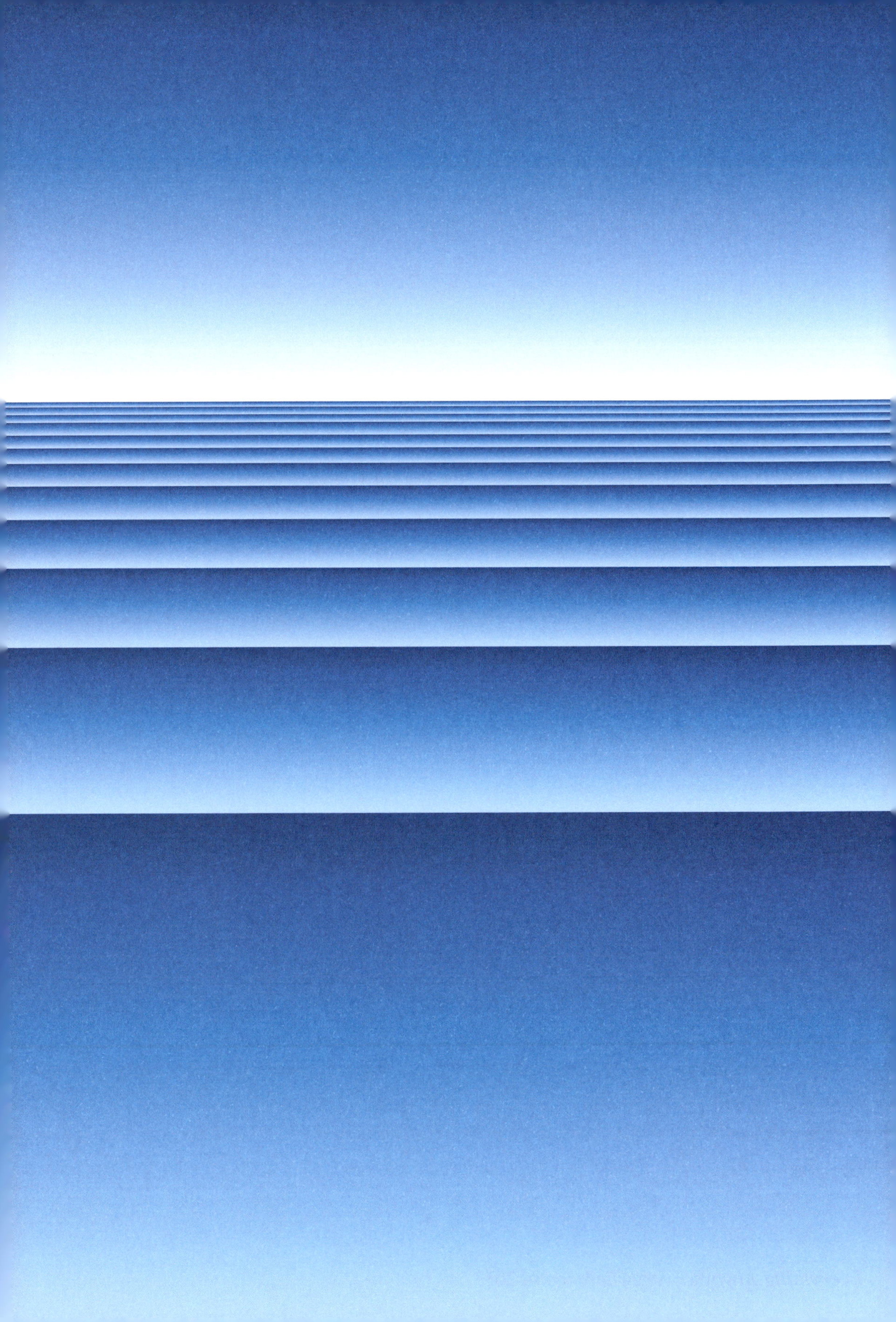

Everything Always Everywhere .com, 2013

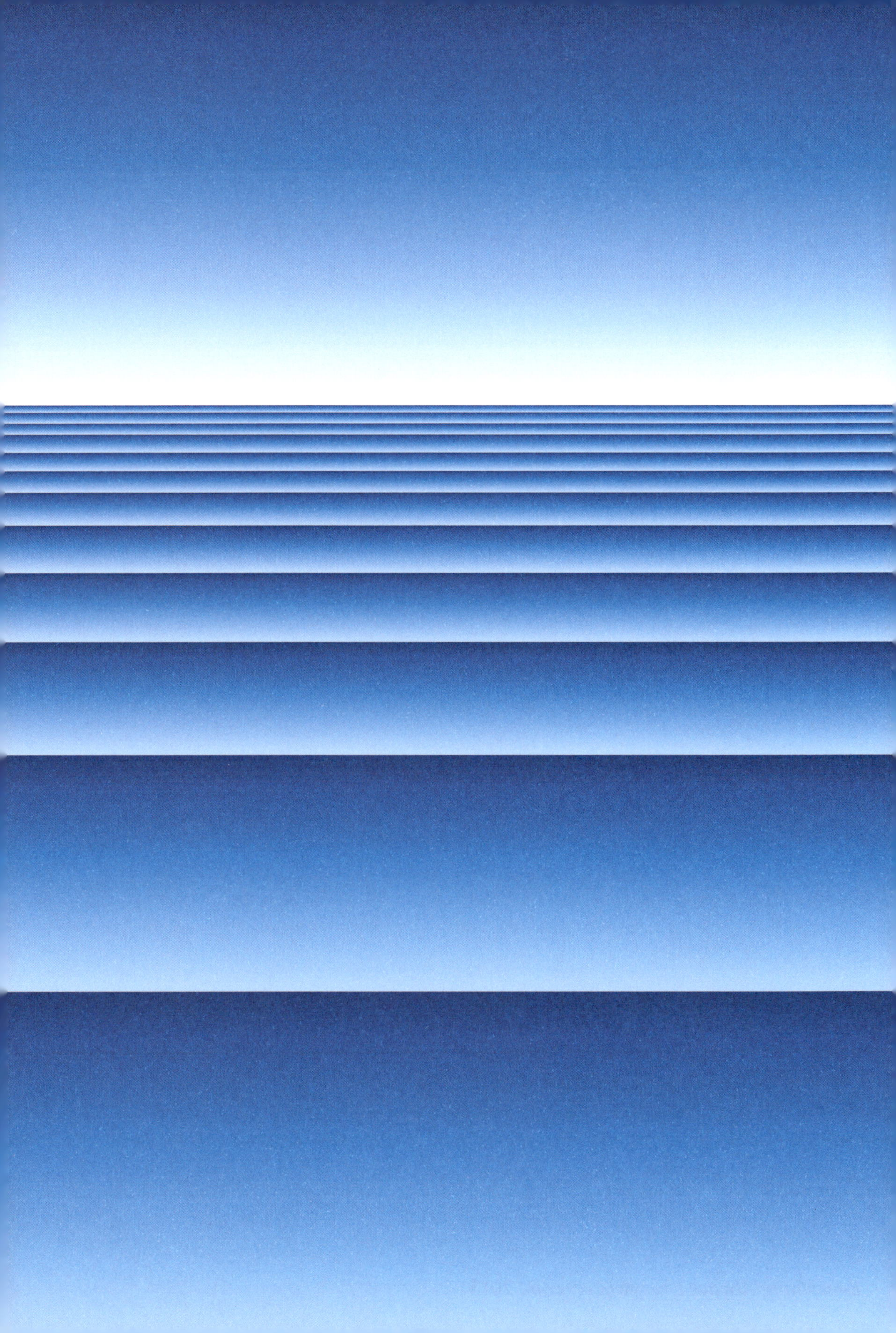

Everything Always Everywhere .com, 2013

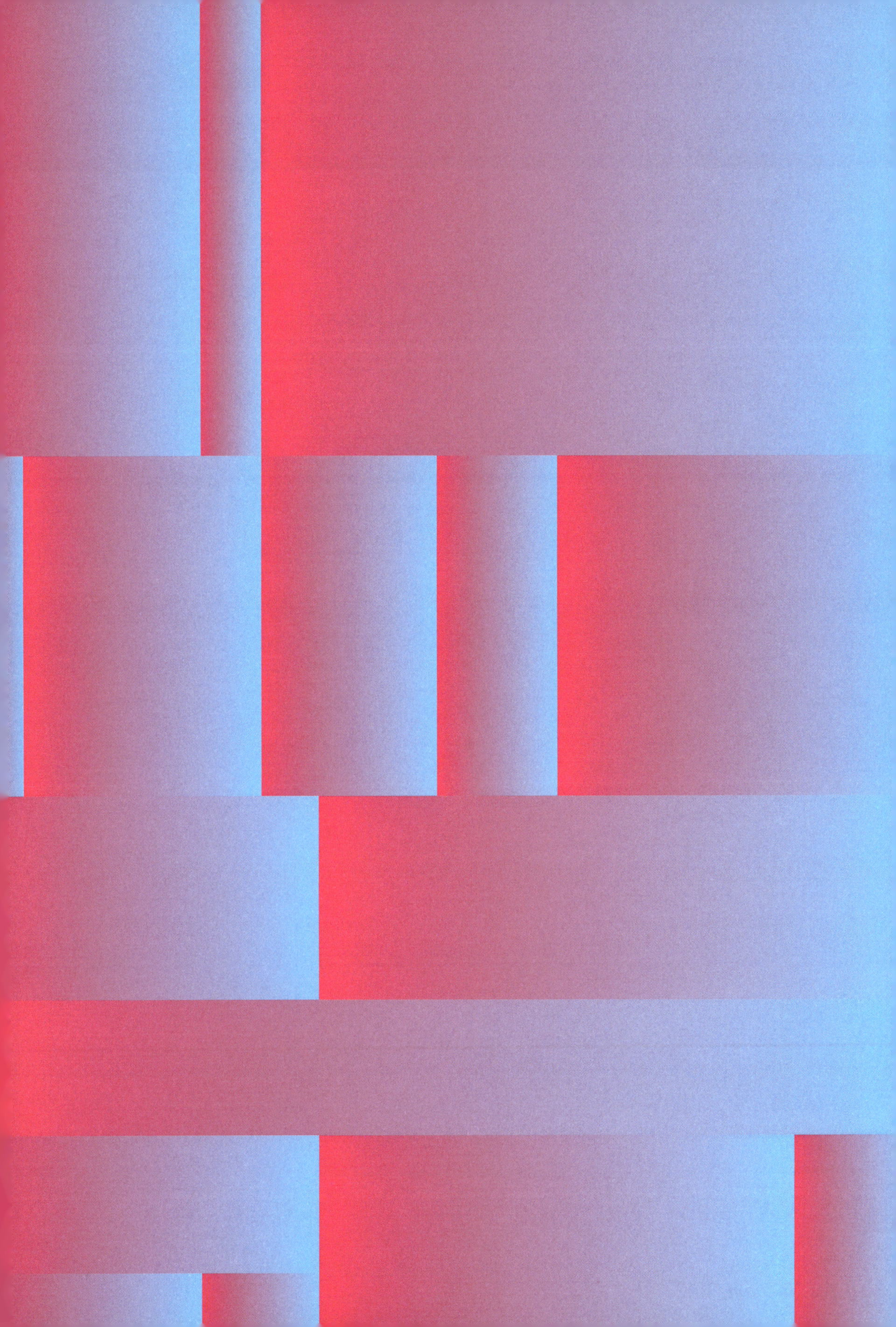

If Yes No .com, 2013

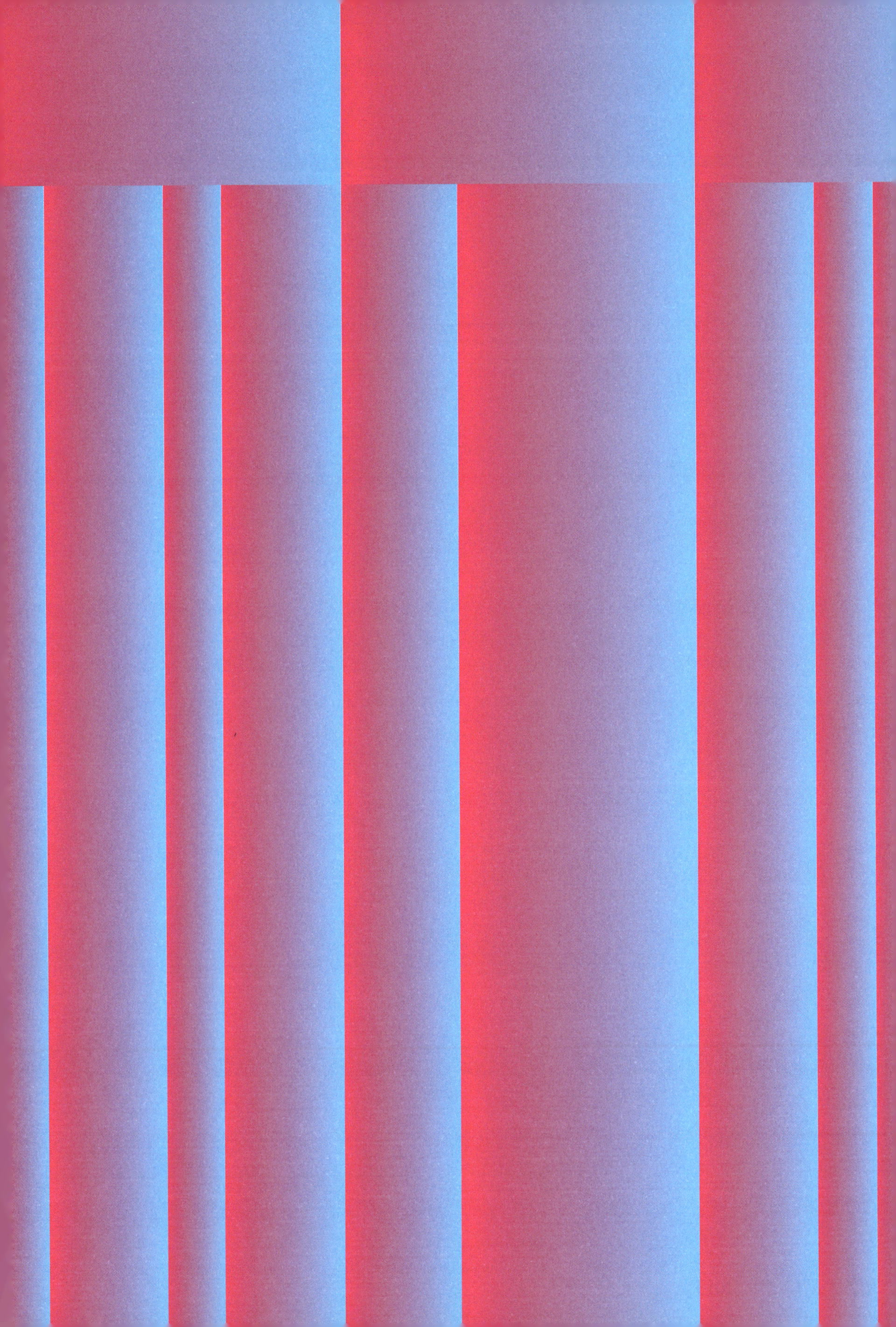

Here That .com, 2015

Here That .com, 2015

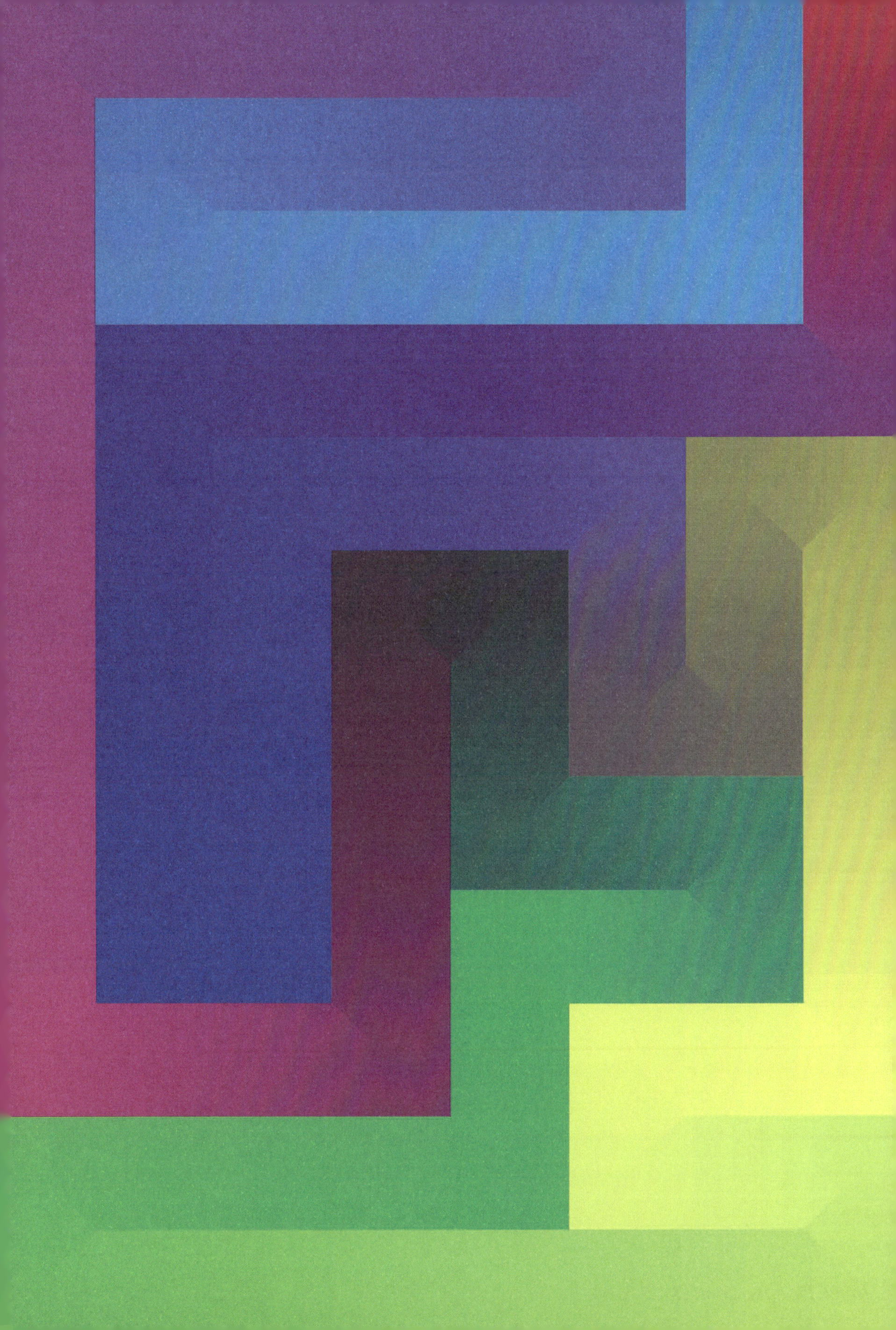

Inner Doubts .com, 2012

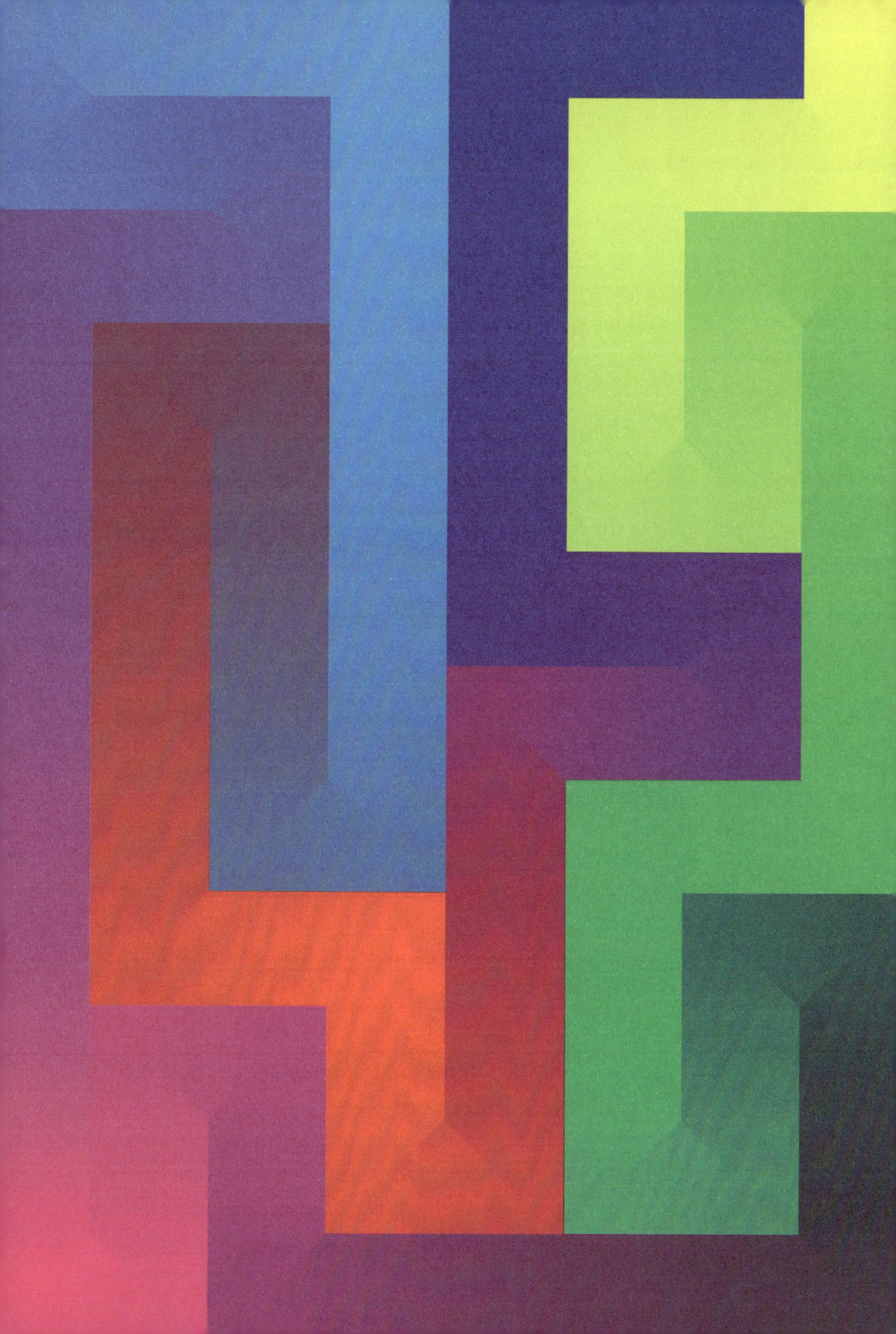

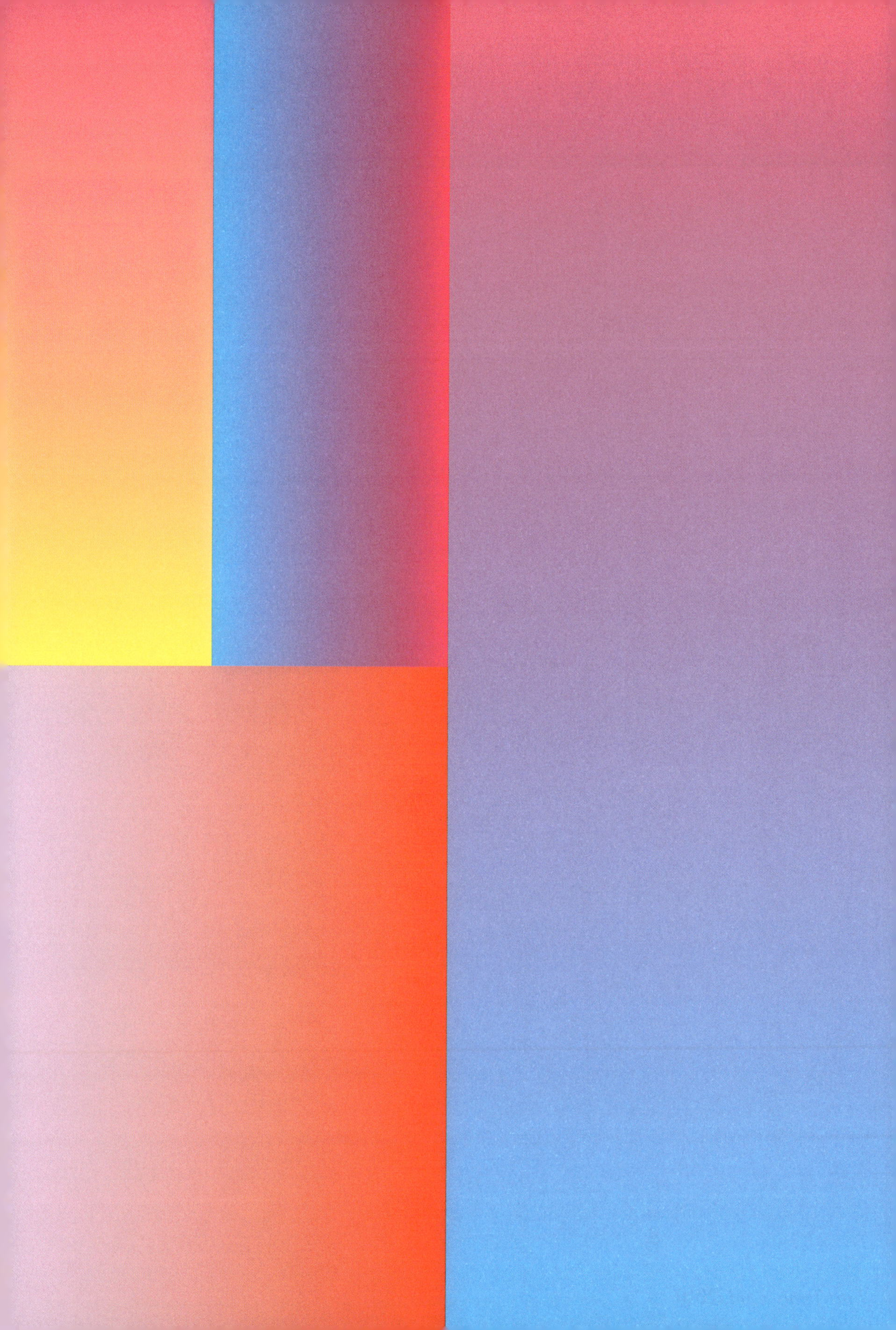

Into Time .com, 2010

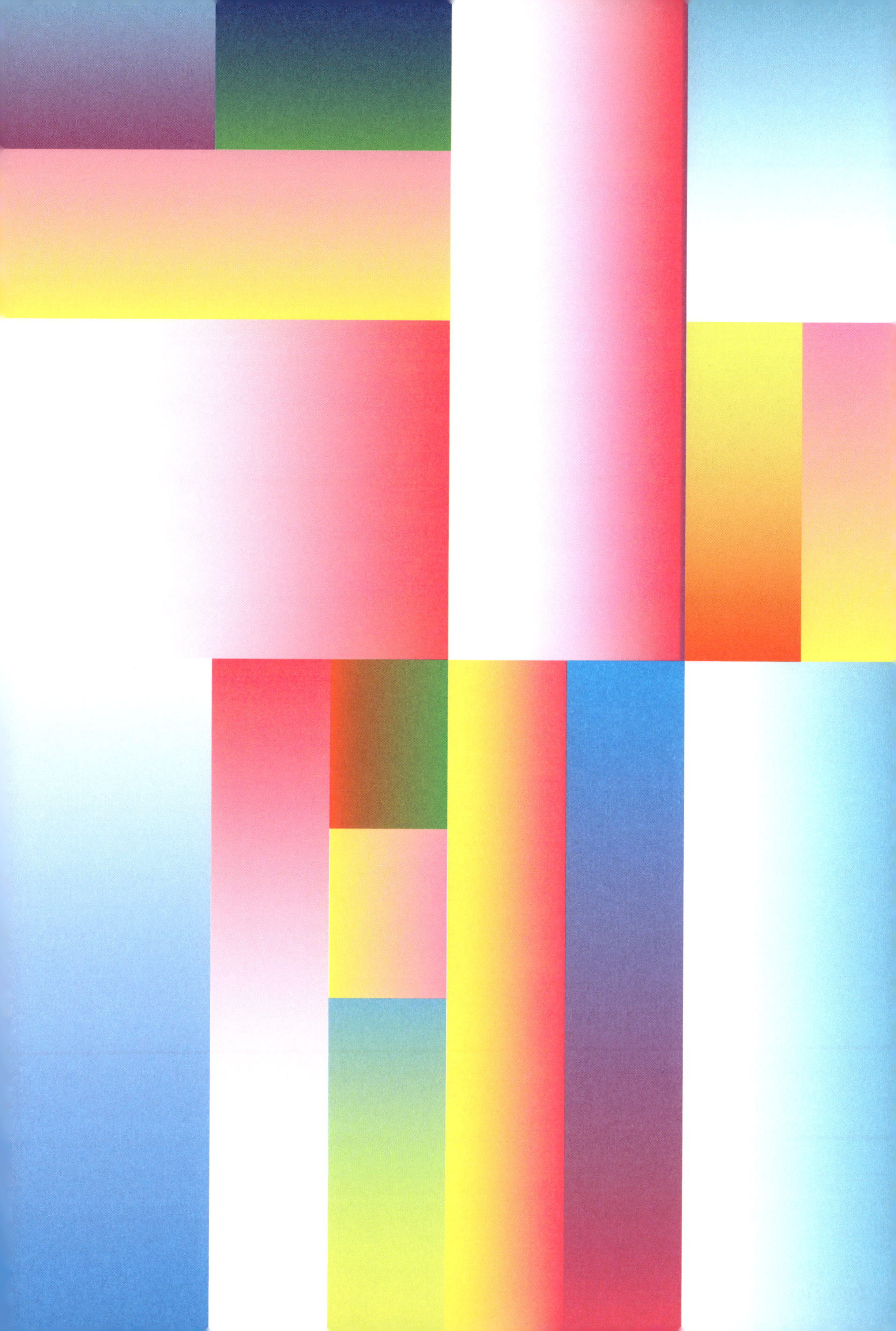

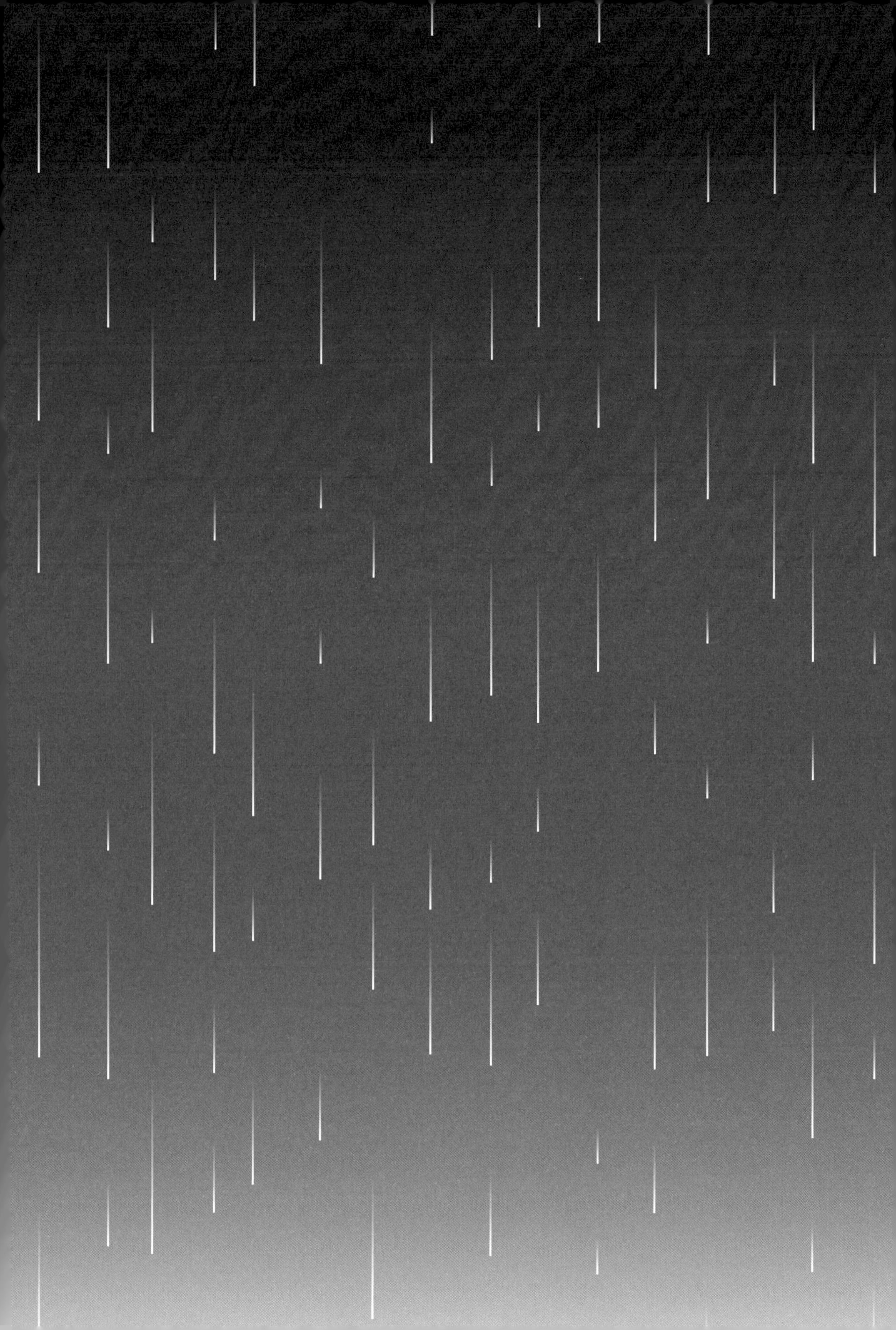

Looking At Something .com, 2013

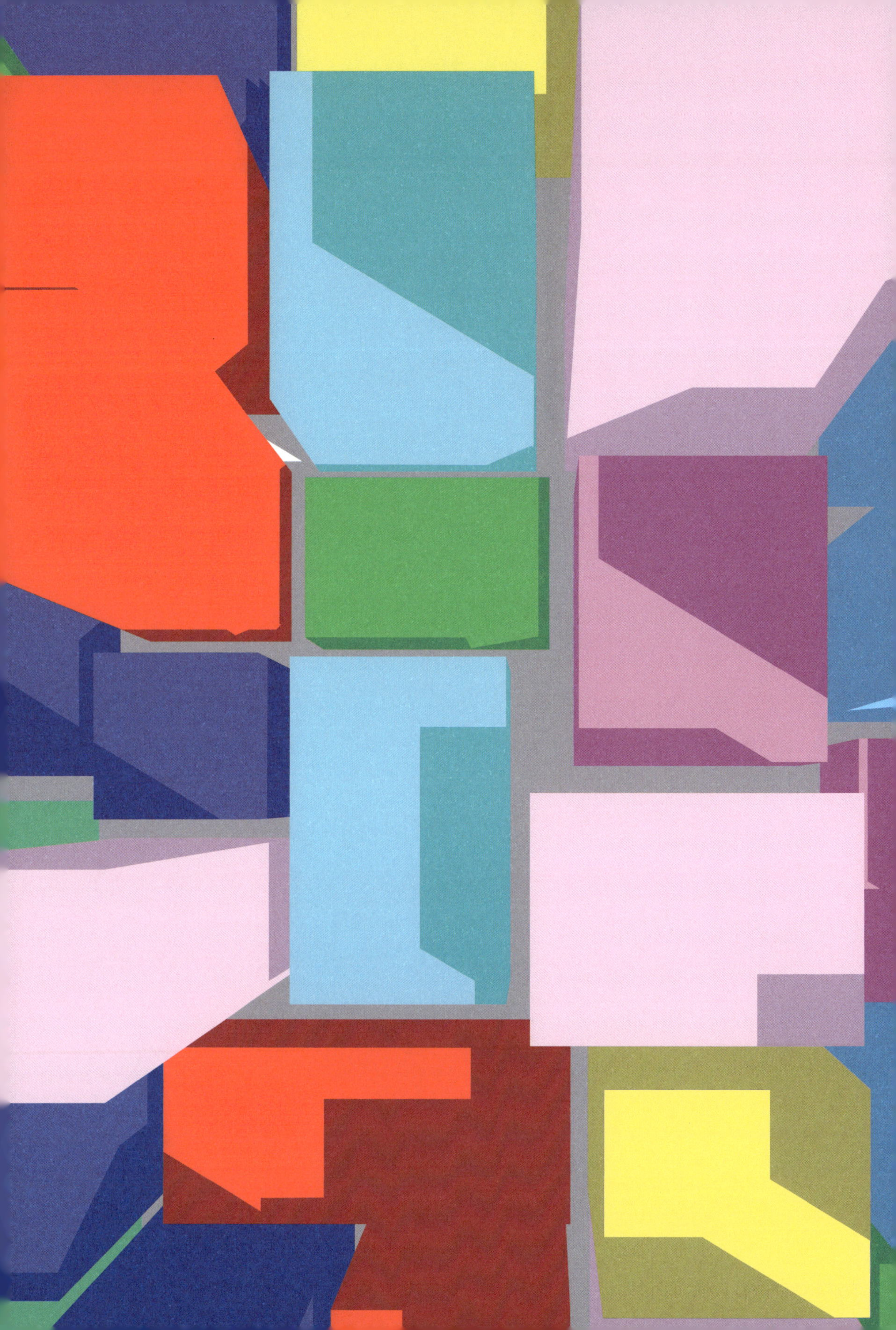

Neo Geo City .com, 2014

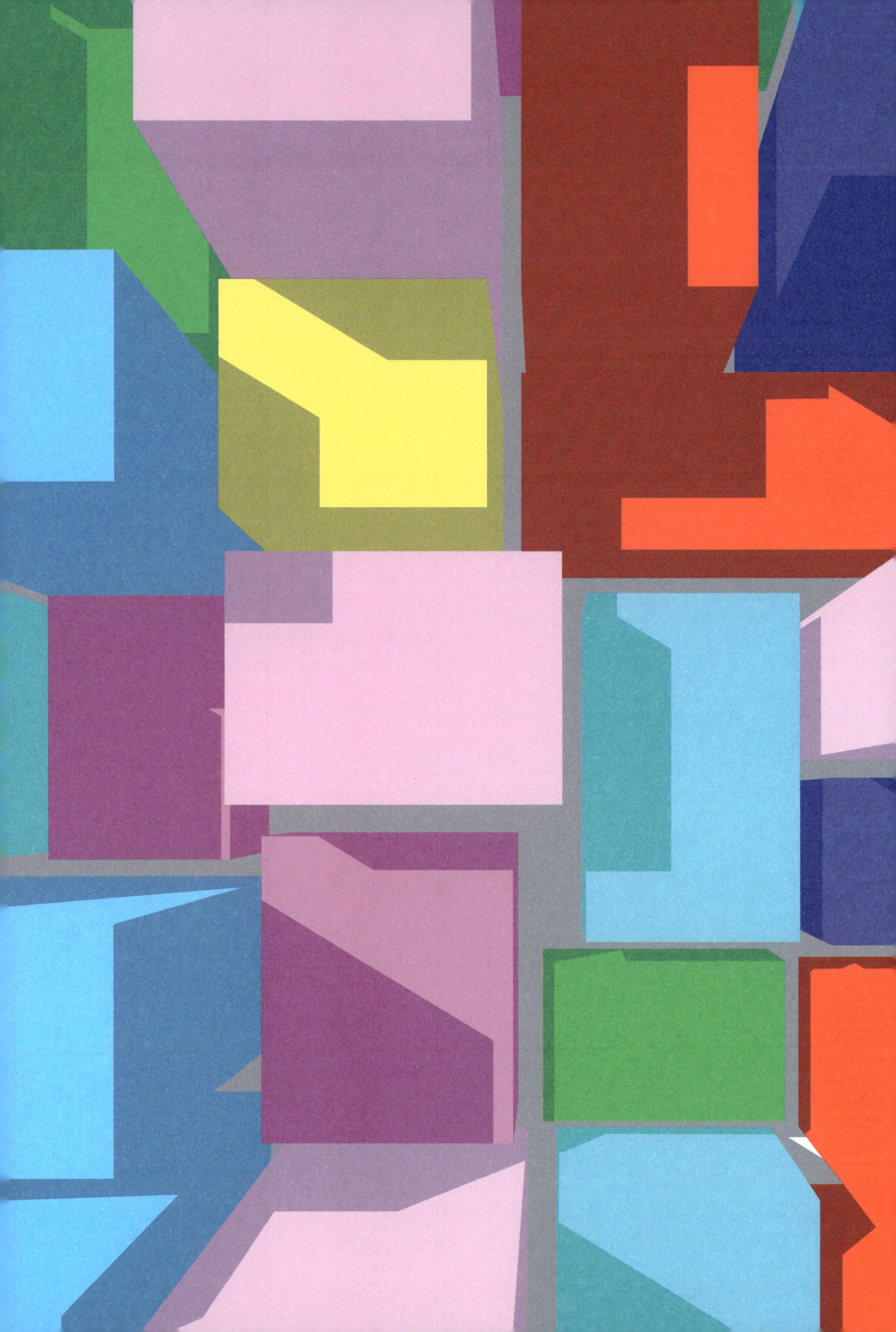

Neo Geo City .com, 2014

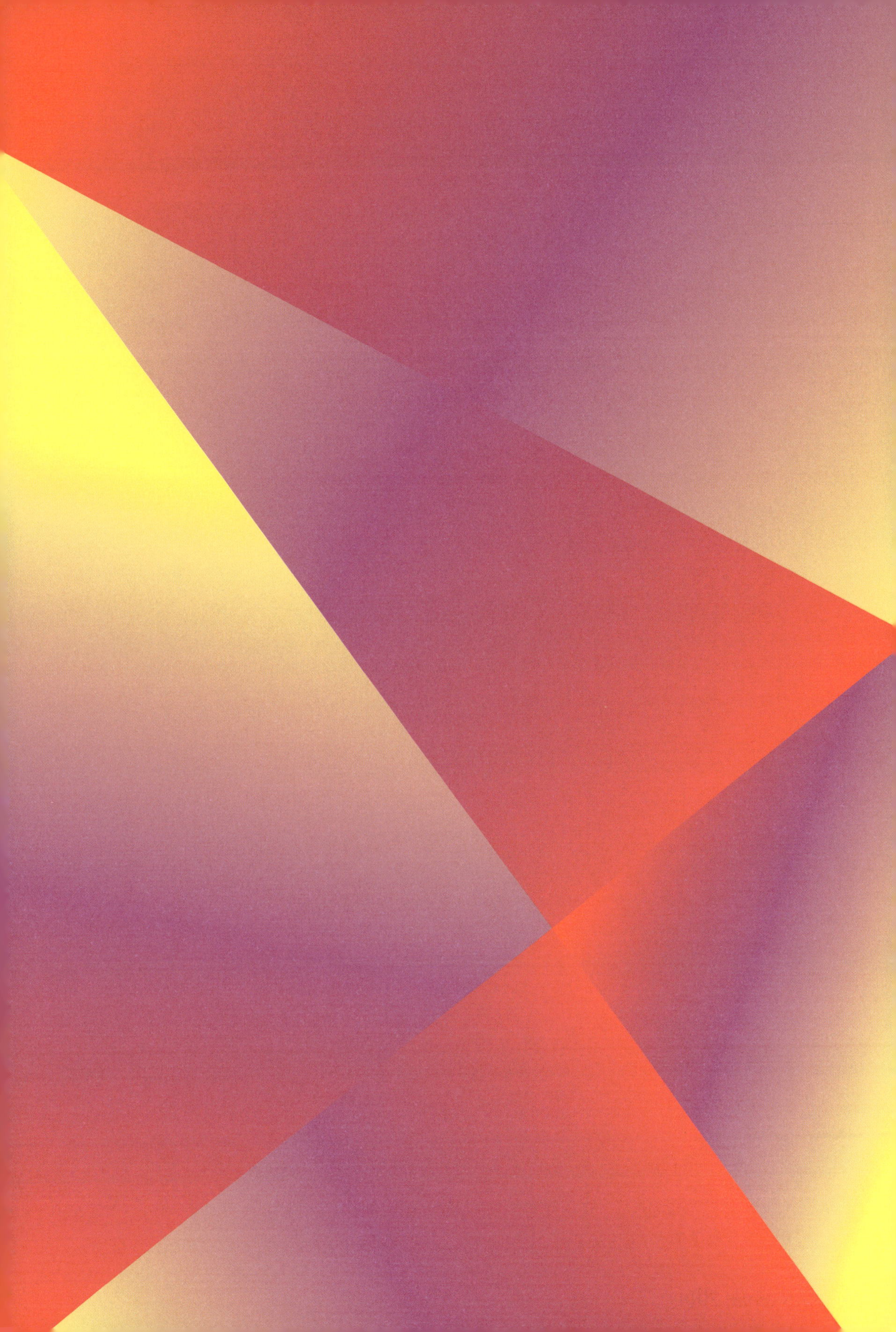

No If Yes .com, 2014

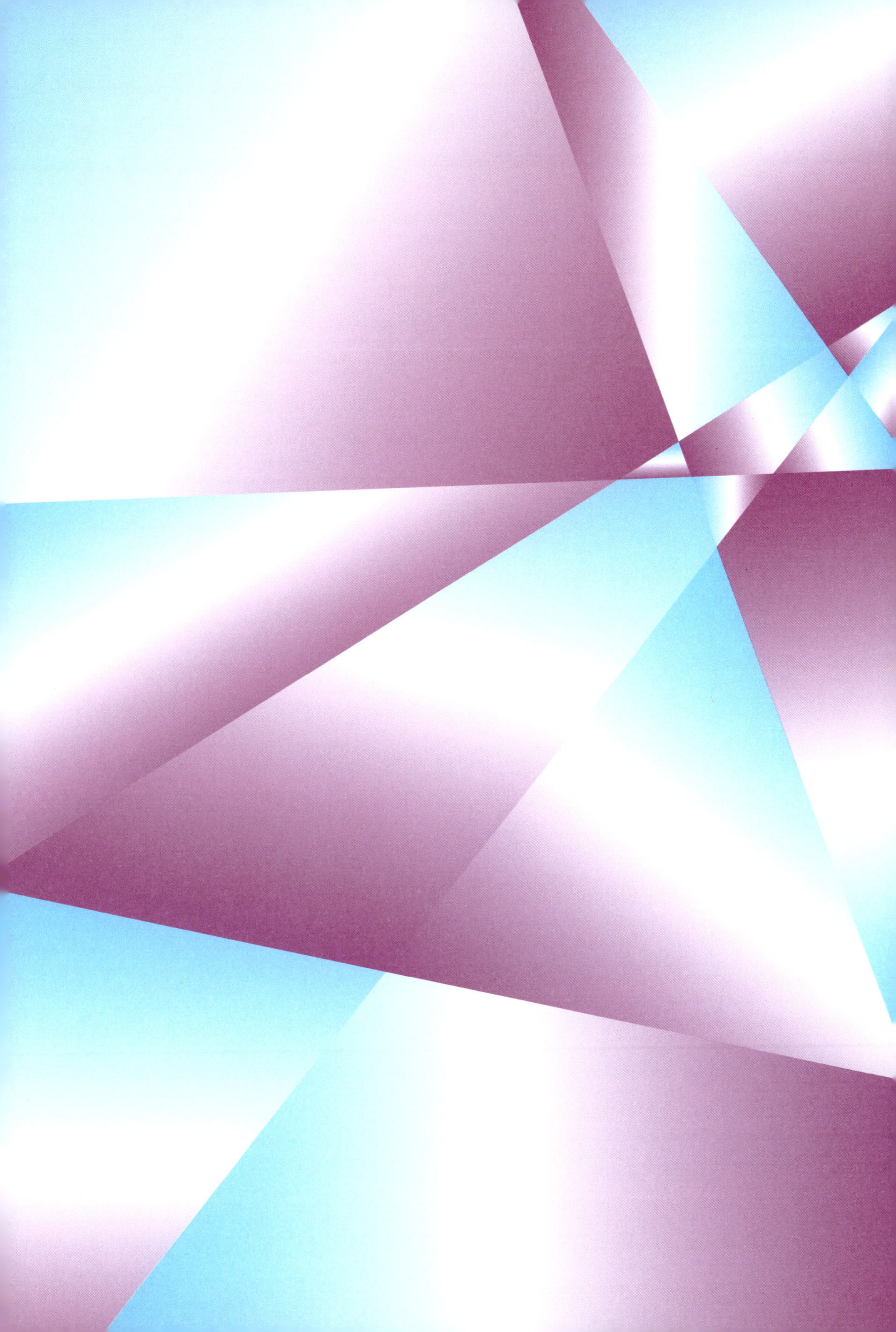

No If Yes .com, 2014

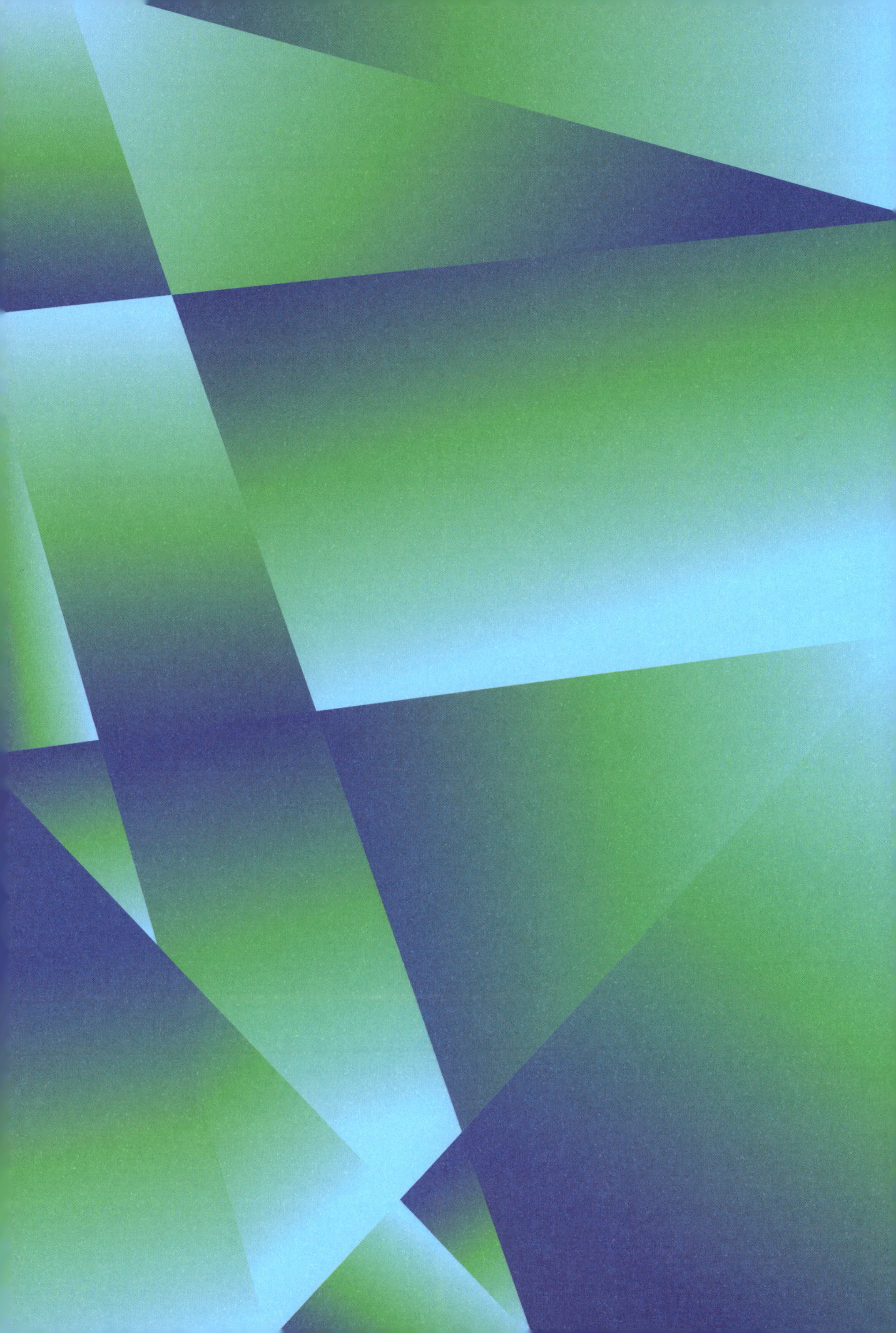

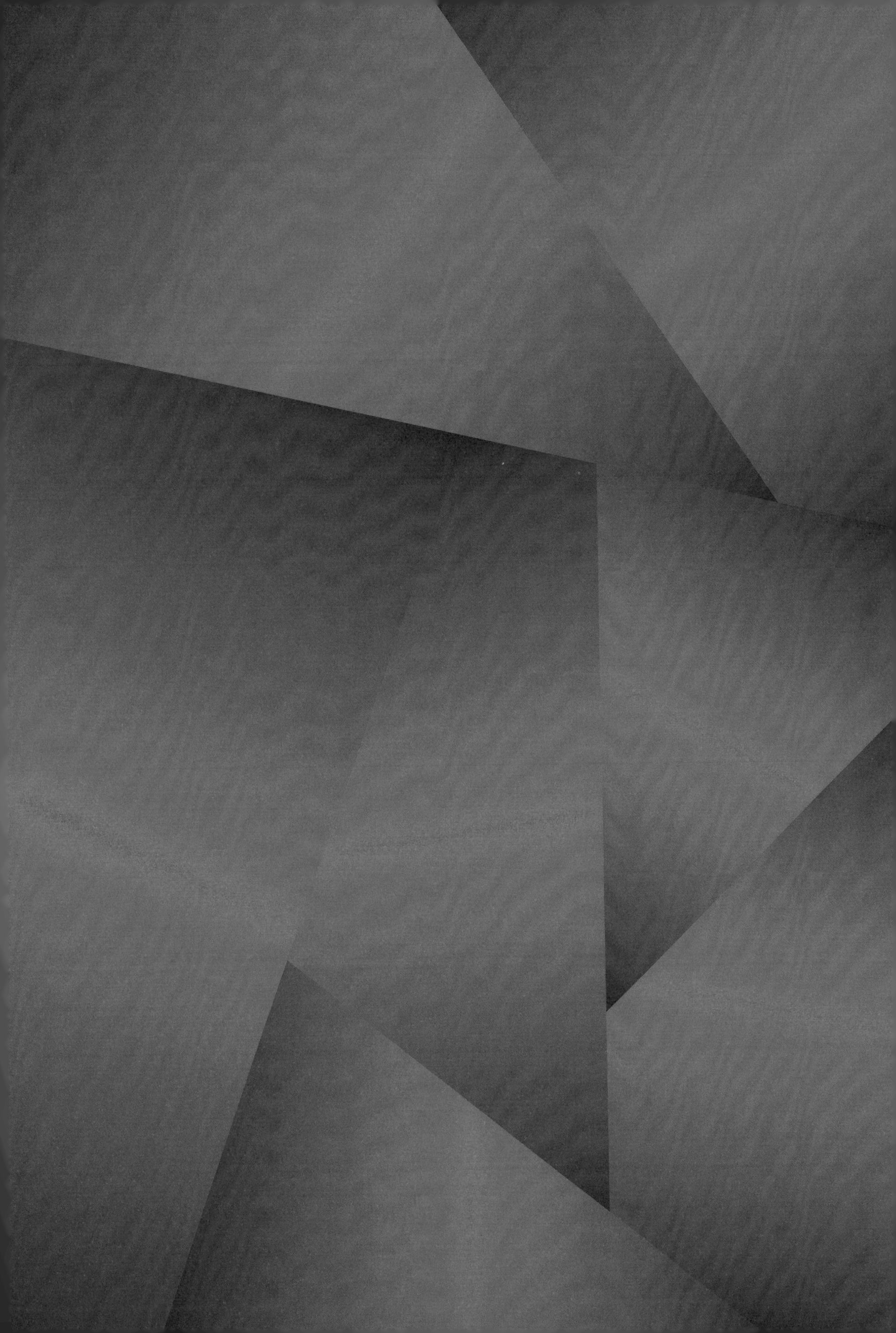

Silent Silence .com, 2014

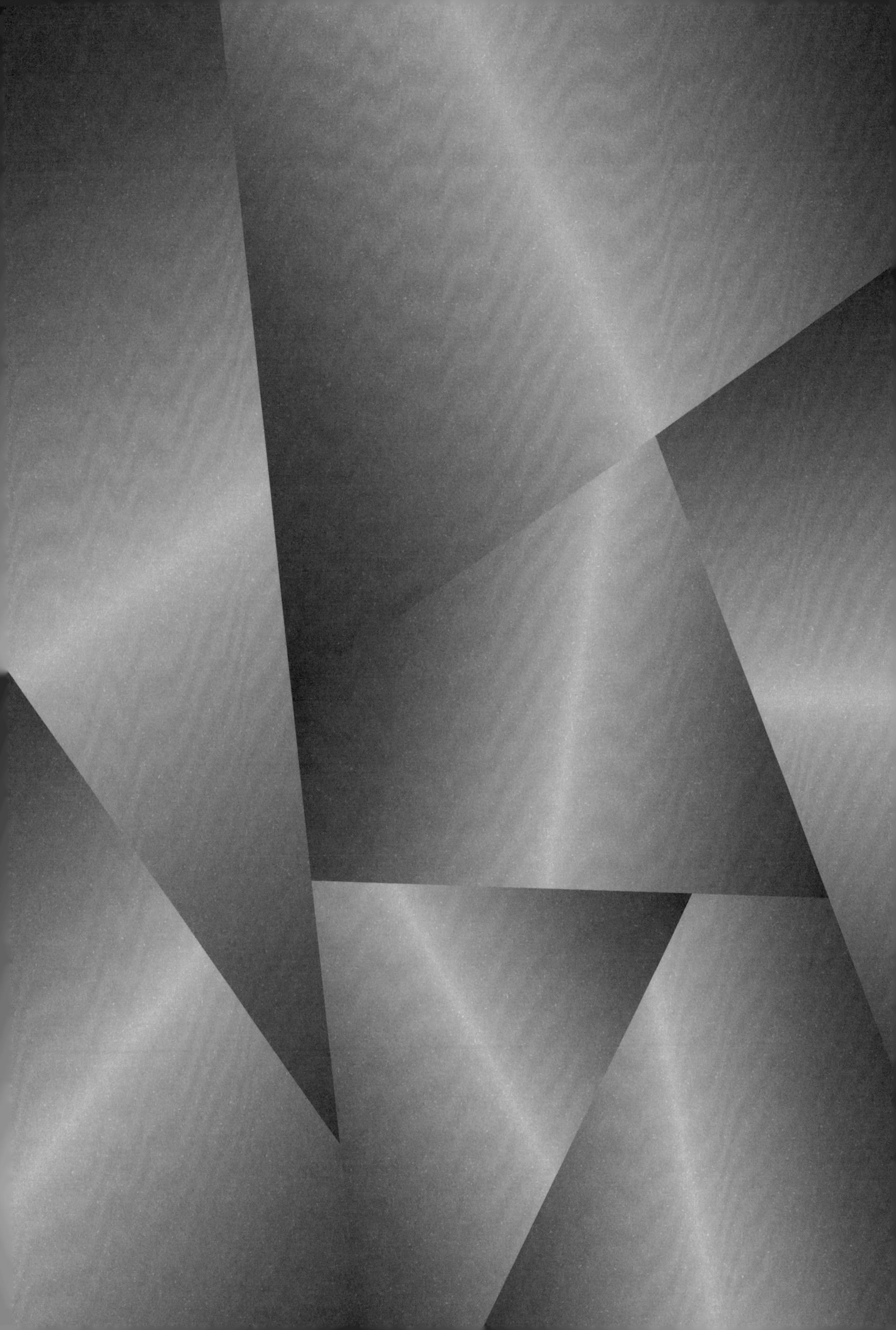

Silent Silence .com, 2014

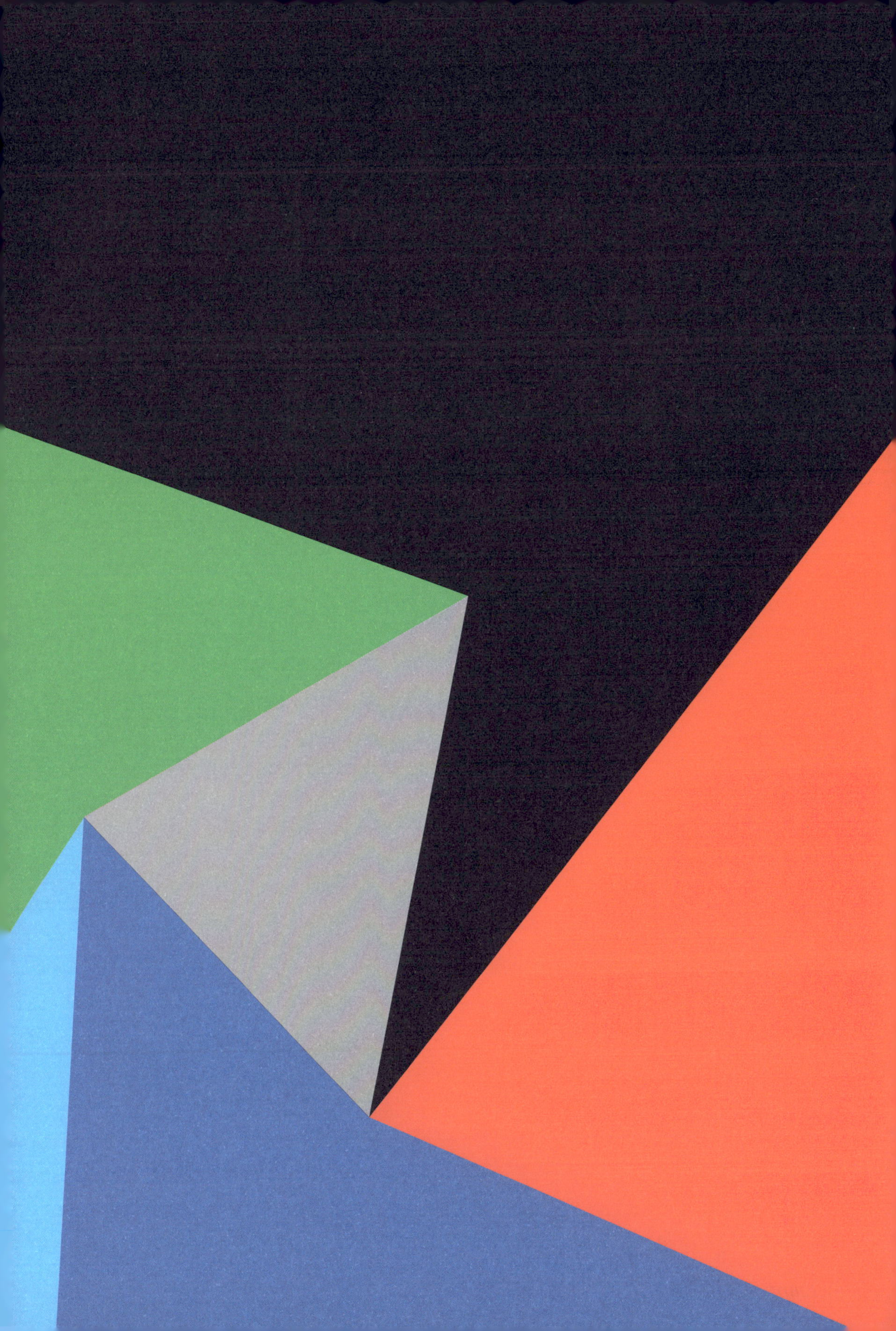

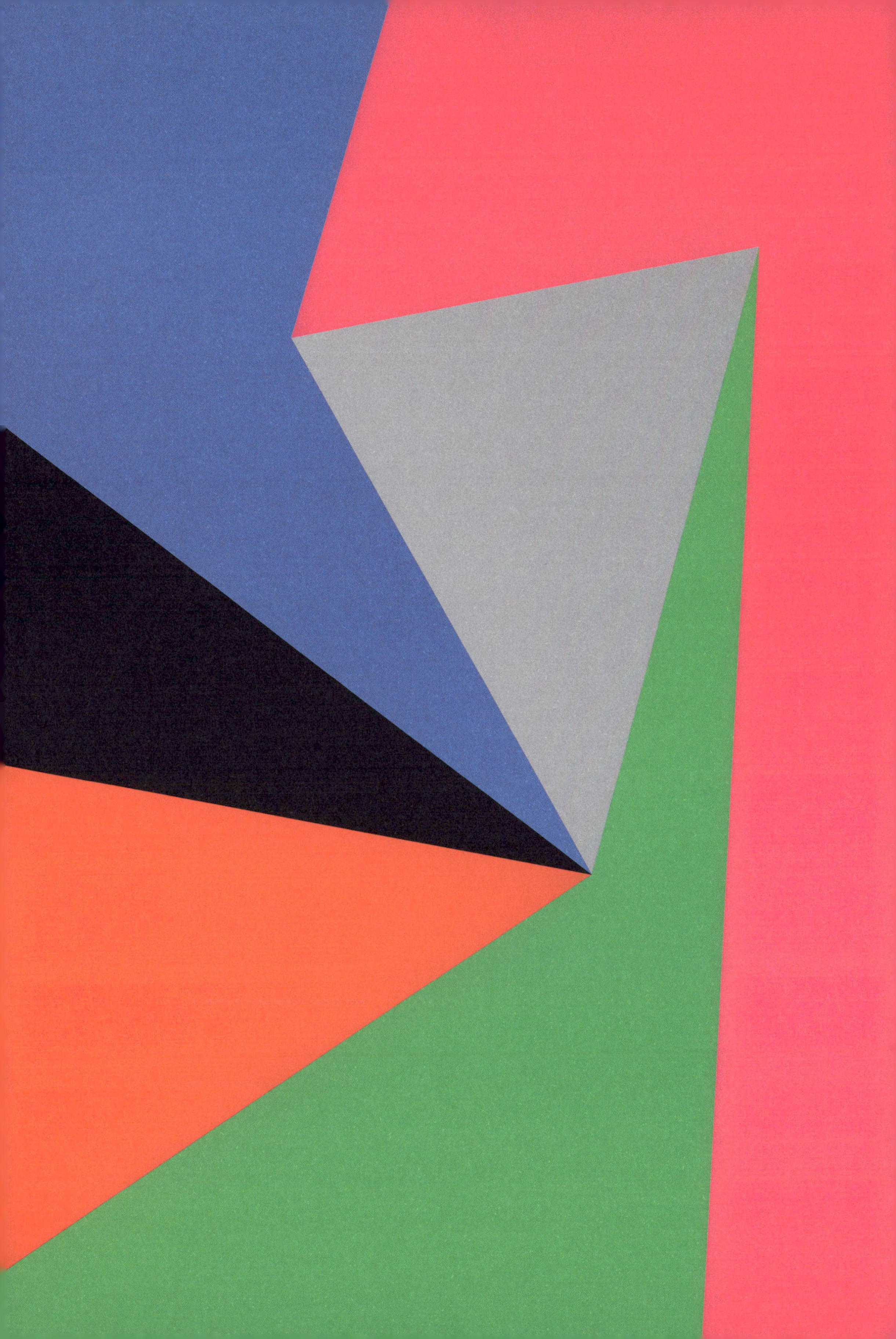

Slow Empty .com, 2013

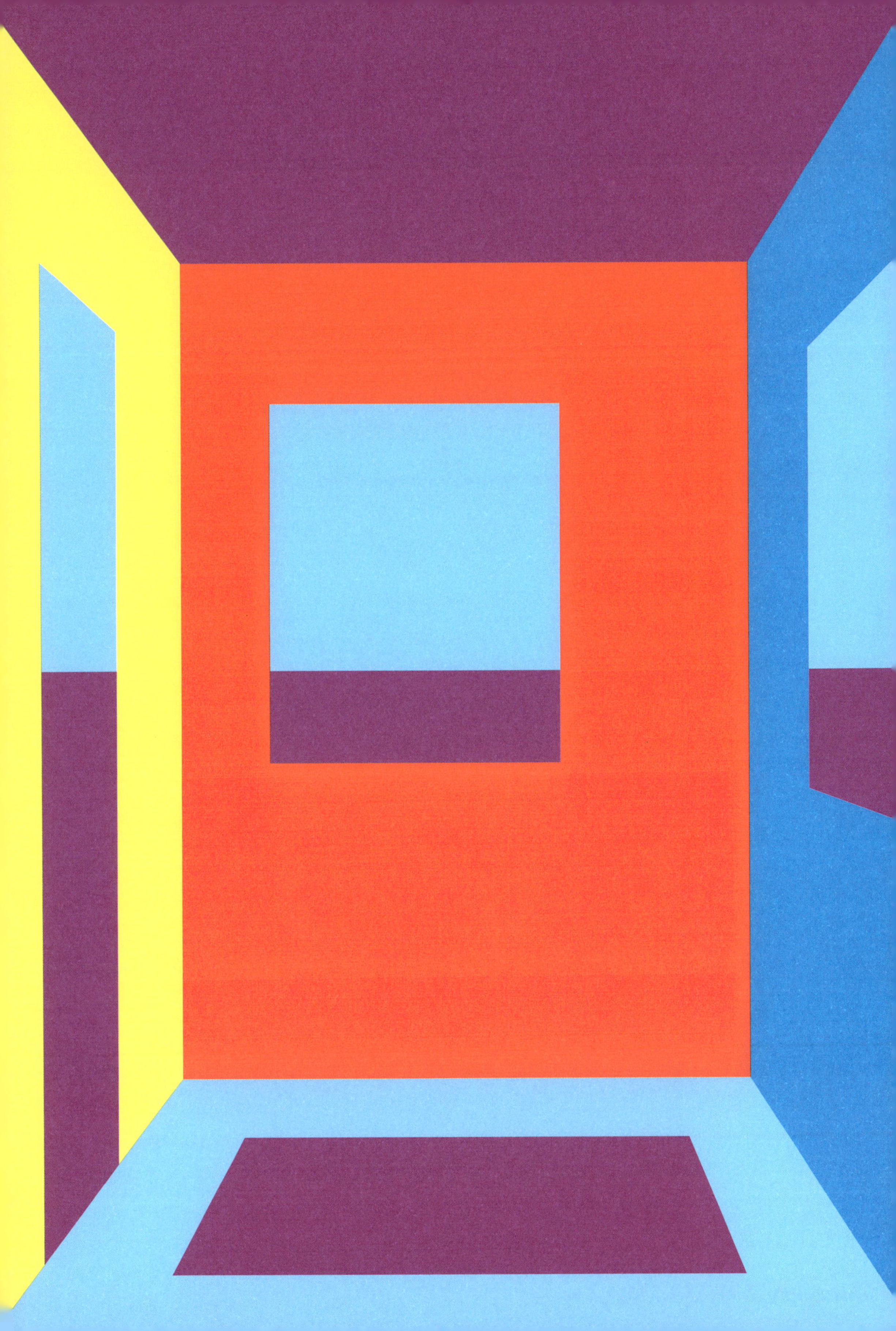

This Empty Room .com, 2015

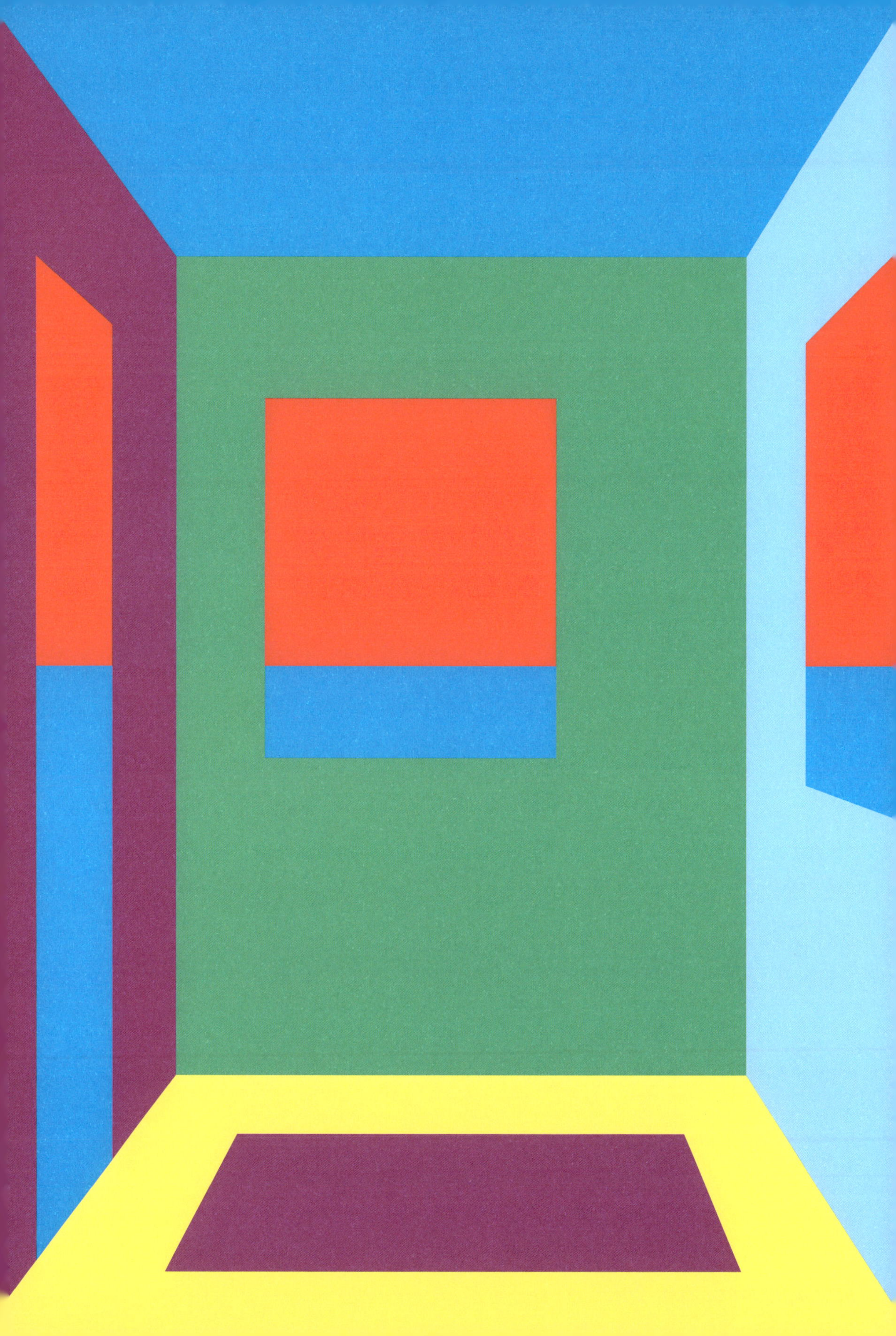

This Empty Room .com, 2015

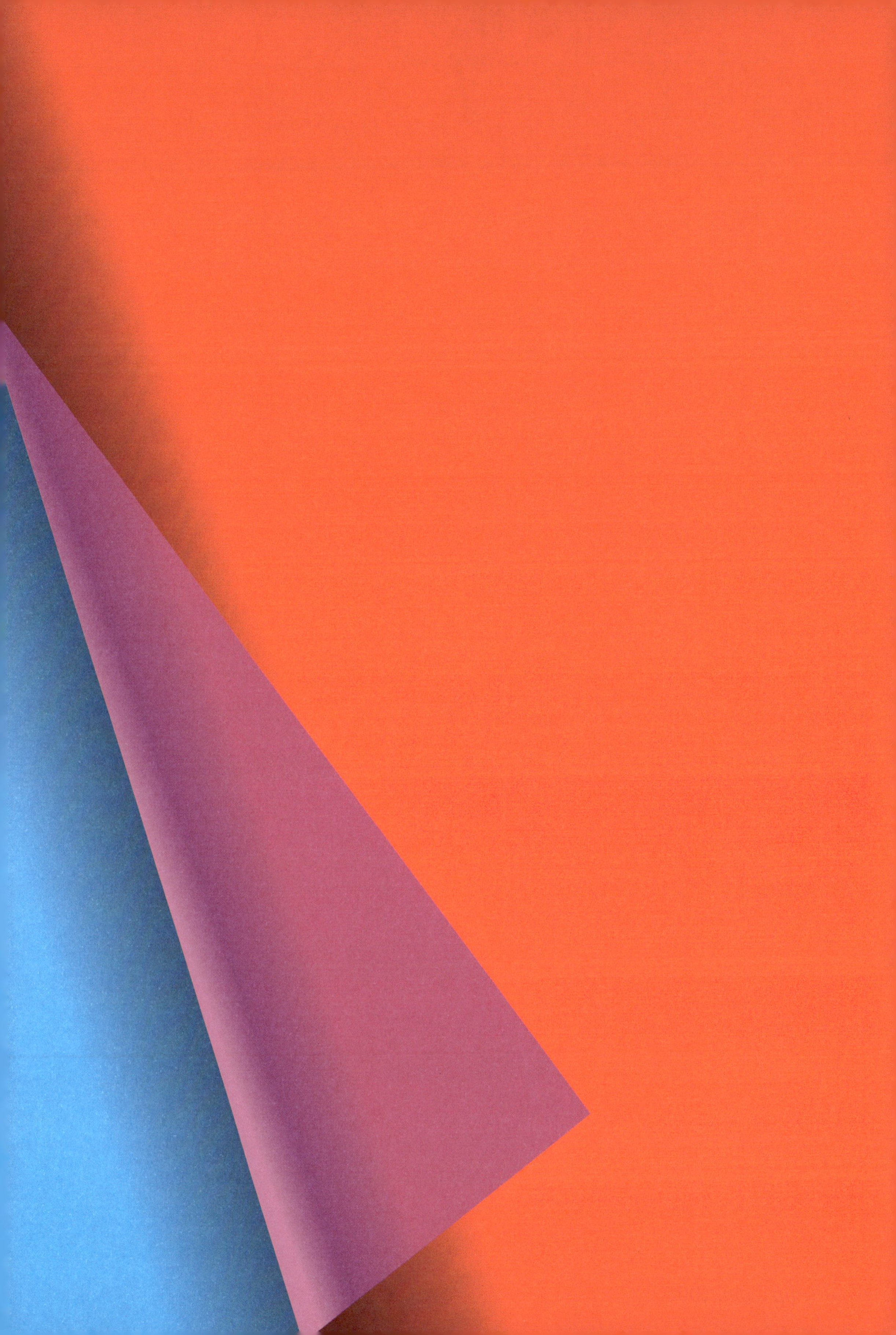

Color Flip .com, 2008

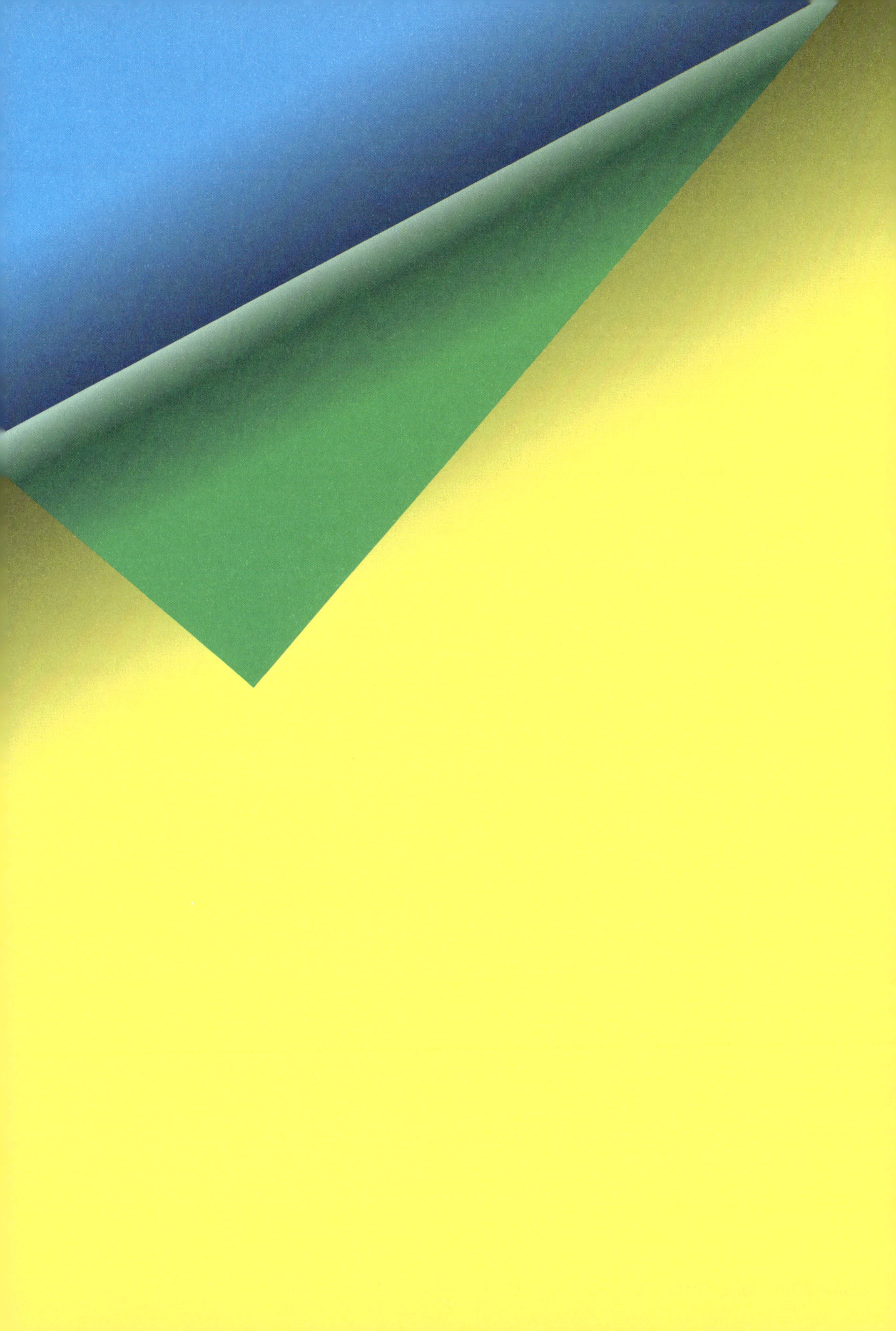

Color Flip .com, 2008

[09–11] *Almost Calm .com*, 2012
Website, dimensions variable,
duration infinite
Collection MW
Courtesy Upstream Gallery,
Amsterdam

[13–19] *Into Time .us*, 2012
Website, dimensions variable,
duration infinite
Collection Cobra to Contemporary
Courtesy Upstream Gallery,
Amsterdam

[21–23] *Never Nowhere .com*, 2014
Website, dimensions variable,
duration infinite
Collection MW
Courtesy Upstream Gallery,
Amsterdam

[25–29] *Random Fear .com*, 2013
Website, dimensions variable,
duration infinite

[31–37] *Falling Falling .com*, 2011
Website, dimensions variable,
duration infinite
Collection Hampus Lindwall

[39–43] *Float Bounce .com*, 2016
Website, dimensions variable,
duration infinite
Takuma Collection
Courtesy Takuro Someya
Contemporary Art, Tokyo

[45–47] *Hex Attack .com*, 2013
Website, dimensions variable,
duration infinite
Collection MW
Courtesy Upstream Gallery,
Amsterdam

[49–51] *Pink Yellow Blue .com*, 2014
Website, dimensions variable,
duration infinite

[53–57] *Yes No If .com*, 2014
Website, dimensions variable,
duration infinite

[59–61] *Ooze Move .com*, 2014
Website, dimensions variable,
duration infinite

[63–65] *Blank Windows .com*, 2016
Website, dimensions variable,
duration infinite
Collection Klinkhamer Family
Courtesy Upstream Gallery,
Amsterdam

[67–69] *Everything Always
Everywhere .com*, 2013
Website, dimensions variable,
duration infinite
Collection Annette Doms

[71–73] *If Yes No .com*, 2013
Website, dimensions variable,
duration infinite

[75–77] *Here That .com*, 2015
Website, dimensions variable,
duration infinite

[79–81] *Inner Doubts .com*, 2012
Website, dimensions variable,
duration infinite
The Ekard Collection
Courtesy Upstream Gallery,
Amsterdam

[83–87] *Into Time .com*, 2010
Website, dimensions variable,
duration infinite
Collection Nur Abbas

[89–91] *Looking At Something .com*, 2013
Website, dimensions variable,
duration infinite
Collection Motoi Sadakane and
Copilot Inc.
Courtesy Takuro Someya
Contemporary Art, Tokyo

[93–95] *Neo Geo City .com*, 2014
Website, dimensions variable,
duration infinite
Collection Jeremy Bailey

[97–101] *No If Yes .com*, 2014
Website, dimensions variable,
duration infinite
Collection Pontus Lindwall
Courtesy Upstream Gallery,
Amsterdam

[103–105] *Silent Silence .com*, 2014
Website, dimensions variable,
duration infinite
Collection Museum of The Image,
Breda
Courtesy Upstream Gallery,
Amsterdam

[107–109] *Slow Empty .com*, 2013
Website, dimensions variable,
duration infinite
Collection Servais Family
Courtesy Postmasters Gallery, New
York

[111–113] *This Empty Room .com*, 2015
Website, dimensions variable,
duration infinite
Collection Museum Voorlinden,
Wassenaar
Courtesy Upstream Gallery,
Amsterdam

[115–117] *Color Flip .com*, 2008
Website, dimensions variable,
duration infinite
Collection Sébastien De Ganay

A HINT OF JAPAN IN THE
WORKS OF RAFAËL ROZENDAAL

Kodama Kanazawa

ラファエル・ローゼンダールの中の日本

金澤 韻

The quiet and meditative quality of Rozendaal's works made me think that they seemed, somehow, Eastern. I also felt a great connection with the artist himself, and would often become so engrossed in our conversations that I forgot I was speaking in English. And then I received a request to write about Rozendaal's connection with Japan. Apparently, I was not the only one who had sensed an affinity with Japan in his work.

In 2013, I invited Rafaël Rozendaal to participate in an exhibition and I remember him saying in his remarks at the opening ceremony that he was thrilled to be able to do an exhibition in the land of Nintendo. The land of Nintendo! A game console launched by Nintendo in the eighties became popular around the world, and Japan led the world in the gaming industry for a while after that. However, Japanese games do not seem to have remained as popular since. Many reasons are pointed out for this, such as that the role-playing games (RPGs) popular in Japan are not quite as popular in other countries, or that the 'save-system' concepts are different in Japan and the West. According to another report, American and European gamers, being used to more realistic graphics, shy away from the planar characters featured in Japanese games. It is true that, with the evolution of high-performance gaming consoles since the early two thousands, American game developers have moved toward more realistic portrayals, as made possible by the higher performance consoles, whereas characters in Japanese games continue to keep their typically unrealistic proportions. Games that are hugely popular in Japan, such as Pokémon and Dragon Quest, are good examples of this.

The trend is similar to what is happening in the animation industry. While the smooth movements of three-dimensional characters and animals in the 3DCG animated films made by Pixar are hugely popular around the world, most Japanese animated films including those made by Miyazaki Hayao's Studio Ghibli are two-dimensional, but also enjoy great popularity, even in terms of box-office records, in Japan.

It is the desire to create a fantasy world that looks real enough to reach out and touch versus the desire to create original pictorial scenes that clearly look different from reality. Or three-dimensionality versus two-dimensionality. Both trends have had their phases of popularity throughout history, sometimes vying with each other for supremacy. In the history of art, for instance, Japonism was a popular trend in the nineteenth century, revealing an infatuation with Japanese art styles. Modern artists such as Édouard Manet, Claude Monet, and Vincent van Gogh were influenced by the compositions and motifs of *ukiyo-e* and other Japanese art so strongly that this influence is clearly visible in their works, even to later generations. Of course, there were also those who, going by the values on which

Western art was based, were critical of Japanese art for its lack of anatomical detail and perspective, lack of integrity, and poor balance in terms of the arrangement of motifs.

> Art historian Shuji Takashina explains it this way. In Western European art, it was considered important that a painting within a frame be a small world, complete in itself, but the frame in Japanese paintings was just that—a frame, a window—with the presupposition that the world existed as a continuum outside that window.[1] In other words, the composition of a scene cut out by the frame in Japanese art was quite novel from the perspective of Western European tradition. The gist of this analysis is that the concepts related to what should constitute the space of a painting are fundamentally different in Western European and Japanese art, and have developed in entirely separate contexts.

I am not trying to convey the impression that Japanese painting is singular or original. In the first place, Japanese art is the result of imitating cultural works from around the world introduced to Japan through the silk road and the arrival of Dutch ships in Japan, developing upon these imitations, and then brewing something original out of it. About a hundred years before *ukiyo-e* influenced the West in the form of Japonism, *ukiyo-e* artists were incorporating the techniques for creating perspective they had learned from Western art. The use of adjectives like 'Japanese,' therefore, is mainly for the sake of convenience. The one thing that can be said, however, is that specific situations make cultural exchange possible, and it is important to discuss these situations when studying history or contexts. For instance, Western artists had arrived at an impasse in expressing the space of a painting in the traditional Western manner, and when a limited number of paintings from faraway Japan were introduced into this situation, they played the role of offering new hints. This could be the context in which Japonism arose.

> What was the context in which Rafaël Rozendaal emerged? One thing that is clear is that the scenes he was gazing at were on a computer screen. Rozendaal has been composing these scenes, visible from this relatively small window and lacking any sense of depth, as works of art.

Let us take another look at some of Rozendaal's works. In *Unknown Landscape .com*, the screen is divided into two color planes, with the bottom one-fourth or so of the screen space in a different color than the top three-fourth, and the colors of each of these planes keep changing.

---

1   Shuji Takashina, 'Branches Drooping from the Sky: The theory of drooping branches,' 'A Collection of Essays on Art History,' 5, 1998.

The line separating the two planes is unsteady, as though drawn by hand, and gives the impression that the bottom plane represents land, while the top plane represents the sky. This kind of 'allusive' space is one of the characteristics of Rozendaal's works, and also, allusion is considered one of the main characteristics of Japanese art. Several of his works, including *This Empty Room .com*, which portrays the inside of a room in the form of a one-point perspective drawing, are good examples of such allusion. When one realizes that the intention is to be allusive, one begins to understand the unique spatial characteristics of works such as *Blank Windows .com* and *Something Open .com*.

> Next, I would like to take up planarity. Many of Rozendaal's works comprise simple color surfaces, expressed by filling in an outlined portion with a single color, which creates an impression quite similar to that created by traditional Japanese paintings.[2] Because of this, they have a very pure and strong visual impact. I would like to point out here, that Rozendaal's works are driven by a very different sense of aesthetics than that seen in the Western tradition, where shadows are used to create realistic images.

The third characteristic of Rozendaal's works is reproducibility. *Ukiyo-e* were made using woodblock printing techniques and sold at affordable prices, so ordinary people could also enjoy them. As works of art, therefore, they existed under very different circumstances than one-of-a-kind paintings and sculptures owned by royalty, titled nobility, or religious institutions as symbols of power. It is held that even before *ukiyo-e,* Japan had a tradition of inexpensive prints sold as souvenirs in tourist spots or as toys and recreational items at local festivals, and today, the trend continues in the country's *manga* culture. Rather than develop as symbols of authority or wealth, art in Japan developed to embody commonality. Rozendaal's works are also oriented in this direction. The artist feels that it is important to make them accessible to everyone, as long as they have an internet connection. Rather than finding the value of a work in its uniqueness, Rozendaal is a believer in value inherent in a concept or phenomenon itself, which is not lost even when reproduced without limit.

> The last point I would like to talk about is simplicity. *Zen*, a religious philosophy that originated in China and evolved in a unique way in Japan, is known and loved all over the world today as a Japanese aesthetic. Zen is a minimalistic aesthetic that attempts to completely eliminate the unnecessary. I think that simplicity, as

2   This method of painting in Japanese art was due to the nature of the glue-based paints, *kousaiga*, which were made by dissolving pigments in glue. *Kousaiga* is thought to have come to Japan from mainland China, but has existed in Japan for over a millennium and evolved into uniquely Japanese styles, so I use the term 'Japanese art' here for the sake of convenience.

Zen suggests, is the most important quality of Rozendaal's works. Waves surging in, unendingly, from the horizon (*Everything Always Everywhere .com*); a rotating fried egg, both the white and yolk of which subtly change in size based on the screen width (*egg alone.com*); a glass window that can be slid open by moving the cursor to the right, revealing a more vividly blue-and-green scene outside (*Open This Window .com*)——the story in all these works could seem inconsequential or even silly, especially when viewed in light of Europe's impressive tradition in the humanities.

Zen says – don't think, don't speak; nothing is real. By the standards of our modern world, this seems a somewhat extreme philosophy, but I think it embodies a hard-earned nugget of wisdom acquired by people in the old days in their attempts to attain the truth. Rather than amassing ideas clothed in words, simply observe, become aware of, and awaken to the various phenomena of this world in which we live; comprehend them in your own mind. I think one of the reasons for the popularity of Rozendaal's art is its simplicity, honesty, and its embodiment of the artist's minute awareness of the surroundings in which he is placed.

Rozendaal's *haikus*, which he says he began to write after his exhibition in Japan, also embody this simplicity. Though using words (we do have to use the basic minimum of tools to express our thoughts and feelings), his poetry pares them back as much as possible while still expressing how he views the truths of life and this world of ours.

(I offer the haiku below as an illustration)

time passes

until

time ends

It is possible that the contemporary world in some ways replicates the state of pre-modern Japan: the *ukiyo-e* era, when the Japanese government at times severely limited the number of ports for trade, and information that people received from the outside world was also limited. We modern folk are always staring at the small screens of our mobile phones, tablets and computers. Filter bubbles limit the variety of information that seeps through to us. Perhaps, in terms of the ability to weave a rich tapestry of images from narrow interfaces and limited sources and create something new out of them, there is a connection between Rozendaal and Japanese tradition.

ローゼンダールの作品に静けさと瞑想性を感じ、どこか東洋的だと思うことがあった。作家本人とのコミュニケーションでも強い親近感を覚え、話しているときに、英語を使っていることを忘れることが度々あった。そこへきて、作家と日本との関係について書いてほしい、という依頼をもらった。きっと私が感じていたローゼンダールと日本との親和性は、さほど唐突なことではないに違いない。

ラファエル・ローゼンダールが、2013年、私の招いた展覧会のオープニングで、「ニンテンドーの国で展示をすることができて嬉しい」と挨拶したのを覚えている。ニンテンドーの国 ── 1980年代にニンテンドーが発売したゲーム機が世界中で人気になって、しばらく日本はゲーム業界をリードしていた。ただその後日本のゲームの人気は一時期ほどではないようである。原因として語られるのは、日本で好まれるRPGが日本以外の国では好まれないとか、セーブシステムの概念が違うとか、いろいろあるのだが、一説に、日本ゲームの平面的なキャラクターが、写実的なグラフィックが好まれる欧米で敬遠されている、というものがある。確かに、特に2000年代に入ってからゲーム機はより高性能なものに進化したが、アメリカがその性能により可能になるリアリスティックな描写を実現する方向に動いたのに対し、日本ではゲームのキャラクターは独自の非現実的なプロポーションを保ったままだ。日本で絶大な人気を誇るタイトル「ポケットモンスター」や「ドラゴンクエスト」などにその例を見てとることができる。

> これはどうも商業アニメーションの世界で起きていることと似通っている。ピクサーが手がける３DCGアニメーションの、立体的なキャラクターや動物のなめらかに動くスペクタクルが世界中で人気を博す一方で、宮崎駿のスタジオジブリ作品を筆頭に、日本で作られるアニメーションは２Dが多く、興行成績でも圧倒的な人気を誇っている。

仮想世界を、リアルに、まるでそこにあるみたいに作り上げたいという欲望と、明らかに現実とは違う見た目の、独自の絵画的空間を作り出したいという欲望。あるいは立体性と平面性。この二つの潮流は、歴史の中で何度となく姿を現し、時にぶつかり合ってきた。例えば美術史の中では、19世紀に興ったジャポニスムにその邂逅の様子を見ることができる。マネ、モネ、ゴッホといった近代の画家たちが、浮世絵を中心とした日本の絵画の構図やモチーフを参照し、後世にもはっきりと分かる影響を見せた。もちろん、伝統的な西洋絵画の価値観から、解剖学、透視図法の知識の欠如、統一性のなさ、モチーフ配置のバランスの悪さによって日本絵画を批判する向きもあった。

> 美術史家の高階秀爾は、次のように言う。西欧においては絵画の枠の中は一つの小宇宙として完結していることが重要と考えられたが、日本の絵画における枠は文字どおり窓そのもので、枠外に世界が続いて存在していることが前提だった、と。[1]つまり、日本の絵画では、枠によって切り取られる光景の構図が、西欧の

伝統からすると斬新なものになり得たということだ。この分析が語りかけているのは、両者の絵画空間における概念の違いが抜本的なものであり、まったく違う文脈の中に存在してきたということである。

もっとも、私が言いたいのは日本絵画の比類なき独自性といったことではない。そもそも日本の美術は、シルクロードやオランダ船などを通してもたらされた、世界中の文物を、模倣し、発展させ、醸成してきたものだ。浮世絵がジャポニスムとして西洋に影響を与える100年ほど前には、浮世絵師が西洋絵画から学んだ透視図法を画面の中に取り入れたりもしている。だから「日本の」と名前をつけてはいるが、便宜的なものであることを断っておかなければならない。ただ一つ言えるのは、文化の交流にはそれを可能にするシチュエーションがあり、それを語ることは歴史や文脈を研究する上で有意義だということだ。例えば、ジャポニスムは西洋の伝統的な絵画空間に行き詰まりを感じていた画家たちのレディネスがあって、そこに地理的に遠方にあったがために供給の限られていた日本の絵画がもたらされたとき、ある種のヒントとして機能したということもできるだろう。

ラファエル・ローゼンダール登場のシチュエーションは何であろうか。確かなことは、彼の見つめていたスクリーンが、パソコン画面だということだ。この奥行きのない、比較的小さい窓から見える景色を、彼は芸術空間として構成しつづけている。

改めてラファエル・ローゼンダールの作品を見てみよう。Unknown Landscape. com は画面の下四分の一くらいの部分で上下それぞれ違う色面に分かれており、それぞれの色面は次第に別の色へと変化していく。二つの色面の境界は手で引かれたような不安定なラインとなっており、そのため、下の色面が大地を、上の色面が空を表しているように見える。このような「見立て」の空間は、ラファエル・ローゼンダールの作品の特徴の一つだ。色面によって一点透視図的な室内を表現したthis empty room.com などいくつかの作品はそのよい例だろう。このような見立てのシステムが内包されていると考えるとき、blank windows.comや、something open.comなどが持つ、独特の空間性を私たちは知ることになる。

次に、平面性を挙げることができる。ローゼンダールの多くの作品は、単純な色面により構成されており、それはアウトラインによって囲まれた部分を単一色で塗りつぶして表現した、伝統的な日本の絵画と近い印象を与える[2]。このため、ローゼンダールの作品は視覚的に素朴で強いインパクトをもたらすものとなっている。ここでは、陰影をつけて、写実的に物事を表そうとしてきた西

1　高階秀爾「空から降る枝－『枝垂れモティーフ論』」『美術史論叢』5、1998。

2　日本絵画におけるこの描き方は、顔料を膠で溶いて絵の具とした、膠彩画の素材の性質によるところが大きい。膠彩画は中国大陸から渡って来たものと考えられるが、千数百年の長い間、日本にも存在し、また独自の表現形式にも発展したことから、ここでは便宜的に日本の絵画と呼ぶ。

　　洋の伝統とは異なる美意識が働いていることを指摘しておきたい。
三つ目の特徴として、複製性を挙げることができるだろう。日本の浮世
絵は、木版技術によって生産され、廉価で販売されたことで、庶民に親
しまれた。王侯貴族や宗教組織がその権力の証として所有した一点物の
絵画や彫刻と、まったく別のありようを示す芸術品だった。浮世絵以前
にも、観光地のお土産、お祭りの日などで販売されるおもちゃ、娯楽品
として販売される廉価な印刷物の伝統があったとされ、また現代におい
ては漫画文化がその流れを受け継いでいる。権力、財力の象徴となる方向
性というより、ある種の公共性を体現していく方向性だ。ローゼンダール
の作品もこの方向を向いている。作品が、ネットにつながっていさえす
ればいつでもどこでも見られるようになっていることが重要だと作家は
考えている。一点もののアウラにその貴重さを見出すのではなく、無制
限に再生されても失われない、コンセプトあるいは現象そのものに宿る
価値を、ローゼンダールは信じている。
　　最後にシンプリシティについて話したい。今日、禅という中国発祥の宗
　教哲学は、日本で独自の発展を遂げて今では日本の美学として世界
　中に普及し、愛されている。それは不要なものを極力排除しようとす
　る、マイナスの美学である。私は、ローゼンダールの作品の最も重要な
　資質はこのシンプリシティにあると考えている。水平線から波が止む
　ことなく押し寄せてくる（everything always everywhere.com）。目
　玉焼きが回転するとき、スクリーンのサイズに合わせて黄身も白身も微
　妙に大きさを変える（egg alone.com）、カーソルを右に動かすとガラ
　ス窓がスライドするようによりはっきりとした緑と青の景色が姿を現す
　（open this window.com）。それらのストーリーは取るに足らない、特
　に、ヨーロッパの重厚な人文学の蓄積を前に眺めると、ほとんど意味
　のない、あるいは馬鹿げたものにも感じられるかもしれない。
禅は、考えるな、語るな、そこに真実はない、と教える。現代に生きる
私たちのスタンダードからすると、やや極端にも感じられるのだけれ
ど、昔から人間が苦闘して得てきた、真実に至るための知見の一つなの
だろうと思う。言葉による思考を積み重ねるのではなく、私たちのいる
この世界に起こる現象を見ること、それを感知すること、気づくこと。
心の内側でその意味を悟ること。ローゼンダール作品の人気の一端は、
素朴で、誠実な態度と、自己と自分を取り巻く環境への気づきに満ちて
いることにあるのではないか。
　　川崎での展示をきっかけに始めたという俳句の作品も、このシン
　プリシティを体現している。言葉を使いながら（どのみち、私た
　ちは思いや考えを表現するために最低限のツールを用いなければ
　ならない）、これ以上ないほど短く刈り込まれた詩に、私たちは
　世界の、人生の真実を見ているのだ。

（以下の俳句は図版として使いたいもの）

time passes

until

time ends

もしかすると、現代の世界は、日本における近代以前の状況をどこかで再現しているのかもしれない。携帯電話、タブレット、パソコンの、小さなスクリーンを常に見ている私たち。フィルターバブルによって外界からやってくる情報は限られたものになっている。その狭いインターフェースと制限されたソースから、豊かなイメージを紡ぎだし、新しいクリエイションへと繋げた精神において、ローゼンダールと“日本の伝統”はつながっているのかもしれない。

all i want

is a little bit more

than anyone else

money

more is better

some is ok

is it good

is it bad

at least i tried

i love you

you love me

we love each other

going home

to see christina

smile on my face

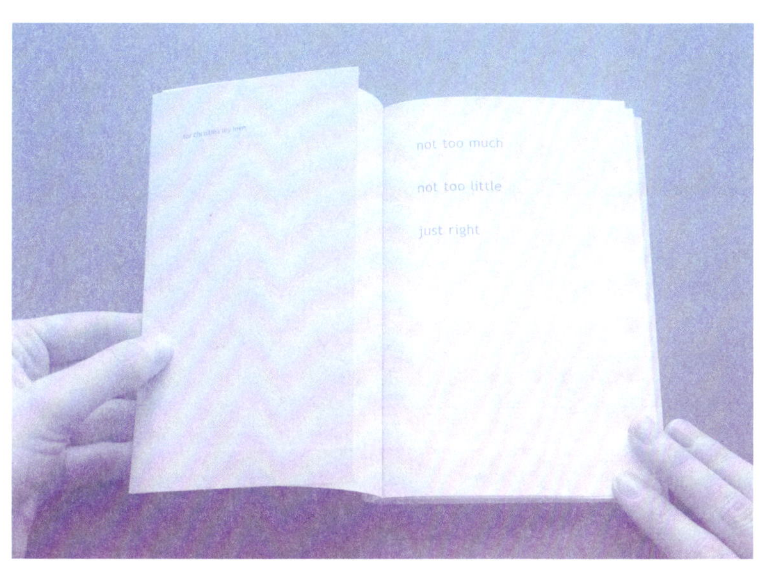
not too much

not too little

just right

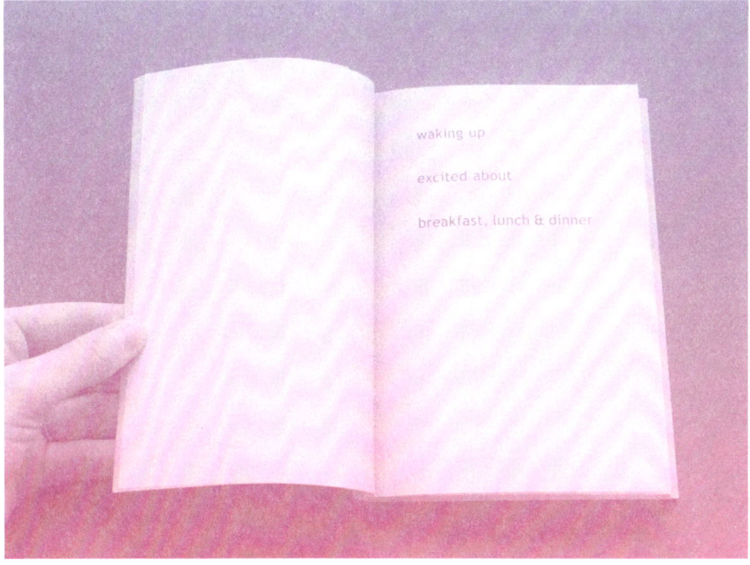
waking up

excited about

breakfast, lunch & dinner

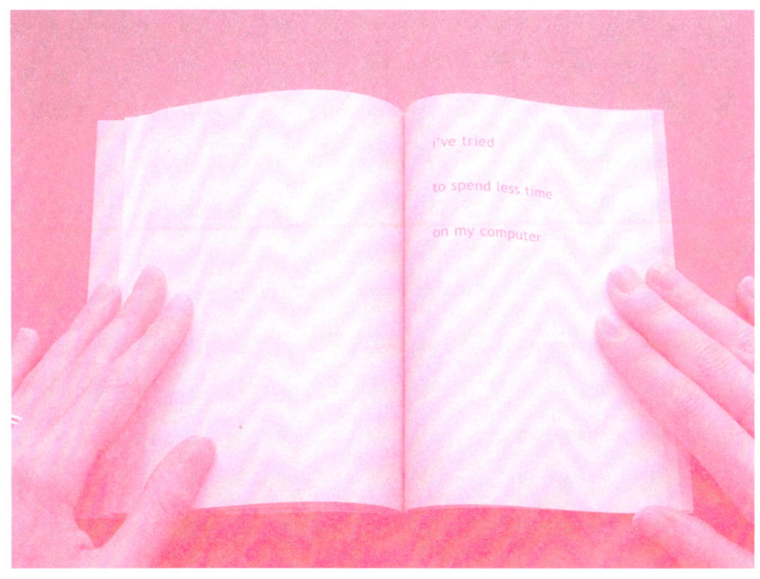
i've tried

to spend less time

on my computer

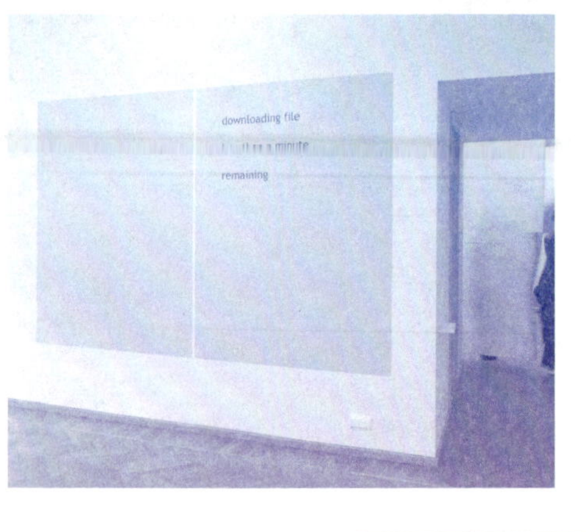
downloading file
it is a minute
remaining
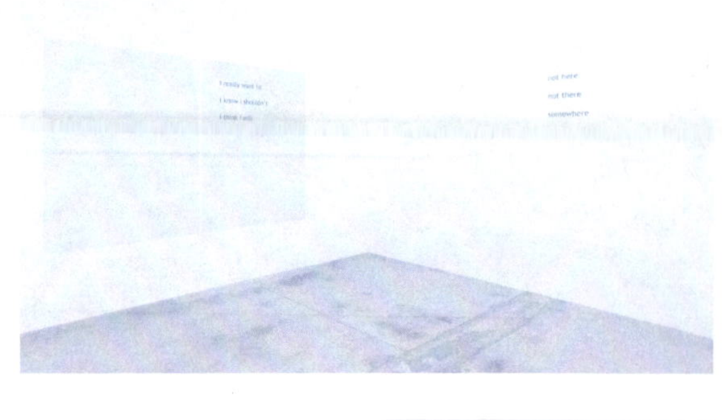
i really want to
i know i shouldn't
i think i will
not here
not there
somewhere
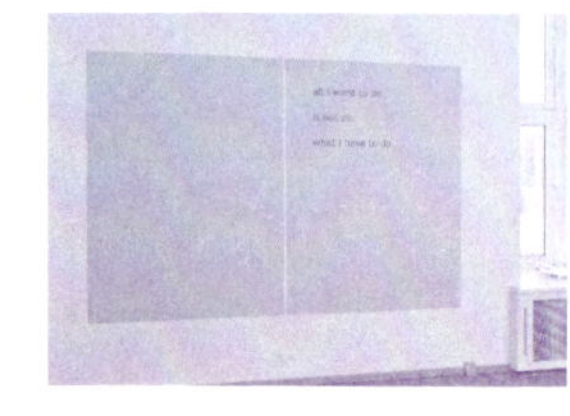
all i want to do.
is not do.
what i have to do
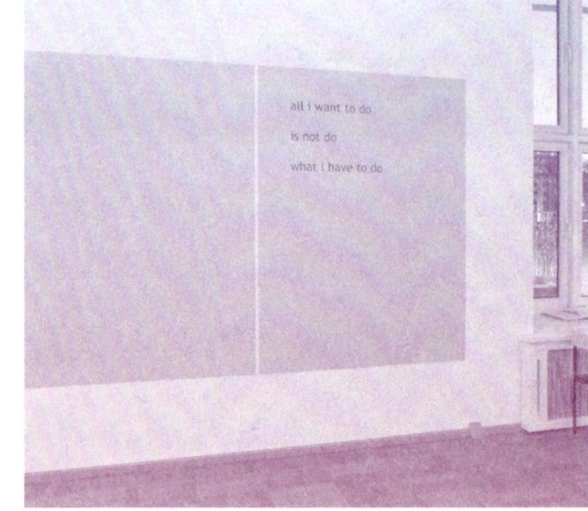
all i want to do.
is not do.
what i have to do
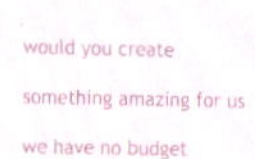
in my chair
wondering if i'm
doing too much

is it good
is it bad
at least i tried

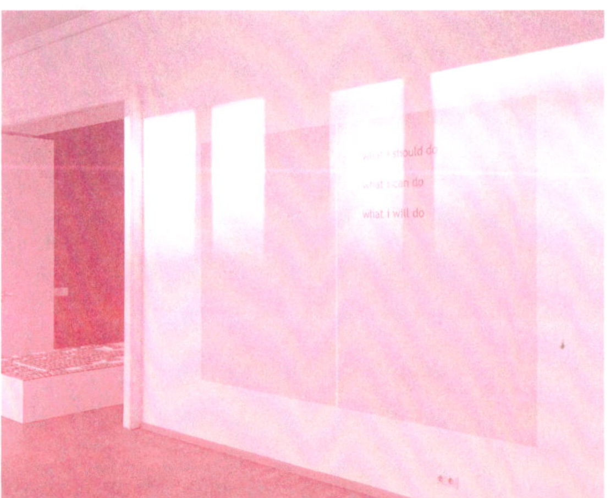
what i should do
what i can do
what i will do

future repairing
rather
not working

trying to remember

something

i forgot

not too much

not too little

just right

not here

not there

somewhere

when there is nothing

i think of something

and dream of quiet

everything's fucked

might as well

be happy

not here
not there
somewhere
what i should do
what i can do
what i will do
would you create
something amazing for us
we have no budget

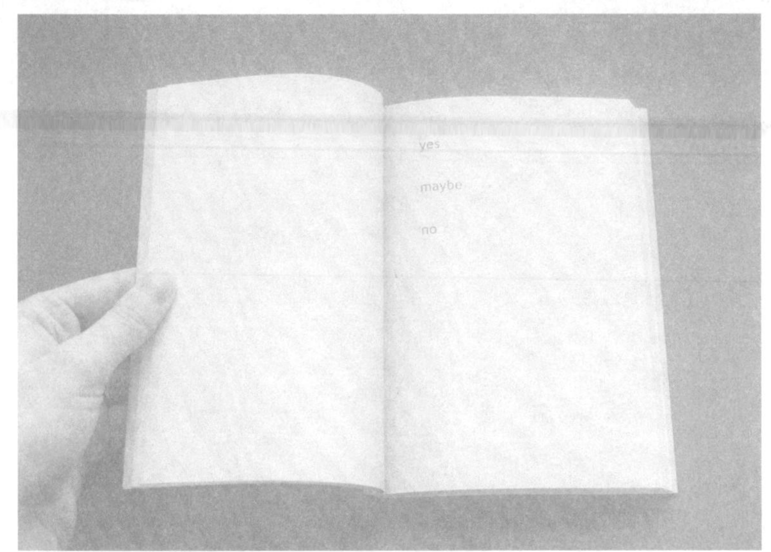
yes
maybe
no

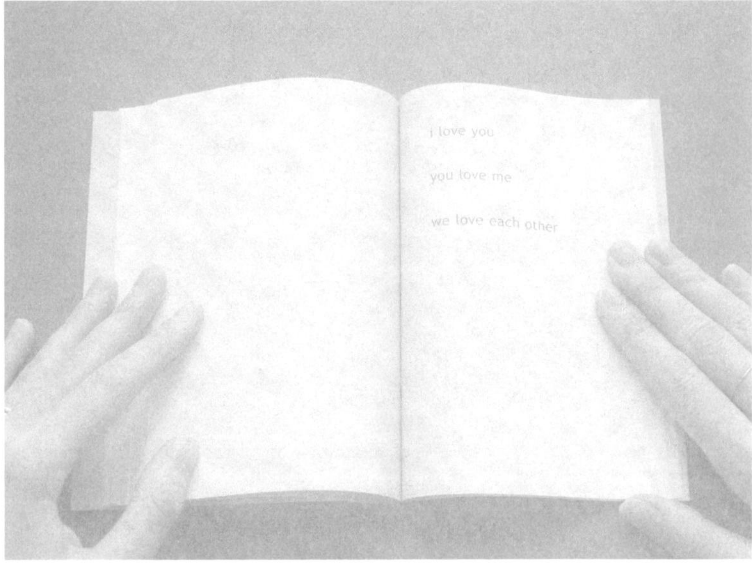
i love you
you love me
we love each other

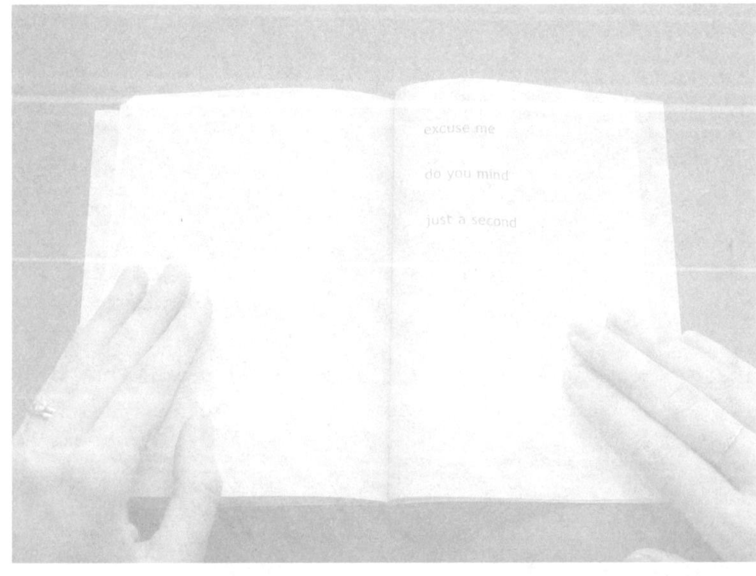
excuse me
do you mind
just a second

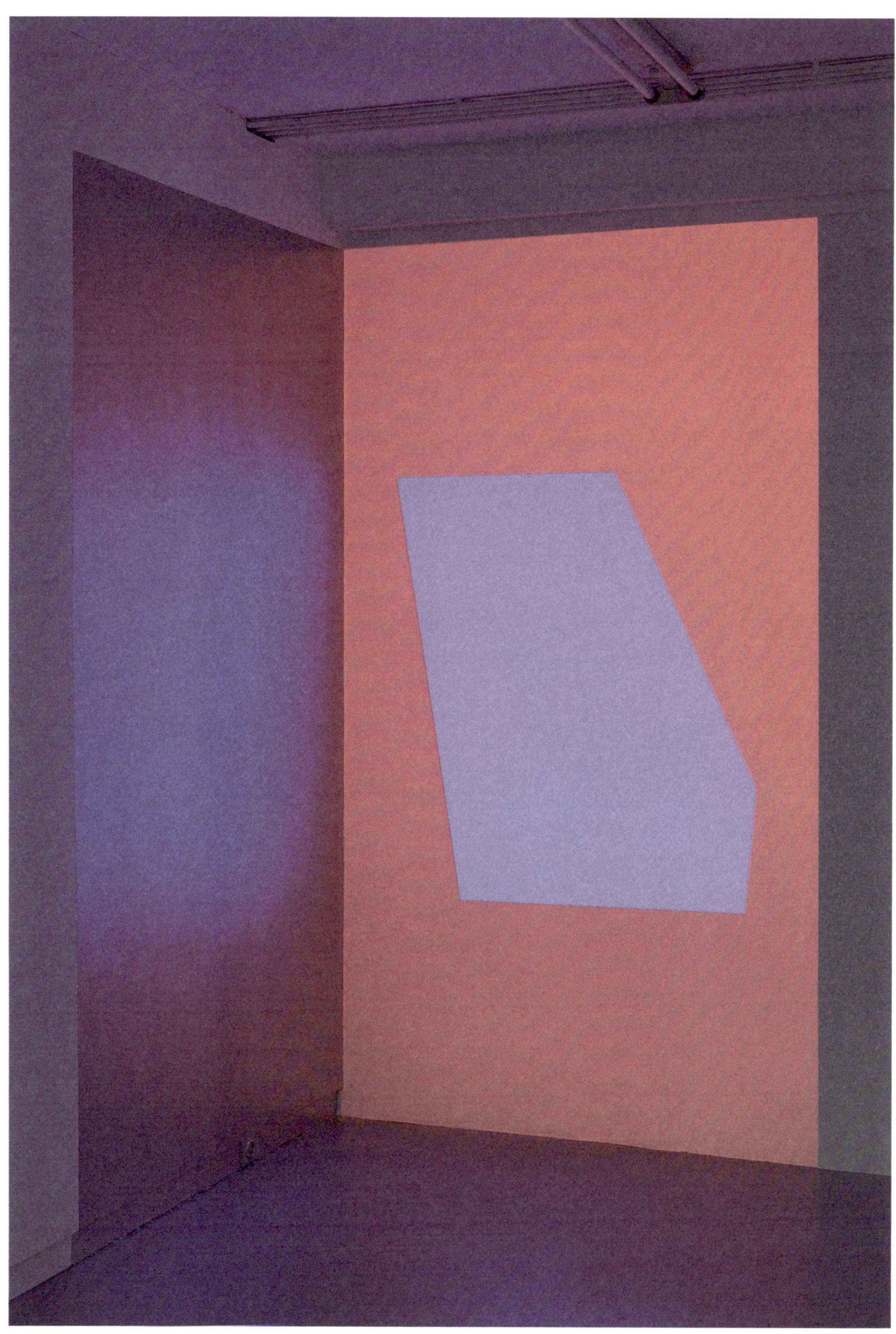

Deep Sadness .com, 2014

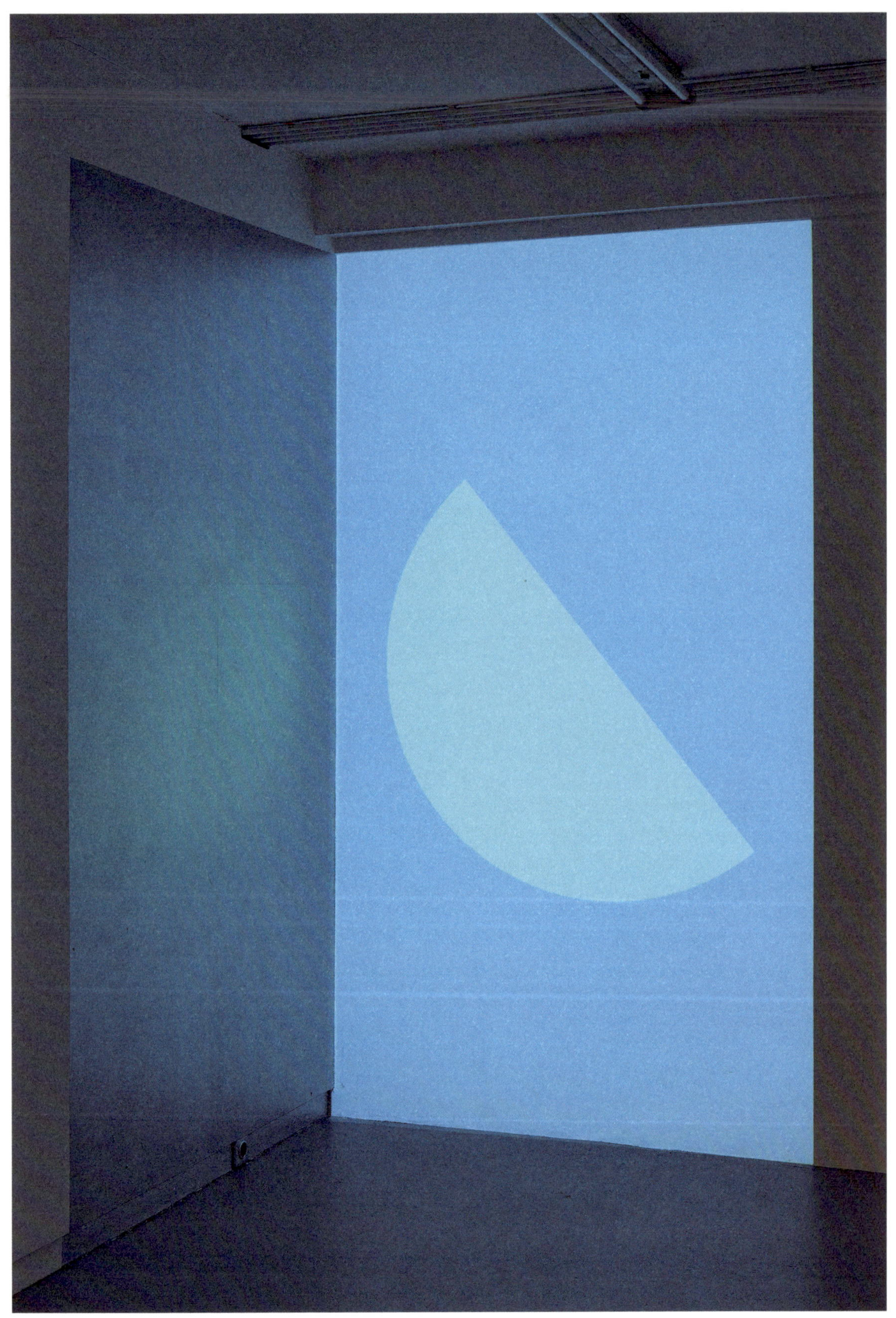

Deep Sadness .com, 2014

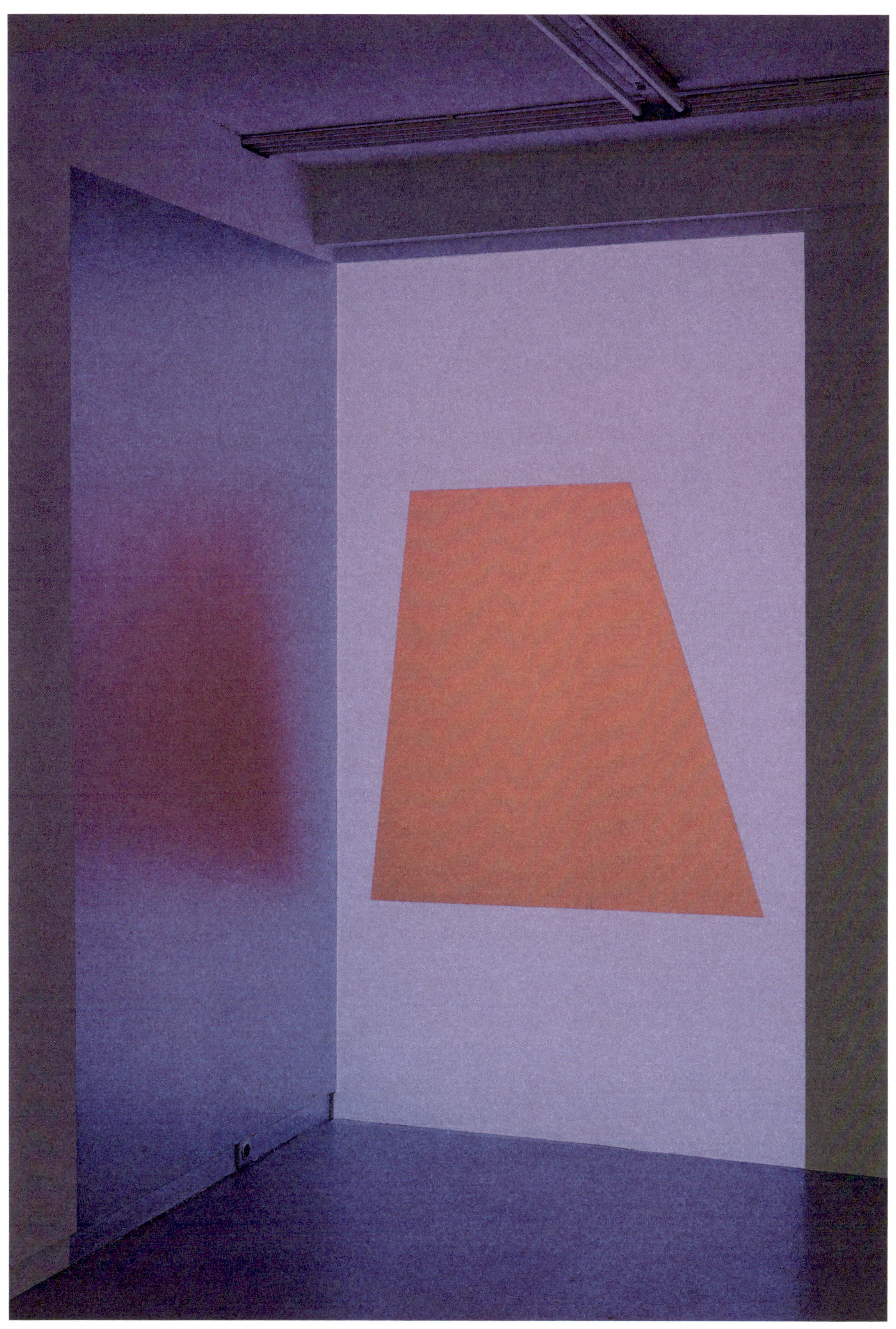

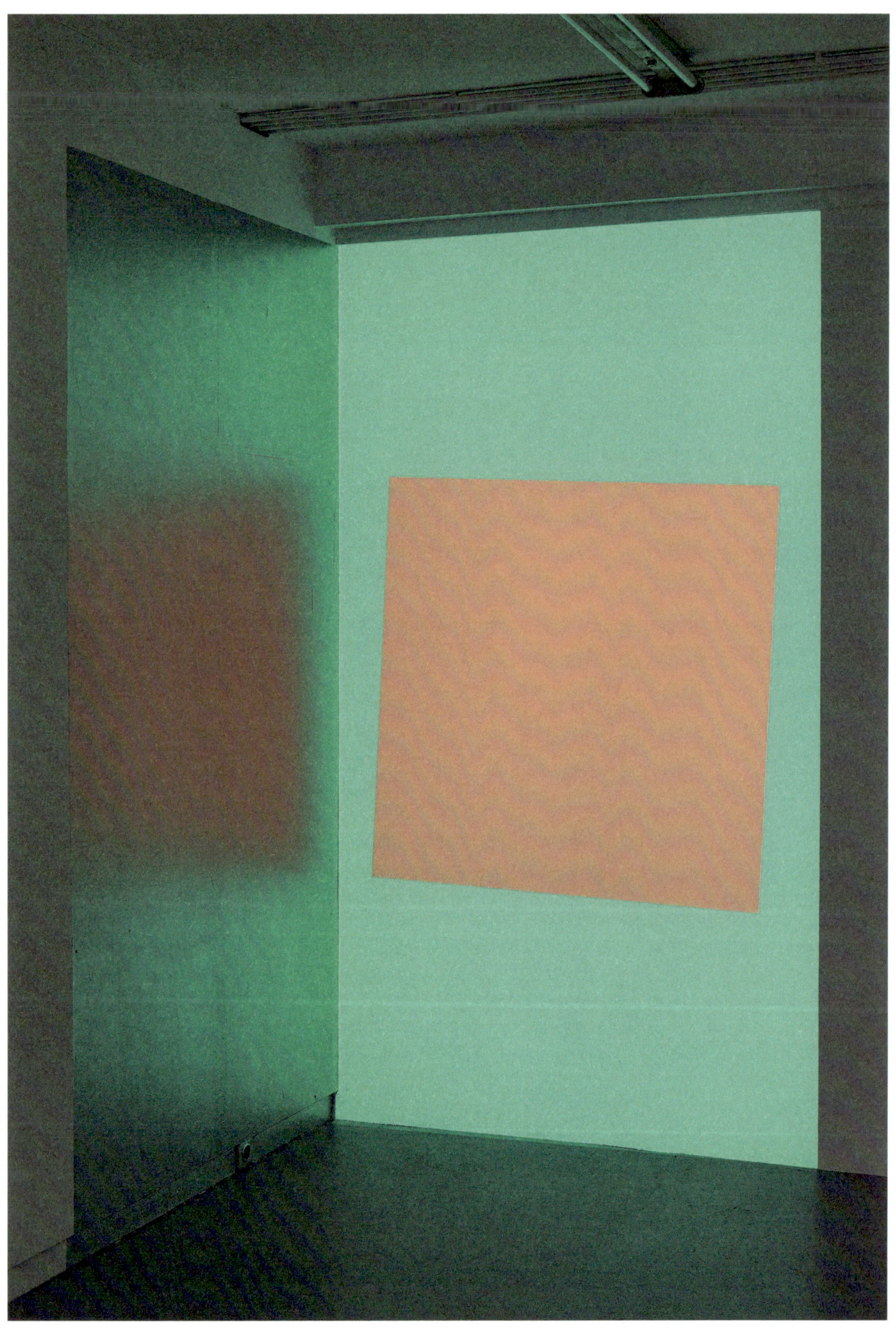

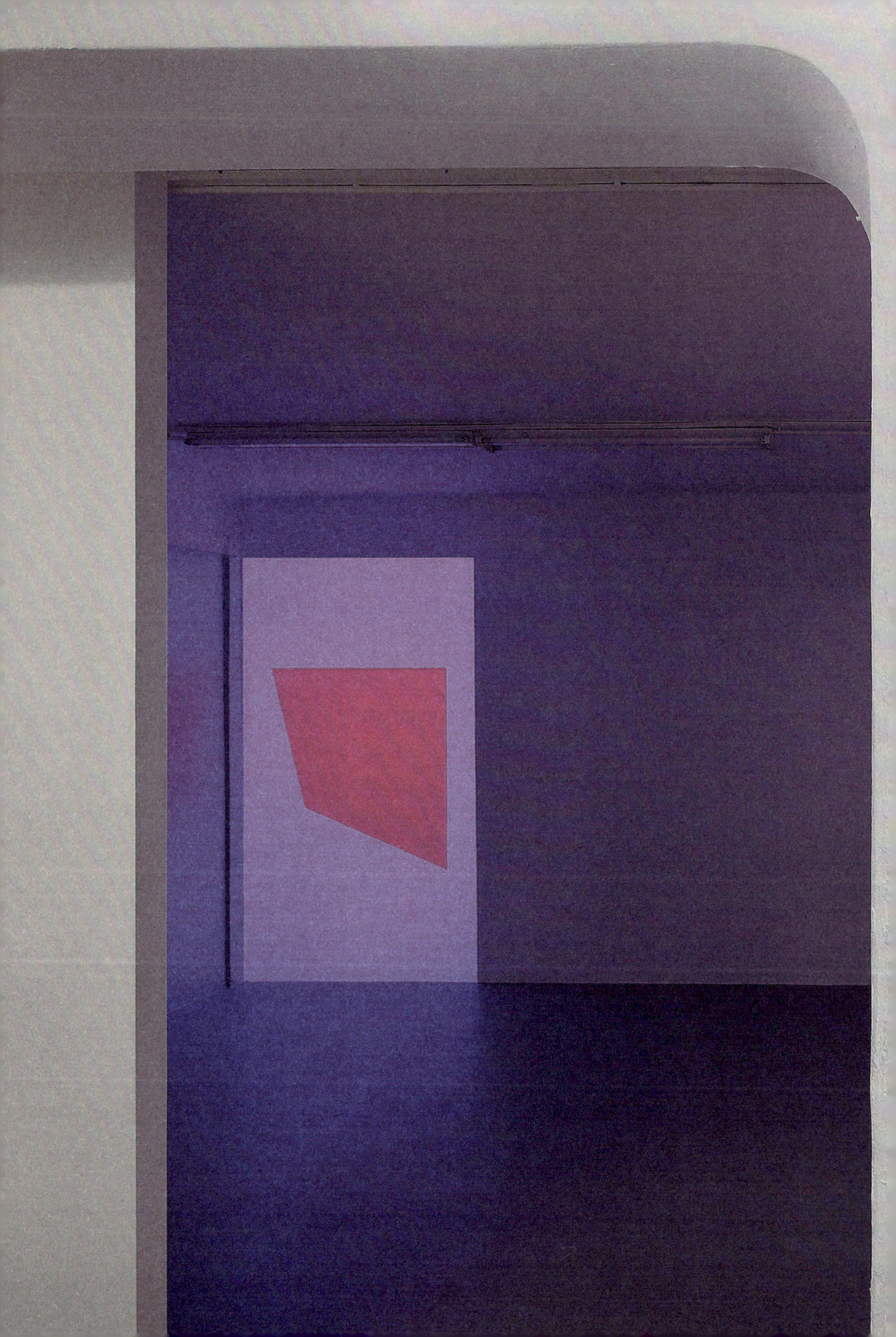

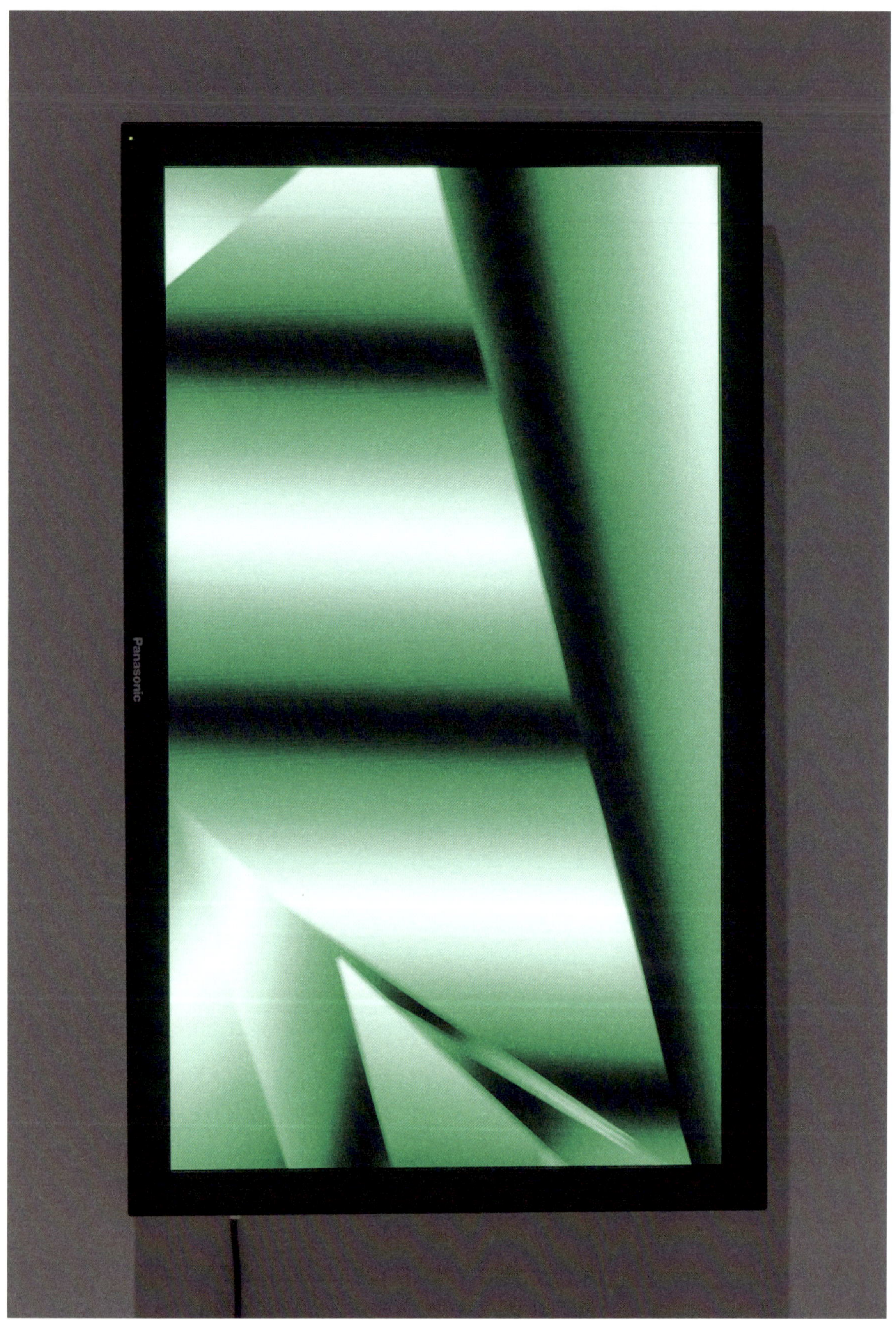

Silent Silence .com, 2014

152 *Soft Focus*, 2015
153 *On and On*, 2015
158–161 *Much Better Than This .com* at Times Square, 2015
164 *On and On*, 2015
165 *Soft Focus*, 2015

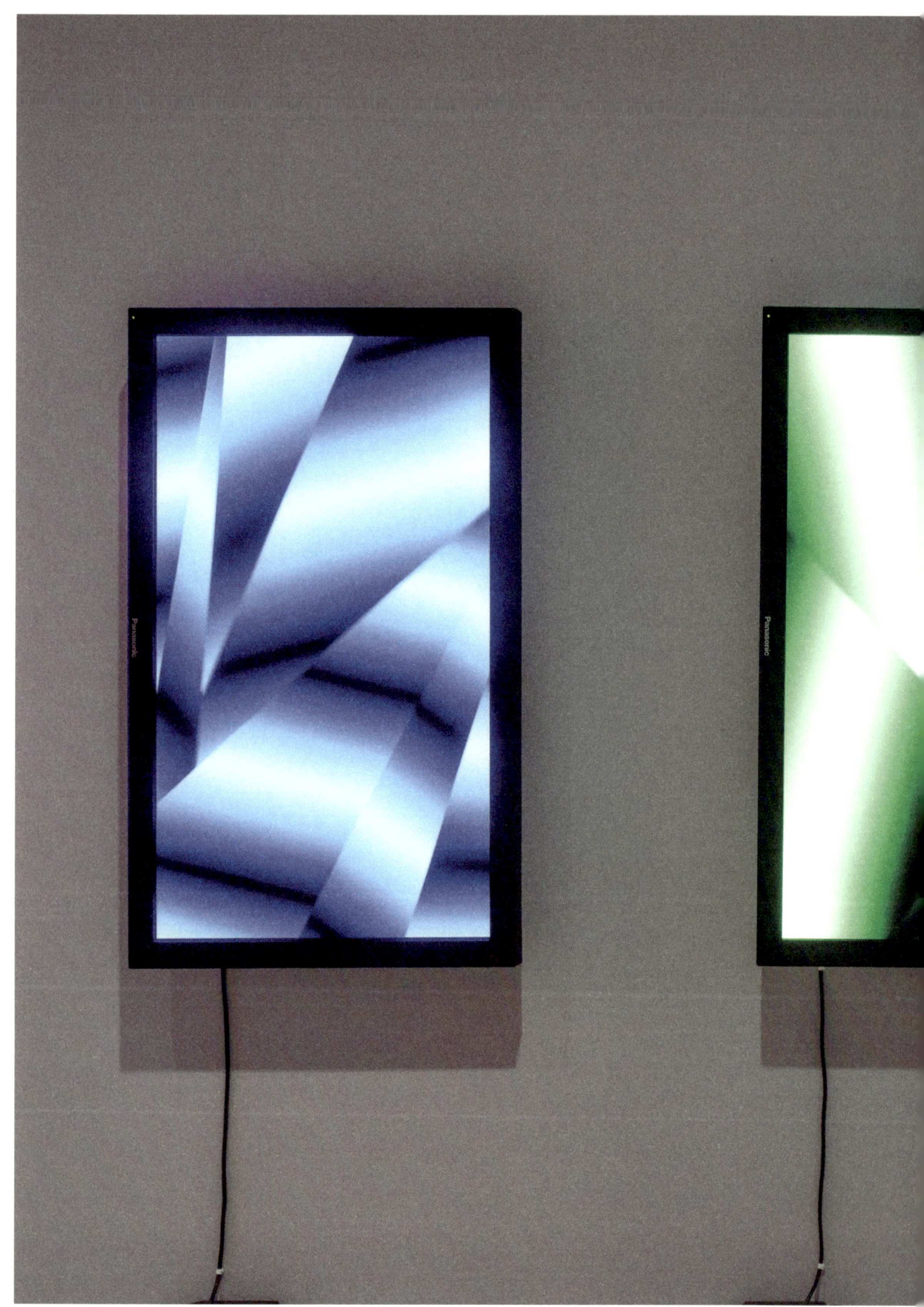

Silent Silence .com, 2014

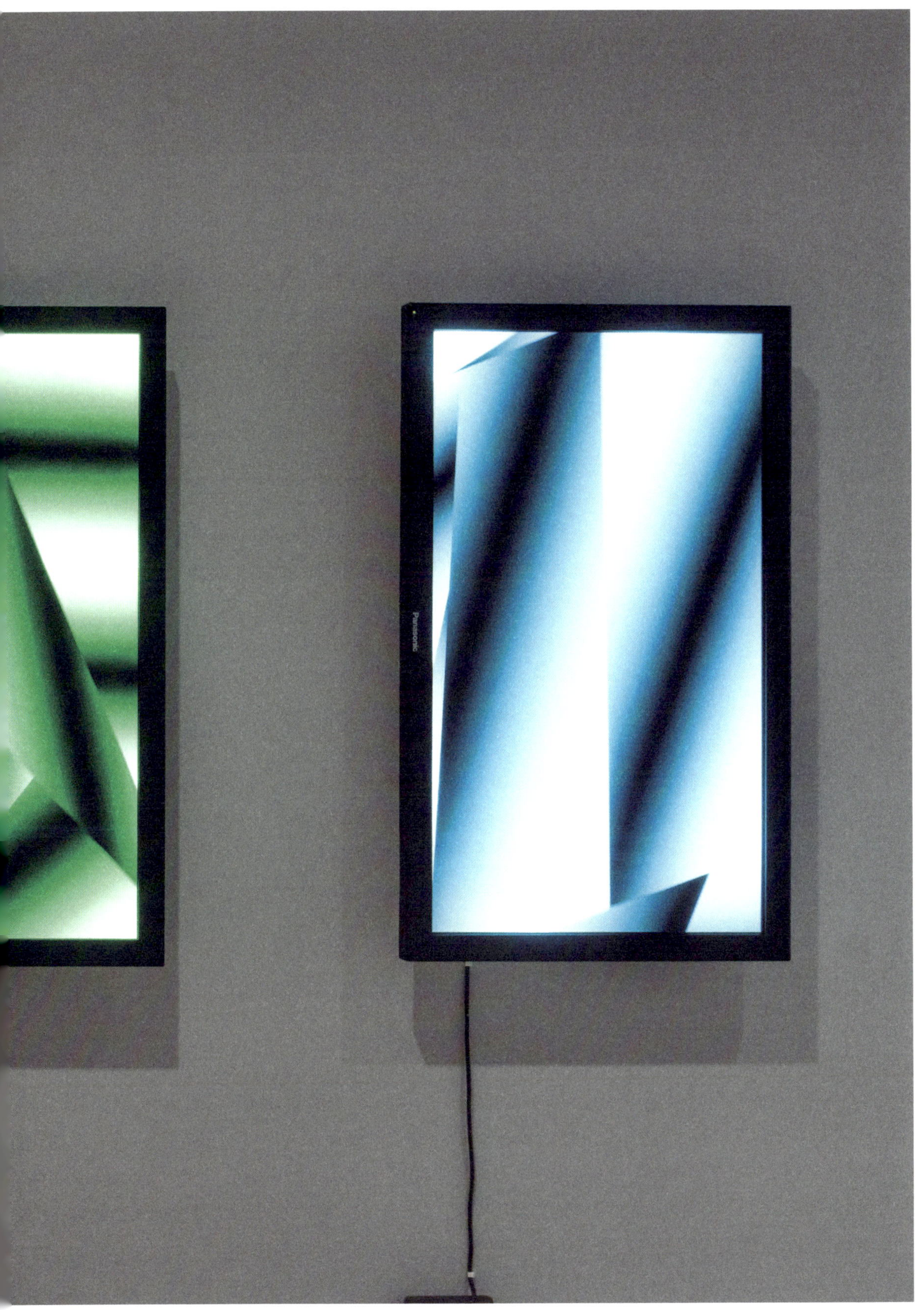

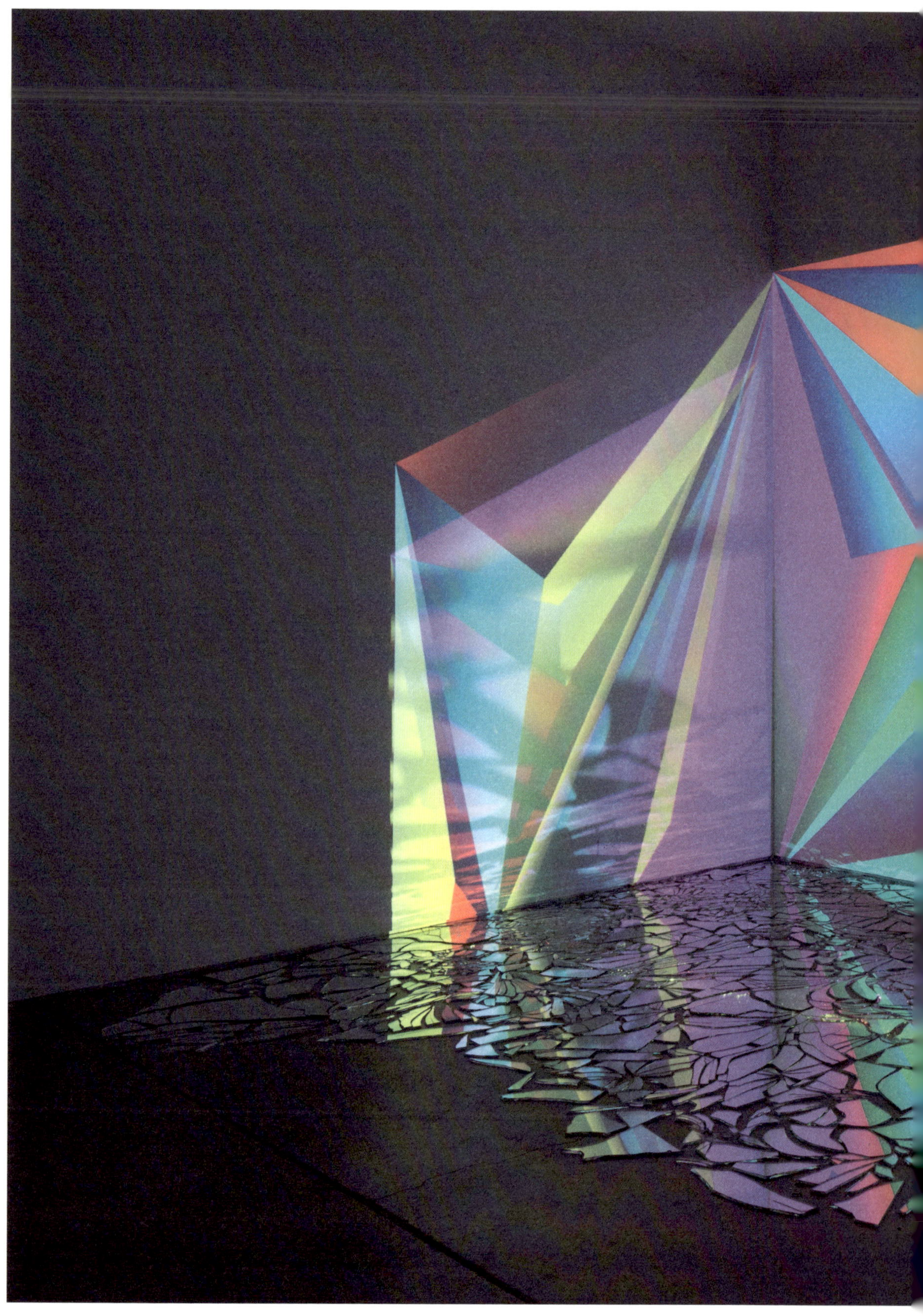

Into Time .us, 2012

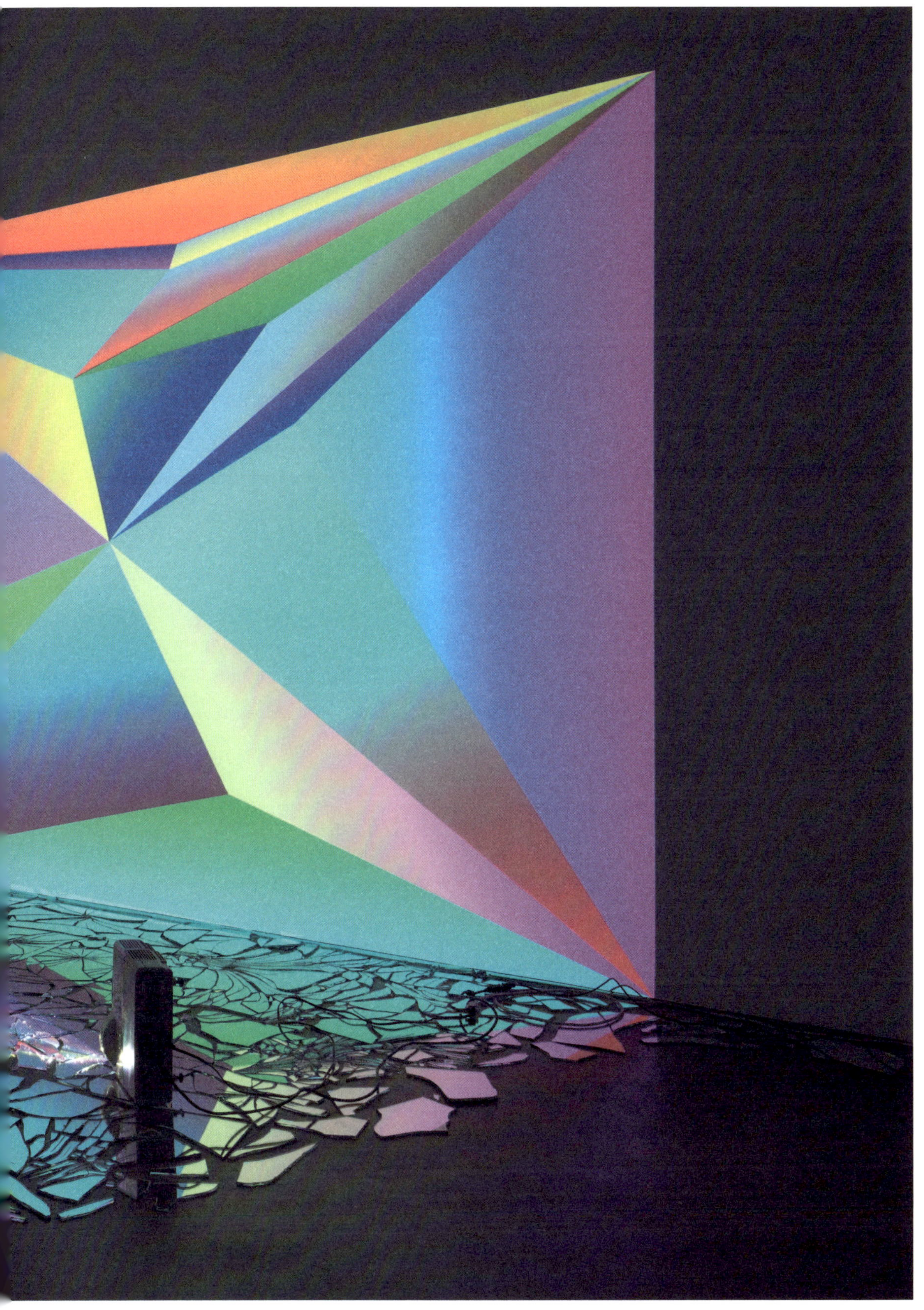

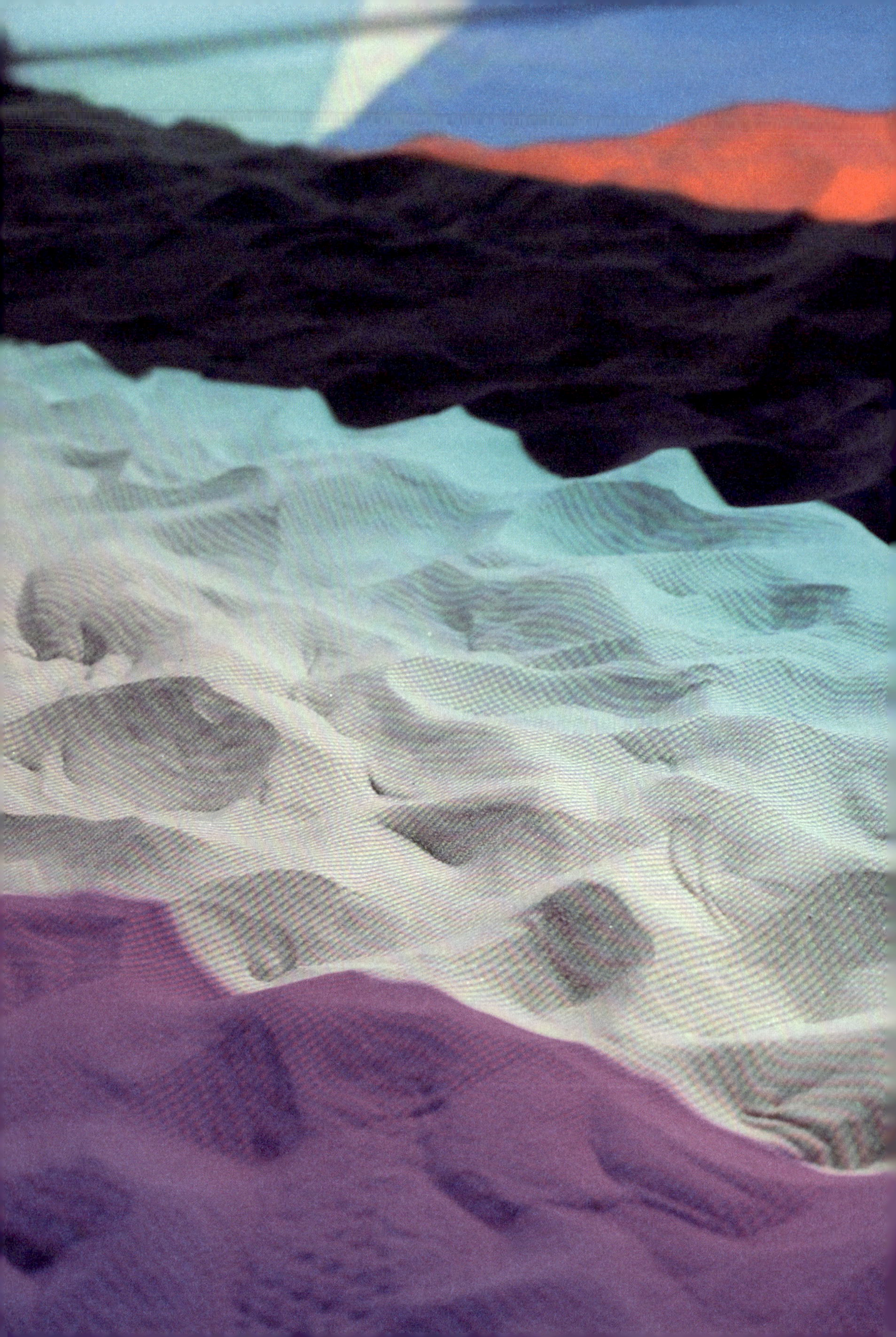

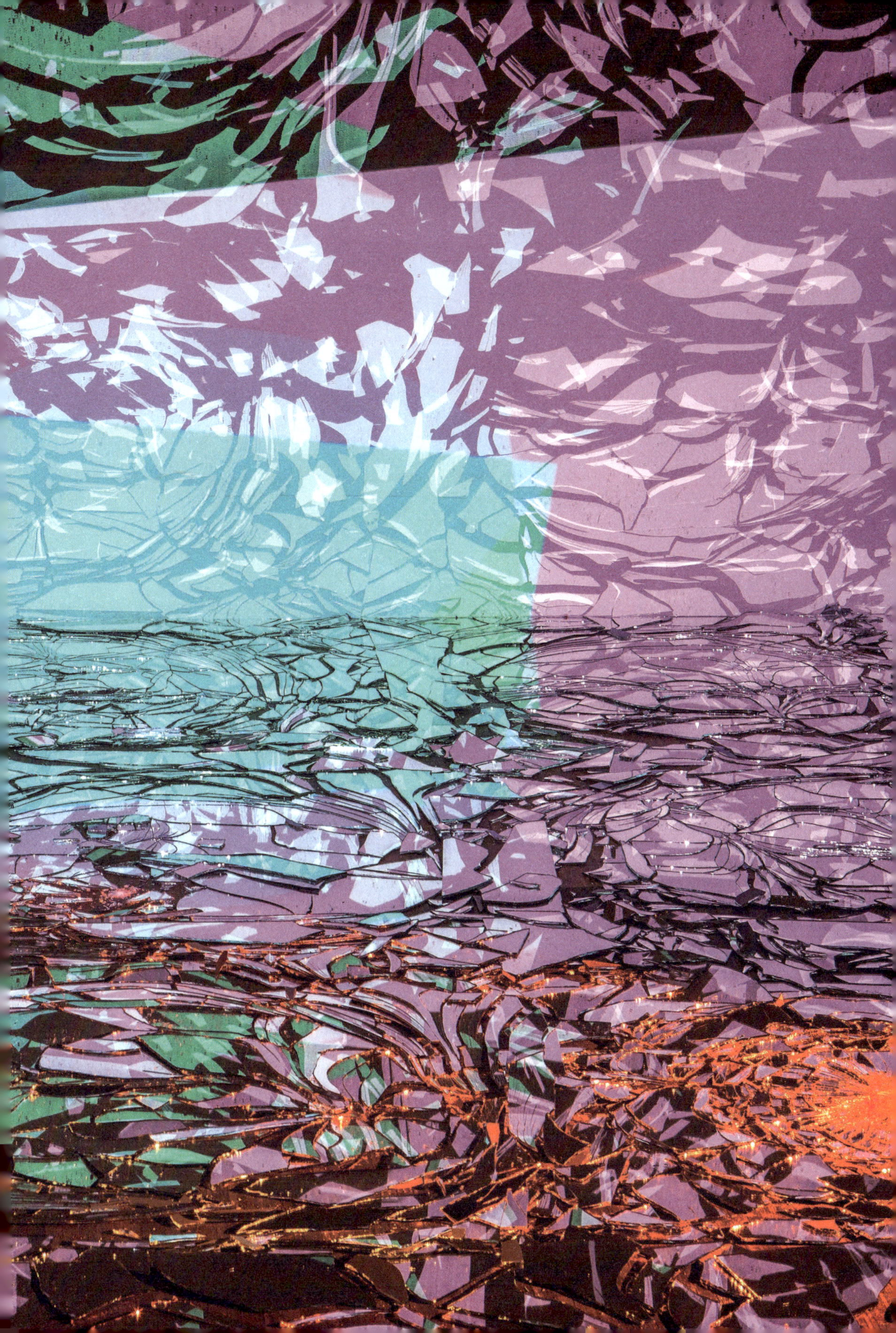

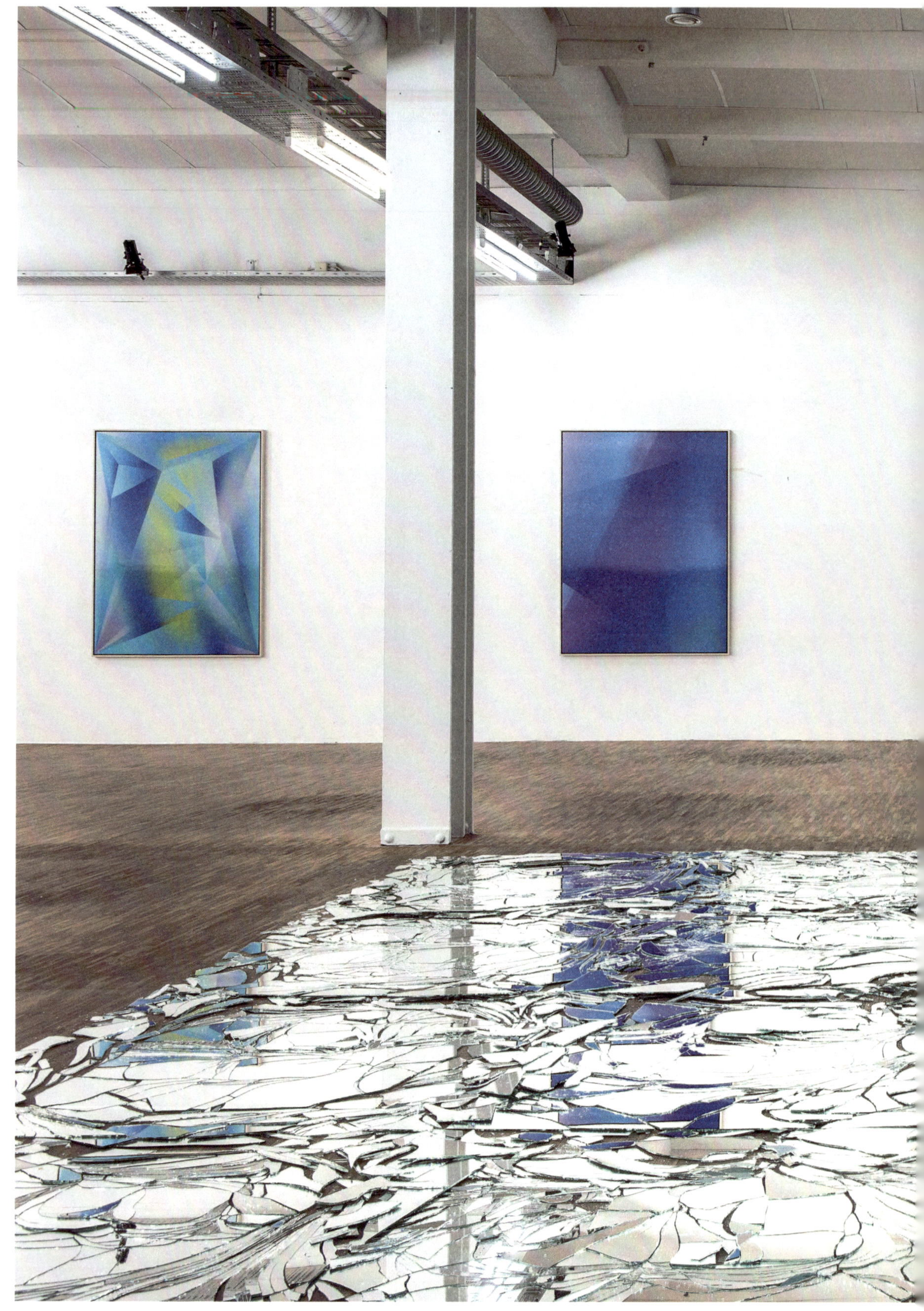

On and On, 2015

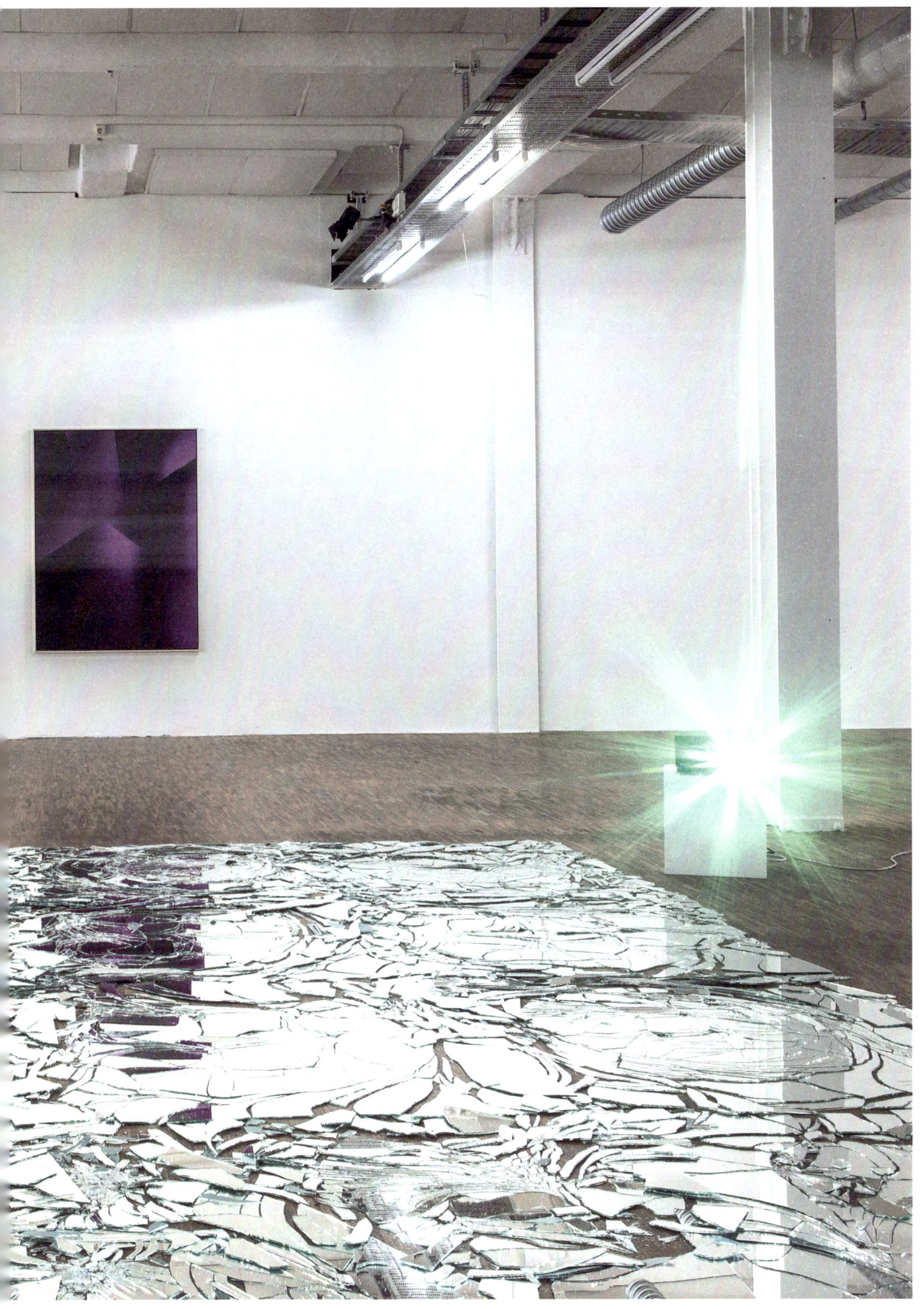

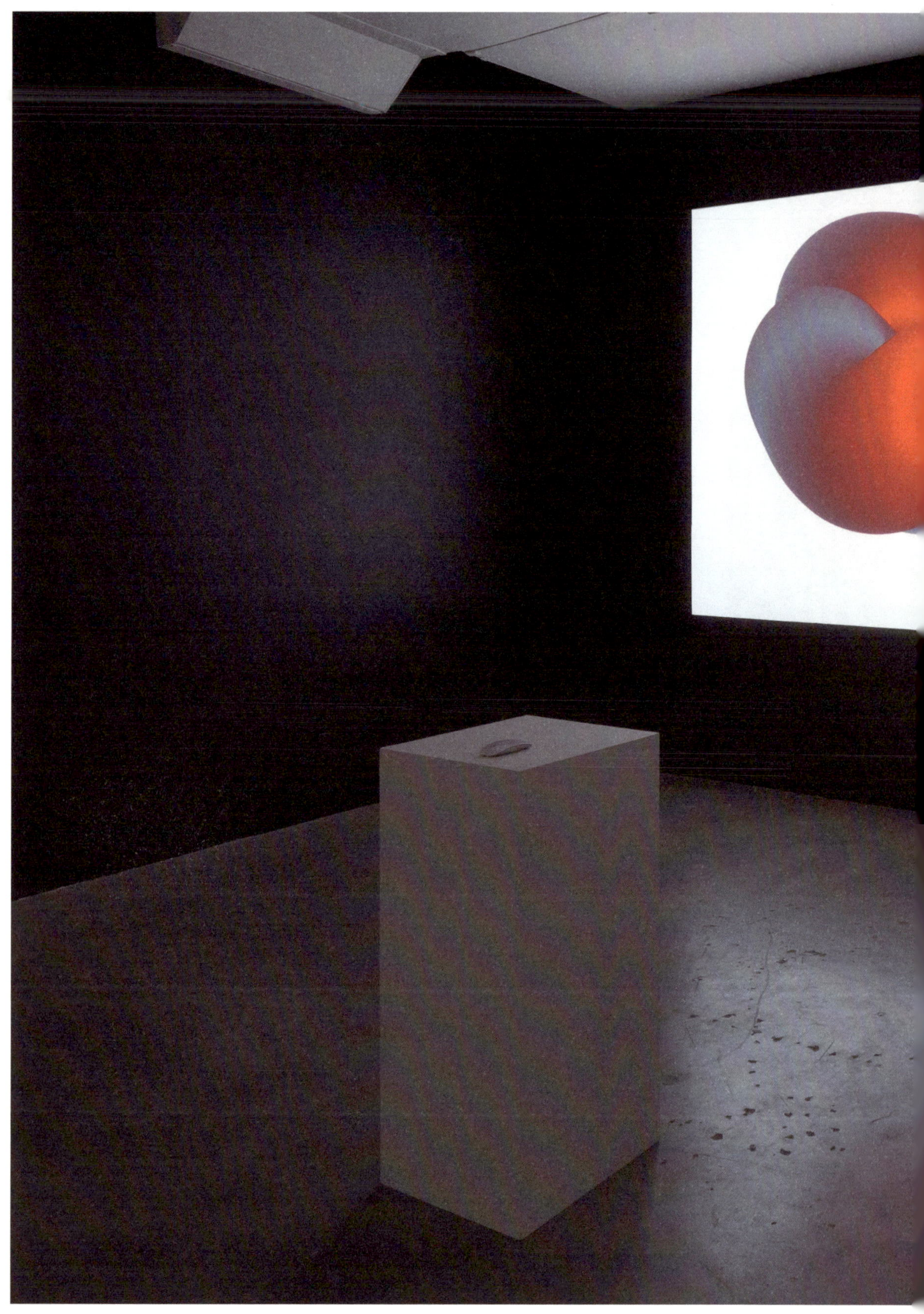

Ooze Move .com, 2014

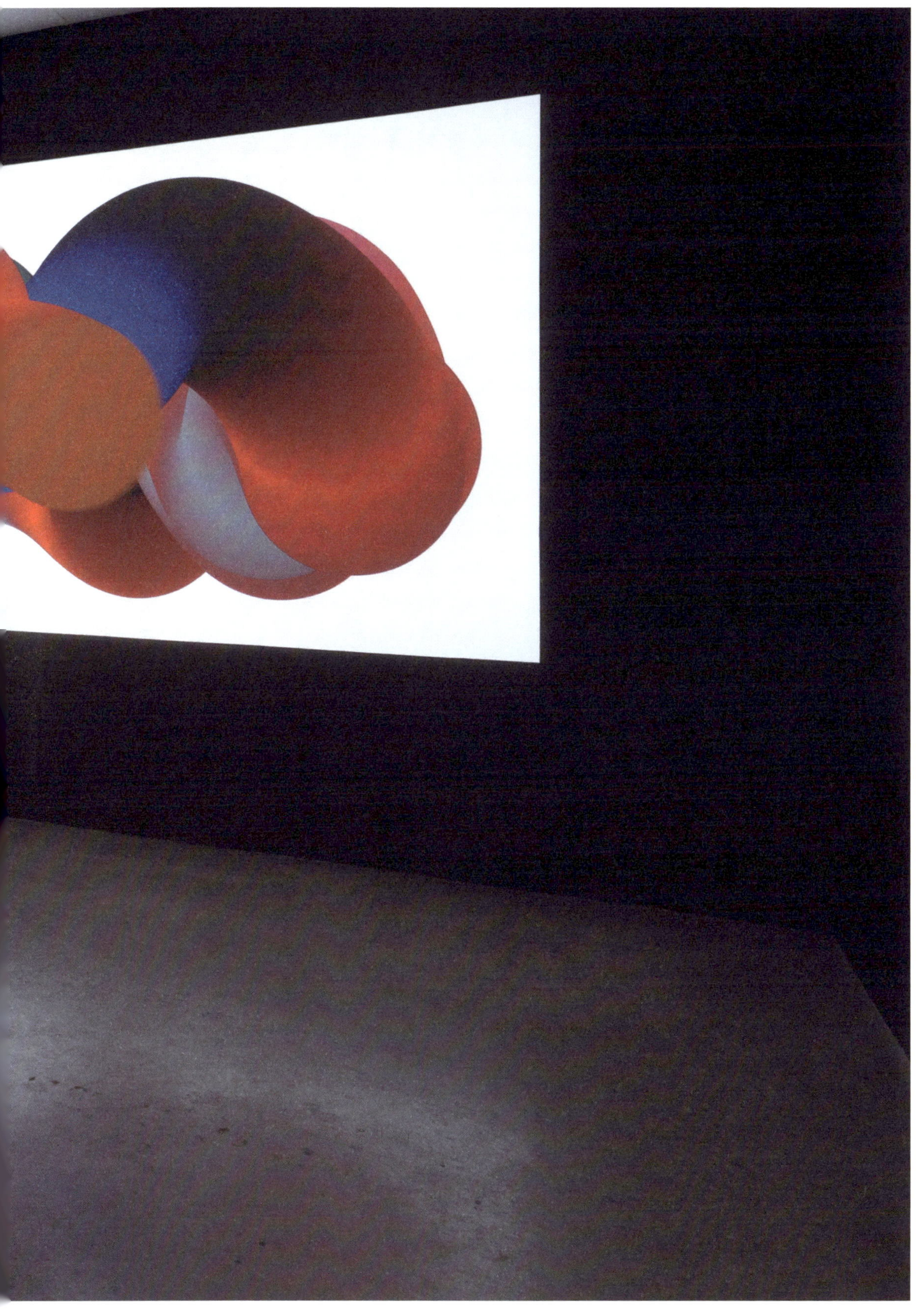

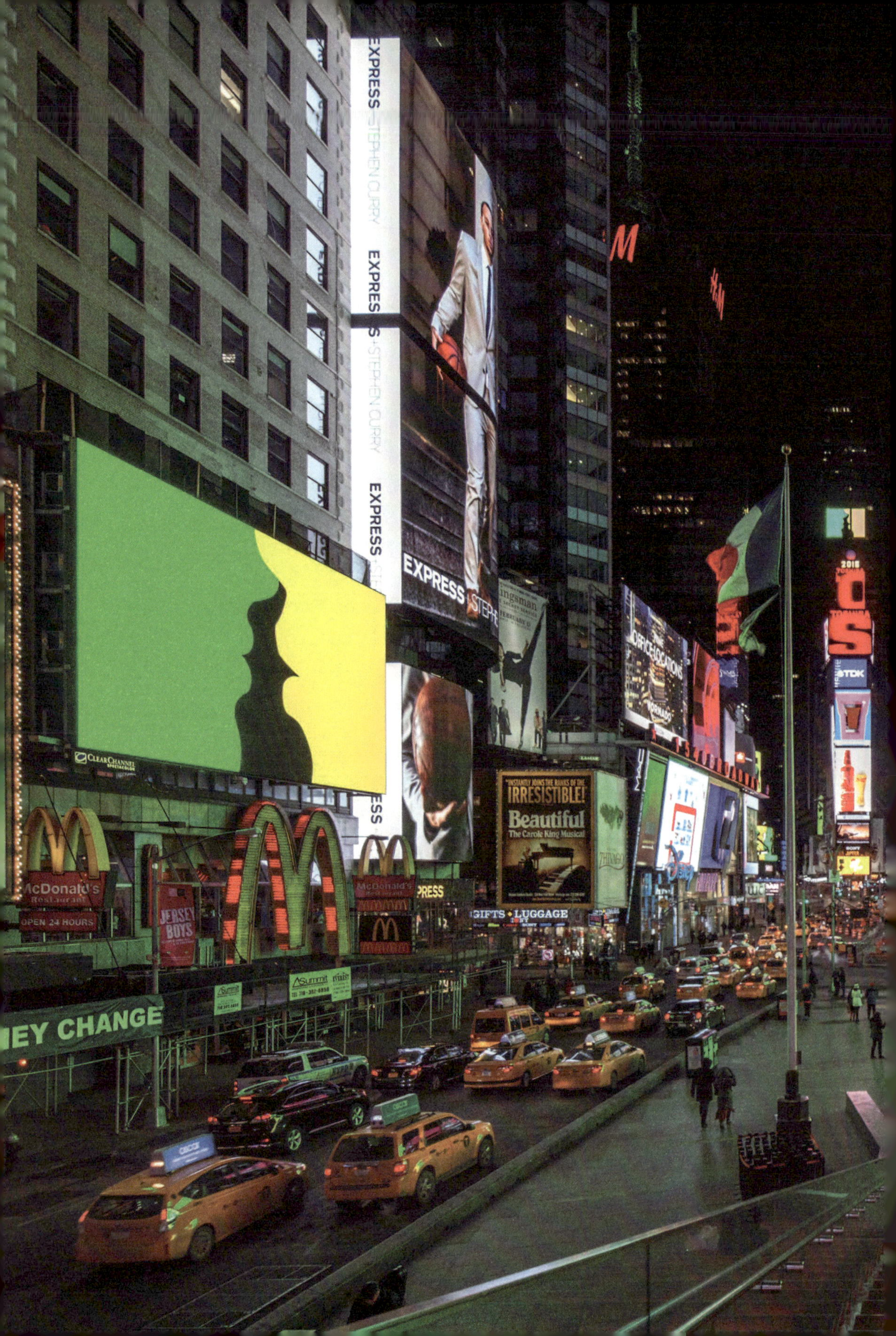

EXPRESS
STEPHEN CURRY
EXPRESS
STEPHEN CURRY
EXPRESS
EXPRESS
Kingsman
H&M
McDonald's
McDonald's Restaurant
OPEN 24 HOURS
JERSEY BOYS
CLEAR CHANNEL
SPECTACOLOR
EY CHANGE
INSTANTLY JOINS THE RANKS OF THE
IRRESISTIBLE!
Beautiful
The Carole King Musical
GIFTS • LUGGAGE
MAC
THE ORIGINAL GANGSTAS
TORNADO
TDK
SONY
2016
ASummit

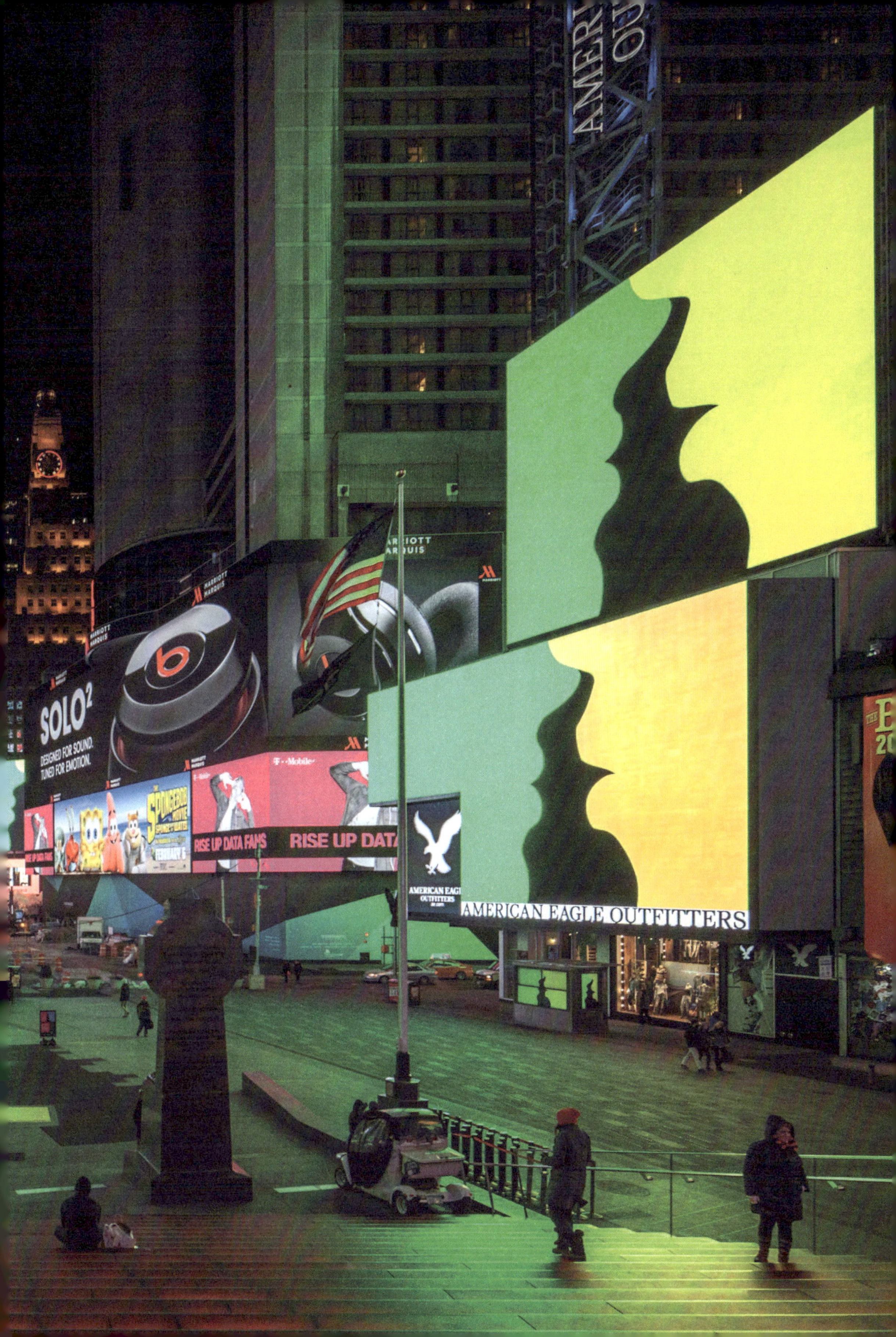

AMERI
MARRIOTT
MARQUIS
SOLO²
DESIGNED FOR SOUND.
TUNED FOR EMOTION.
THE SPONGEBOB MOVIE
FEBRUARY 6
RISE UP DATA FANS
RISE UP DATA
T Mobile
AMERICAN EAGLE
OUTFITTERS
AMERICAN EAGLE OUTFITTERS

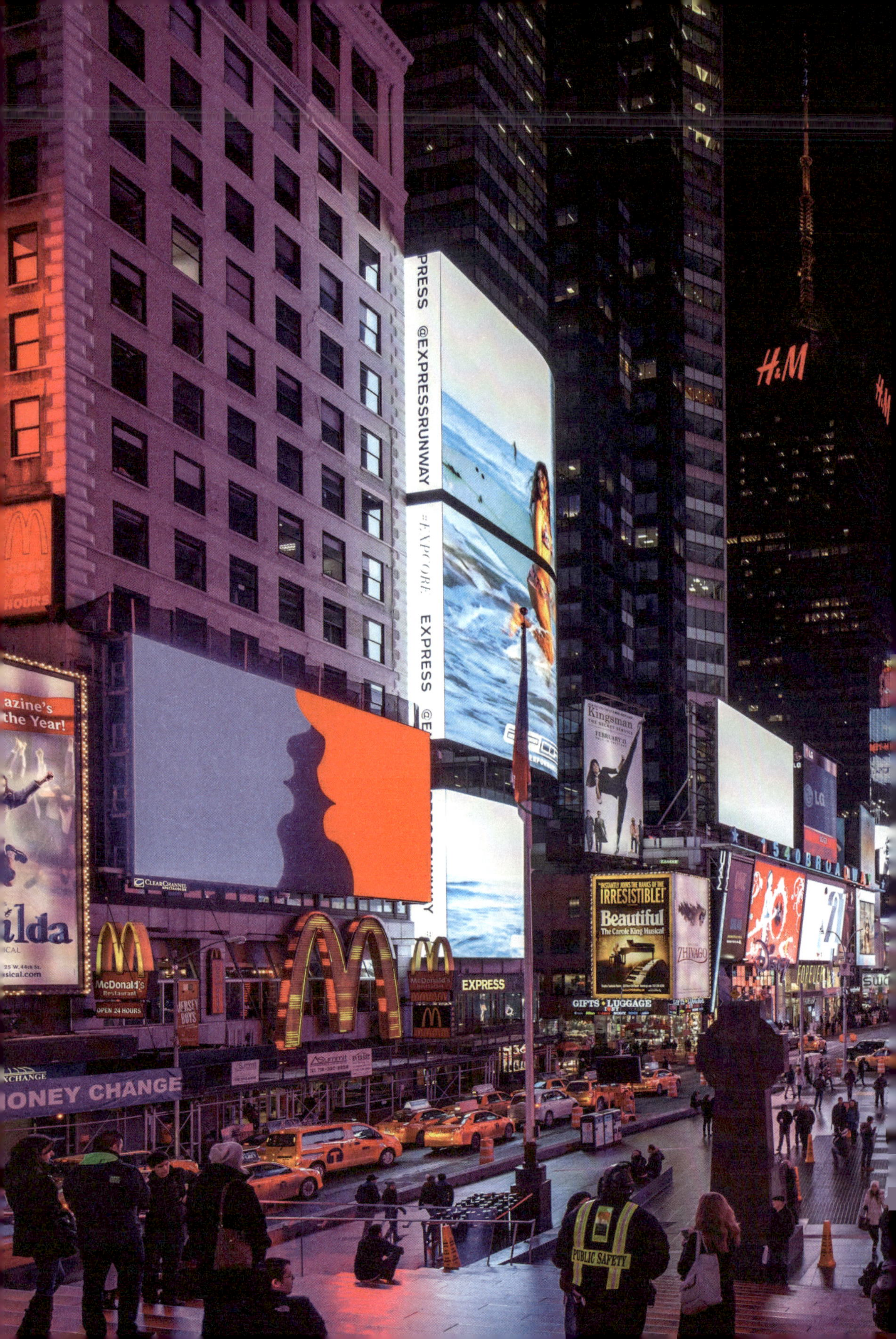

PRESS @EXPRESSRUNWAY
EXPLORE
EXPRESS @E
H&M
H&M
LG
LG
1540 BROADWAY
azine's
the Year!
ilda
asical.com
25 W. 44th St.
McDonald's
Restaurant
OPEN 24 HOURS
JERSEY BOYS
Kingsman
THE SECRET SERVICE
FEBRUARY 13
IRRESISTIBLE!
Beautiful
The Carole King Musical
ZHIVAGO
EXPRESS
GIFTS + LUGGAGE
ClearChannel
McDonald's
HOURS
ASummit
MONEY CHANGE
EXCHANGE
PUBLIC SAFETY

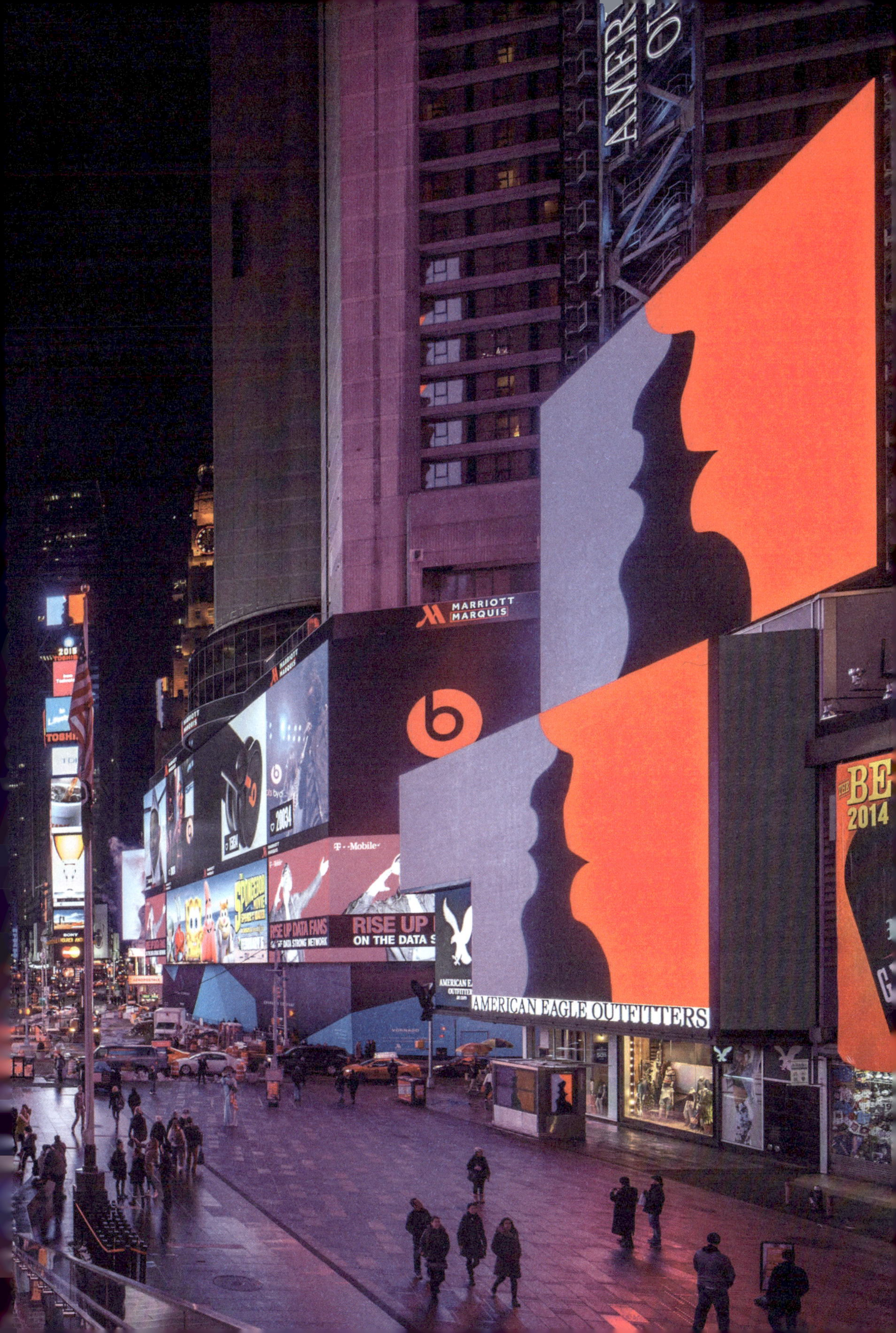

MARRIOTT
MARQUIS
MARRIOTT
MARQUIS
beats
T-Mobile
RISE UP DATA FANS
ON THE DATA S
AMERICAN EAGLE OUTFITTERS
AMERICAN
EAGLE
OUTFITTERS
TOSHIBA
THE BE
2014

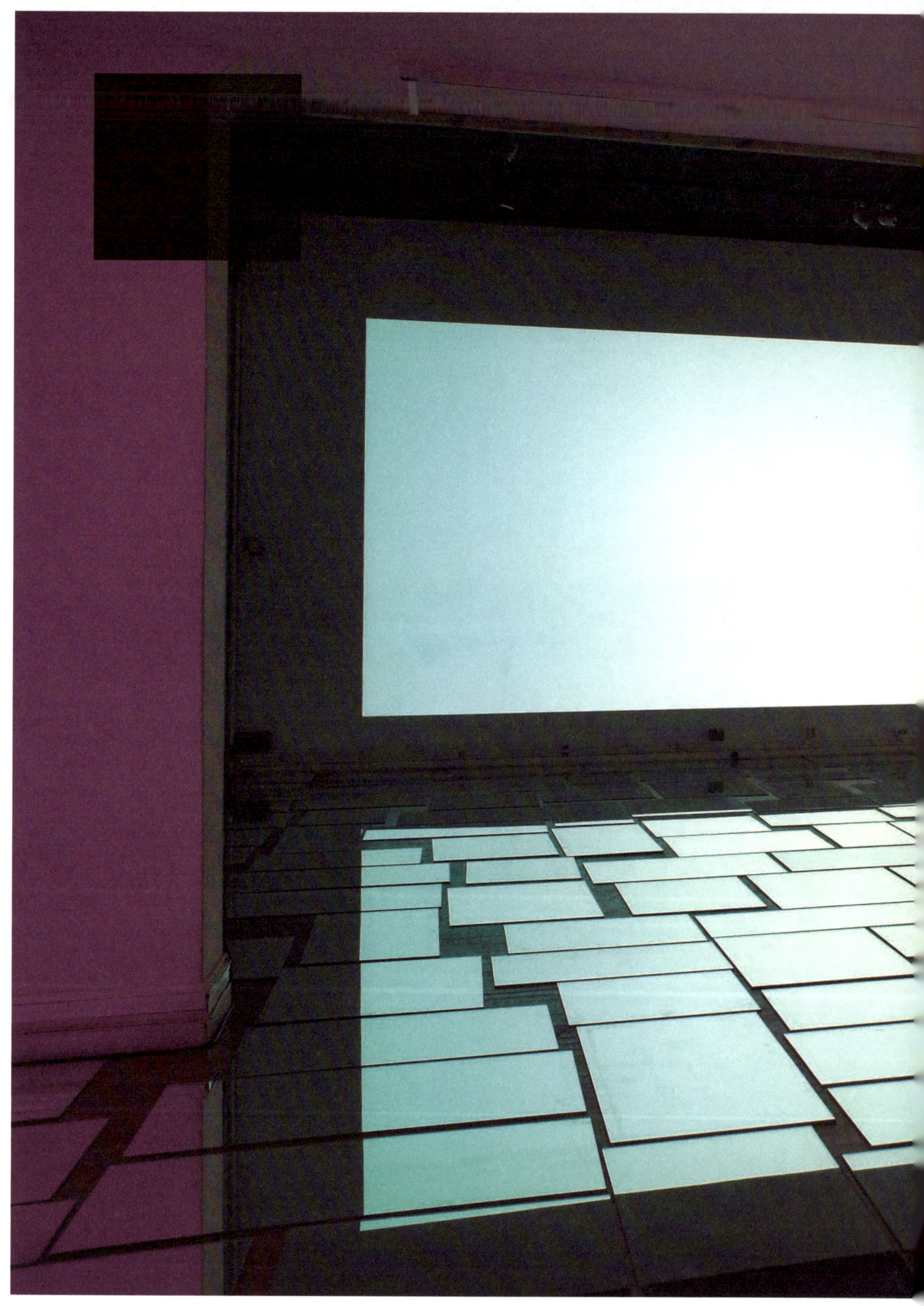

Yes For Sure .com, 2010

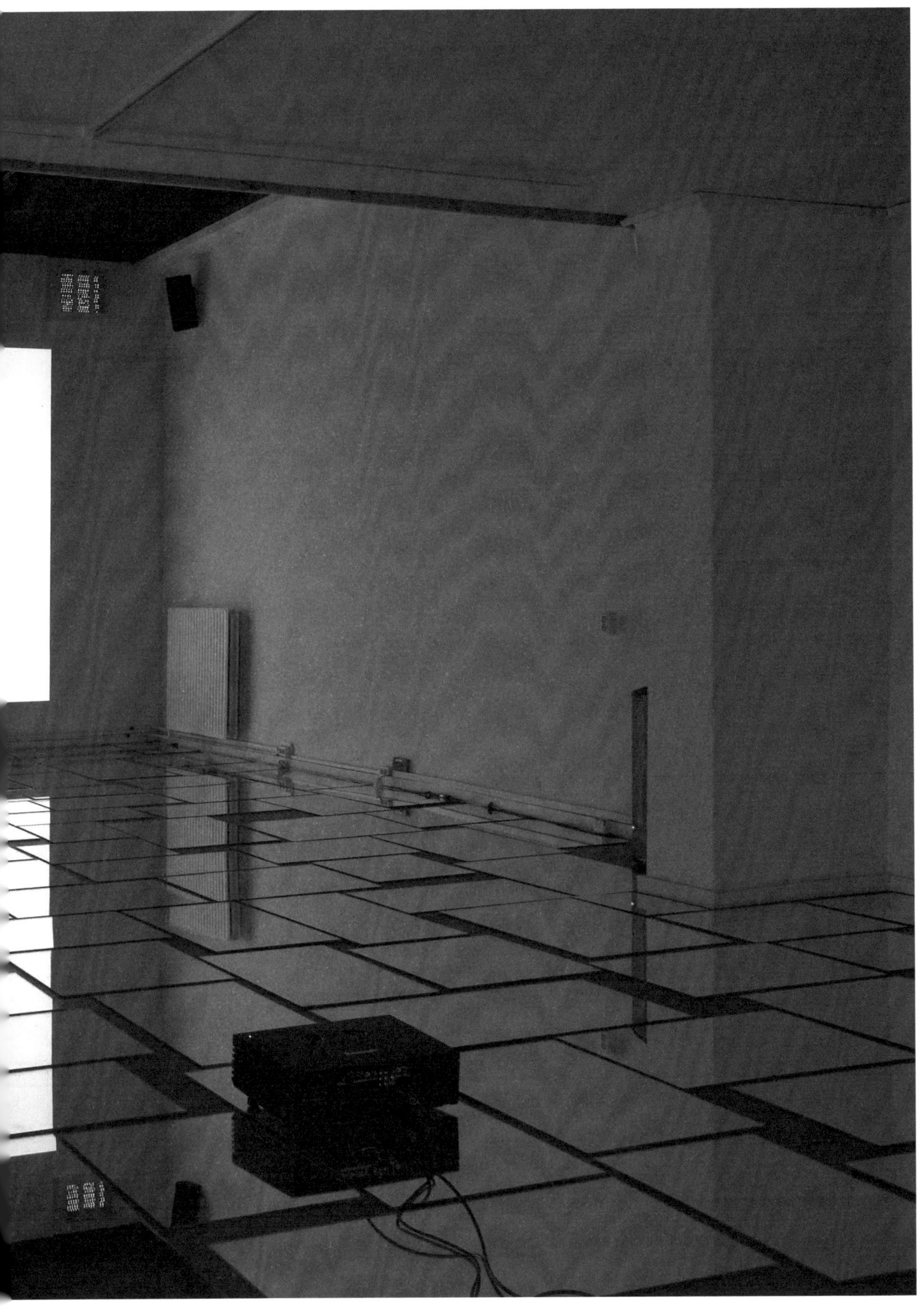

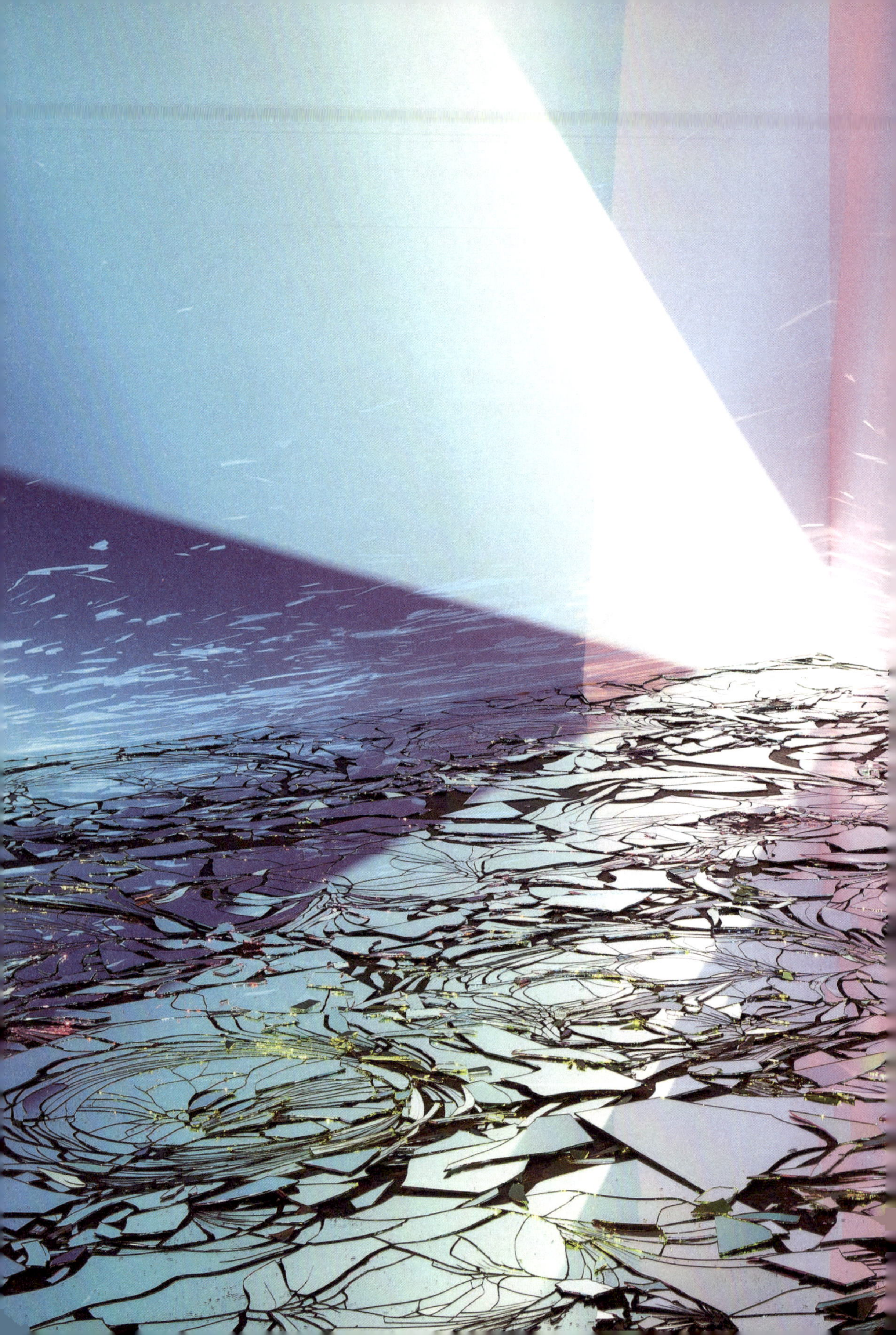

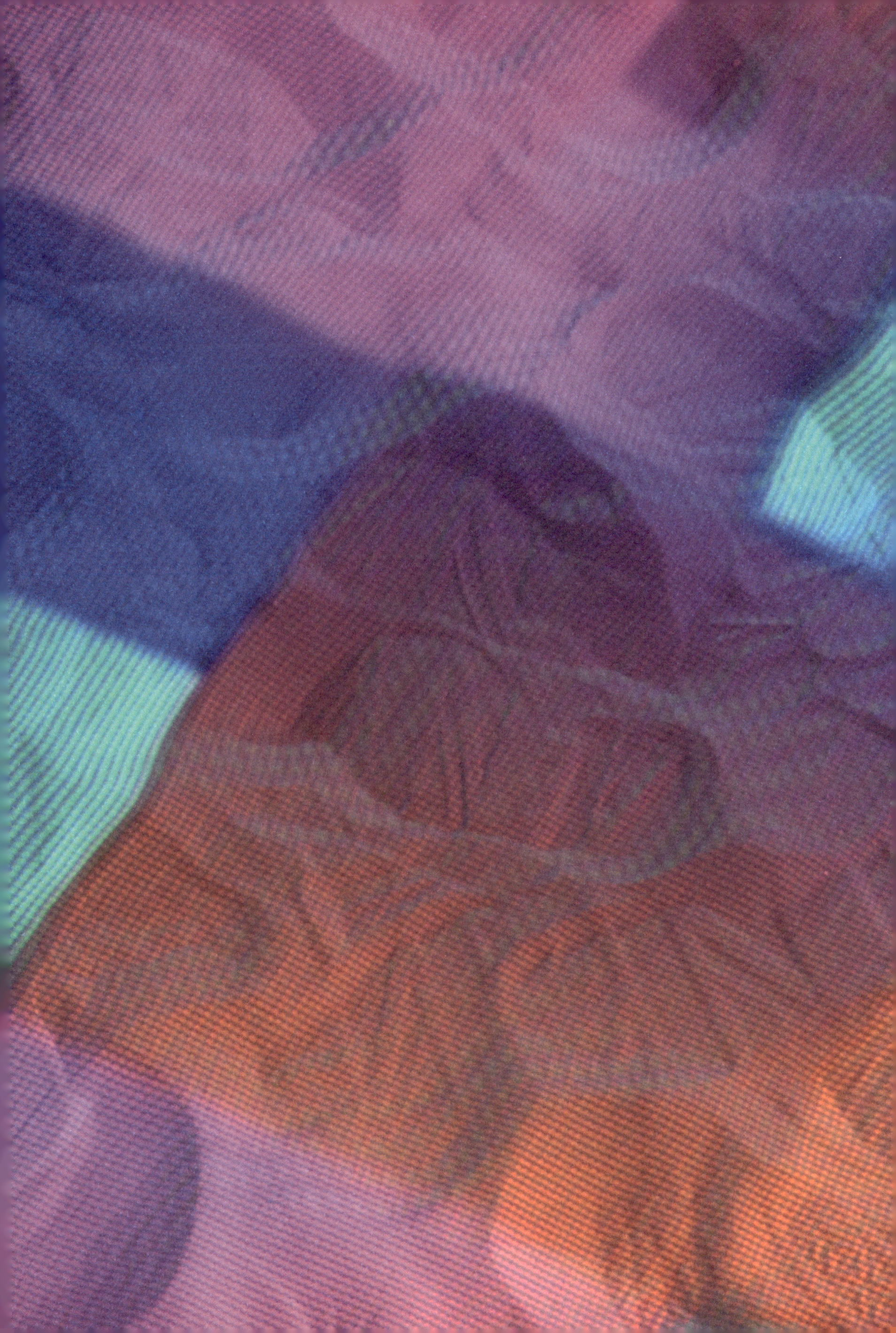

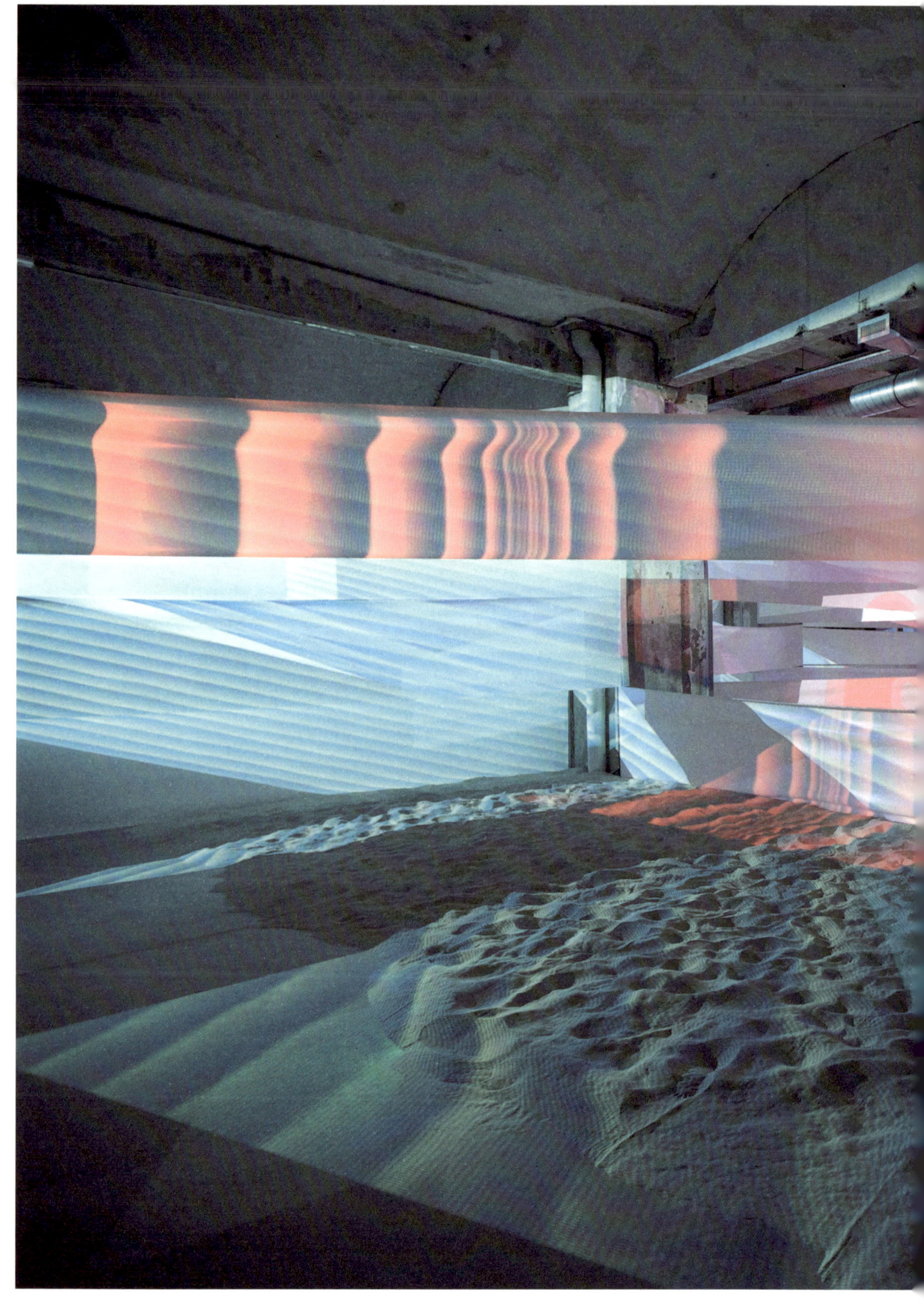

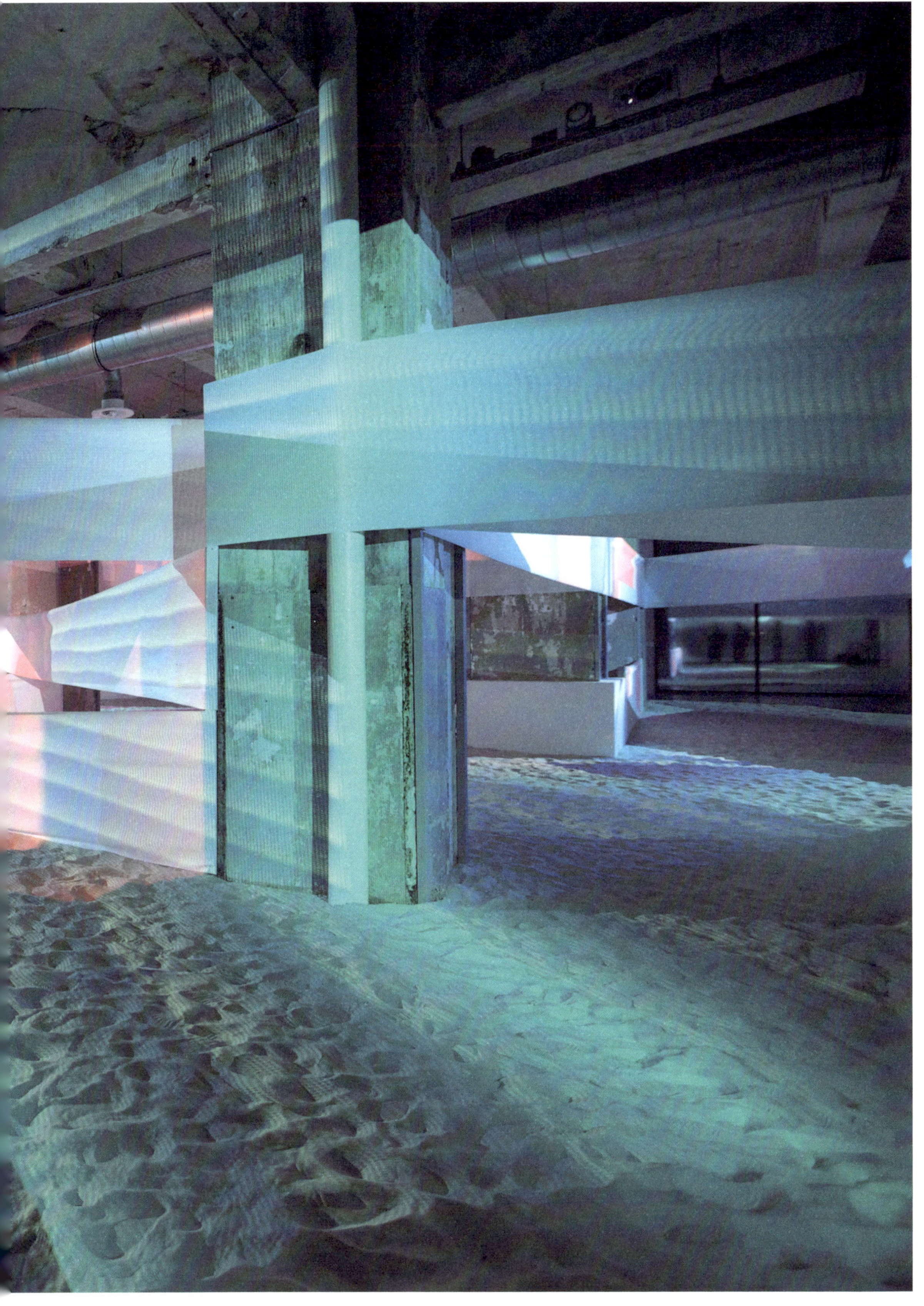

(UN)FRAMING RAFAËL ROZENDAAL
Margriet Schavemaker

I

Since the last decades of the twentieth century, Dutch artists such as JODI, Constant Dullaart, Jan Robert Leegte, Peter Luining, Geert Mul, and Han Hoogerbrugge have been working on a vast oeuvre in which the digital world is a key denominator, both as medium and as a topic. Like Rozendaal, these artists have been enjoying the wonderful climate in the Netherlands for experimental art consisting of a generous subsidy system and a healthy network of presentation- and production platforms. Due to the crisis and with coming budget cuts in the arts, a significant part of this rich cultural infrastructure has been eradicated over the past five years. However, it still seems relevant to root Rozendaal's internationally renowned production of websites and related objects and installations in this national context: it was a daily reality for this generation of (post)internet and media artists, facilitating an absolute freedom in transgressive practices and radical innovation.

To frame Rozendaal's artistic practice on other levels as 'typically' Dutch seems a more than slippery business. Operating on the on-line global web and interlacing with an international network of like-minded artists, it seems to defy national readings. Like Rozendaal, most artists have left their home country to work elsewhere, they travel most of the year and collaborate with an international pool of galleries, which represent them all over the world. Rozendaal seems a case in point when he presents himself on his website as 'a Brazilian-Dutch artist, living and working in New York,' Augmenting this international identity we find an accompanying portrait of the artist eating Japanese food with sticks (dressed in a blouse that makes Rozendaal merge with the Japanese wall design behind him). Rozendaal's dedication to the haiku (also published on his website) also testifies to this love for Japanese culture, even though his short three-sentence poems do not meet the required 5-7-5 meter). In the poems Rozendaal often reflects on his personal life as a globally working artist.

For example, in haiku 231:

> i miss rio
>
> i miss tokyo
>
> i do not miss berlin

Or haiku 227:

i feel at home

when i'm

not at home

However, when talking to Rozendaal about his work it is surprising how the artist brings national identities into play. For instance, zooming in on the bright colors, clear lines and abstract forms of his websites, comparisons are made to key figures in Dutch art history such as Johannes Vermeer and Piet Mondrian. At other times, he describes these formal qualities as influenced by what he refers to as 'American Golden Age cartoons, like Disney and Fleischman.'[1] This latter framing seems to be translated into his appearance as well: dressing in monochrome bright colors and having a sharp haircut, giving him an almost cartoonlike look alluding to, for example, Mickey Mouse.[2]

In the hour-long dialogs between Rozendaal and fellow internet artist Jeremy Bailey, published on Rozendaal's website as 'the Good Point podcast,' they often talk at length about references to issues of national identity as well. The on-line conversations between the two artists always start with a spacey musical intro after which Rozendaal and Bailey greet each other with a somewhat over the top American intonation: 'Hi Jeremy, how are you doing?' 'Hi Rafaël, how are *you* doing?' The dialogue continues with the artists reflecting on where they currently are in world, or where they have been travelling to that past week (often mocking their status as 'successful artists') after which they turn to the topic of the day. These range from the art world at large (for example studio visits or the art market) to how they were raised and how this cultural background has influenced them and differs from the American society in which they are currently working and living. For instance, in podcast *07– Small Countries* Bailey's Canadian background is compared to Rozendaal's Dutch roots and we can listen to elaborate reports on typical national breakfast habits, national holidays, the schools and academies that they have attended as well as comparisons of the national subsidy systems and cultural politics in general.[3]

In other words, Rozendaal hovers between internationalism and nationalism. Is it a form of schizophrenic dissociation or a healthy

1   Mail to author (February 16, 2017).
2   Gidi Heesakkers, 'The Artist is Online', *de Volkskrant*, March 14, 2015.

3   https://soucloud.com/goodpoint/07-small-countries.

combination? I would say it most of all shows that embracing the Internet does not mean that technology is taking over: on the contrary, it leads to a ceaseless production of human communication, a flux of texts and dialogues in which the artist performs his identity as both free floating and grounded by multiple national identities.

II

This (inter)national discourse produced by Rozendaal brings me to another probing question, namely what is the status of the haiku, podcasts and other discursive practices? Are they extra layers contextualizing the core body of work (i.e. the websites and objects)? In a way this feels a bit like a shame. Following Marcel Duchamp, who claimed that he wanted to quit producing art for the retina and instead focus on the mind, since the start of the twentieth century many artists have been producing texts, performances, events and all possible alternatives to the conventional visual art practices. Their ephemeral output became a core practice. Or, as the French philosopher Jacques Derrida explained it, the division between the frame and what is inside the frame, was dissolved in both modernist en postmodernist practices. The so-called 'parergon'—that which envelops the main text—has become part of the main text. The distinction between work and non-work does not hold anymore. Instead, artists are working on a network of practices in which 'the work' is presented, performed, contextualized, framed, narrated, criticized, disrupted, negated and opened up for dialogue and participation.[4]

> In the past it was especially the sixties generation of neo-avant-garde artists, for example those aligned with Fluxus, who started producing experimental projects in this context. Think for example of the event scores by George Brecht in which the audience got an absurd or puzzling assignment like 'exit' (word event, 1961). He or she could take action and exit the room or look at an exit sign or perform any other relevant interpretation. These event scores, as produced by Brecht, Yoko Ono and many others, were not meant as art works in themselves, but as instructions for a future realization: periphery to an art work that may or may not exist in the future. And of course the artists themselves were allowed to produce concrete realizations of the scores as well. Brecht for instance realized several performances and objects of the aforementioned 'exit' score.

4   Jacques Derrida, 'The Parergon,'
    October 9 (Summer 1979), pp. 3–41.

The conceptual artists of the late sixties, such as Joseph Kosuth and the British Art & Language group were more purist and started deploying language to move beyond the visual/material paradigm that in their mind reduced all art to commercial goods. The idea prevailed that focusing on the discourse conventionally surrounding the art, they could avoid commodification and 'dematerialize' art.[5] Often art in the digital domain from the nineties onwards echoes this more hard-core conceptual strategy. Websites and other on-line artworks are considered by nature an ephemeral, non-commercial free zone that could keep the art world and its accompanying institutionalization and economic forces at bay. Rozendaal's *Bring You Own Beamer* events (organized since 2010 up to the present) can be read as a playful platform for and homage to this ephemeral and decentering positioning of internet art.

However, Rozendaal's dedication to selling his artistic websites seems to be part of a completely different paradigm. His claim to fame is the fact that he has been able to do what so many of his peers have not succeeded in doing and that is finding buyers for that was is accessible to everybody around the globe. He has found an egg of Columbus: a business model for open access content. By presenting himself as both artist and CEO of his company called www.newrafael.com, he stages the economic transaction as core business. Adding the names of the collectors and museums to the URL of the acquired websites is also a case in point (for example: www.welikethisforever.com is transformed into www.welikethis-forever.com -allen & overy collection, welikethisforever.com by rafaël rozendaal, 2011).

Chronologically presented on his website, Rozendaal's artistic websites appear to have a clear visual signature. Bright colors and a simple score that is often a funny pun. The interaction is simple, often reduced to one click or type of interaction. Sometimes the works consist of direct references to art history (for example www.electricboogiewoogie.com makes Mondrian's last work, the *Victory Boogie Woogie*, move like small cars on the New York streets or www.leduchamp.com, which makes Duchamp's bicycle wheel spin by clicking on a specific spot). Recently, Rozendaal started producing material objects and installations in addition to this growingly abstract oeuvre. Paintings, prints, sculptures, carpets and installations that look like analog children of his on-line art production and bring to mind classical abstract painting or minimal art.

Is this, despite the direct referencing to his work, the absolute opposite of Duchamp's anti-retina art and its legacy? Is it a return

5　Lucy Lippard, *Six Years: The Dematerialization of the Art Object from 1966 to 1972*, Berkeley, 1973.

to the conventional art world in which the visual/material paradigm prevails and the discursive is just a secondary envelop? Although we can stay with the Fluxus artists and their dedication to moving out of the studio and starting stores through which buyers could directly engage with the artists (think of the two stores by Ben Vautier, George Brecht and Robert Filliou in the South of France and the Flux Store opened in Amsterdam by Willem de Ridder), I feel it might help to bring the work of Marcel Broodthaers to the table. This Belgian artist started to copy the commodification of the art world. He placed his poetry publications in a chunk of plaster and sold them as a sculpture. He also created his infamous *Musée d'art moderne—Département des Aigles* (1970–1971) in which he added underneath each object the text 'this is not a work of art' (which was both true as the objects were mere artefacts, and untrue as they were part of Broodthaers' art installation). The work was fueled by frustration about his unsuccessful career as a poet and a growing awareness that the conceptual rigor of his contemporaries was failing (museums started to collect the ephemeral linguistic practices anyway and put them on display). It is post-conceptual art in which the ruling paradigm and power structures are not countered but copied.

Rozendaal is practicing a similar kind of ironic yet critical mimicry, but the context is opposite to that in which Broodthaers was operating. Rozendaal's generation is *not* suffering from an unwanted incorporation and commodification by museums and the art market of their ephemeral works. On the contrary, as art historian and media theorist Lev Manovich formulated it already twenty years ago, 'Turing Land' (referring to Alan Turing, the founding father of the computer) and 'Duchamp Land' (the world of contemporary art) are continents removed from one another.[6] And contemporary art theorist Claire Bishop asserted still in 2012 that we continue living in a time of a 'digital divide,' meaning that the digital art world and the contemporary art world remain operating miles apart.[7]

Rozendaal can be seen as one of the most important artists of his generation who has been able to bridge that gap. And he does so by miming all possible rules of both the art world and the world of online start-ups. He creates a buzz around his experimental art, delivers a signature-style visual commodity with clear interaction. And sells it via a sharp performance and the necessary explanatory language in which the work is framed. The minimalist poetry depicts him as a twenty-first-century multi-talented Renaissance

6   Lev Manovich, *The Death of Computer Art*, 1996, www.manovich.net/TEXT/death.html.

7   Claire Bishop, 'Digital Divide: Contemporary Art and New Media,' *Artforum*, September 2012.

man (proving to be a true 'new rafael')and his dialogues with Bailey, interviews and lectures provide the relevant background information. In other words: Rozendaal uses all possible means and media to become complicit in the art world. As Broodthaers placed his books in plaster, Rozendaal sells his websites as paintings, claiming that the world wide web is the new picture canvas. Language is used as the envelop, the conventional periphery, in which the digitally born visual/material practice is being framed, explained, interpreted and made to speak as a desirable commodity, stating over and over again 'this *is* a work of art.'

III

What do museums learn from this practice? Most of all, Rozendaal serves them on a golden platter everything they need to know in order to finally annex 'Turing land' to their Duchamp habitat. Or does that sound too colonial? I remember the emotional outburst of Geert Mul on Facebook when in 2016 the Stedelijk Museum in Amsterdam acquired a significant body of works by Dutch internet artists: 'Finally part of the collection!' The world has changed: the digital artists do want to be collected, presented and preserved. Regarding the latter: Rozendaal has recently recorded a twohour video in which he explains the concept and deployed technique of all his websites so that they may be translated to next generation platforms in the future.[8] It is, like his earlier mentioned dialogues with Bailey, a rich source of oral history, something that most museums are just starting to produce concerning the multimedia art in their collections. This means that there is absolutely no excuse anymore for not acquiring on-line practices.

However, there is a very real risk that museums move too slow or only acquire the more conventional pre- or post-digital output (i.e. videos, websites and objects) and forget about the discursive practices framing and unframing it. It would not surprise me if Rozendaal takes over. He has already started curating an exhibition on screensavers in Het Nieuwe Instituut in Rotterdam ('Sleepmode: The Art of the Screensaver', January 27–August 20, 2017) showing his interest in the recent past of on-line culture. Moreover, he has produced a video on the groundbreaking websites of Dutch artist duo JODI.[9] Could it be that what Hollywood director Martin Scorsese is doing for the preservation of and research into the history of color film is the next model for Rozendaal to mime? I hope so…

8   https://www.youtube.com/watch?v=GjR1lsem6tw.

9   https://www.youtube.com/watch?v=YuxLGvkg-3k&t=1693s.

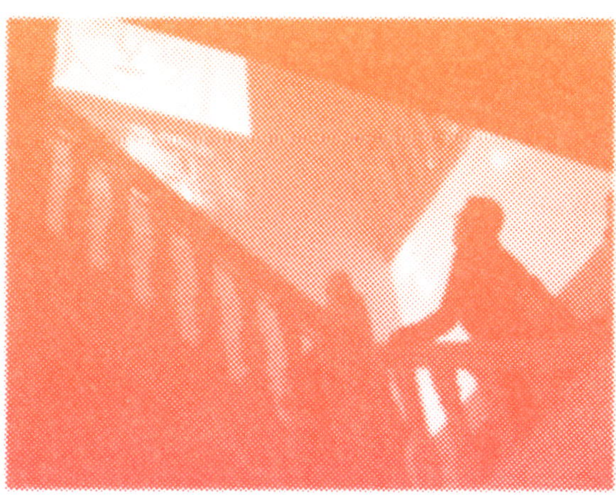

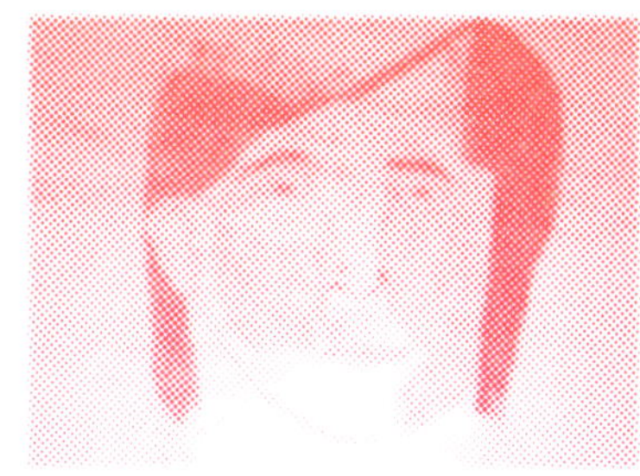
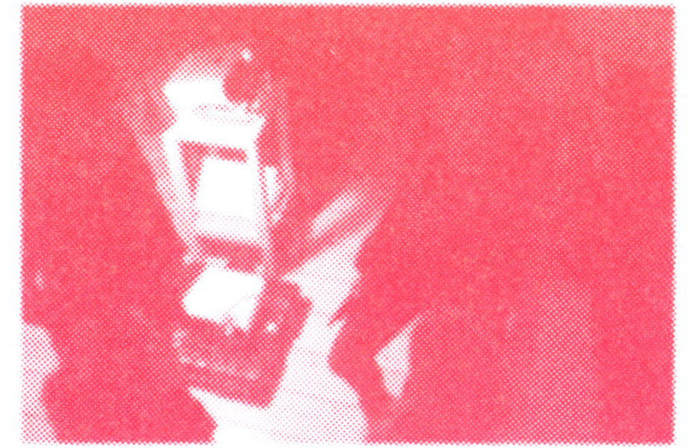

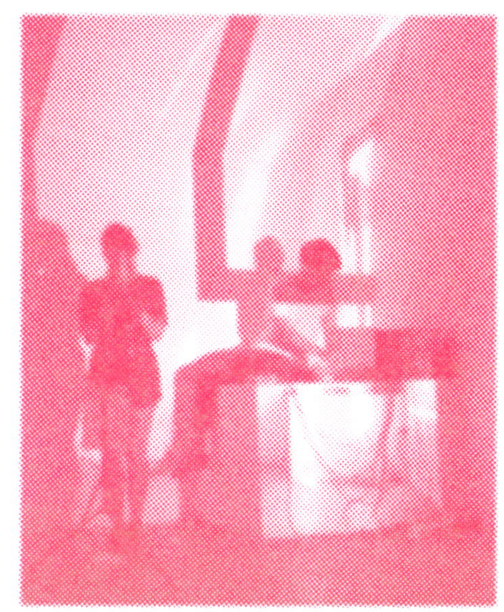

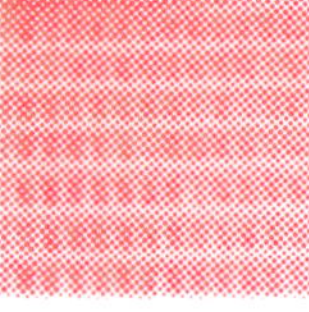

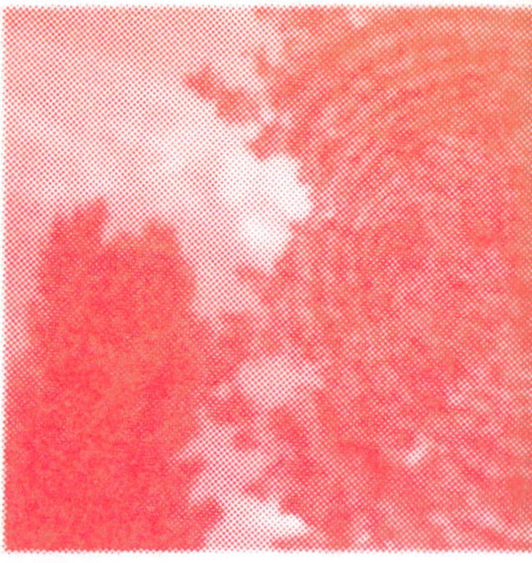
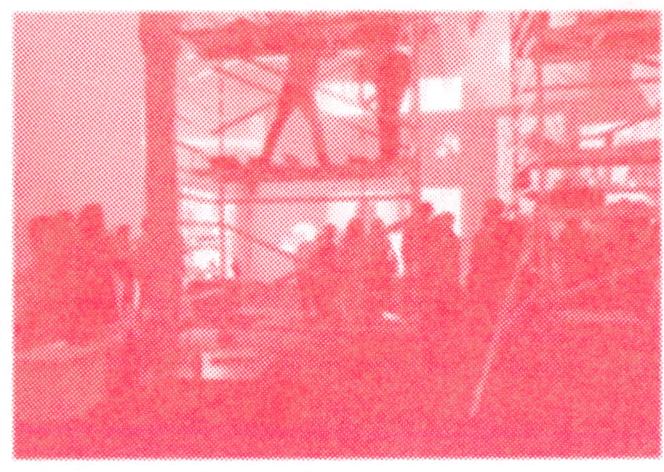
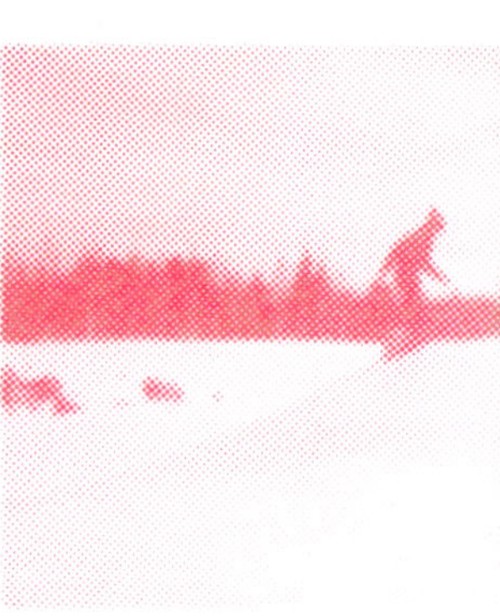
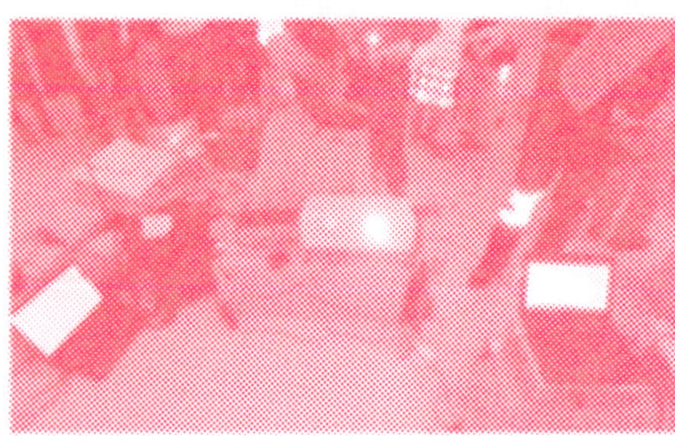
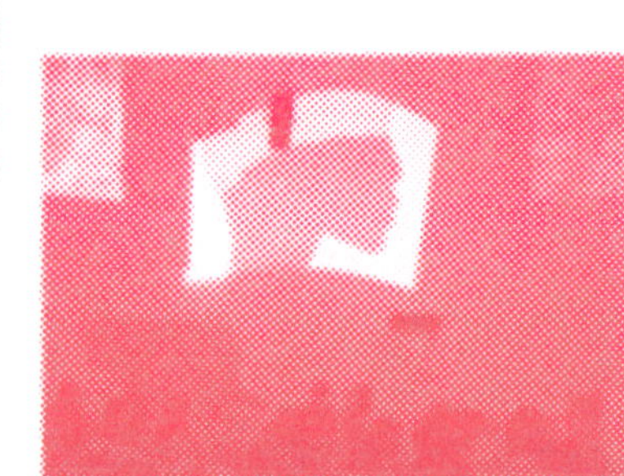

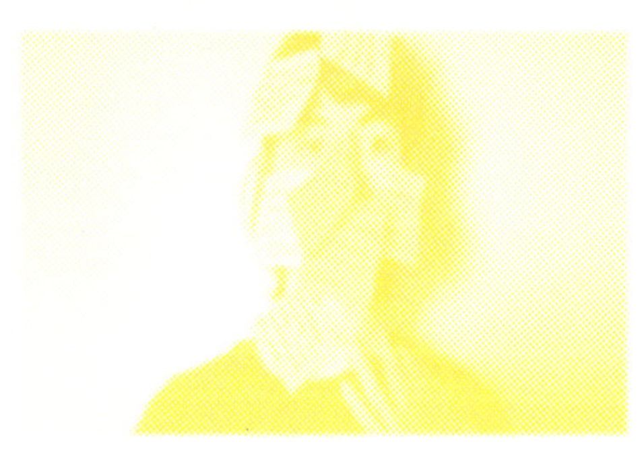

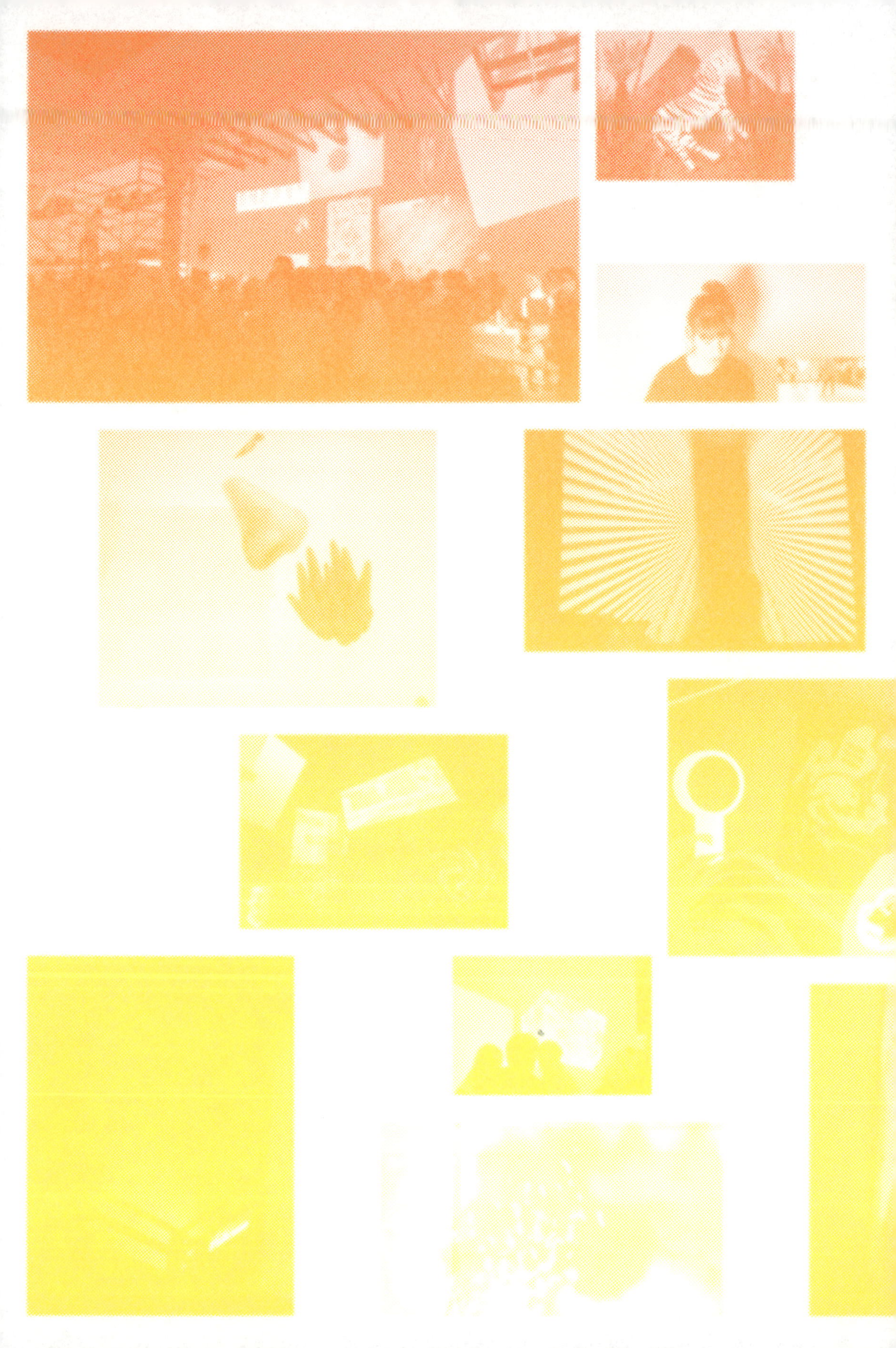

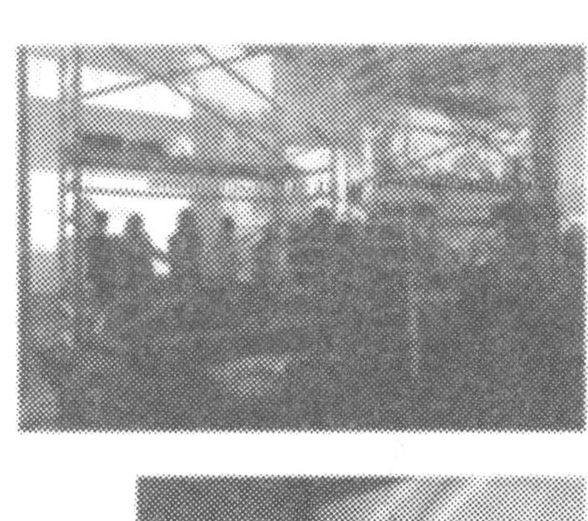
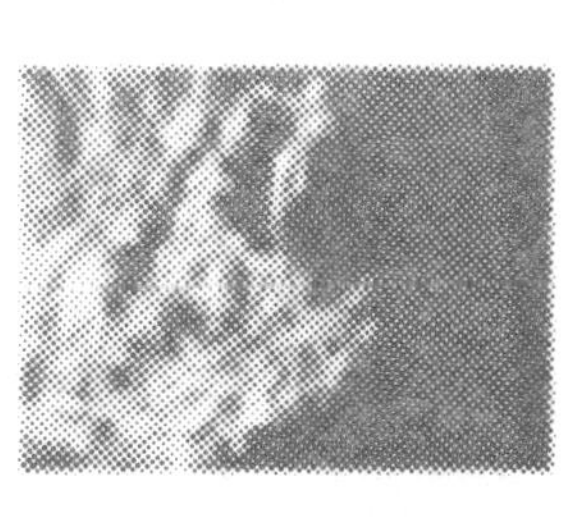
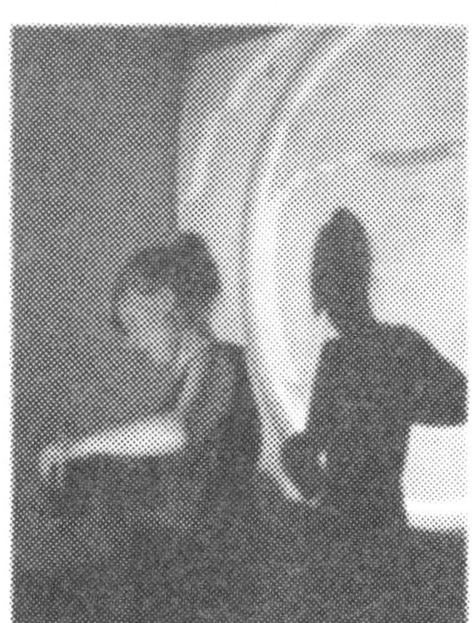
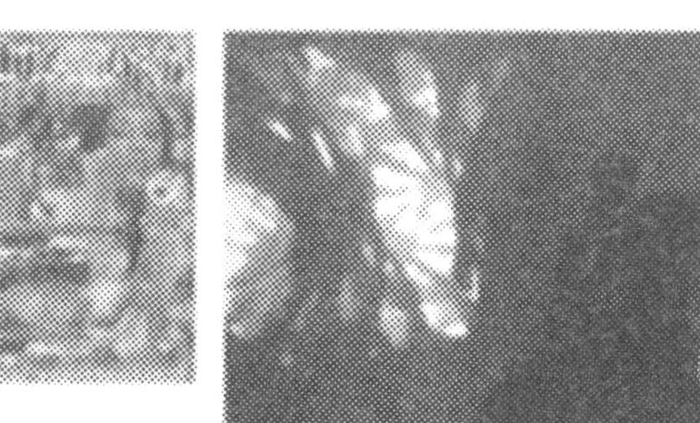
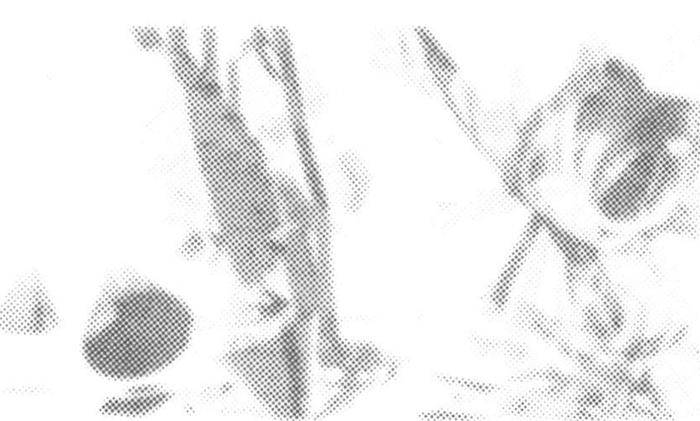
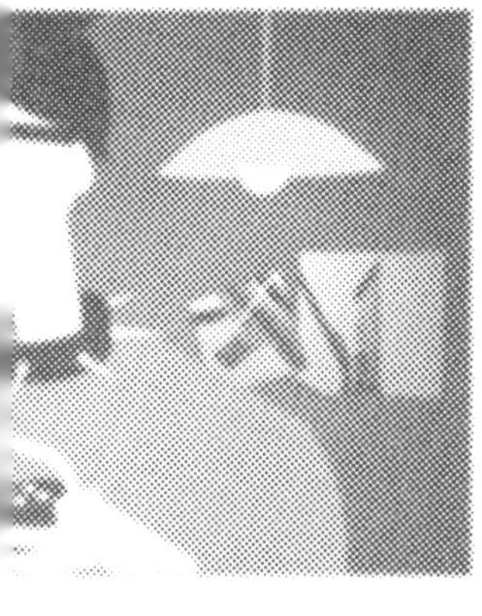
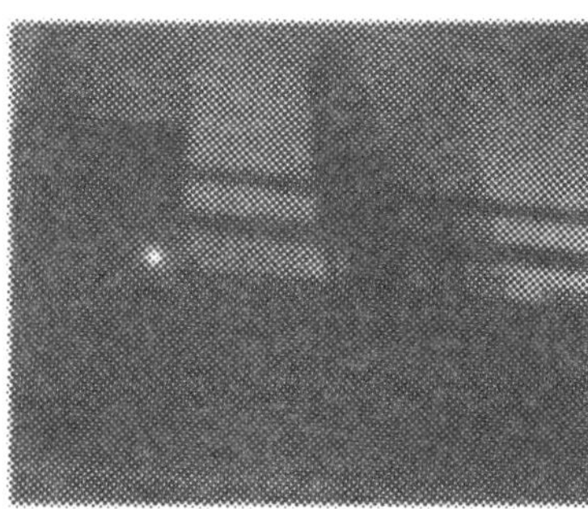
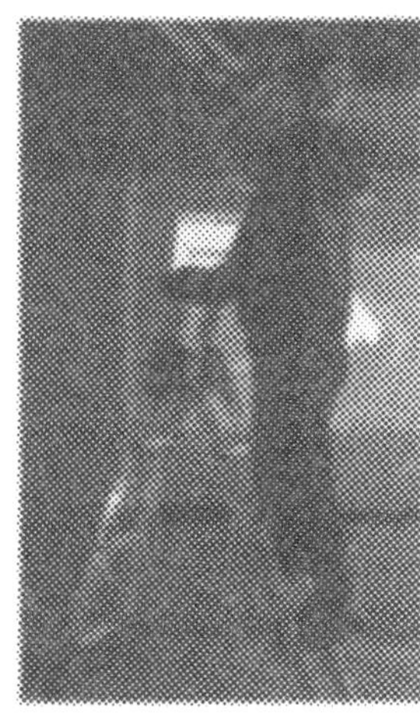
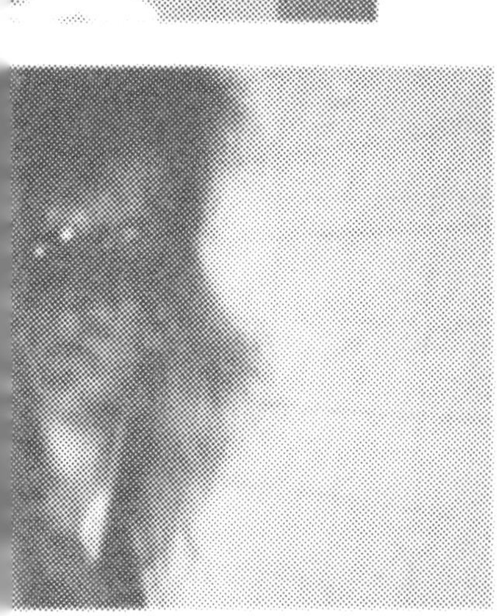
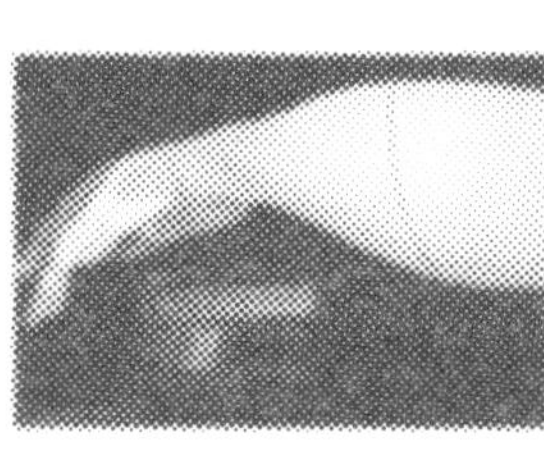
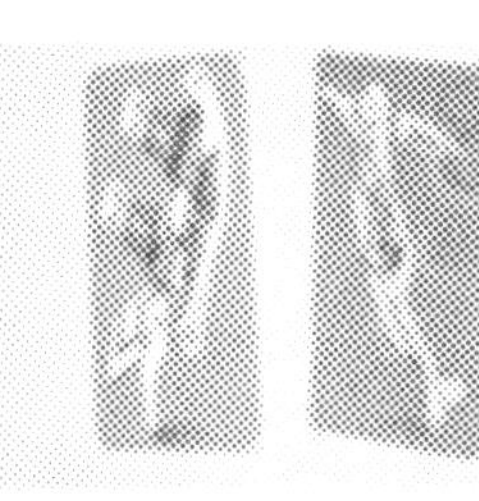

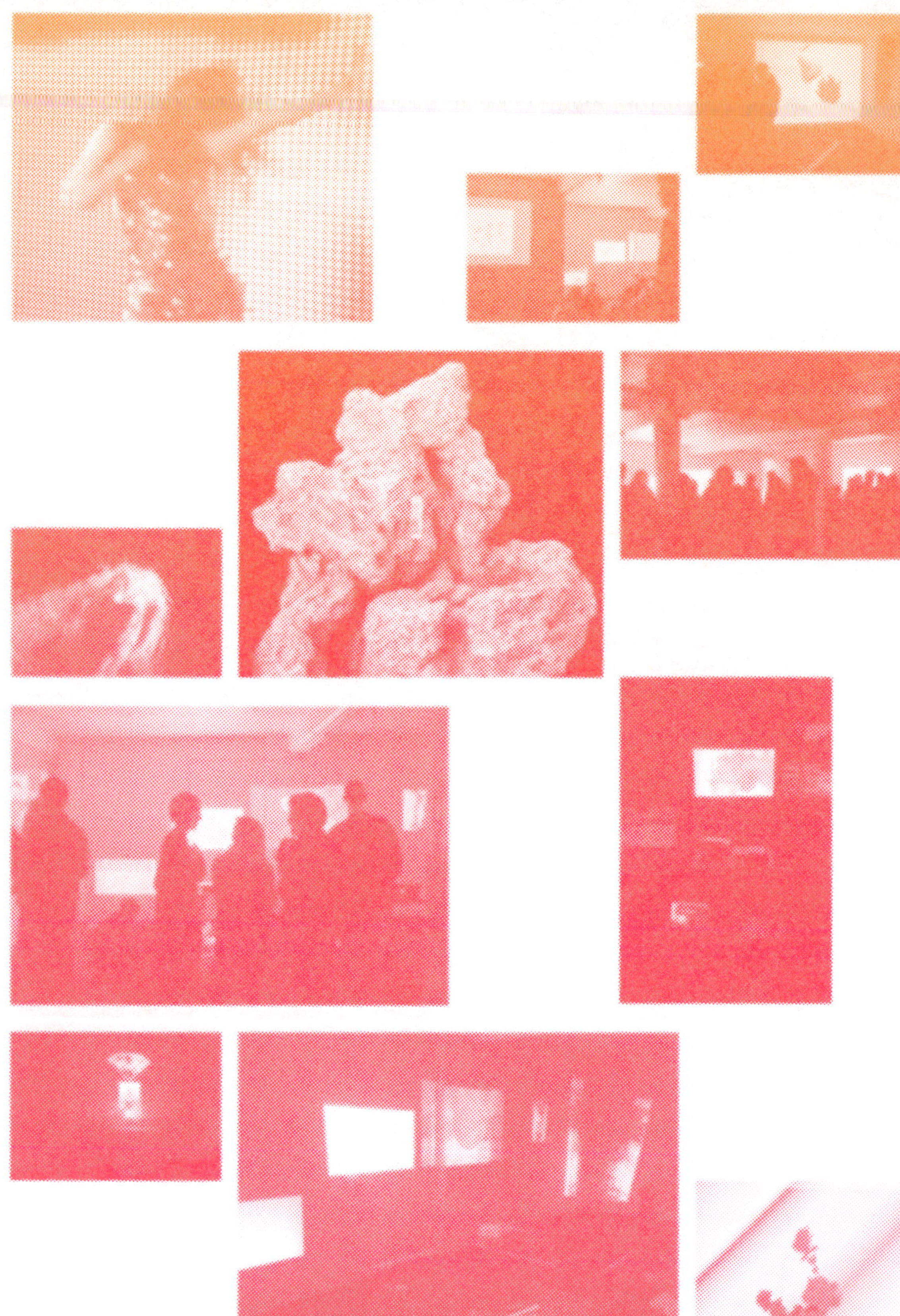

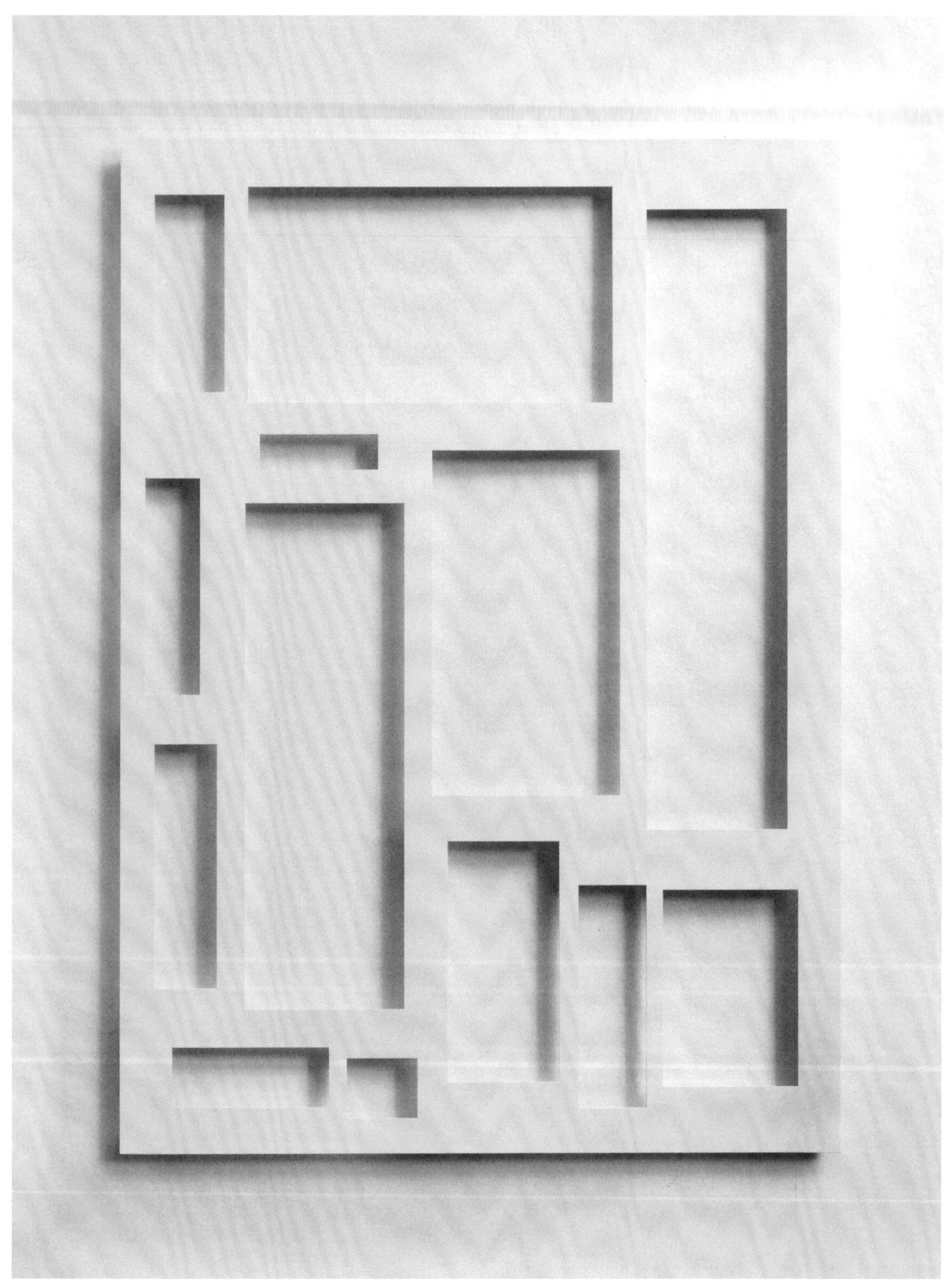

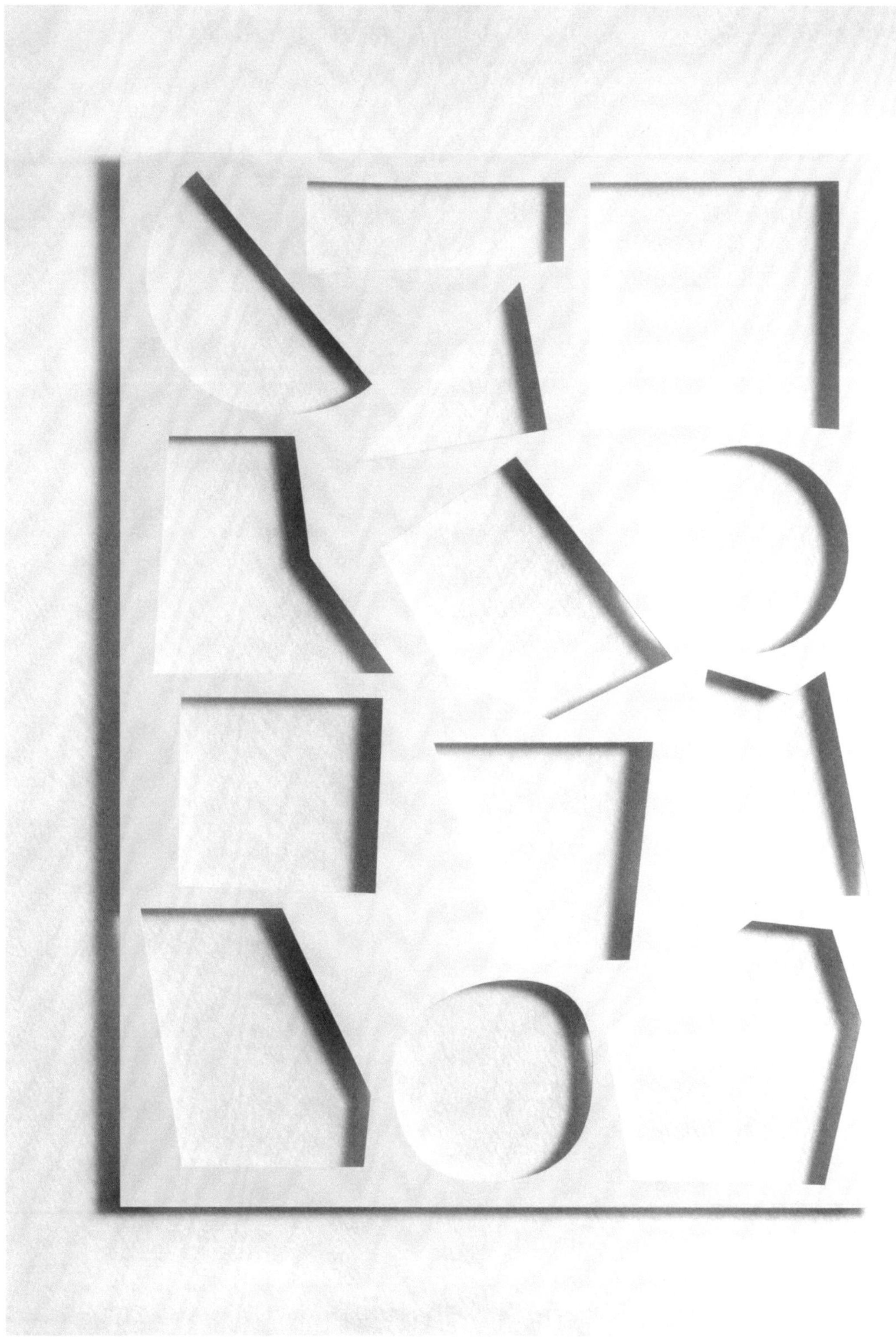

Shadow Object 16 07 05, 2016

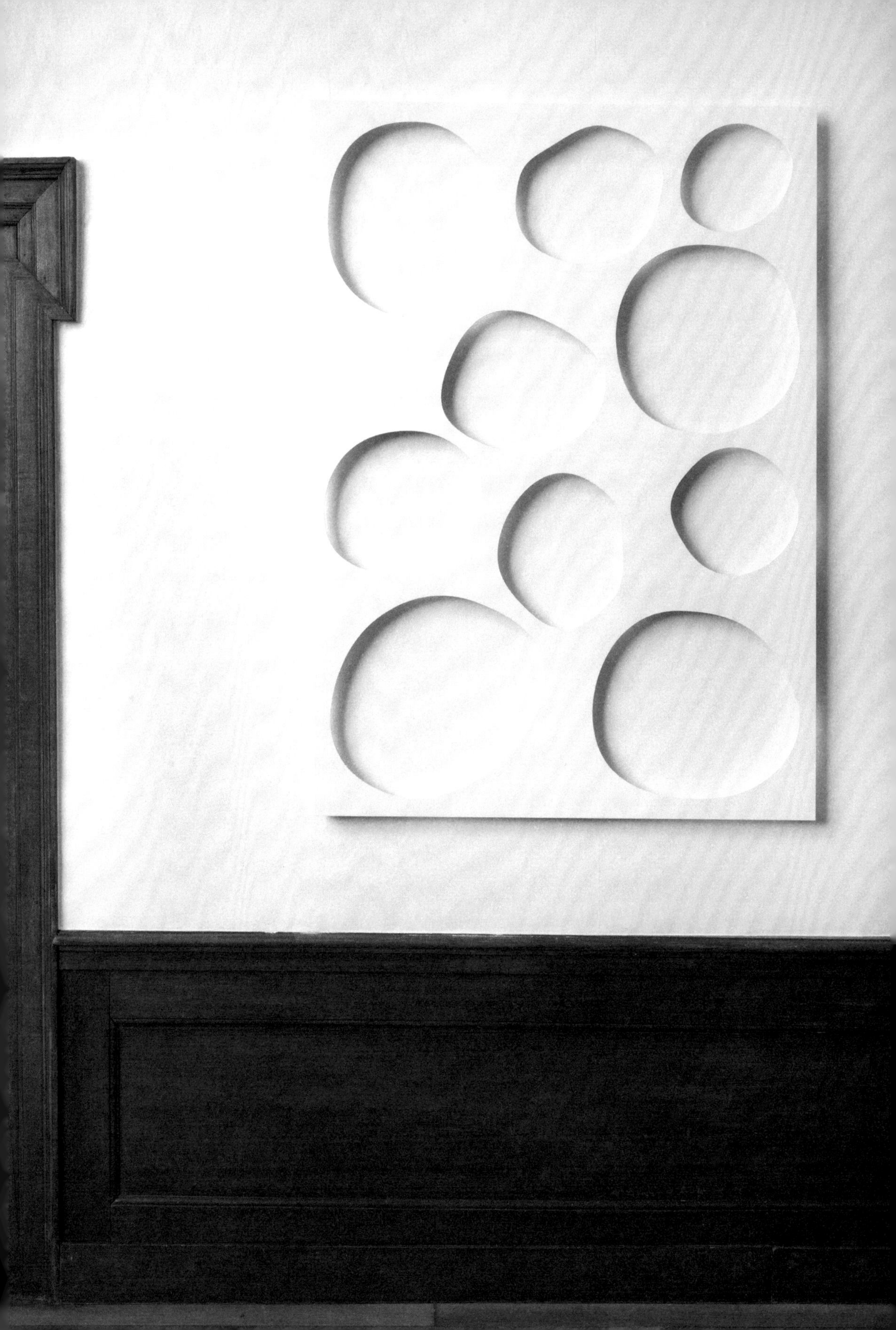

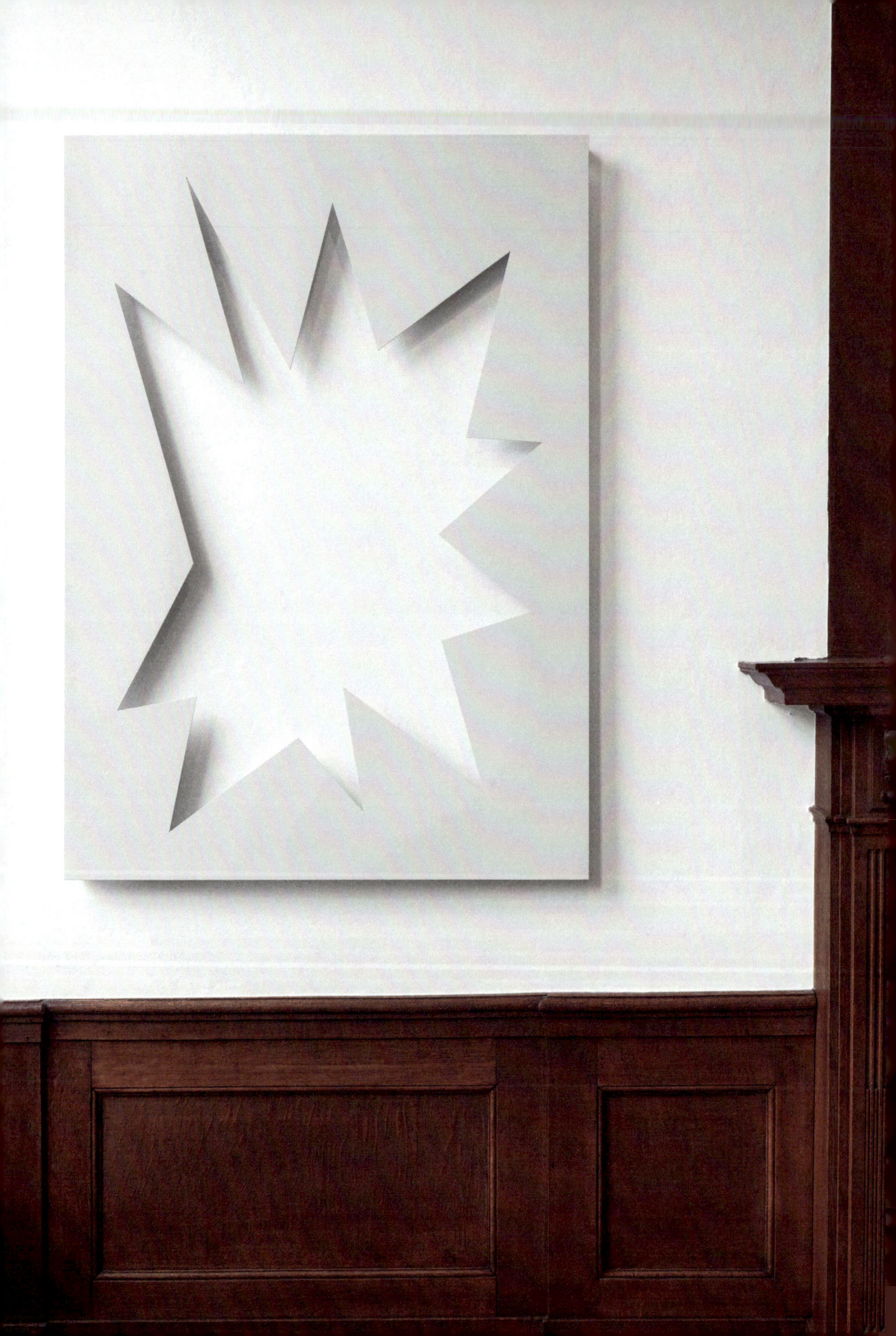

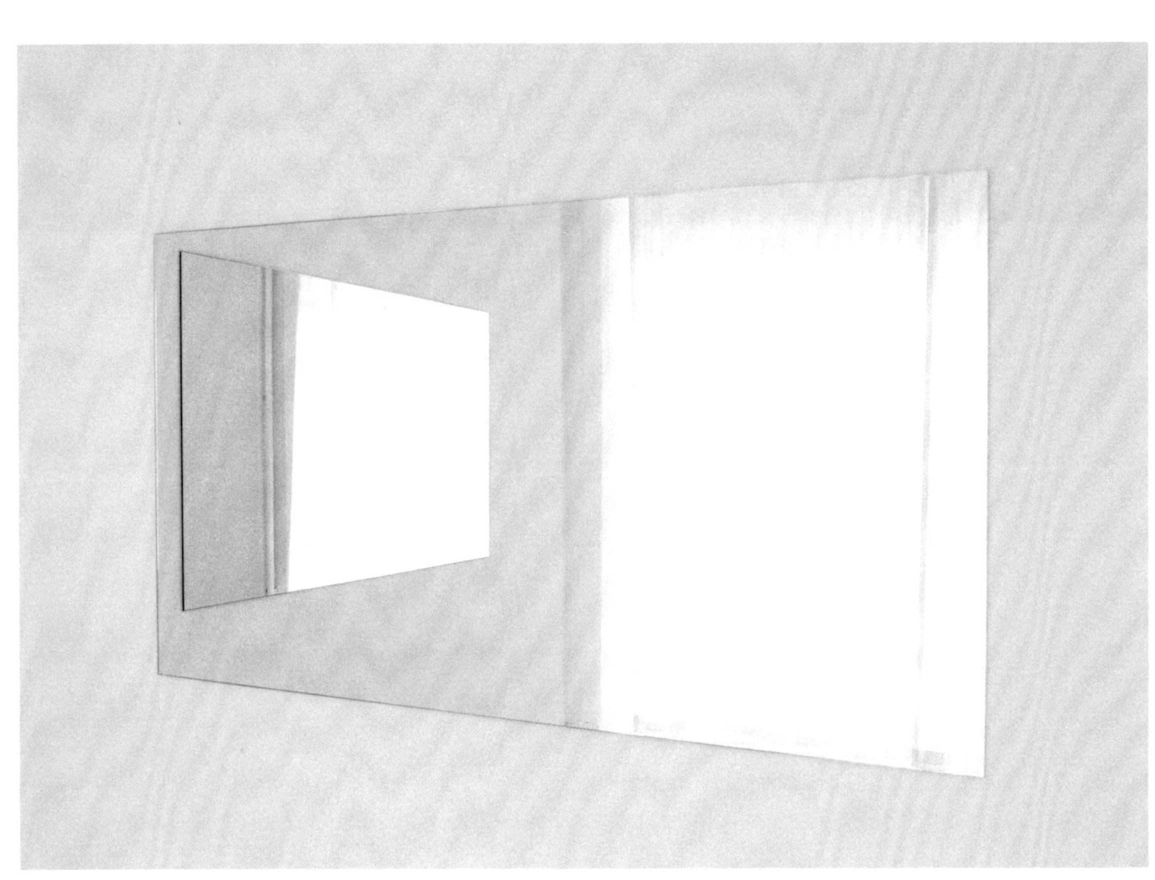

Popular Screen Sizes (60", 55", 46", 40", 32", 27", 24", 21",
19", 17", 15", 13", 11", 9.7", 7", 4", 3.5"), 2011

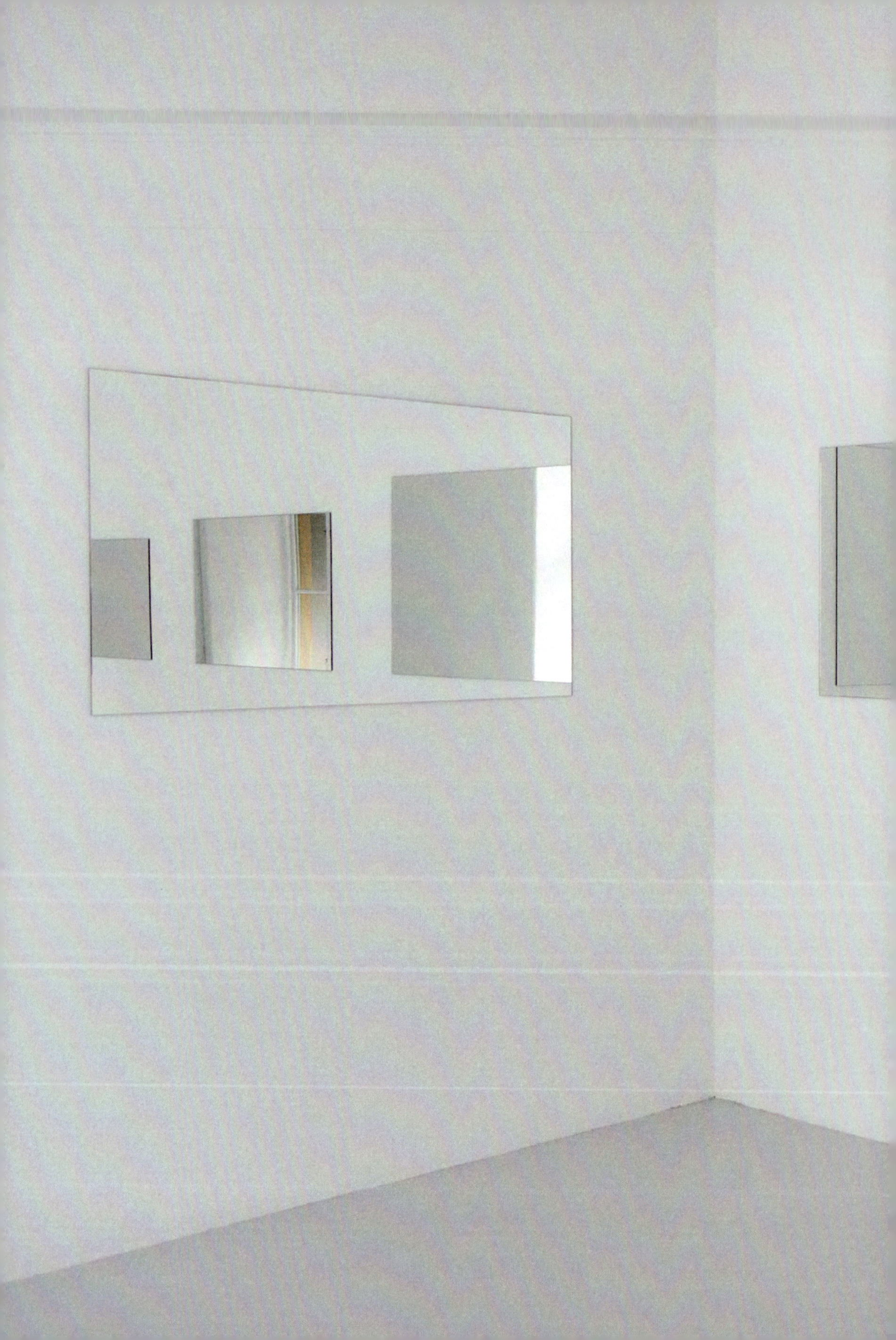

[194–195] *Popular Screen Sizes (60", 55", 46", 40", 32", 27", 24", 21", 19", 17", 15", 13", 11", 9.7", 7", 4", 3.5"), 2011*
[197–199] *Popular Screen Sizes (60", 55", 46", 40", 32", 27", 24", 21", 17", 15", 13", 9.7", 7", 3.5"), 2016*

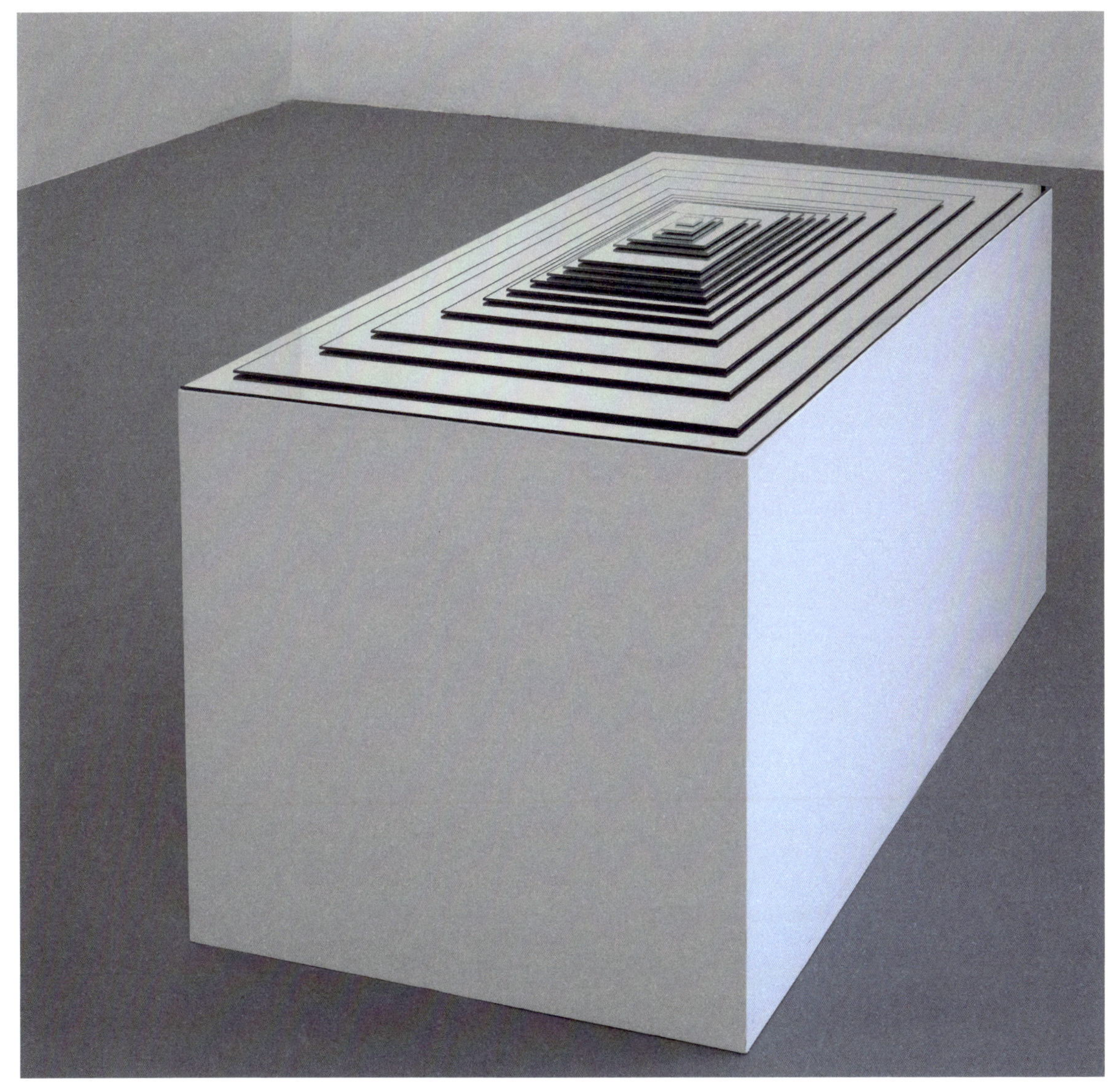

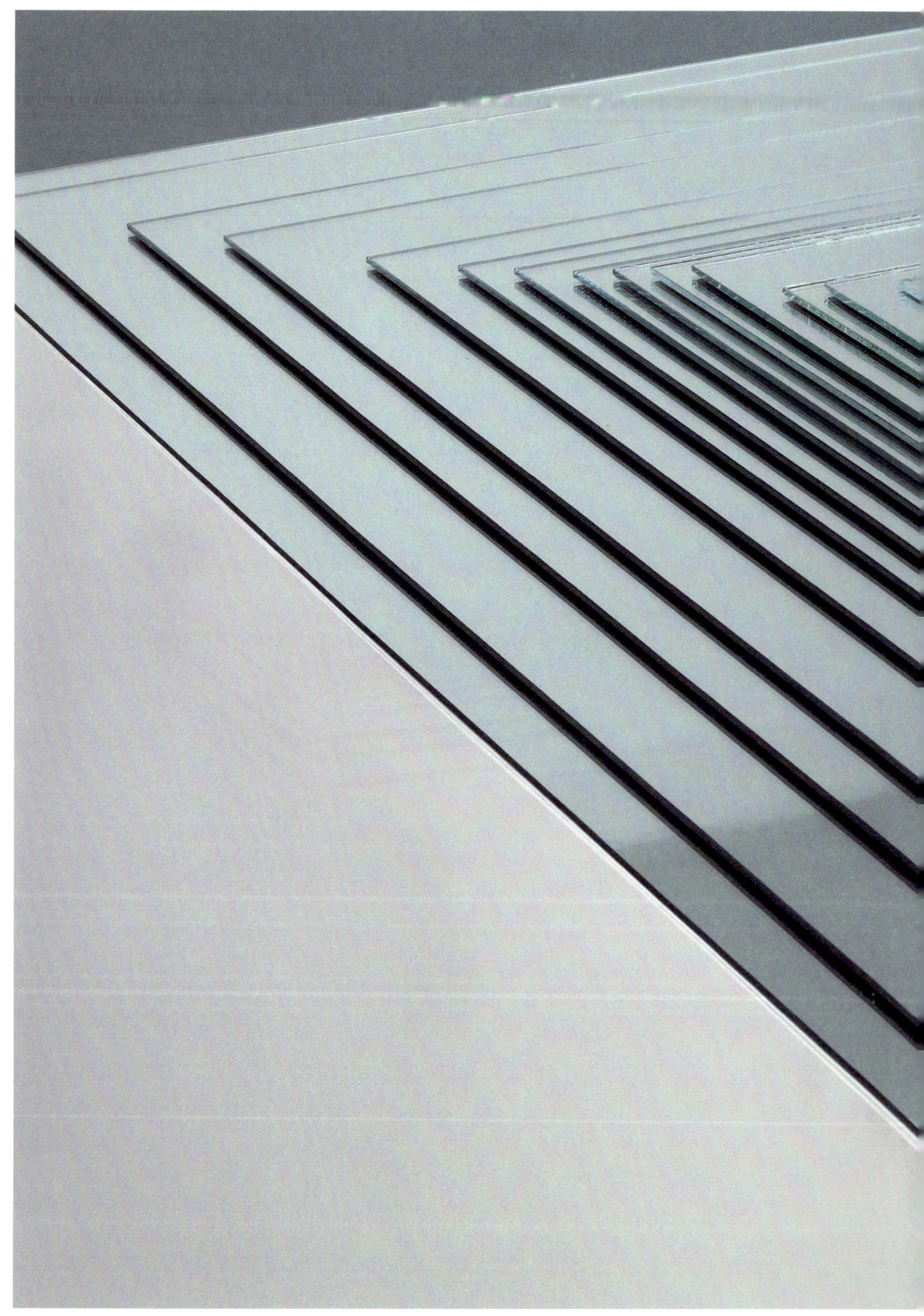

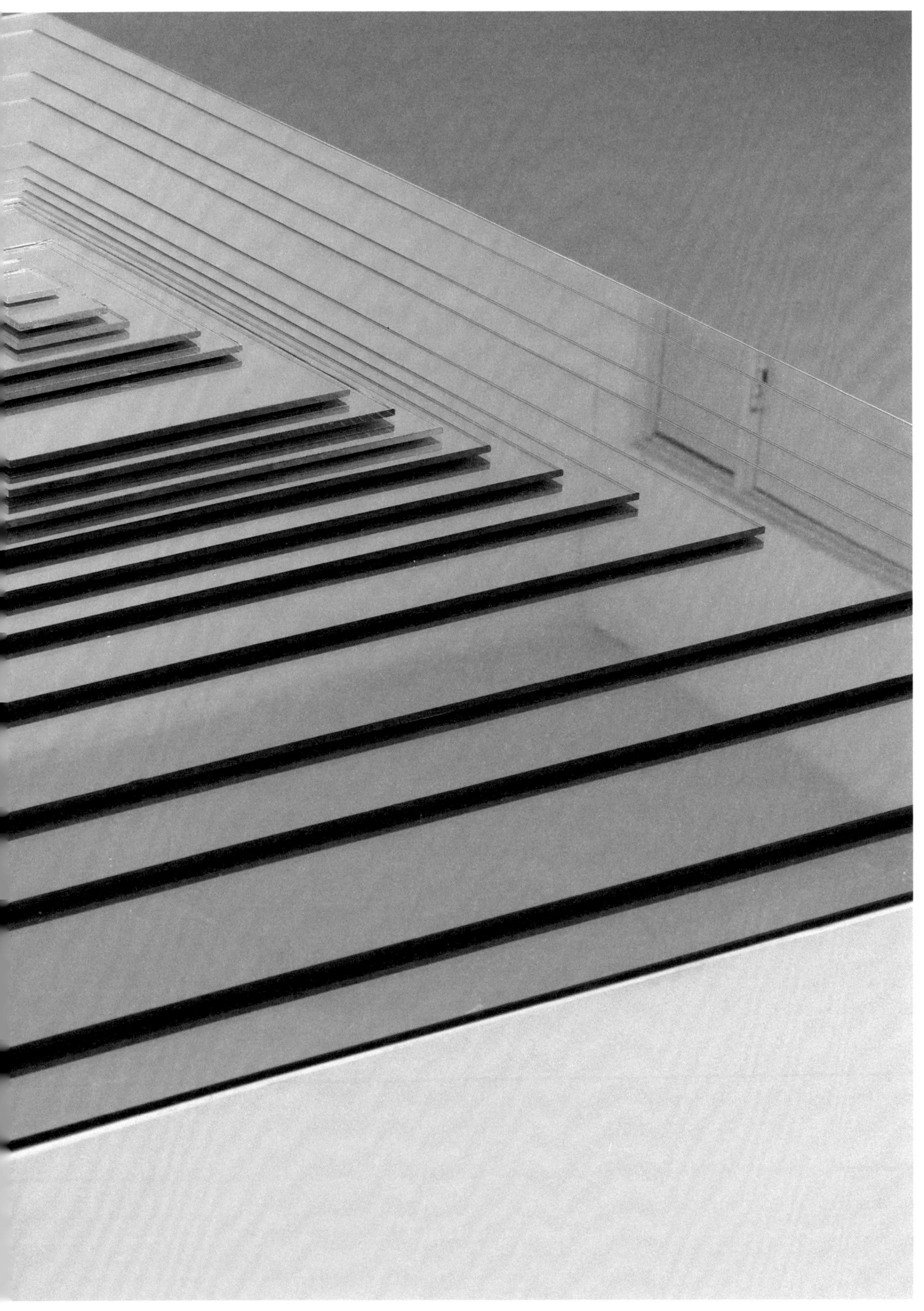

REMOTELY DISTANT NEVER NOWHERE
THE ART OF RAFAËL ROZENDAAL
Christiane Paul

Since its official emergence in the sixties, digital art has evolved in cycles with regard to its materiality, negotiating its inherent physicality and immateriality. While artists started experimenting with digital moving images early on—navigating the limited capacities of rendering work to the screen—digital artwork in the sixties often took the form of physical 'computer drawings.' Artists wrote their own code, which would be stored on punched cards or tape and then output as plotter drawings on paper. In the eighties and throughout the nineties, notions of the digital environment were profoundly shaped by the concepts of virtuality or 'cyberspace' envisioned in novels such as William Gibson's *Neuromancer* (1984) and Neal Stephenson's *Snow Crash* (1992). These concepts found their manifestation in the potential of the World Wide Web, as well as in the 'embodied virtuality' of immersive virtual reality environments accessed through Head Mounted Displays (HMDs) and data gloves; and were critically analyzed from various theoretical perspectives in books such as Michael Benedikt's *Cyberspace, First Space* (1991) and Sherry Turkle's *Life on the Screen* (1995). The new millennium saw the advent of a new phase of physicality through the wide-spread use of mobile devices, such as smart phones and tablets, and the Internet of Things as a networking of physical devices and architectures with embedded software, sensors, actuators, and connectivity.

Over the decades, digital technologies and digital art expanded, challenged, or even redefined concepts of what constitutes public space, the public domain, and public art. Networked digital technologies—the infrastructure of the Internet, mobile devices, as well as wearable computing—brought about formal redefinitions of what we understand as 'public' and opened up new spaces for artistic intervention. These new public spaces range from the Internet itself and a merging of the physical and virtual sphere (or mixed reality) to the augmentation of physical sites and architectures through 'smart' technologies that read data pertaining to their physical environments and make them programmable. Compared to more traditional forms of public art practice, networked art and Internet art, in particular, exist in a distributed non-local space, introducing a shift from the site-specific to the global and collapsing boundaries between the private and public. As opposed to public art in physical space, artworks in the public space of networks are largely not regulated or sponsored by the government, although they are increasingly dependent on corporate platforms.

By the early two thousands, digital technologies had begun to 'infiltrate' almost all aspects of art making, becoming a commonly used tool in the creation of art objects ranging from photography to sculpture and painting. The recent surge of interest in virtual reality aside, the concepts of ubiquitous and pervasive computing enabled by sensors, microprocessors, and mobile devices gradually counter-balanced, if not superseded, the notion of a predominantly virtual cyberspace as the quintessential model of the 'digital environment.' Many artists, curators, and theorists pronounced an age of the 'post-digital' and 'post-Internet' that is deeply informed by digital technologies and networks but takes their language and vernacular for granted, embracing a fusion of art, commerce, advertising and design. The terms post-digital and post-Internet also attempt to describe a condition of artworks and objects that are conceptually and practically shaped by the Internet and digital processes yet often manifest themselves in the material form of objects such as paintings, sculptures, or photographs. While digital or new media art was originally understood as art that was created, stored and distributed via digital technologies, post-digital art still speaks to and about the digital but may not be stored or circulated by means of these technologies. Whether one believes in the validity of the terms or not, post-digital and post-Internet capture a condition of our time—the effects of digital technologies on societies—as well as an aesthetics of representation and form of artistic practice.

It is in this space of a deep understanding of the aesthetic language of the digital and fluid transition between materialities—from the immateriality of software to the physicality of prints—where Rafaël Rozendaal's work resides. While he became widely known for net art projects that use the browser window to create abstract pictorial spaces, his work also translates that space across media and physical forms. His artistic practice comprises websites, installations, prints and writings, and his distinctive visual style has to be understood in the context of the language of digital technologies and the evolution of the Web as a space for artistic expression. Rozendaal's online work both builds on and undermines principles of the Internet art of the nineties.

From the early nineties through the the two thousands, net art underwent a process of 'versioning,' moving from its 1.0 to 2.0 release. In the Web 1.0 era of the nineties, net art consisted of work that existed mostly as discrete websites, commonly comprising sequences of hyperlinked pages that were accessed from one's home or office computer. With the advent of the Web 2.0 era and increasing use of smart phones and tablets in the new millennium, net art transformed into networked art, accessible on multiple platforms (from one's computer to one's smart phone) and often combining various forms within one project, from a website to an

installation or accompanying app. While the corporate metaphor
of Web 2.0 entails a fair amount of hype, marketing, and mone-
tizing, it can also provide an interesting framework for outlining
the ways in which networked art has initiated and responded to
changes in concepts such as virtual and public spaces and the
construction of identity. Networks, particularly social ones, have
evolved and profoundly shaped contemporary art and culture over
the past twenty years. In the Web 2.0 landscape public space is
created on social media platforms by means of highly accessible
and scalable publishing technologies. Artistic practice has both
helped to initiate and responded to the move from the 1.0 to 2.0
version of networked environments and their respective articula-
tion of concepts.

The recent hype surrounding the post-Internet as 'a revolutionary movement'[1] mirrors that which accompanied the arrival of net art in the nineties. The term genre rather than movement may be a more helpful construct for understanding both net art and post-Internet art. In the case of
post-Internet art, the genre also very much is a condition of the medium in
that the art often returns to material forms. While the so-called post-digital and post-Internet art builds on its predecessors, it also distinguishes
itself from them in that it takes the intersections of corporate platforms
and personal identity and of virtual and physical spaces for granted.

The cross-media exploration of aesthetic concepts, both on the
Web and in physical form, is an underlying thread of Rafaël
Rozendaal's work and connects it to the post-Internet genre.
However, his projects do not only cross media literally—exploring
similar concepts online or as prints—but also merge them within
the space of a given work. At the core of Rozendaal's online work
lies a fusion of animation and painting as artistic forms of expression. As opposed to the net art of the nineties, which often placed
emphasis on its hyperlinked, networked, collaborative features
and the architecture of the Web, many of Rozendaal's websites
are reminiscent of paintings in that they are completely contained
within the browser window. At the same time this seemingly

1   Ian Wallace, 'What is Post-
Internet Art? Understanding
the Revolutionary New Art
Movement,' *Artspace*, March 18,
2014, www.artspace.com/magazine/
interviews_features/post_internet_
art?utm_source=Sailthru&utm_
medium=email&utm_term=Master
&utm_campaign=March_23_2014_
Editorial_Weekly.

painterly space is rooted in the digital vernacular that frames how
we experience the online environment through the virtual real
estate of the browser window and the movement it supports.
Growing up, Rozendaal would watch his father, an abstract painter, contemplating his brushstrokes and became accustomed to the concentration
and precision that the act of painting entails. He also became attracted
to animated content at a very young age, watching cartoons on TV. His
interest in animated movement is rooted in a preference for abstraction in
the moving image and for the role the artist's hand plays in it. The human
translation of movement into an abstracted form—such as the hand-
drawn frames of traditional animation—combined with the concentration
involved in painting are essential elements in his work. For Rozendaal
the narrowing down of the visual language in the abstraction of animation and the narrowing down of the narrative in the moment depicted by
a painter, is where animation and painting meet. From an art-historical
perspective his works can be seen as in dialogue with both the abstract
musical animations of Oskar Fischinger and the abstract paintings of Piet
Mondrian or Hélio Oiticica.

> Rozendaal's attraction to the artist's hand in the transformation of
> movement into abstraction is counterbalanced in the display mech-
> anism for his websites, which is far removed from that manual
> element. The high-res computer screen does not have texture and
> emits rather than reflects light. This tension between the human
> hand in the creation of the work and the simultaneous elimination
> of its traces in the display mechanism is one of the distinctive
> characteristics of Rozendaal's style.

The simultaneously cartoonish and painterly visual language of
Rozendaal's net art projects is created through his use of vector animation,
which allows for a cleaner, smoother motion than moving pixels since
images are rendered and resized using mathematical rather than stored
pixel values. His choice of vector graphics was driven by both practical
and conceptual reasons. When Rozendaal started working on the Internet
he quickly became aware that his animations, while looking good on his
own computer screen, would not display the same way when distributed
over the network and perceived by an audience on screens of variable
sizes and at different network speeds. For one thing, Rozendaal saw the
small file size and scalable quality of *vector* graphics—which are based
on paths with a defined start and end point—as a practical solution to
that problem. At the same time, he was intrigued by the vector shape as a
conceptual construct that only gets executed once the viewer of the website activates the script. The work therefore is never completely defined
and also resolution-independent; it remains scalable and, rather than

deteriorating, potentially improves over time as technological advances in displays are being made.

Finding the simplest solution to the visual problem of translating motion into abstraction is one of the driving forces of Rozendaal's on-line art and results in the precision and elegance of his projects. The visual environments of his websites frequently remain in suspension, never arriving at the place evoked by their movement or suggesting a state of infinity through their potential of endlessly reconfiguring themselves. They mesmerize the viewer by contemplating a distance that can never be bridged. This state of suspension between smooth movements is frequently captured in the titles of the websites—*remotely distant, almost there* or *never nowhere.*

Rozendaal's net art projects do not only resist the architecture of hyperlinked space but also frequently undermine one of the essential characteristics of the digital medium: the potential for interaction. Digital media and the Internet as a public space increased the technological possibilities for interaction even if these possibilities are not necessarily always fulfilled. Audience participation is an important element in all public art and how much agency it provides manifests itself in the possibilities for influencing, changing or creating institutions and events, or acting as a proxy. Degrees of agency are measured by the ability to have a meaningful effect in the world and in a social context. Within technological environments one needs to consider the respective degrees of the agency of authors and participants, software and systems. The fact that digital art is inherently interactive, participatory or even collaborative and, in its networked forms, potentially open to exchanges with trans-local communities, moves questions surrounding agency and the authority of authorship central to digital art practice. The degree of participation is partly determined by the levels of mediation unfolding within an artwork.

Rafaël Rozendaal's choice to express his ideas as software is not only rooted in the advantages of scalable expression but driven by his desire to reach a broad audience over the Internet. Connecting with people is most important to him, which makes the Internet an ideal distribution platform for engaging with his audience. Despite Rozendaal's desire to connect, interaction per se is not necessarily a component of his online projects. Many of them perform their own logic of abstraction without a viewer's intervention, and those that allow the audience to interact tend to playfully undermine the conventions of online navigation. Hyperlinks from one Web page to the next provide the defining architecture of the Web, but the endless river of information produced by the traversal of links from one webpage to the next made Rozendaal want to create

dead ends. His websites explore interaction for interaction's sake,
keeping the viewer in the contained space of one page. Interaction
takes place within the confined territory of one browser window,
leading to transformations within that space rather than using the
language of the montage, jump cut, and pause of transition that
is characteristic of hyperlinked net art. The interactions provided
by Rozendaal's works are not driven by goals and do not lead to
easily definable rewards but instead generate pleasure by reflecting
on the conventions and expectations of interaction itself.

While the Internet as distribution platform allows artists such as
Rozendaal to connect to a wide audience, the context it provides still has
some limitations. Net art has been created to be seen by anyone, any-
where, anytime—provided one has access to the network—and does not
need a gallery or museum to be presented or introduced to the public. In
the online world the physical gallery context does not necessarily work
as a signifier of status any longer. At the same time, online distribution
does not allow net art to be seen in the context of other art forms, such as
painting or sculpture, and physical art spaces can still play an important
role in building art-historical connections for net art and further expand-
ing its audience. The presentation of net art in the physical gallery space,
however, has always been a curatorial challenge, and various models for
displaying net art in an institutional context have been widely debated.
Although net art exists in a virtual public space, it is not necessarily an art
form that is easy to connect to the public space of a gallery. The multiple
approaches to showing this art form all have advantages and disadvan-
tages. Some people have argued that it should be presented only online
and that 'it belongs on the Internet'—which is where it resides in any case.
Some works of net art lend themselves to presentation in an installation
because they address notions of space. Others translate well as a projection—for example, works that have not been created for a browser window
and beg to get out of it. Still others need to maintain their inherent 'net-
ness' and require one-on-one interaction by way of a computer. Net art
often requires a relatively private engagement over a longer period of time
and, to create an environment for the latter experience, has often been
presented in a separate area of a public space, which in turn raises the
criticism of 'ghettoization.'

With the more recent developments in wireless technologies and
mobile devices, the Internet has become increasingly accessible
from a range of technological platforms. The numerous require-
ments for viewing net art projects range from browser versions
to plug-ins, minimum resolution, screen size, and so forth, which
have to be fulfilled on the viewers' end in order to have an appro-
priate experience of the art. The fact that websites are viewed by

their audience in very different ways—depending on the speed of the computer and network connection and the brightness and size of the screen—was one of the reasons why Rafaël Rozendaal started experimenting with the presentation of online projects in the gallery and show the same project in different manifestations. Moreover, his works tend to reflect on the possibilities of form and movement in a defined space, which requires negotiating the relationship between medium and spatiality in a translation of projects from online space to a gallery installation. Rozendaal sees every exhibition as another opportunity to create new work through a change in the display of a given project. Over the course of different shows he has created variations of the same piece, including straightforward projection on the gallery wall; overlapping projections; placement of broken mirrors across the floor to create chaotic reflections and expand the space; and projections on fabric, sand or the audience itself. He also has played with exhibiting the same website on a range of different screens hung next to each other, thereby highlighting the element of randomness in the same script. Rozendaal thinks of websites as gas that can fill up any potential space and strives to configure displays in proportion to the space they occupy. As he puts it, viewers experiencing websites at their home are not looking at a laptop or desktop but at the Internet and webpage itself, while an audience in a gallery tends to be much more aware of the screen hung on the wall. For him, the differences in presentation of the same artwork are comparable to those in the experience of music, which people might listen to on their phone, a high-end stereo, or at a concert. The work becomes part of its audience's life in various listening scenarios, with a live performance as highlight or defining moment. Even if they are technologically uneven, these instances remain emotionally and conceptually connected.

The transitions between virtual and physical space in Rozendaal's work do not only play out in the installation of software-based projects in the gallery. They also manifest themselves in the exploration of compositions in both websites and lenticular prints—in which lenticular lenses and interlacing of images are used to produce printed images that have an illusion of depth and change or move when viewed from different angles. To create his lenticulars Rozendaal creates four frames for each print, which are then subjected to computer code that slices them into thin stripes and alternates stripes from each frame consecutively. His websites and lenticulars are engaged in an ongoing dialogue with each other, and similar concepts and movements may take shape as both online project and print. The visual movement that viewers perceive when walking back and forth in front of a lenticular, thereby changing angles, might be similar to the one they experience when they interact with one of Rozendaal's web projects. A viewer's body thereby becomes the 'cursor' that generates movement through a switch of perspective in physical space.

While ideas about composition move back and forth between the virtual space of the website and physicality of the lenticular, the process of working within each medium remains very different. Rozendaal compares the creation process of the lenticulars to 'slow programming' taking place over the course of years. The programming of websites is a direct process in which results are immediately visible, but the lenticulars are the outcome of an ongoing experiment with changing a few variables in every new group that is produced. Rozendaal describes the lenticulars as foggy, dreamy, and more nuanced in their visual expression. At the same time he has less control over their outcome, learning about the potential of each composition only as it is produced. Achieving the nuance of a lenticular within a browser window would go beyond the processing power of the average computer, so the Web projects remain grounded in the line of the vector graphics, simpler and more faithful to their medium. Rafaël Rozendaal's work takes shape through a range of translations and transformations—from movement into abstraction, from virtual into physical space, and from website to print—with all of them informing each other. It may not be easy to pin down and locate his work in the 'somewhere' of a concrete, clearly defined conceptual space, but its visual aesthetics are always precise and never nowhere.

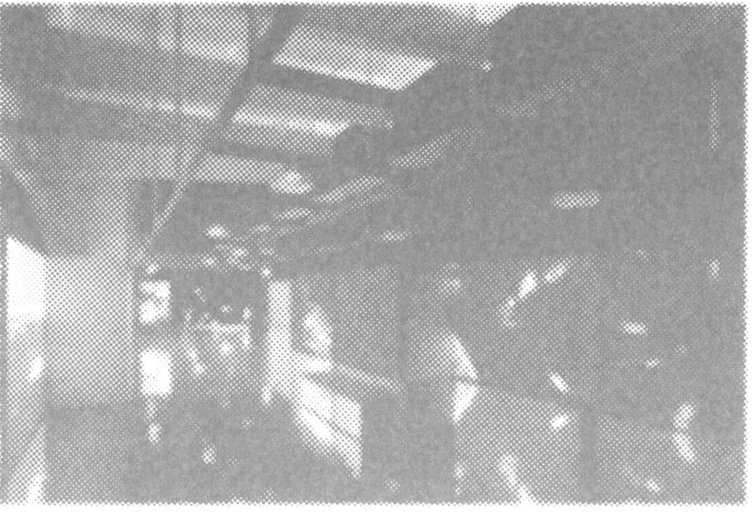
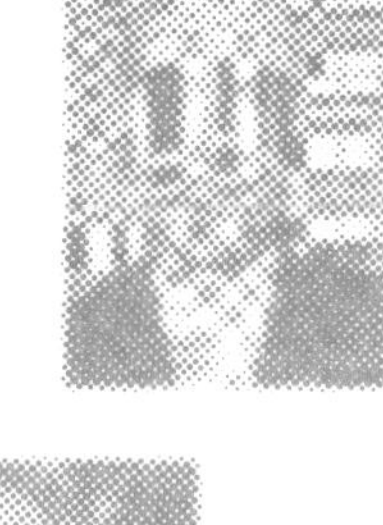
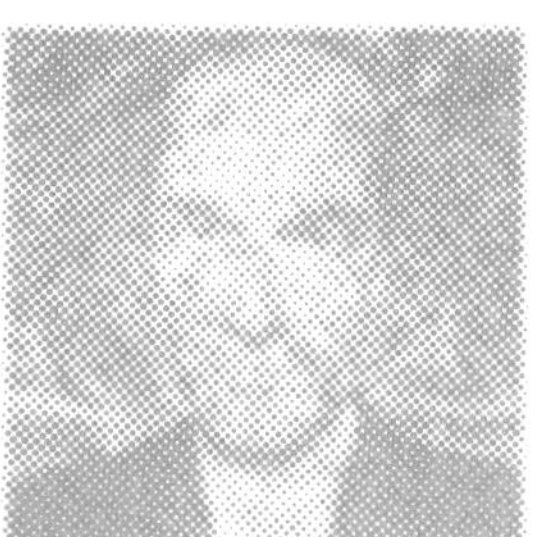
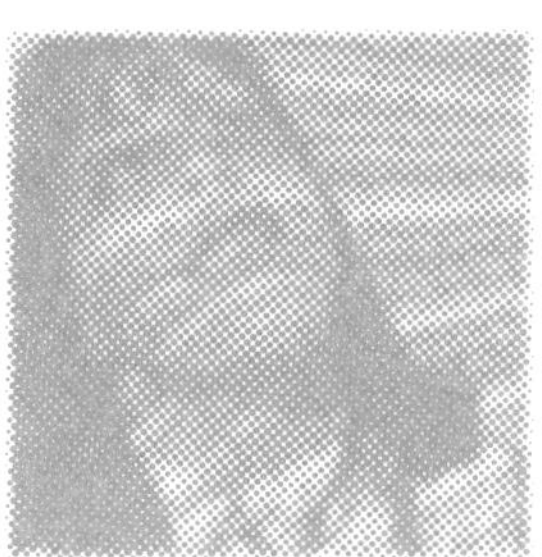
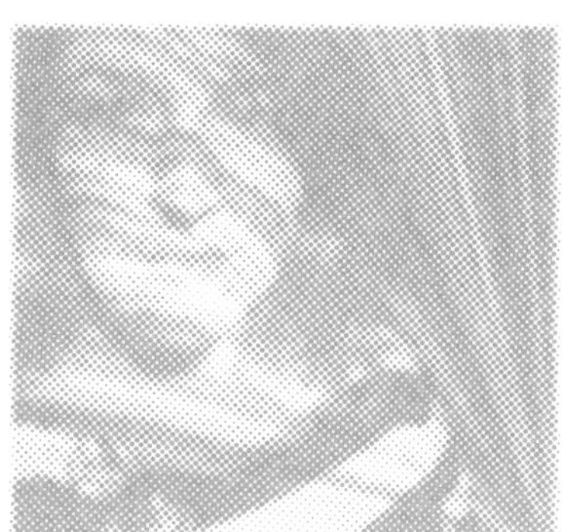
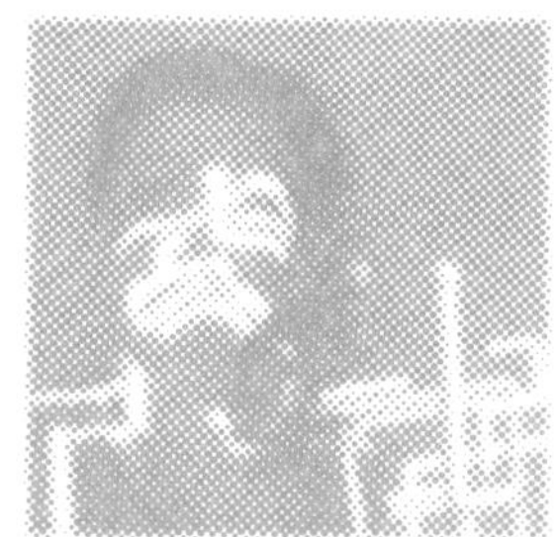
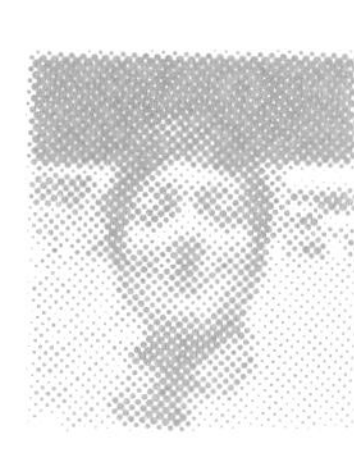

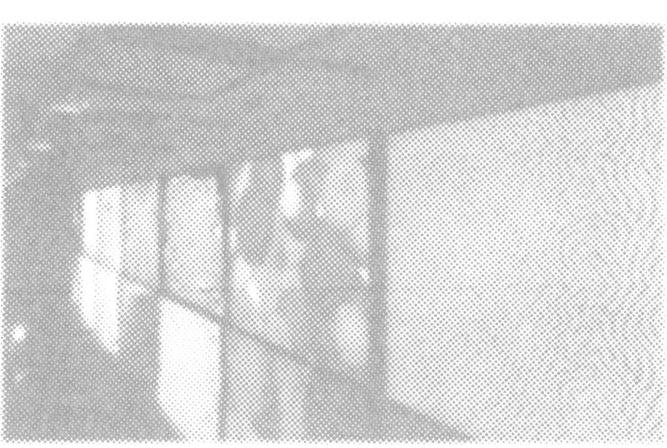
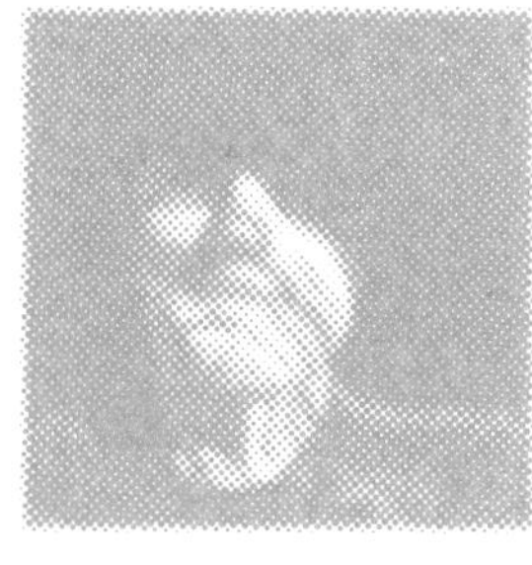
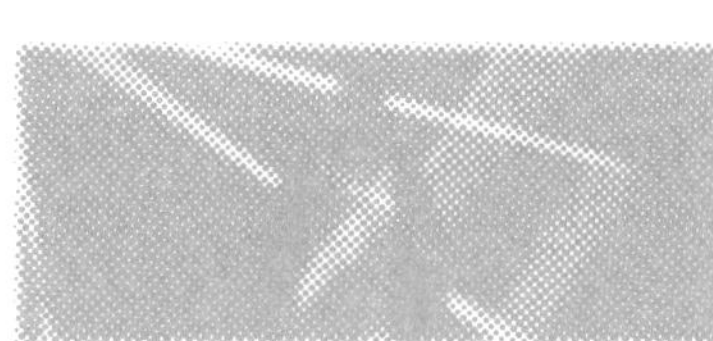

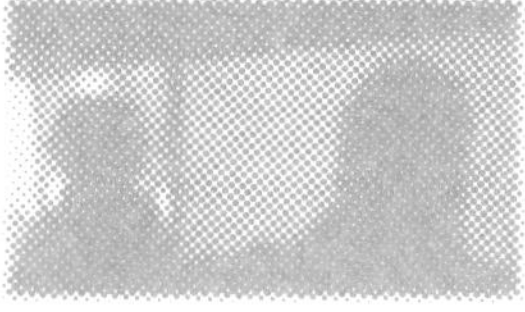

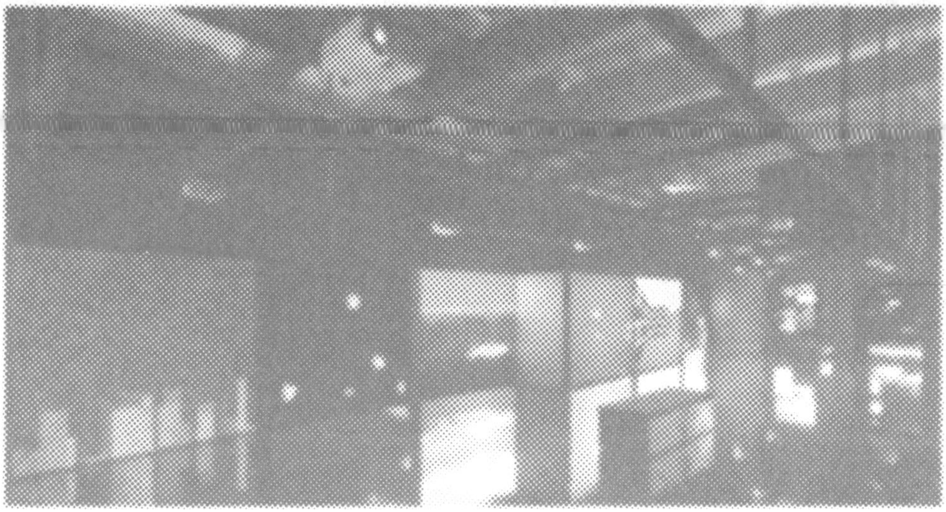

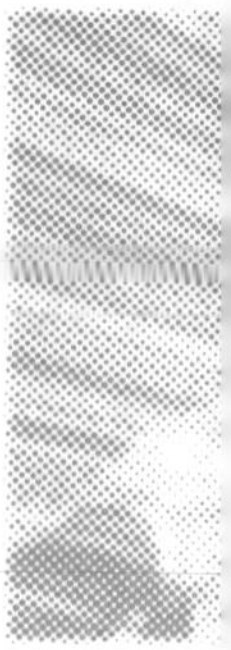

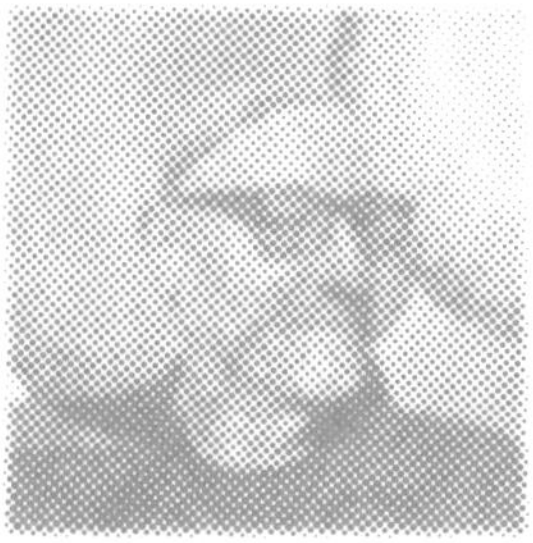

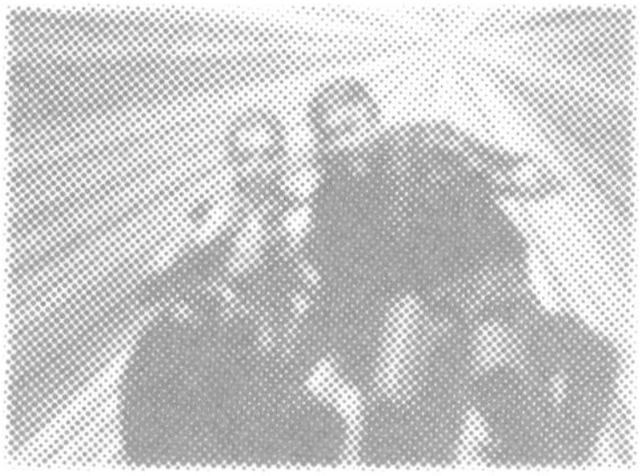

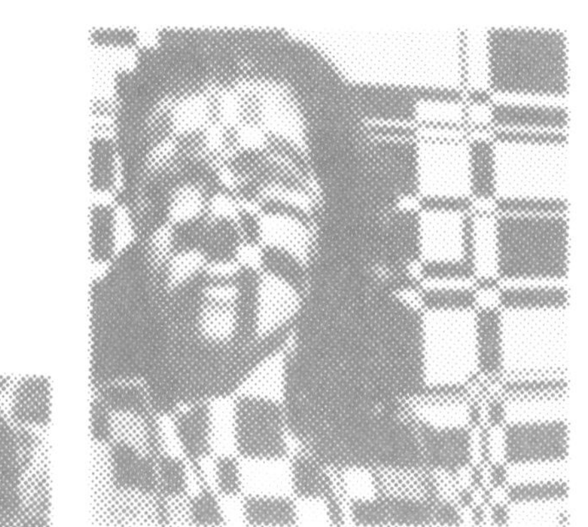

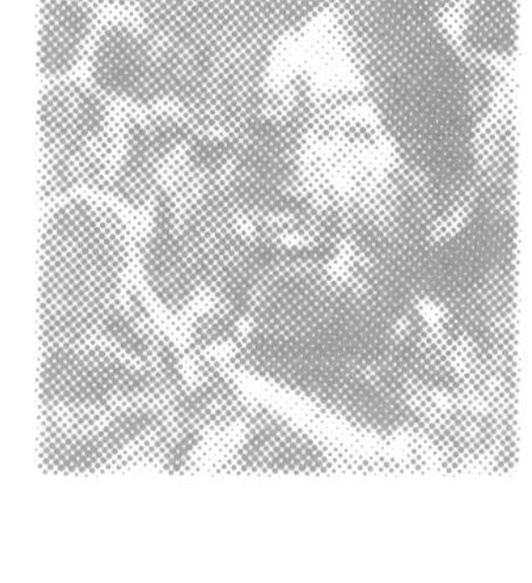

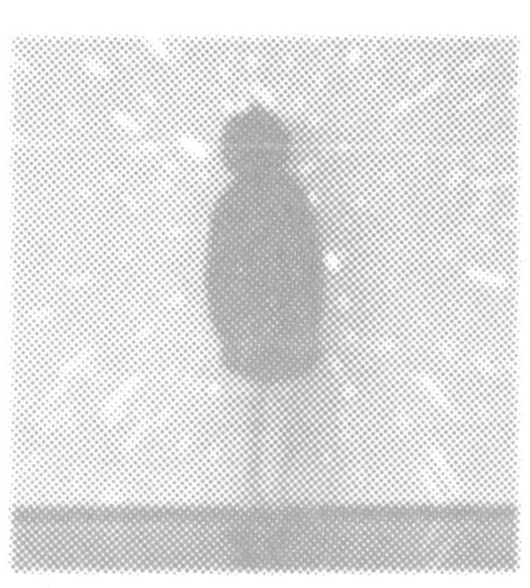
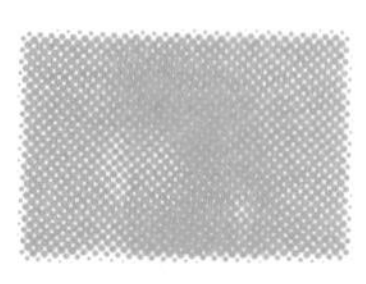

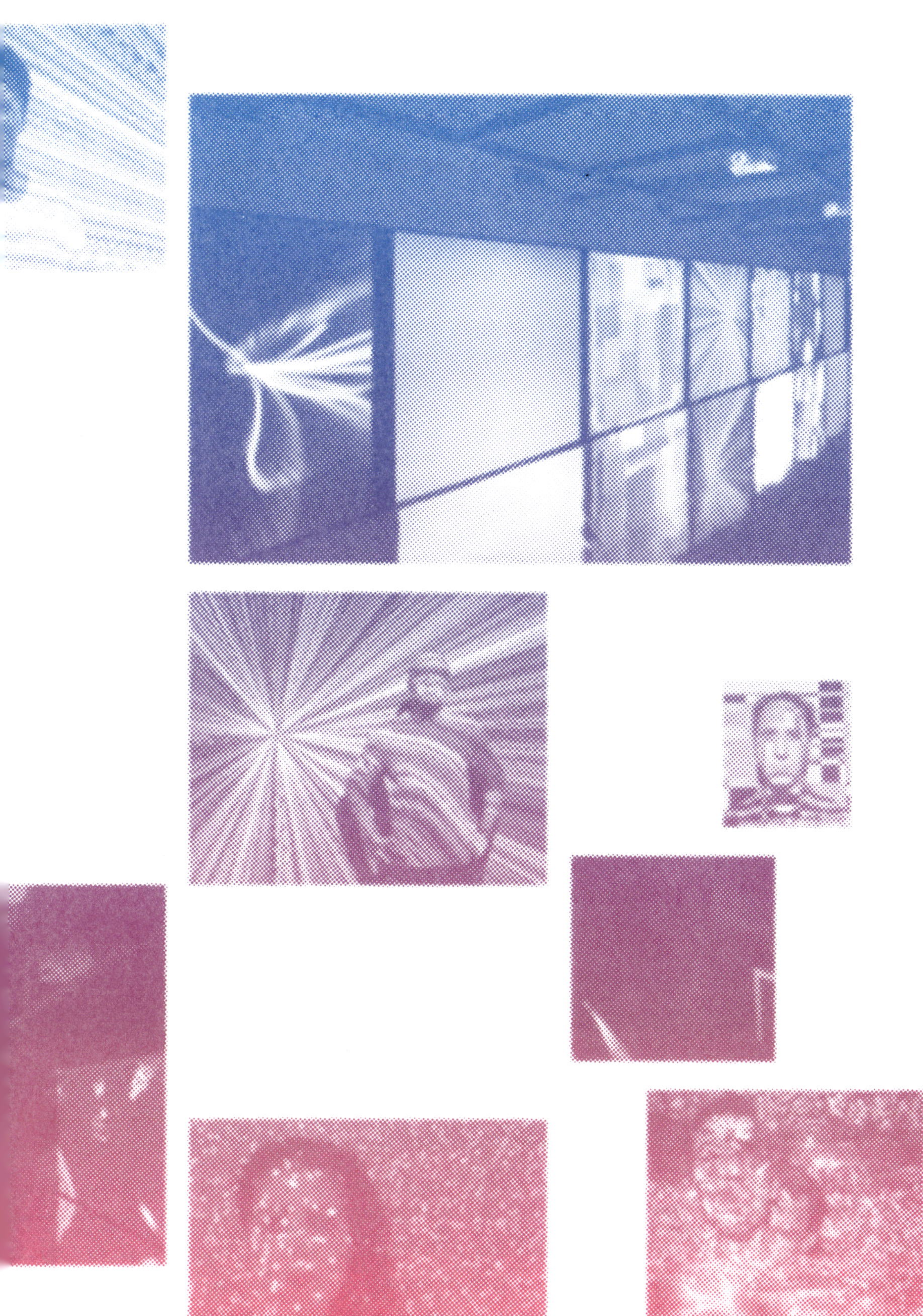

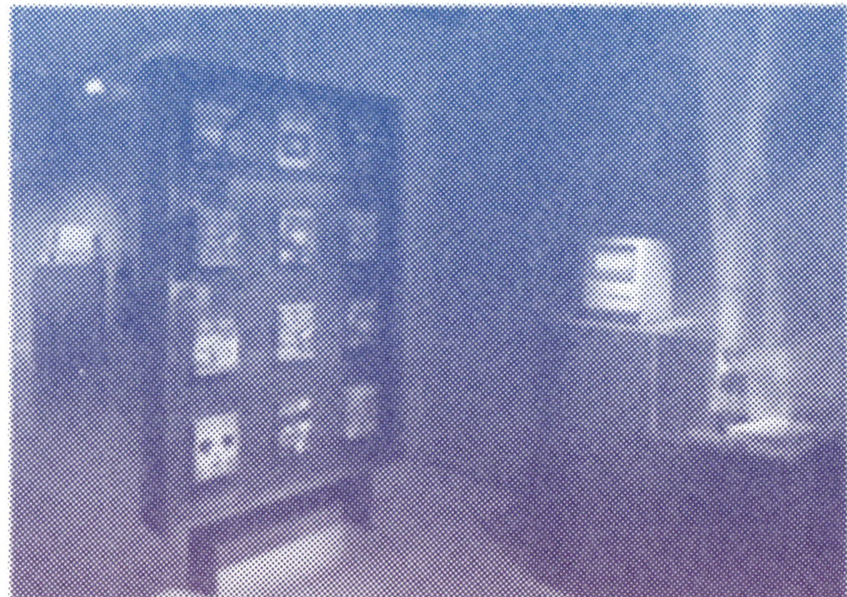
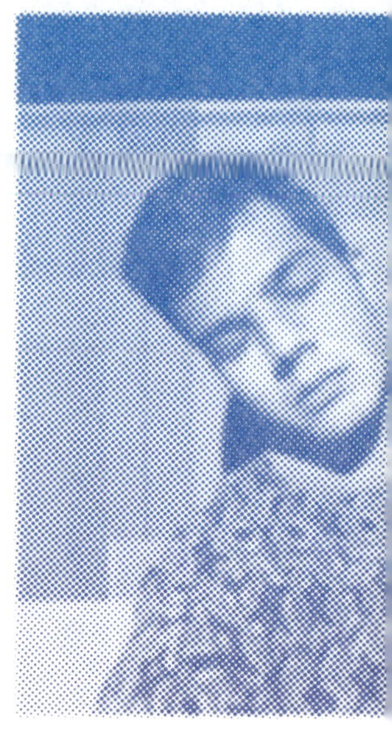
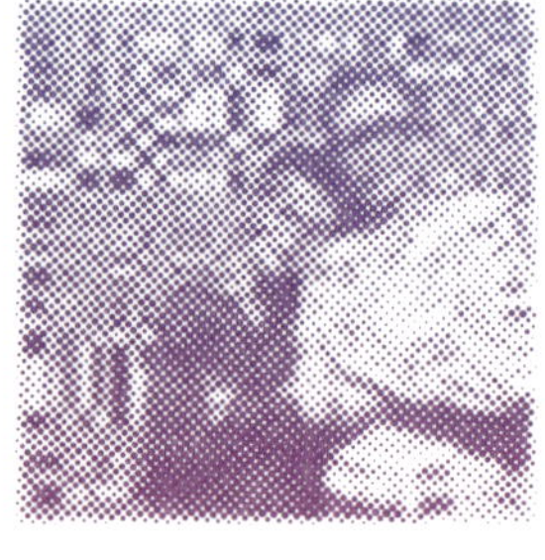
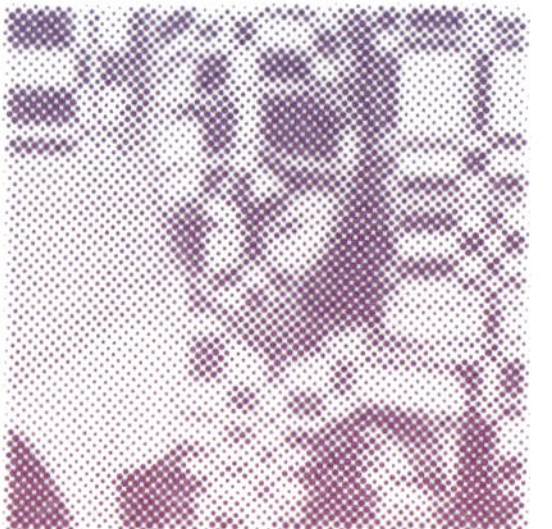
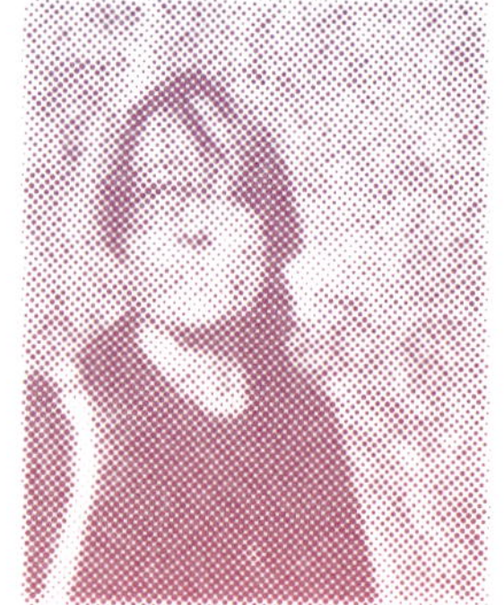
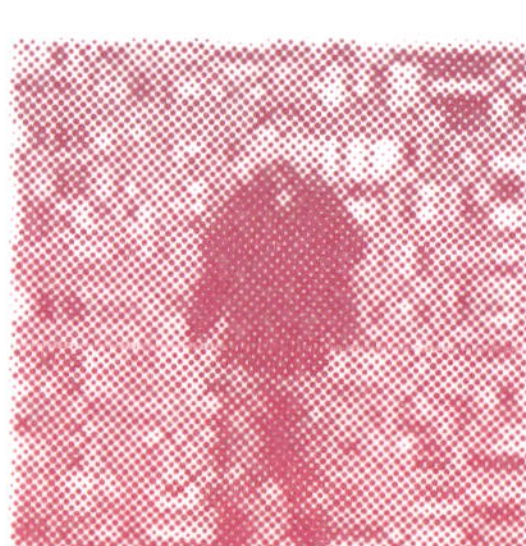
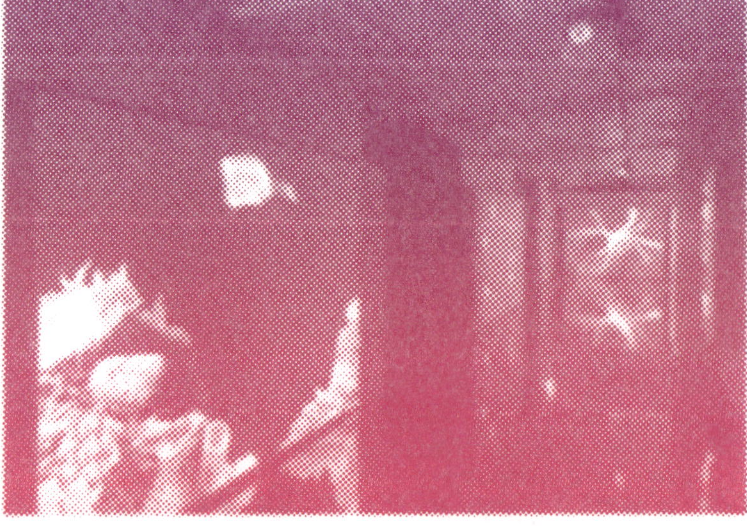

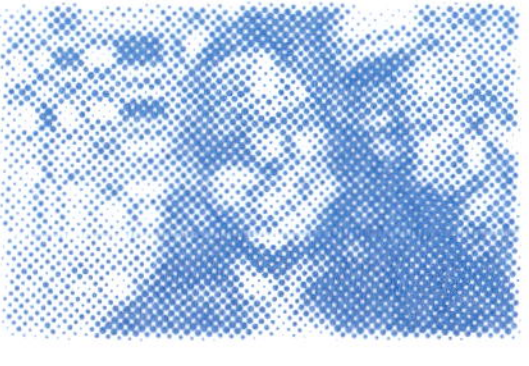

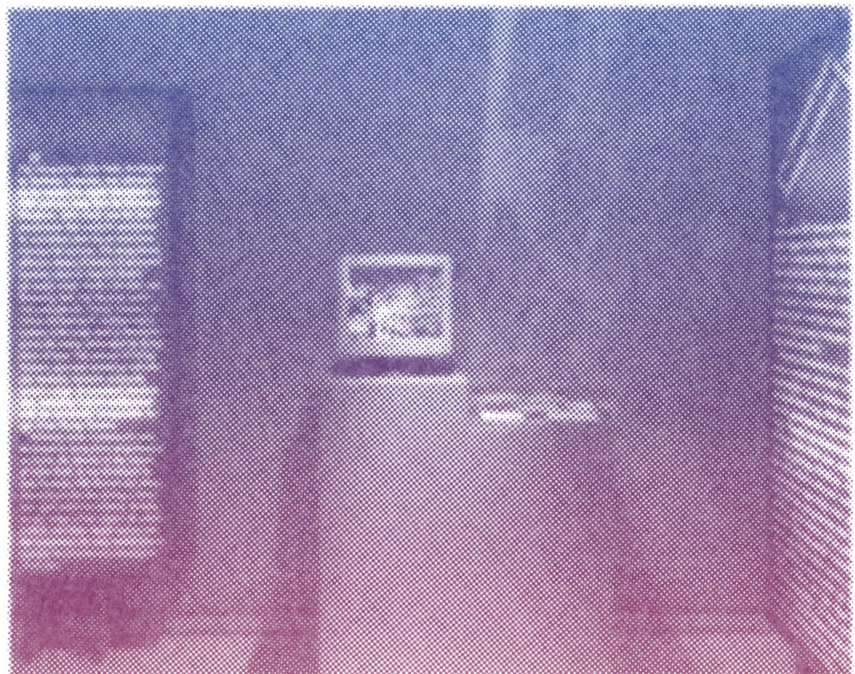

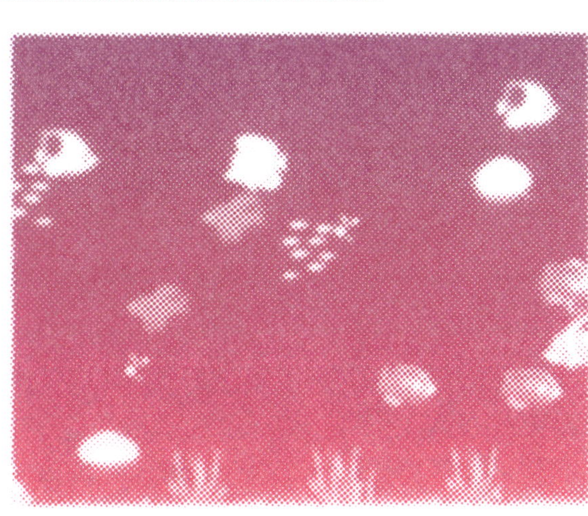

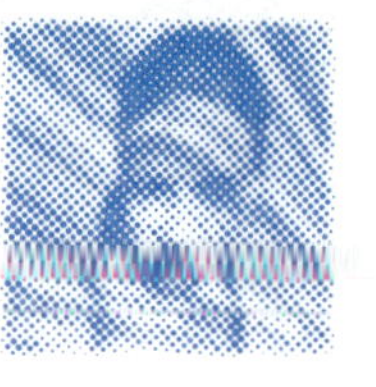
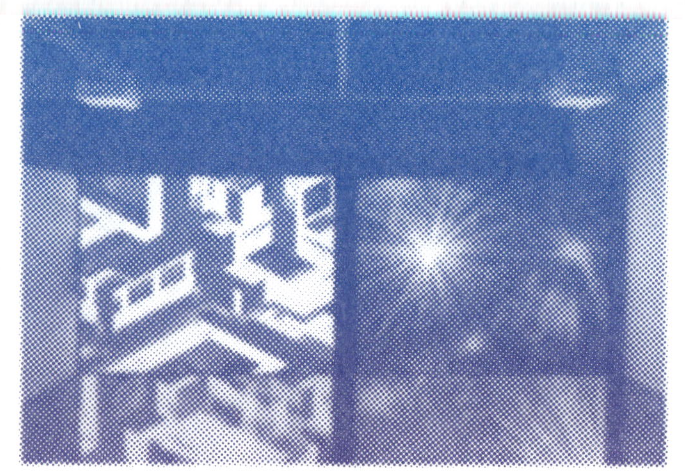
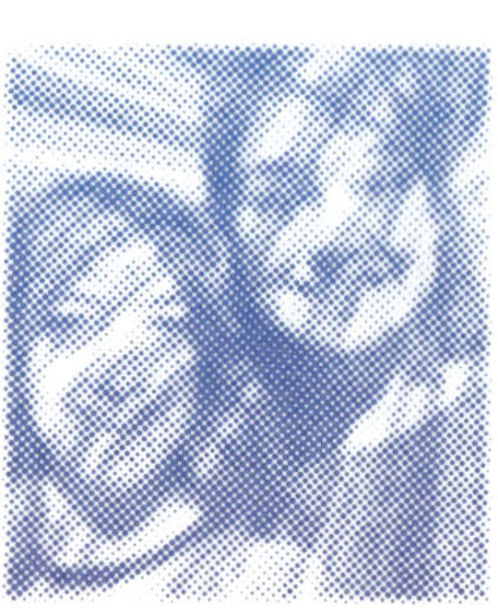
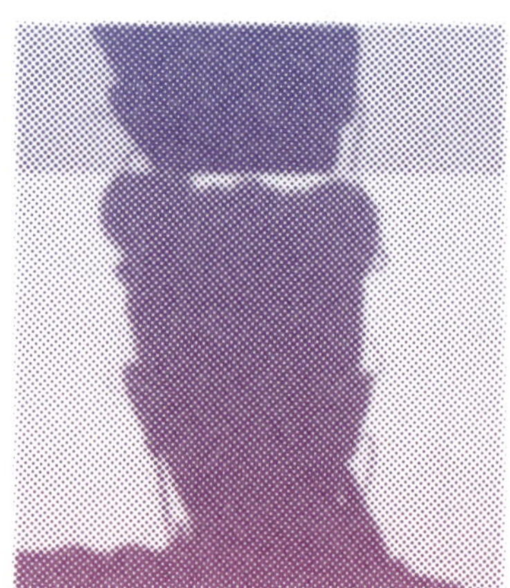
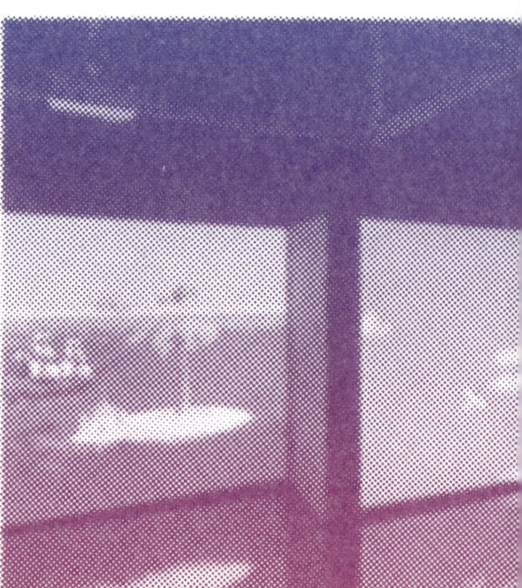
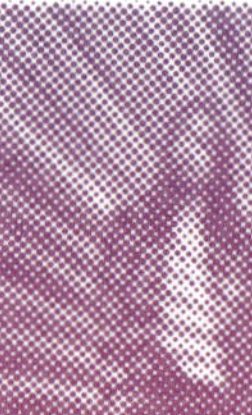
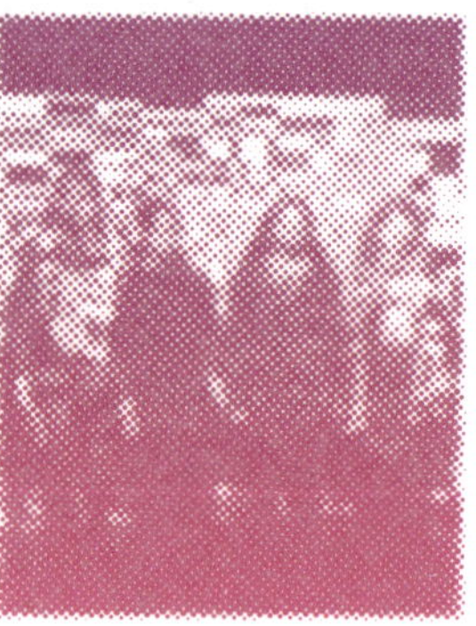
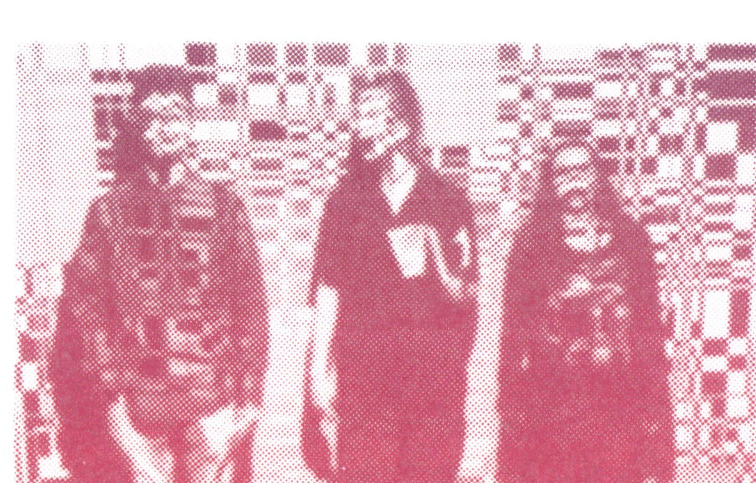
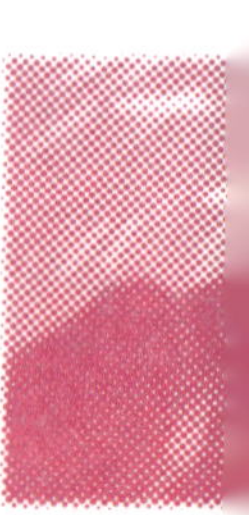

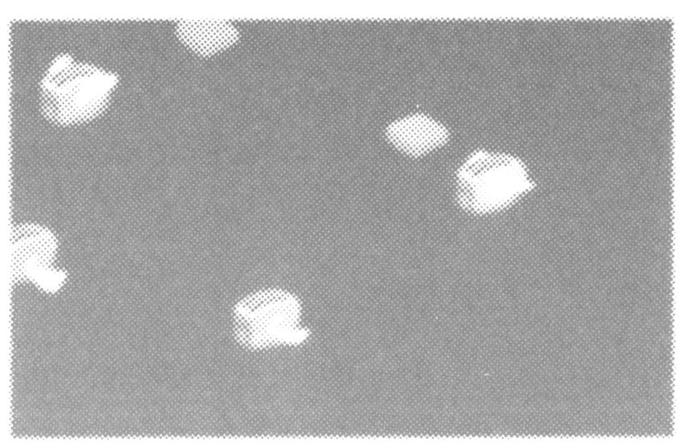
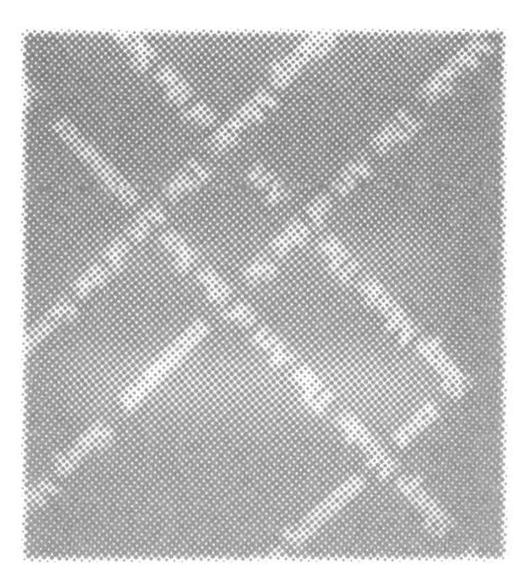
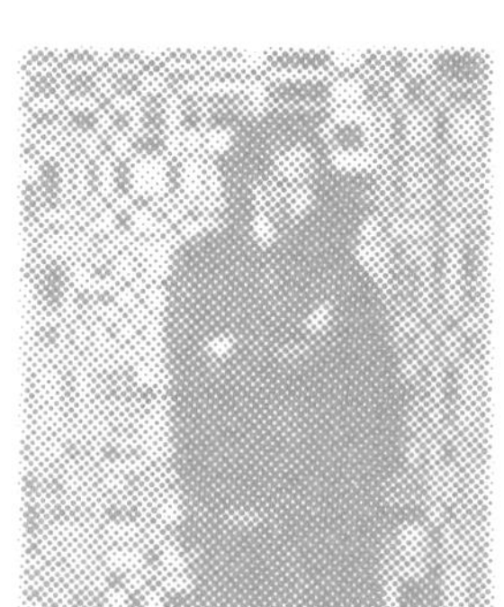
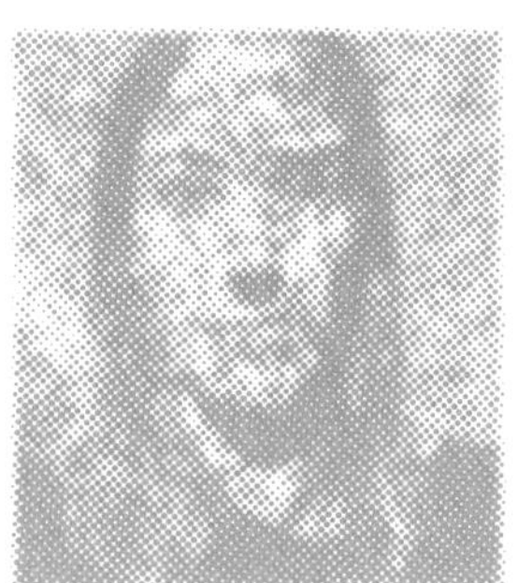
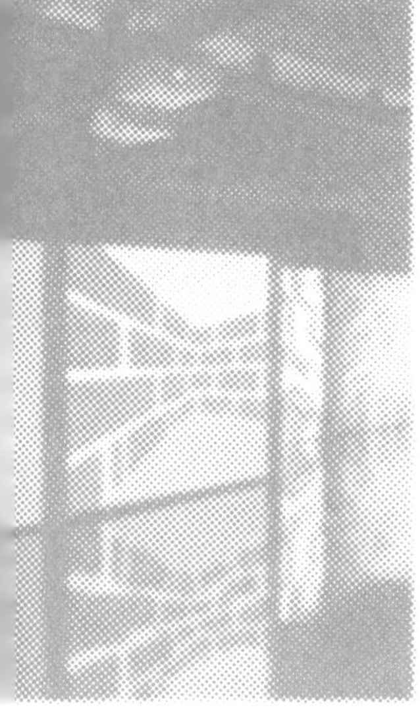
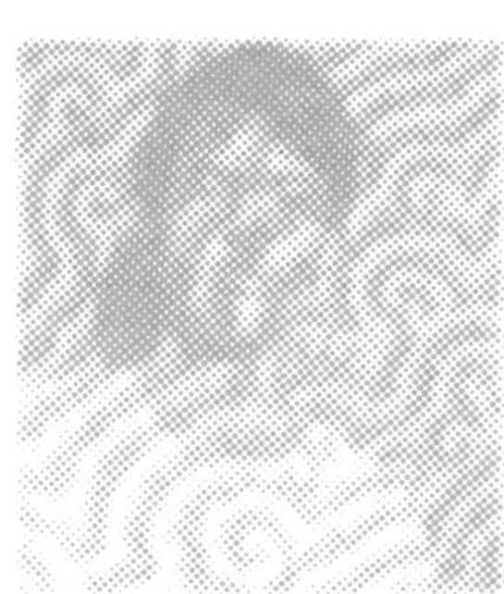
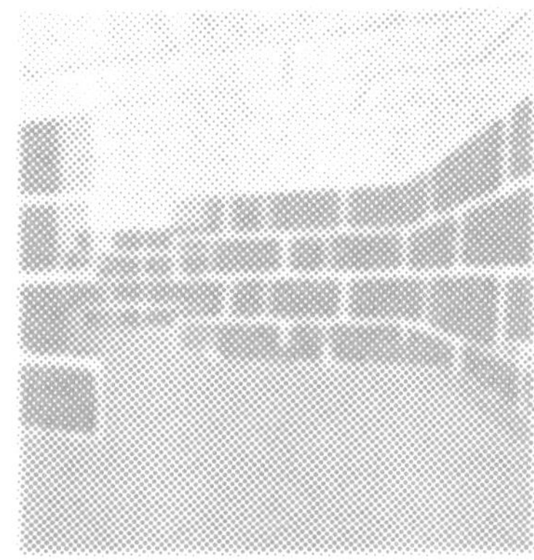

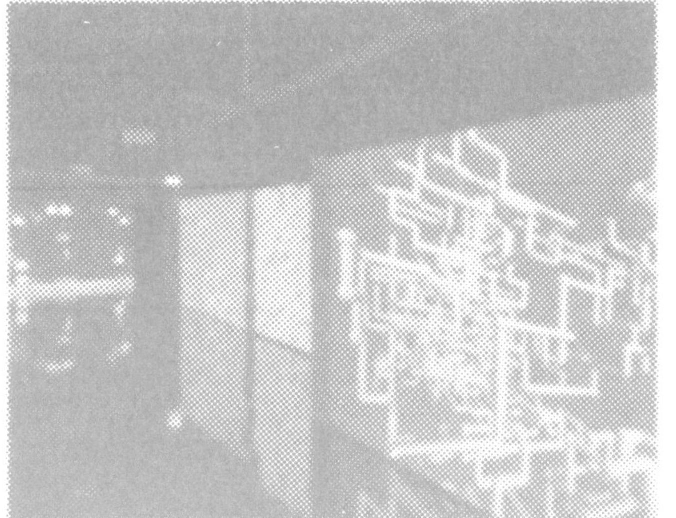

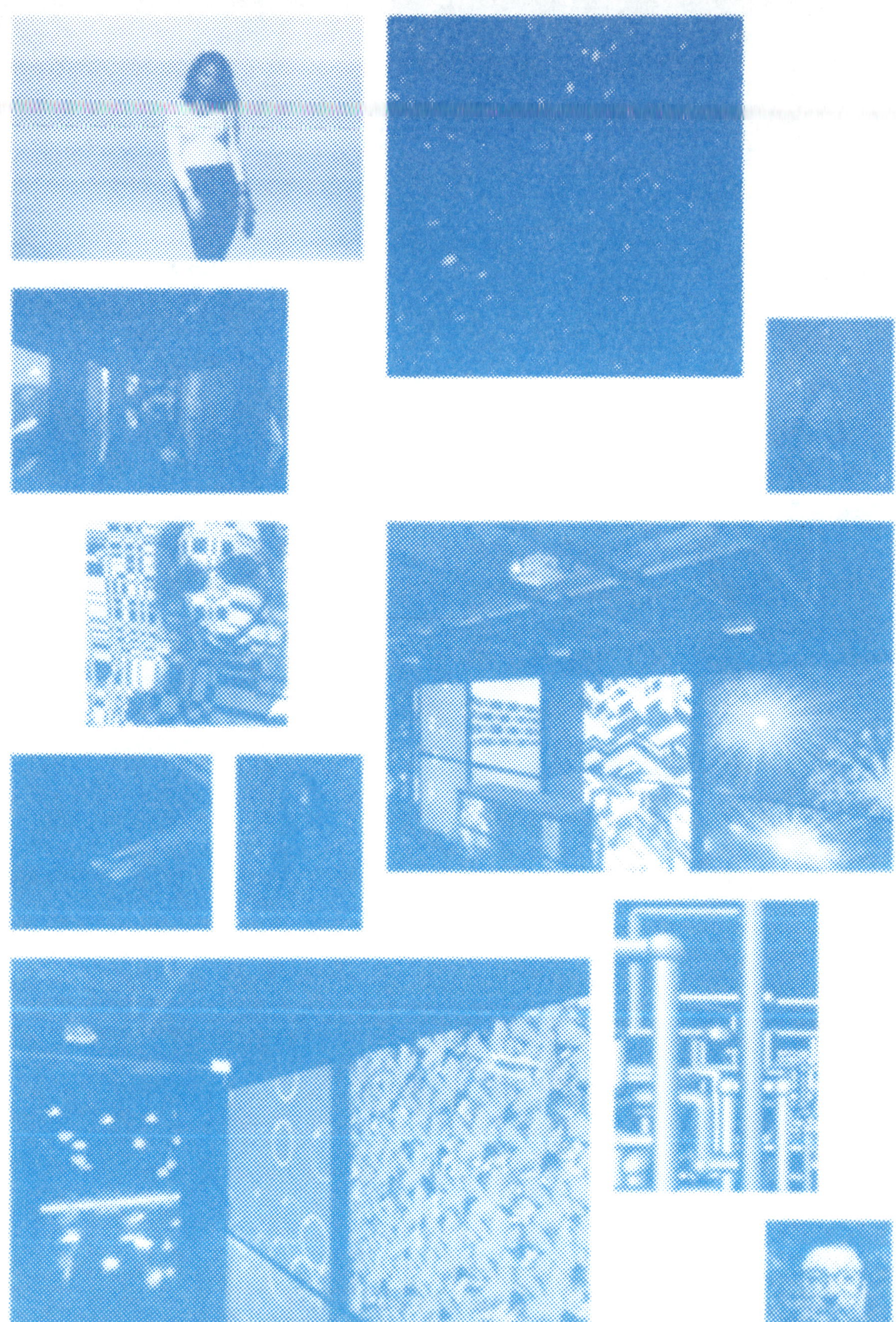

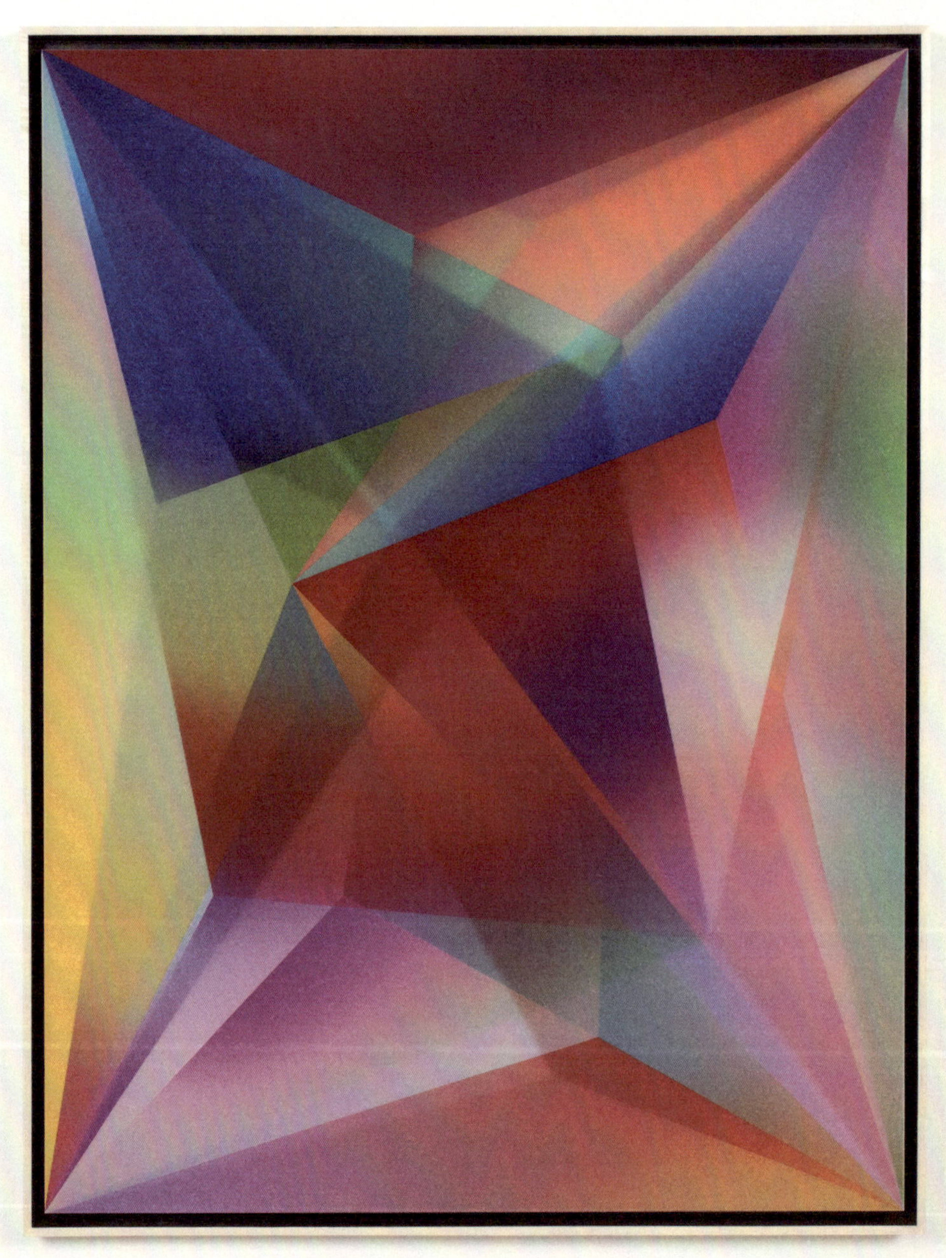

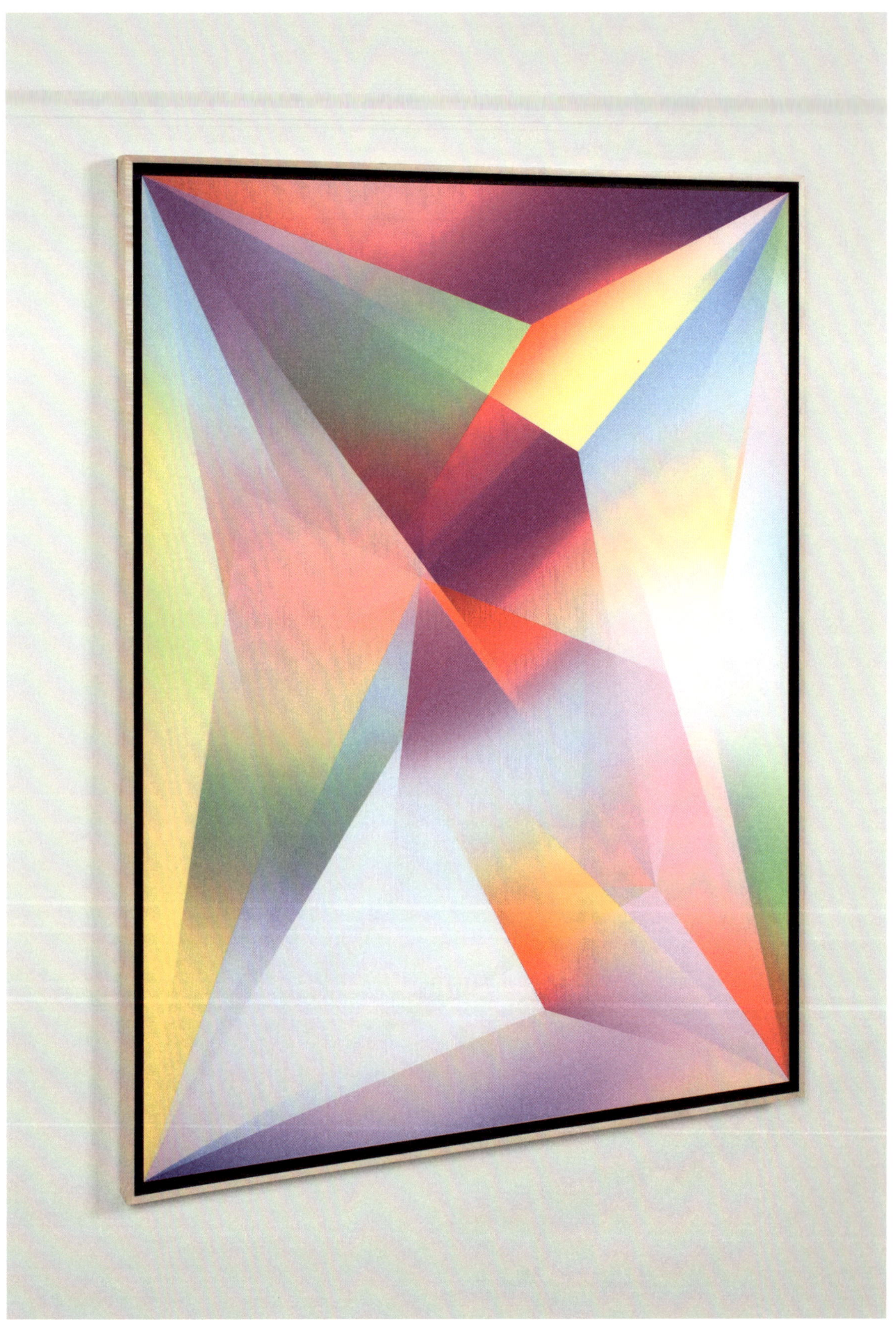

Into Time 13 08 23, 2013

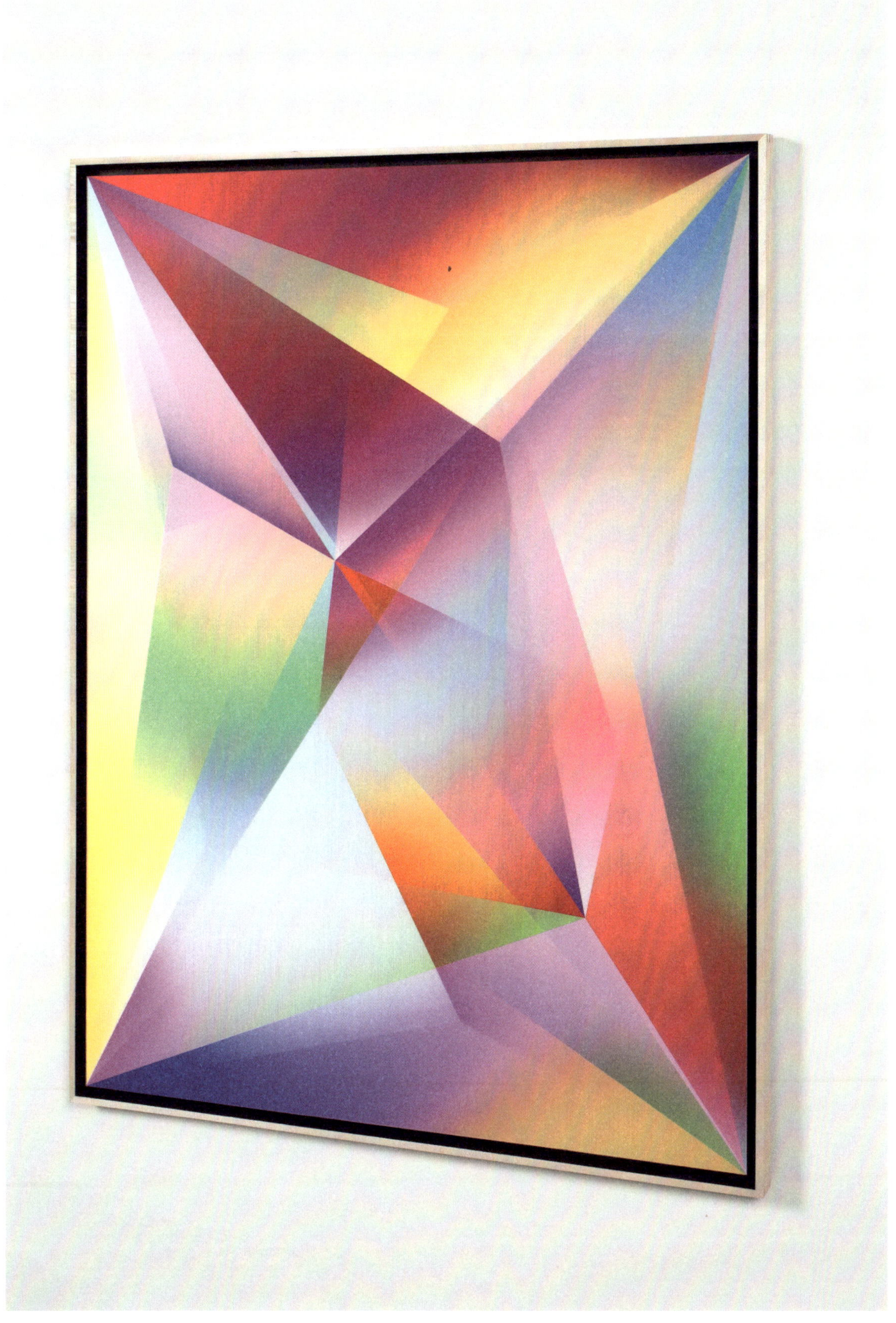

Into Time 13 08 23, 2013

221

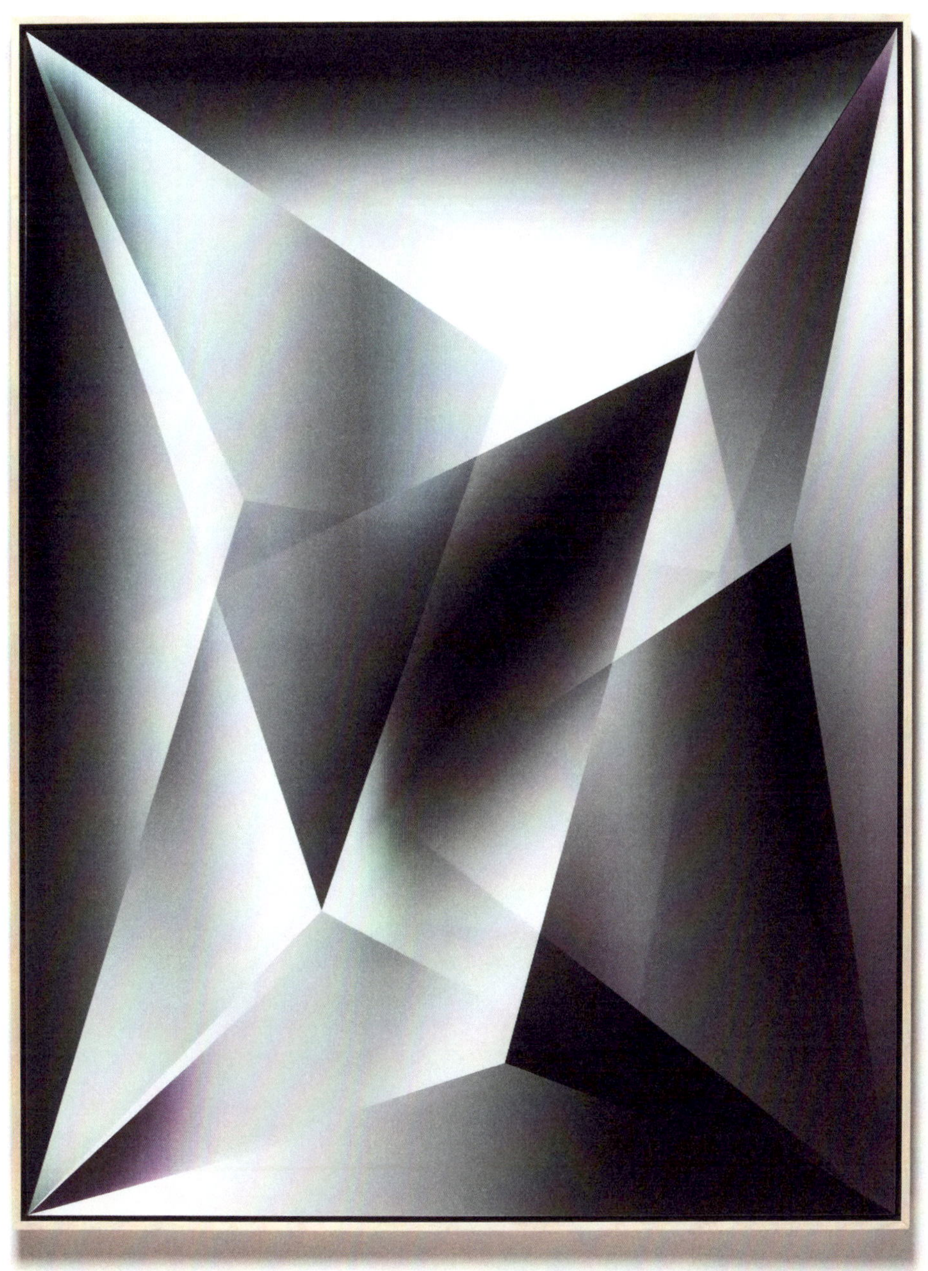

Into Time 14 09 16, 2014

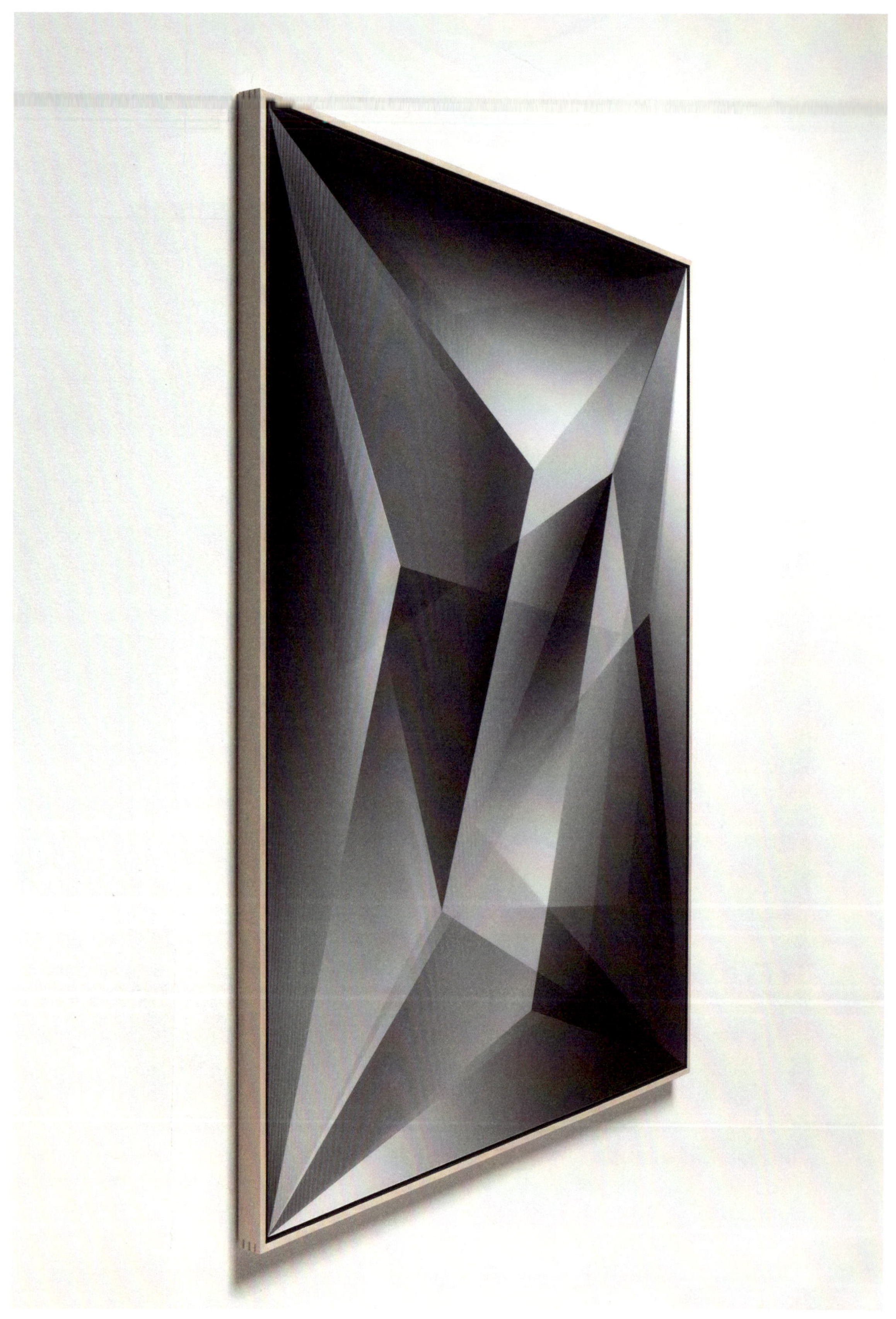

Into Time 14 09 16, 2014

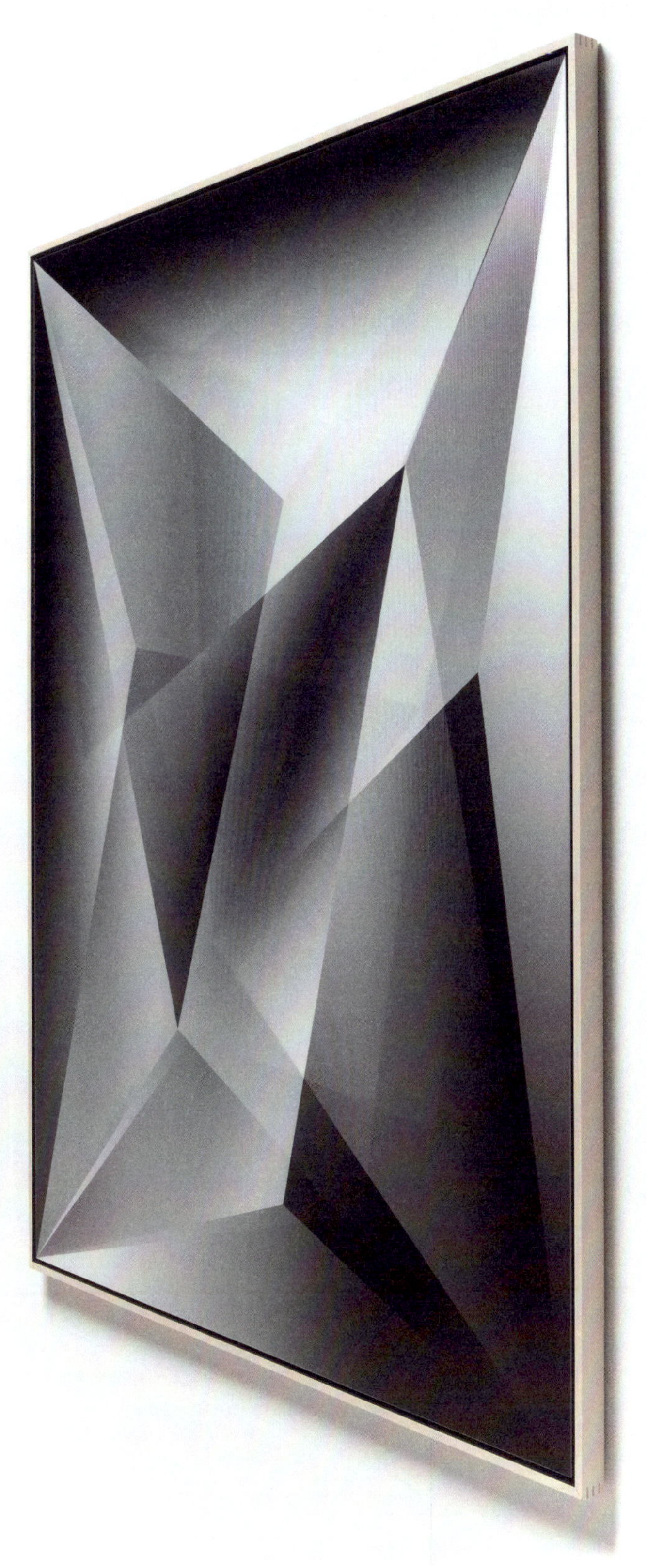

Into Time 14 09 16, 2014

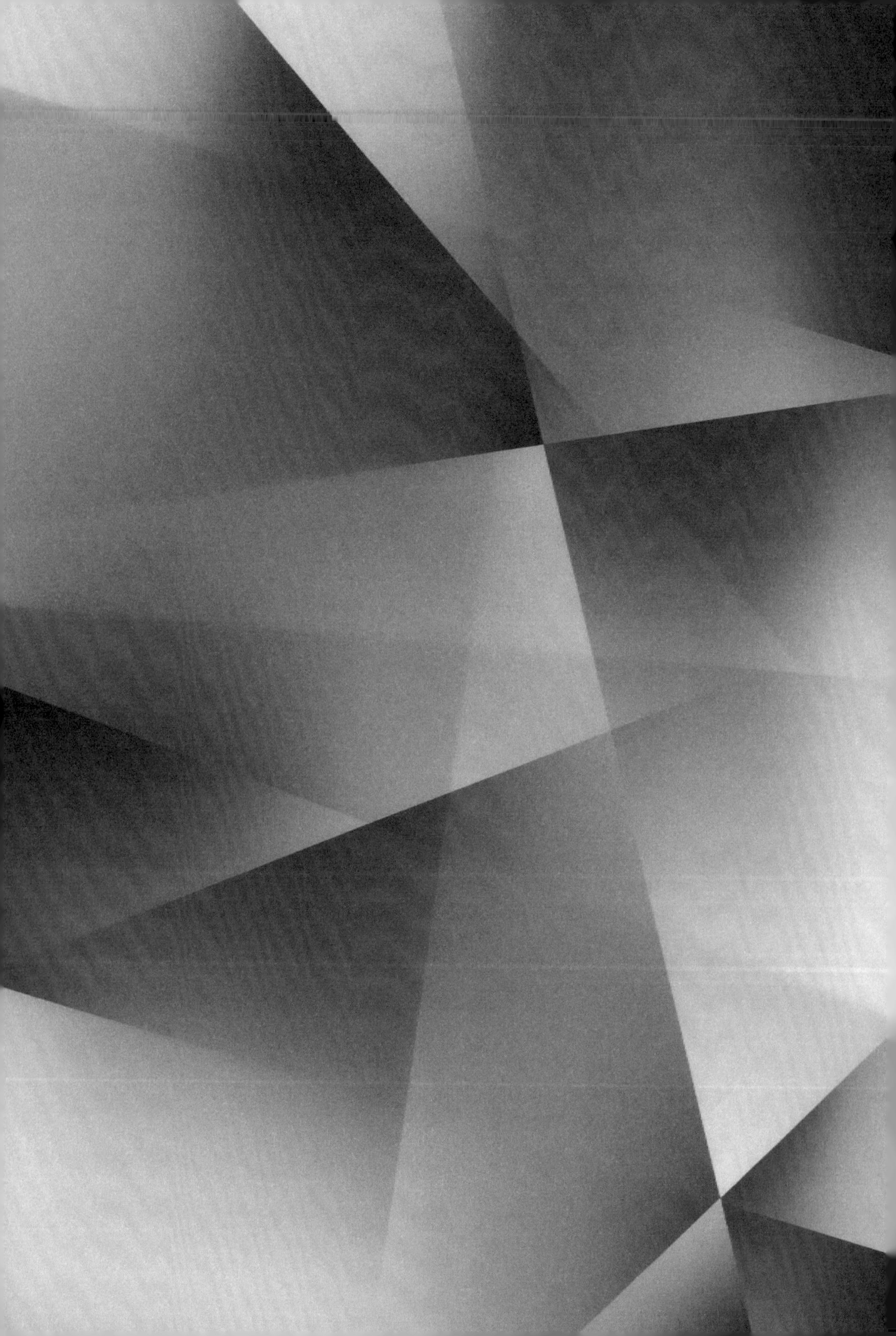

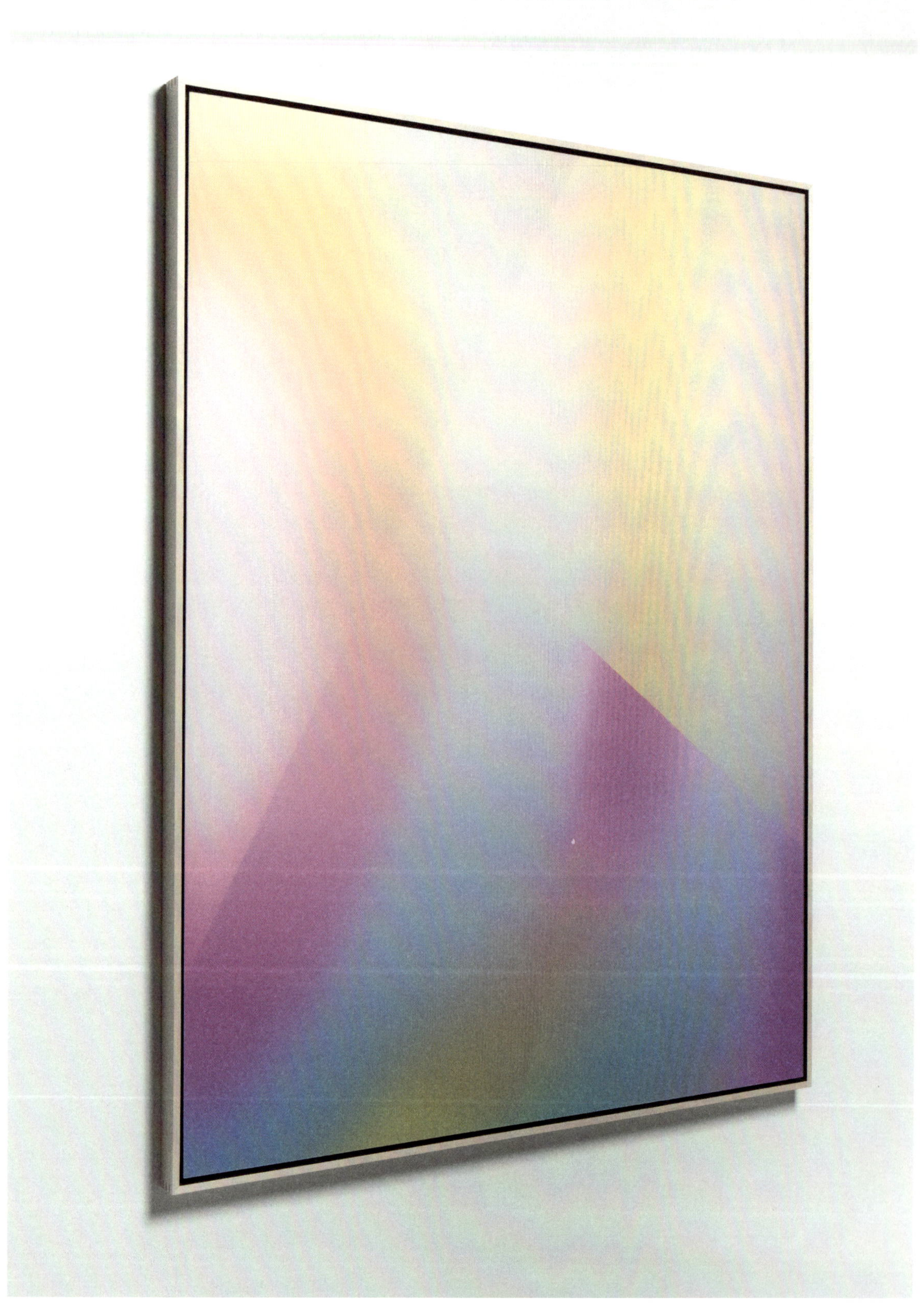

Into Time 14 09 10, 2014

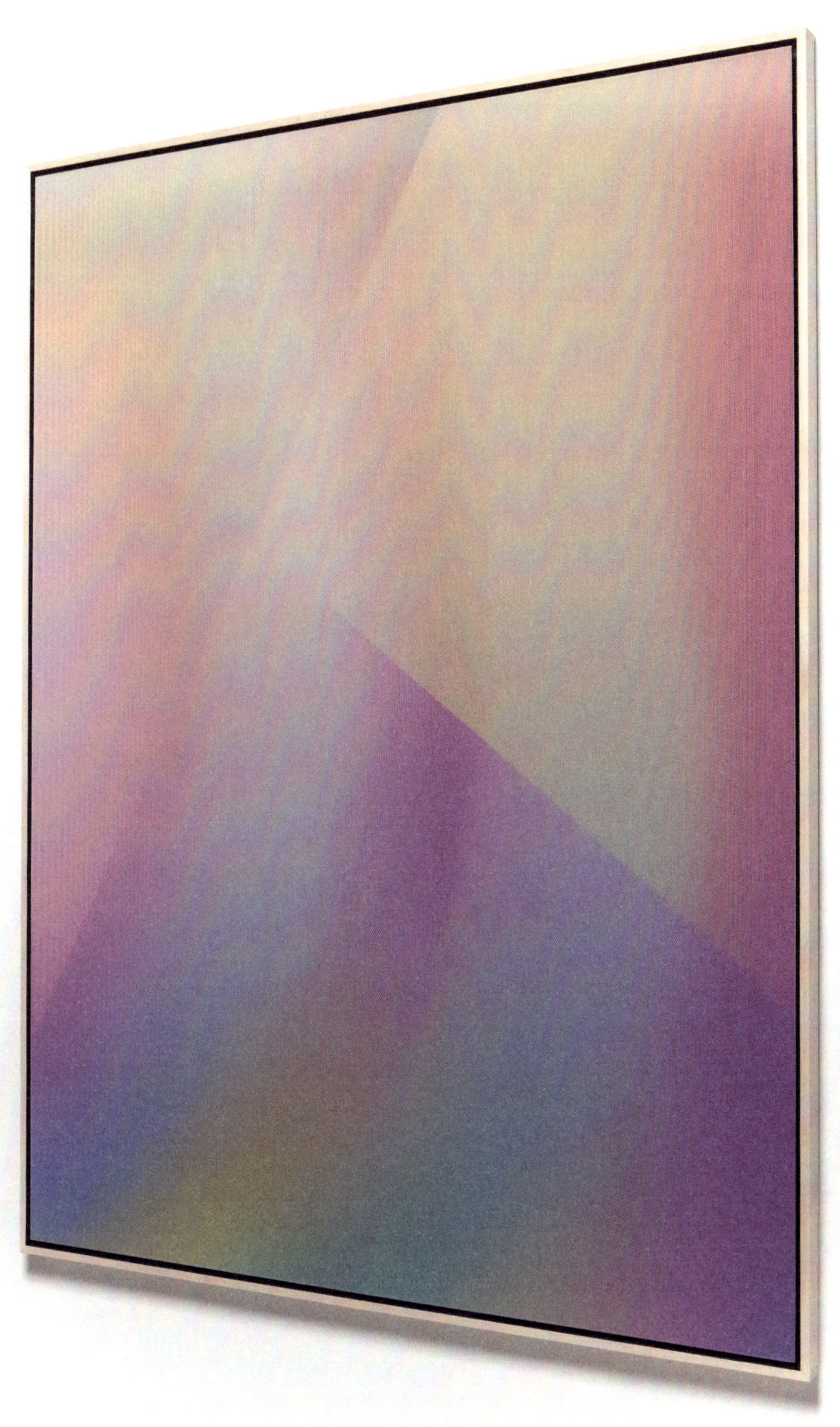

Into Time 14 09 10, 2014

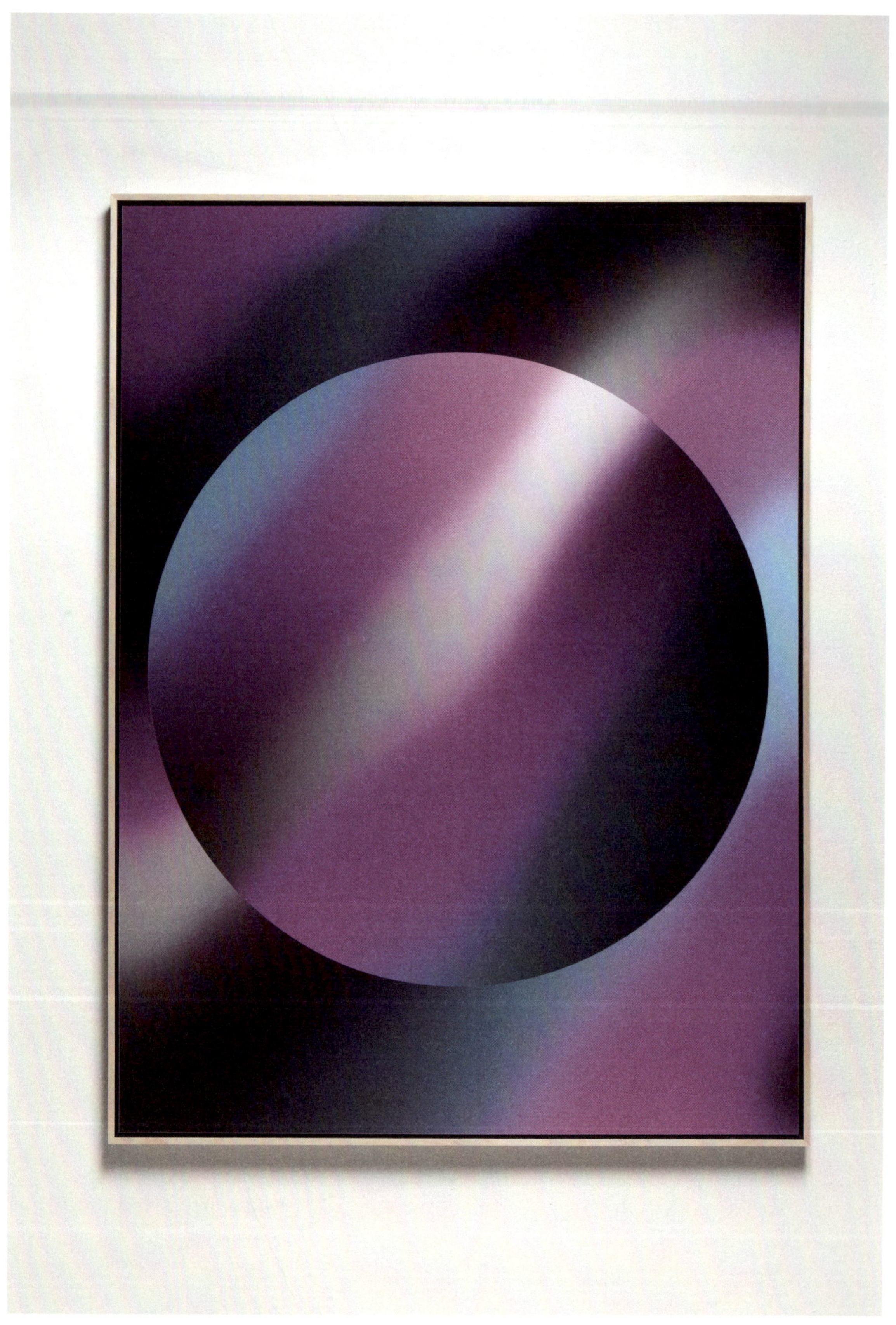

Into Time 14 09 14, 2014

[226] *Into Time 14 05 24*, 2014
[227] *Into Time 14 09 10*, 2014

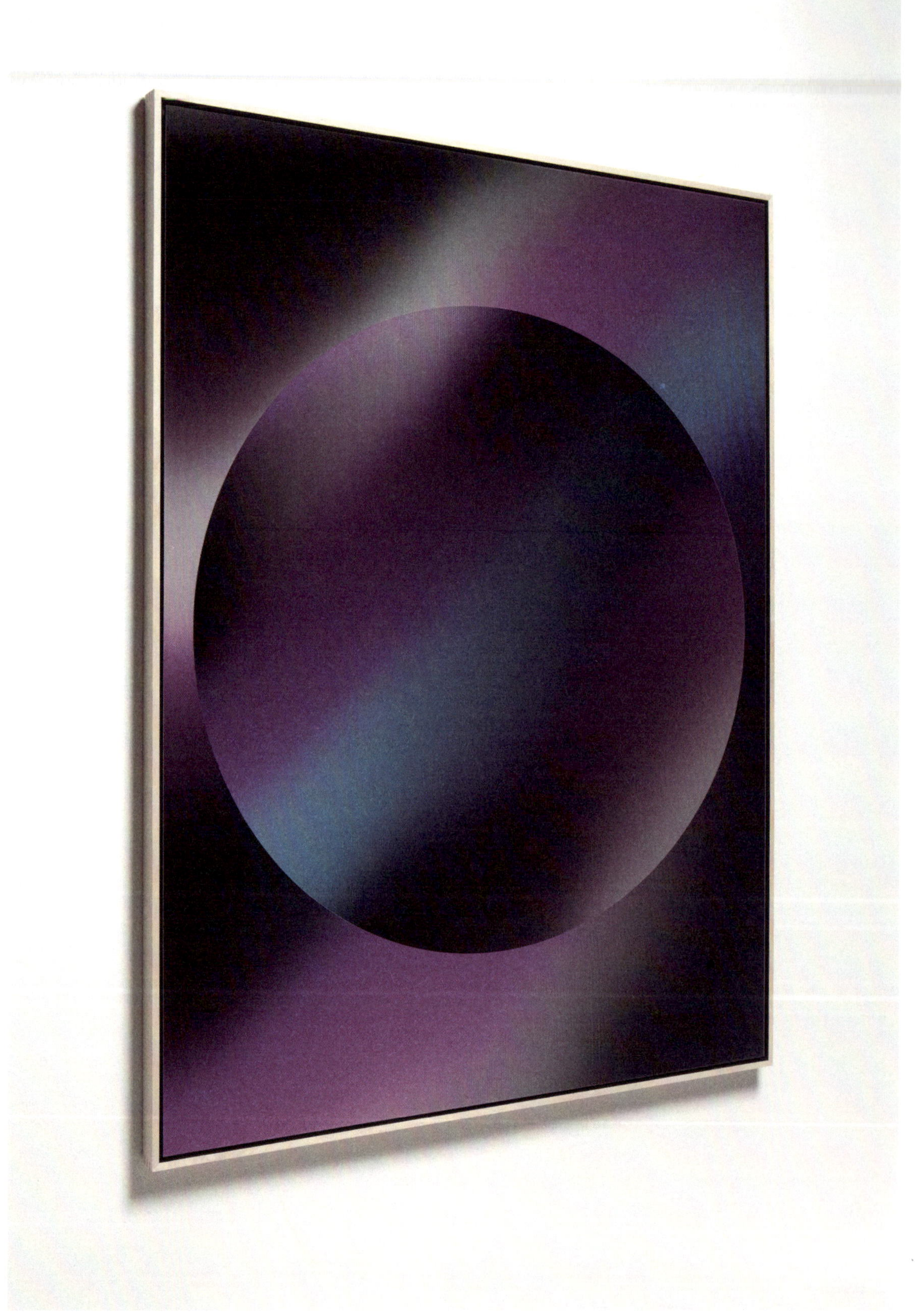

Into Time 14 09 14, 2014

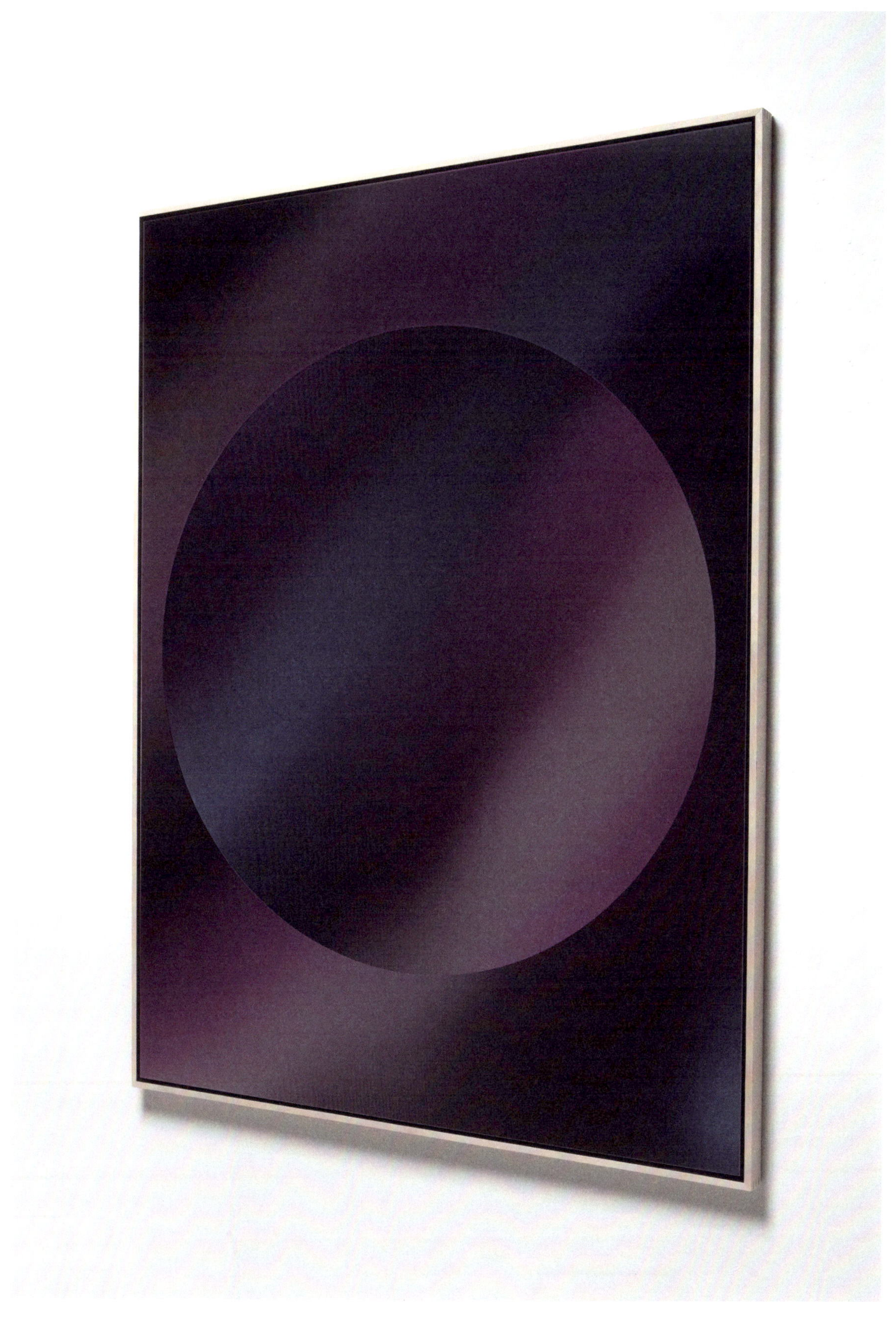

Into Time 14 09 14, 2014

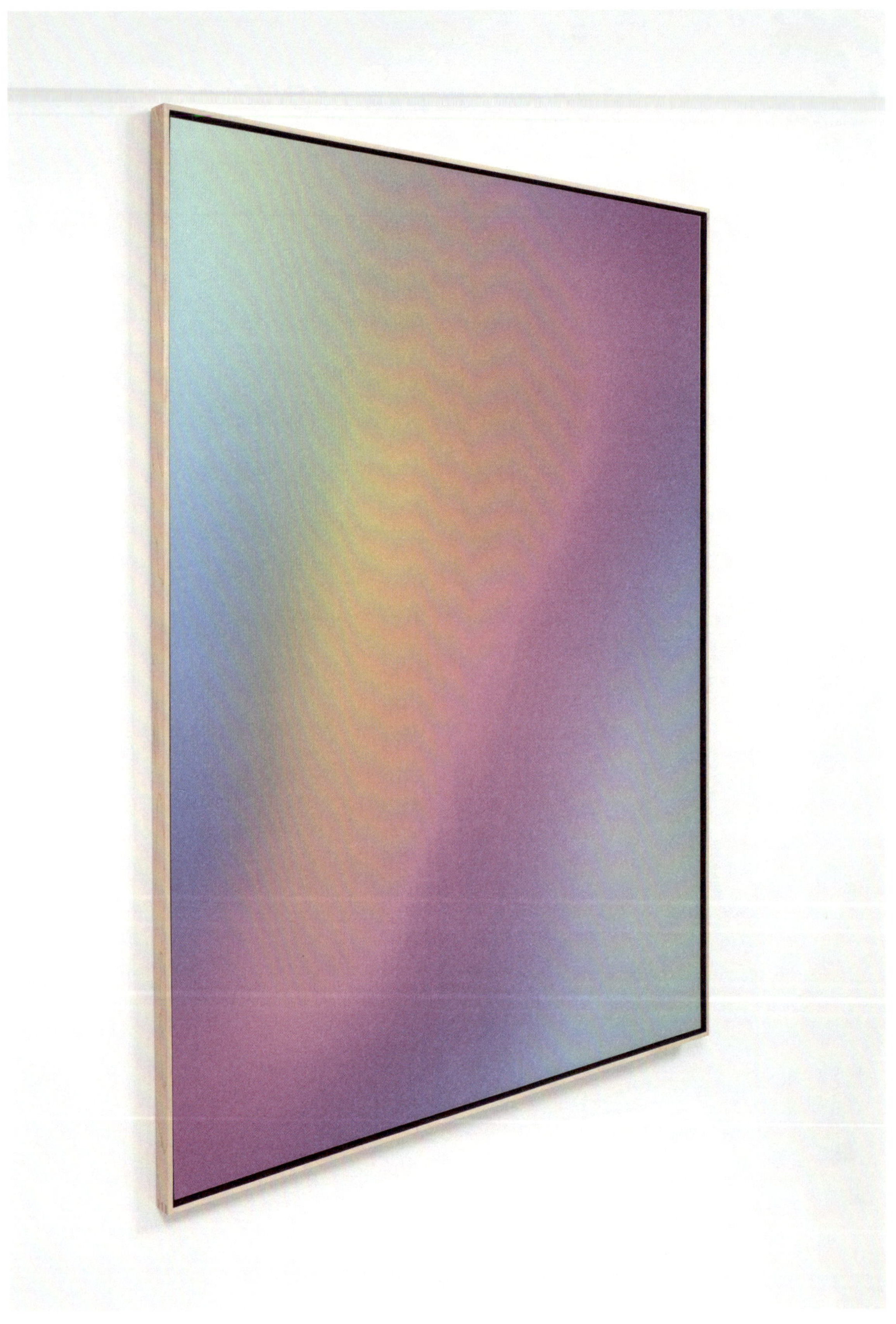

Into Time 16 04 01, 2016

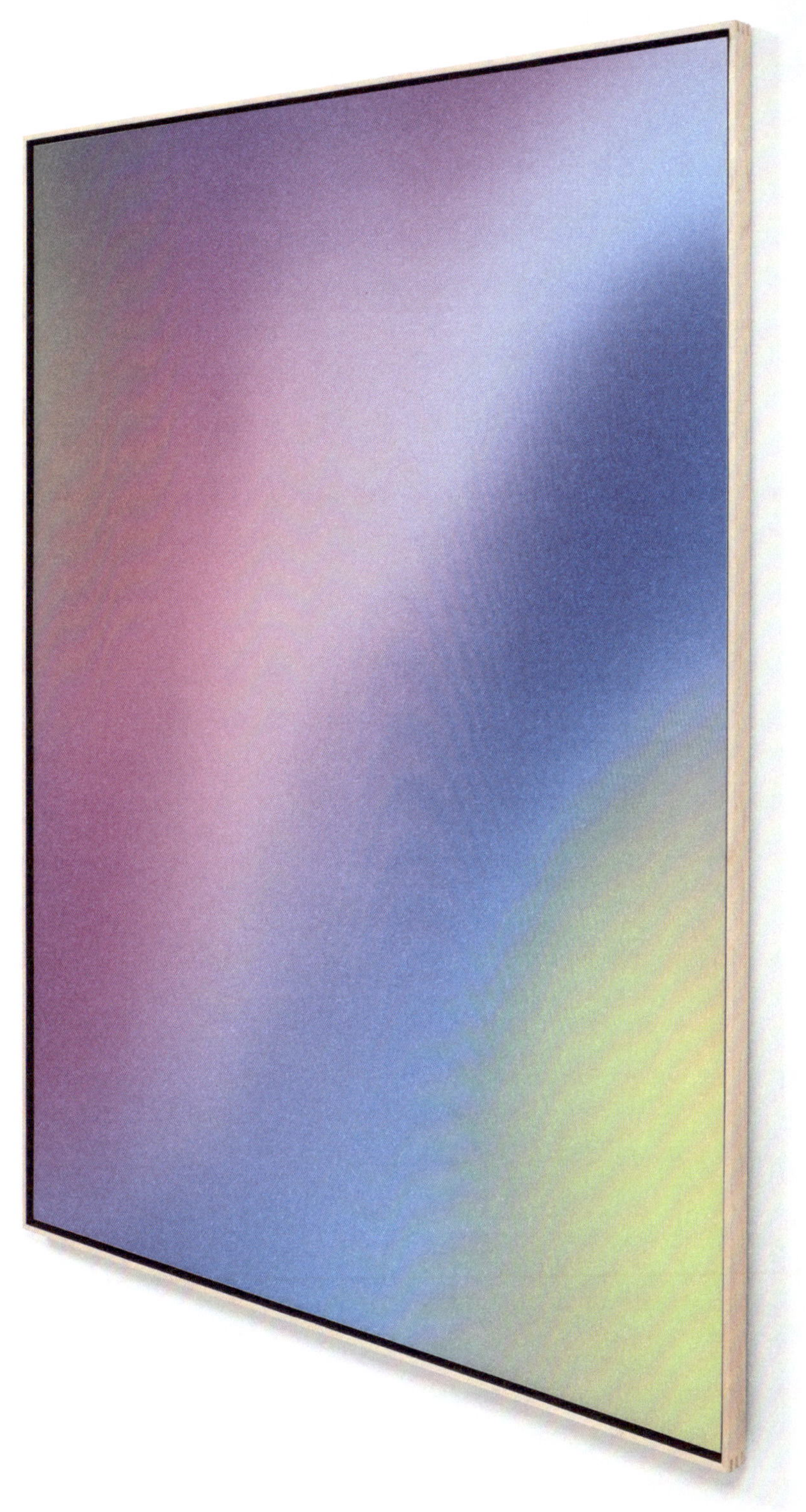

Into Time 16 04 01, 2016

235

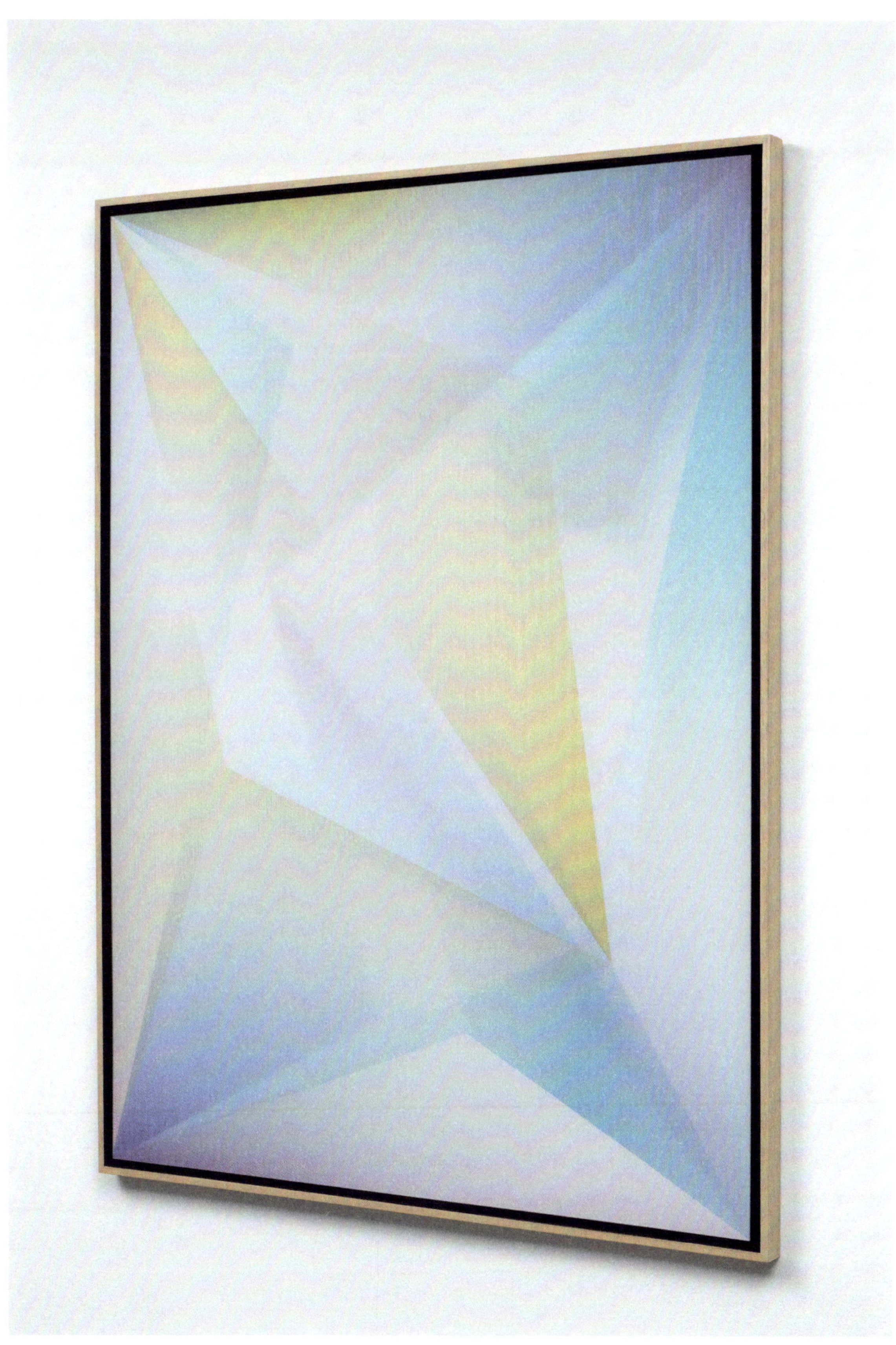

Into Time 14 05 08, 2014

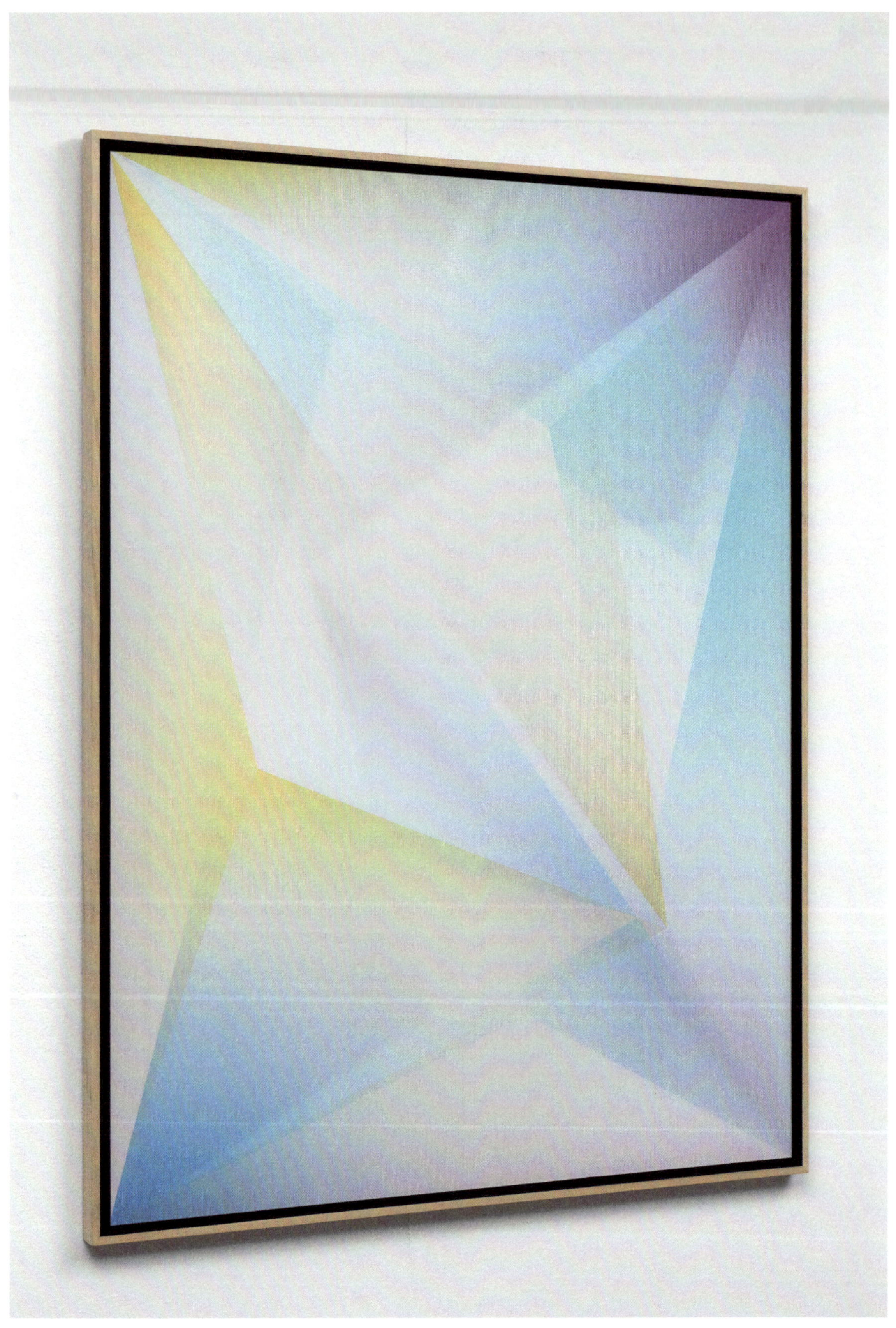

Into Time 15 06 02, 2015

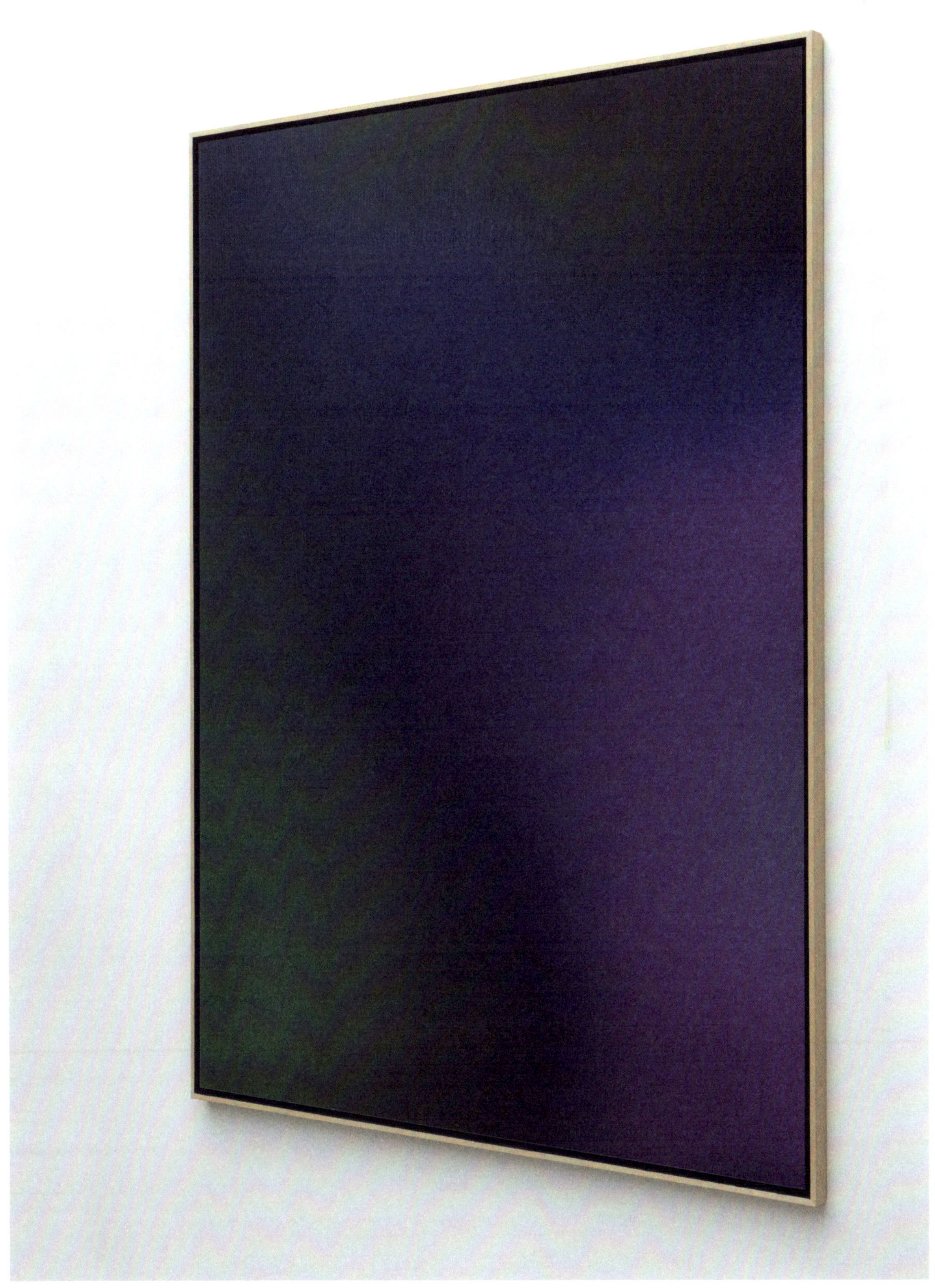

Into Time 15 06 02, 2015

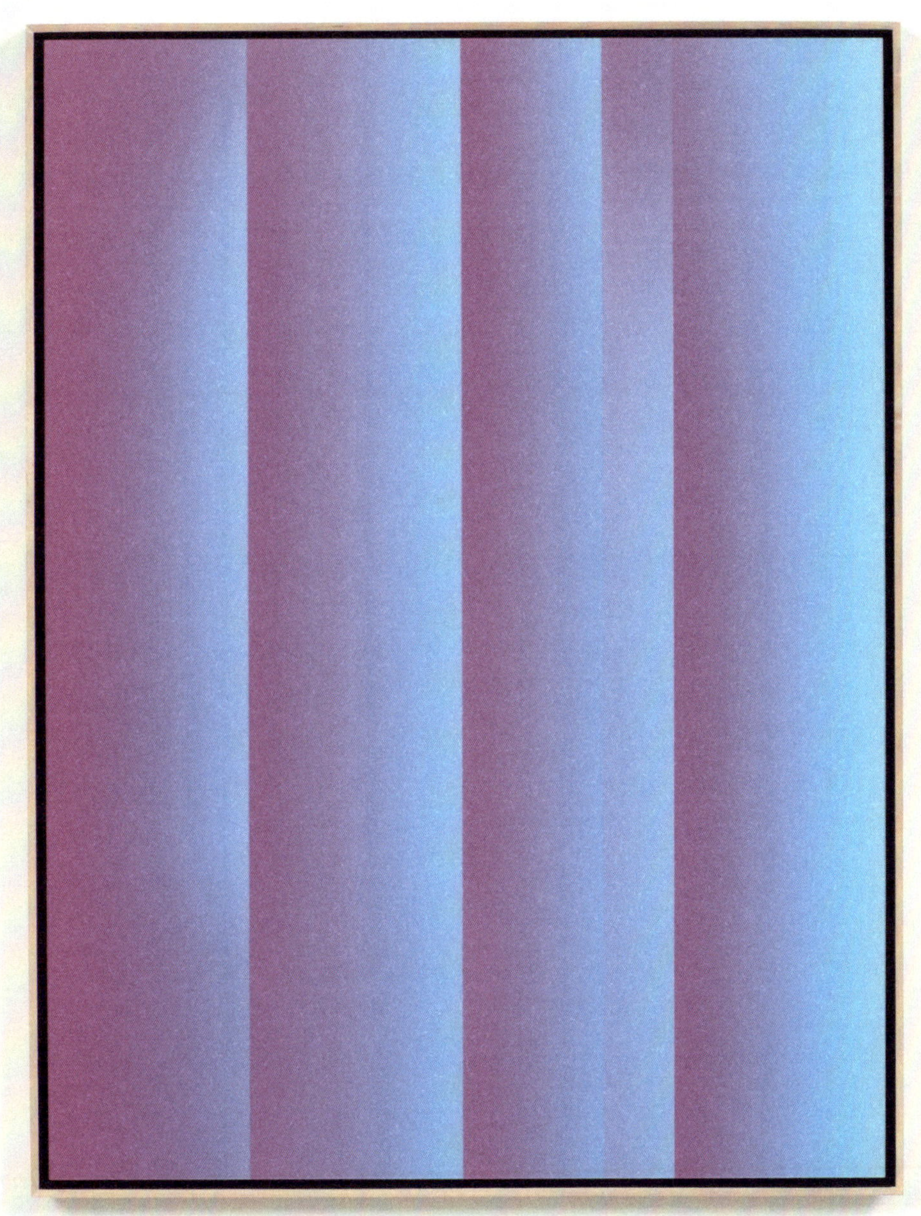

Into Time 14 06 01, 2014

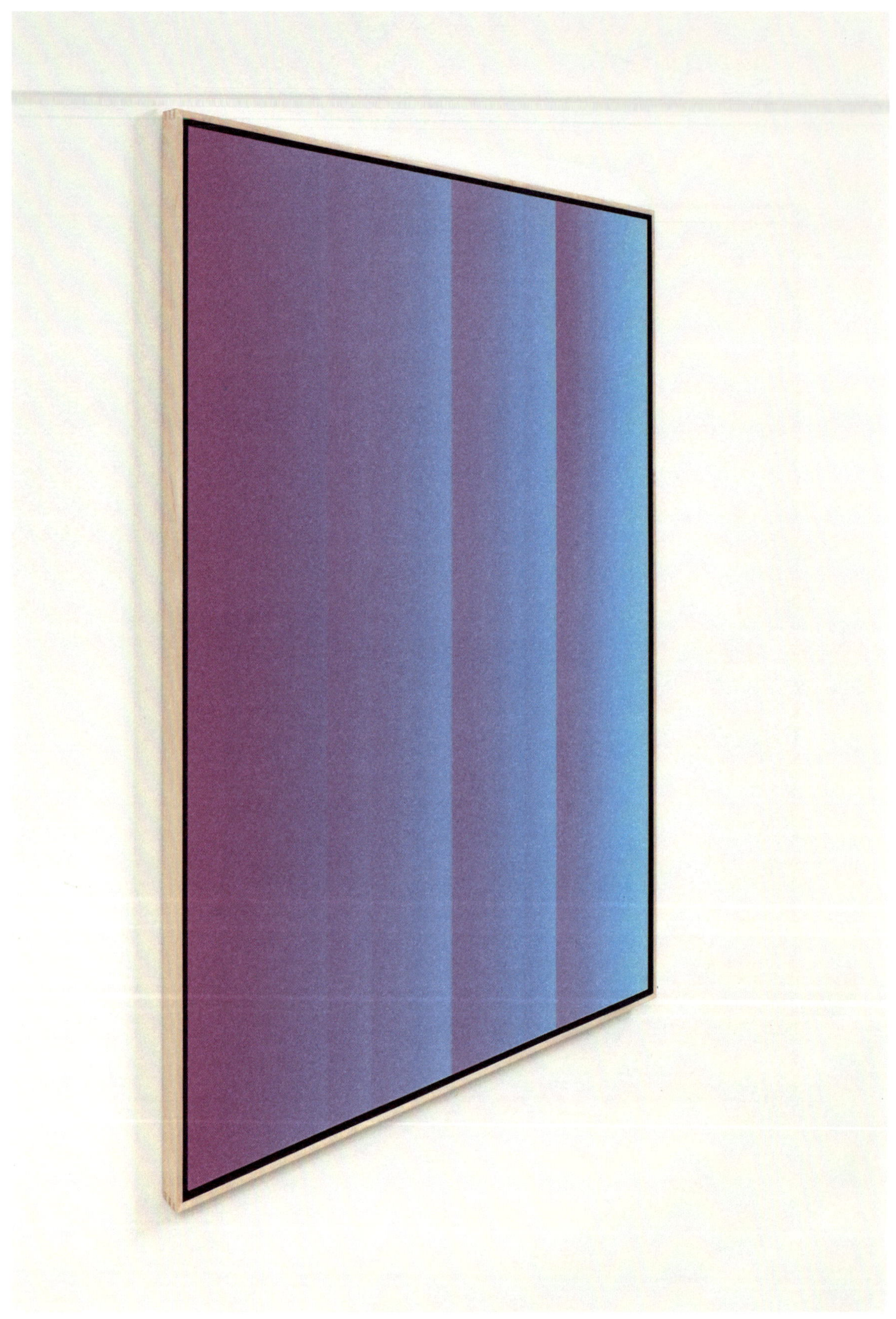

Into Time 14 06 01, 2014

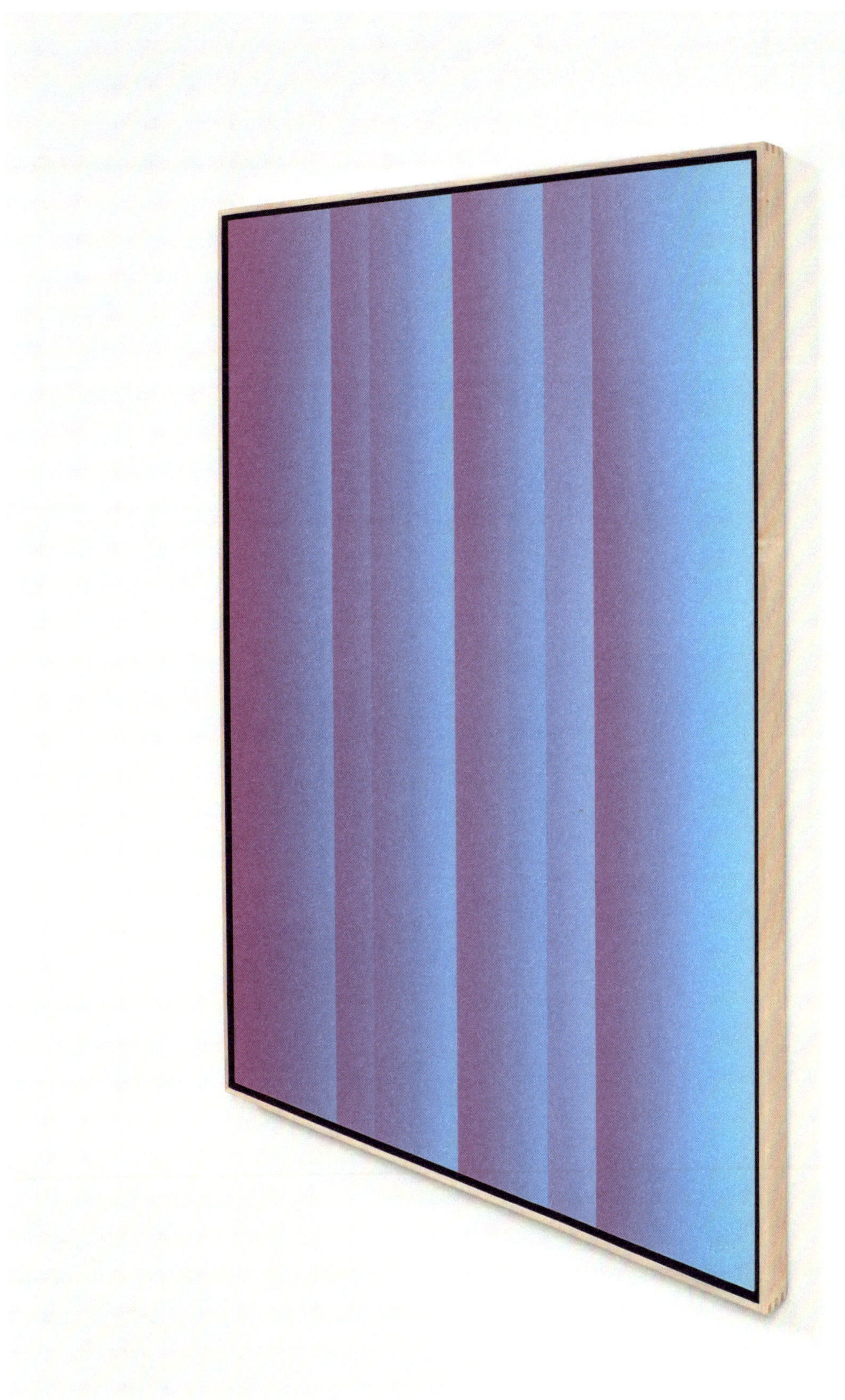

Into Time 14 06 01, 2014

Into Time 14 06 03, 2014

Into Time 14 06 03, 2014

Into Time 14 06 03, 2014

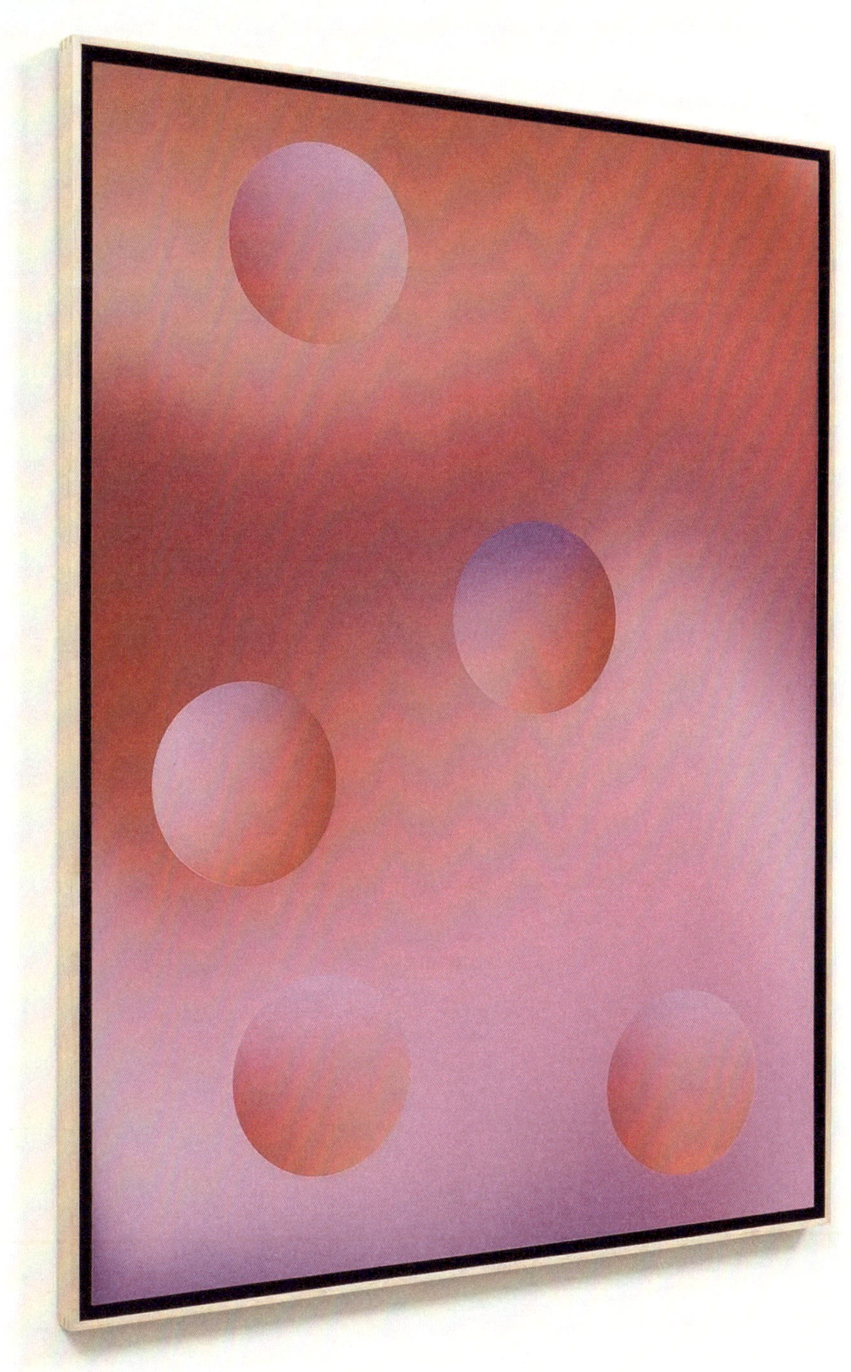

Into Time 14 07 01, 2014

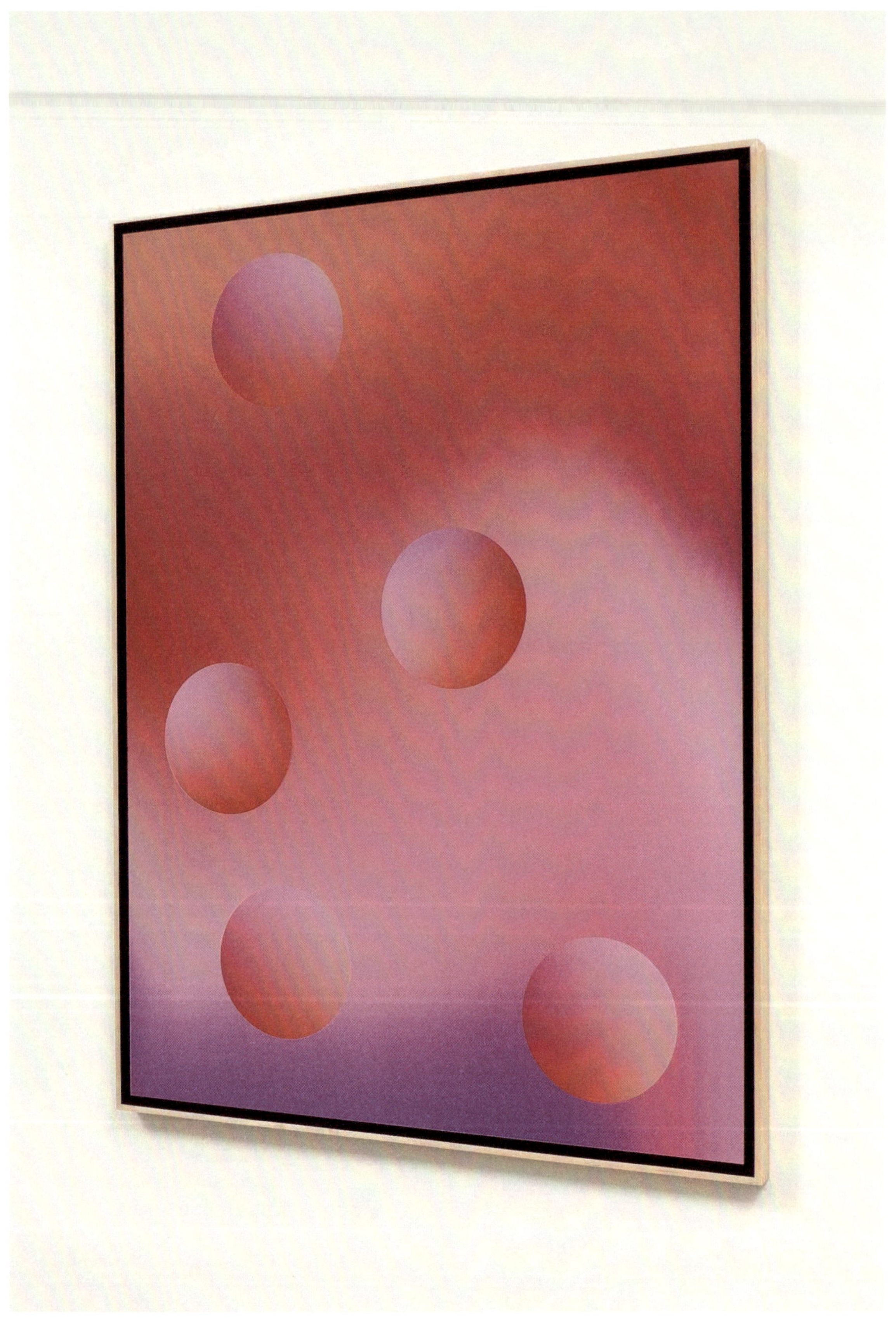

Into Time 14 07 01, 2014

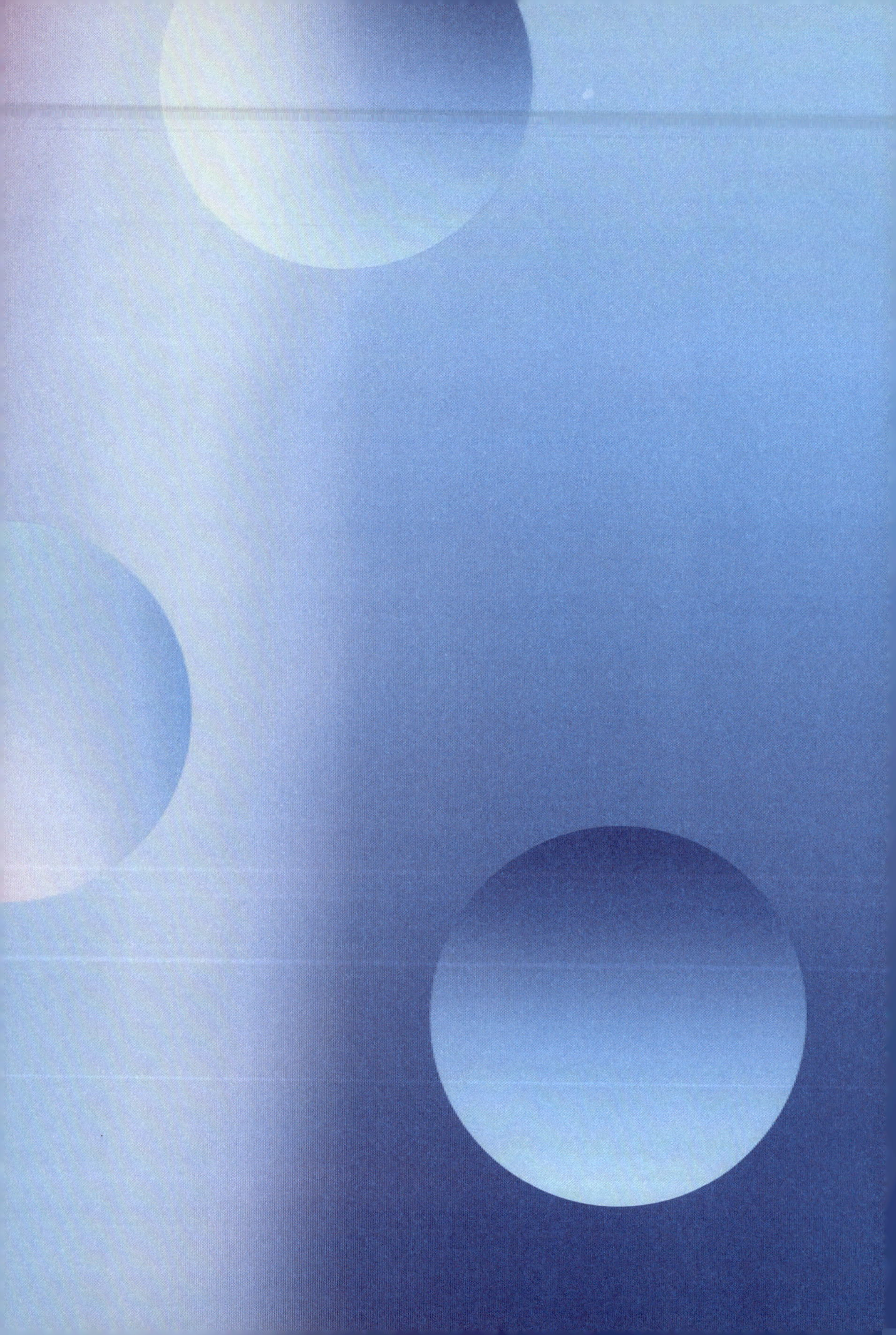

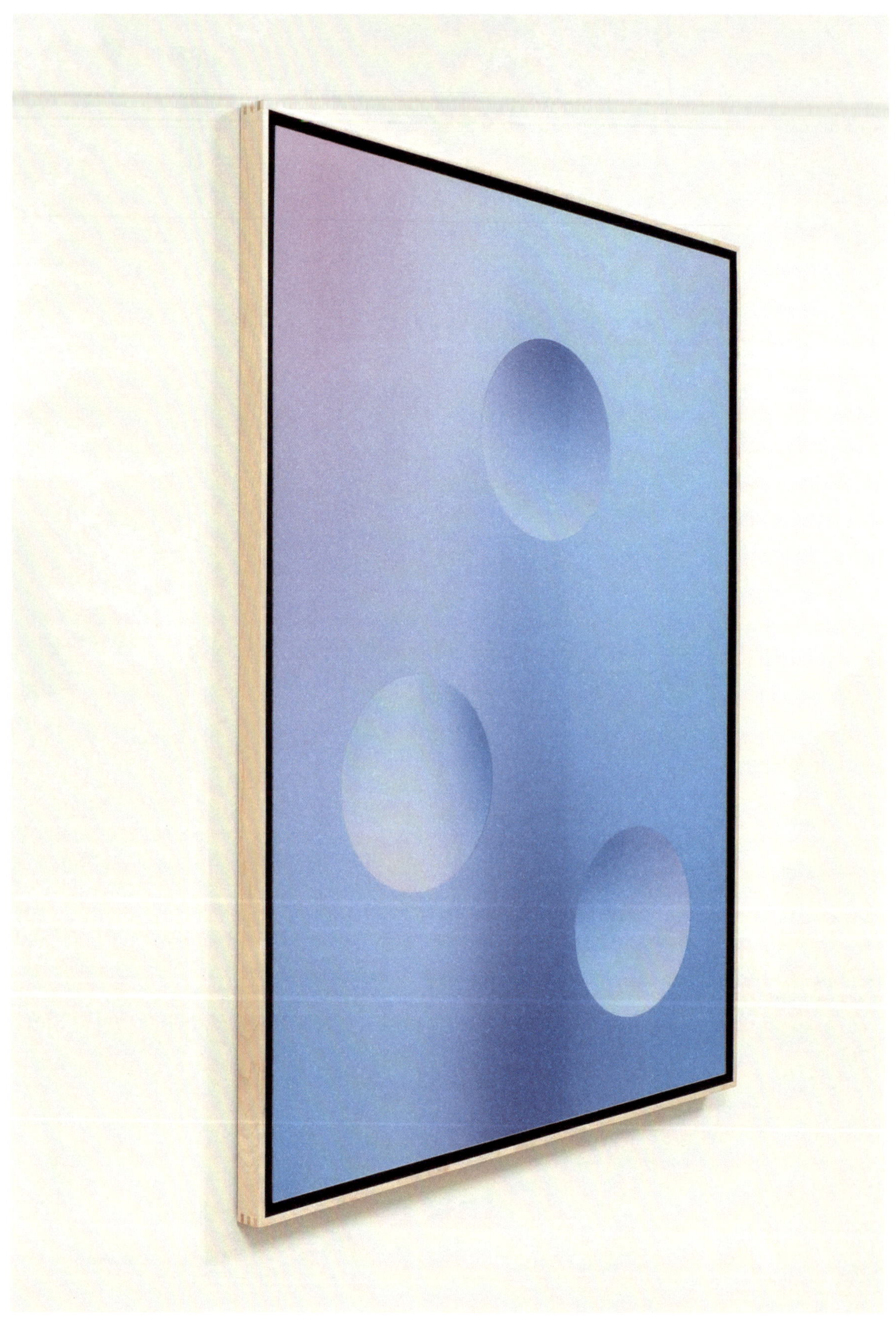

Into Time 14 07 02, 2014

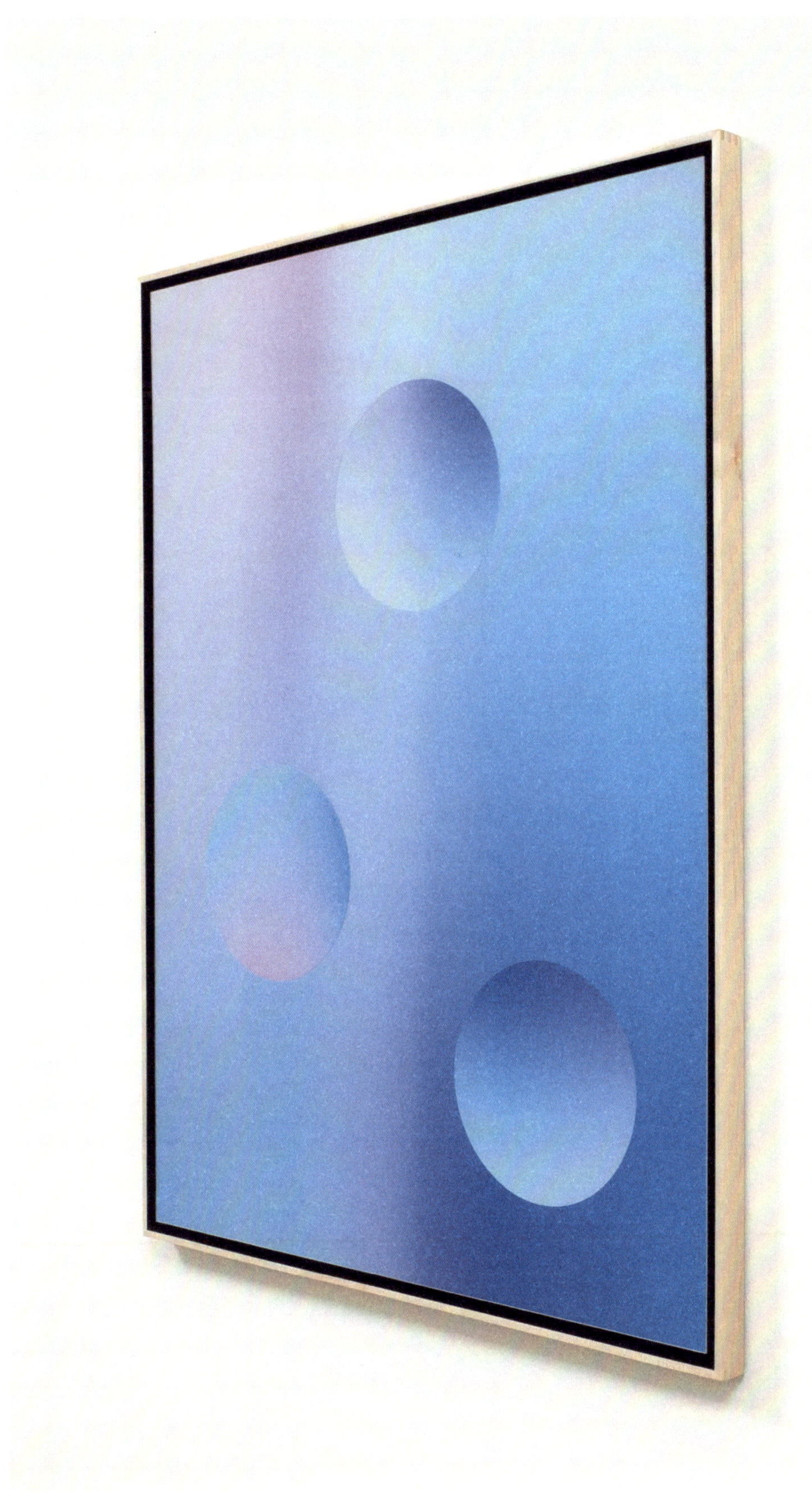

Into Time 14 07 02, 2014   261

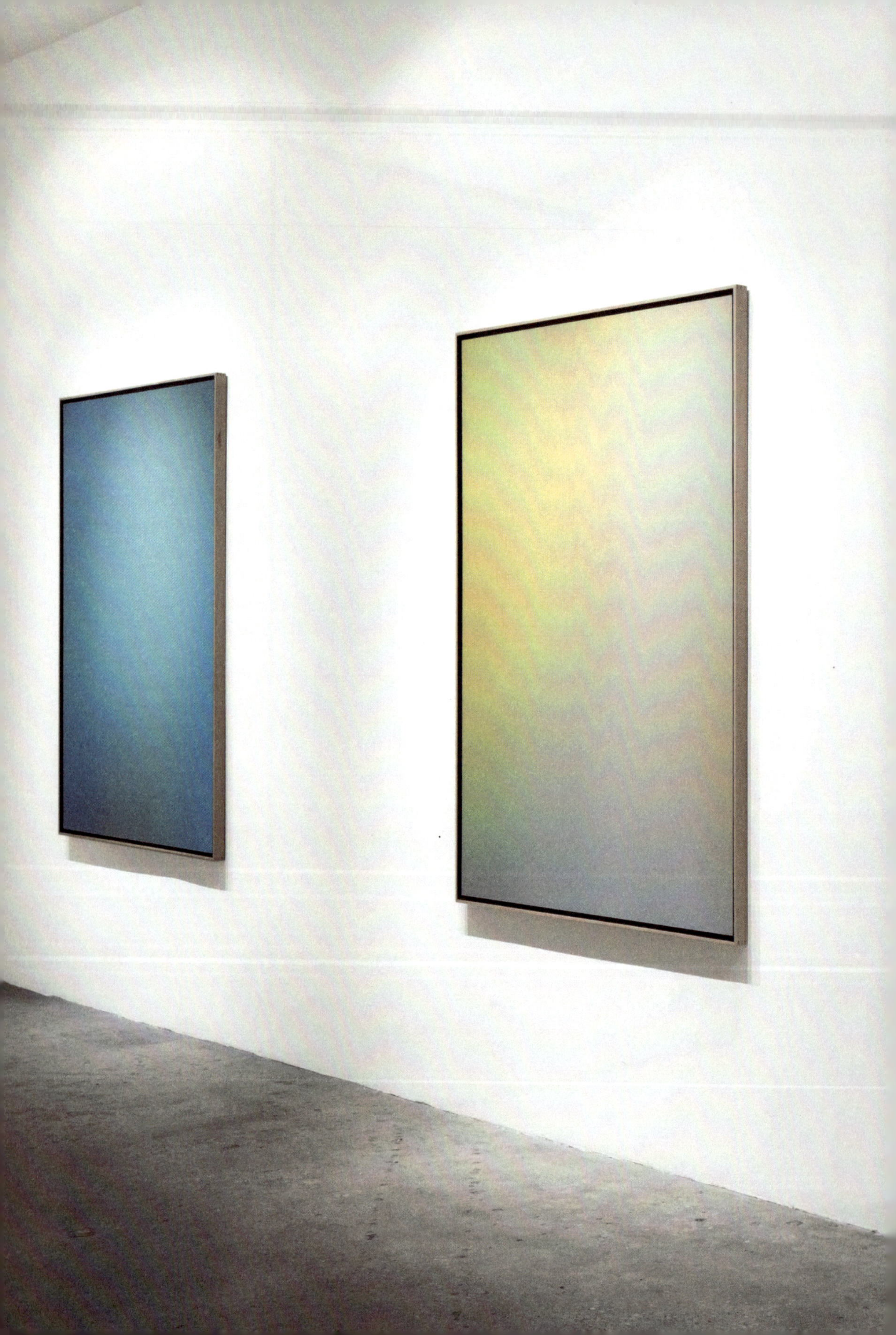

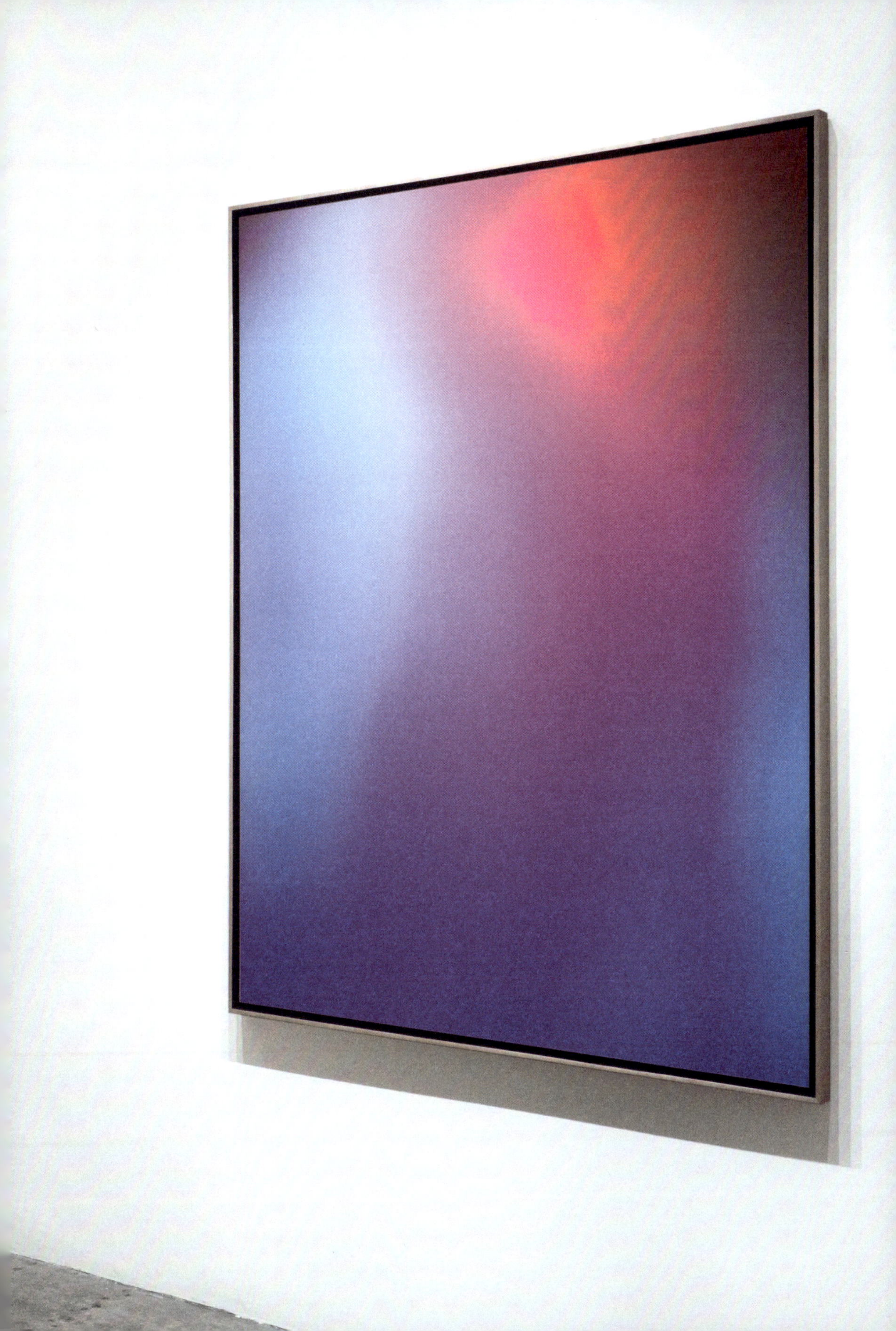

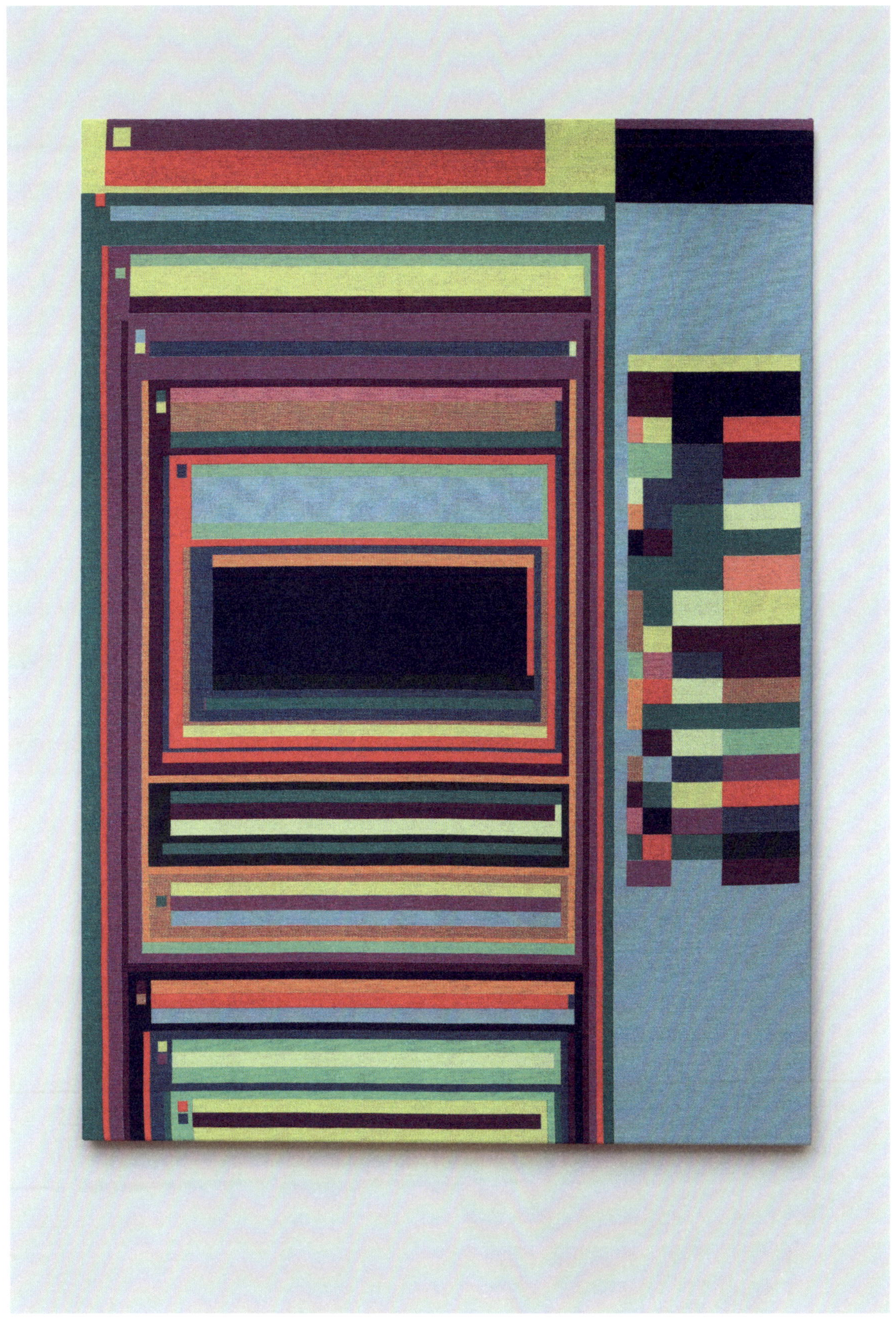

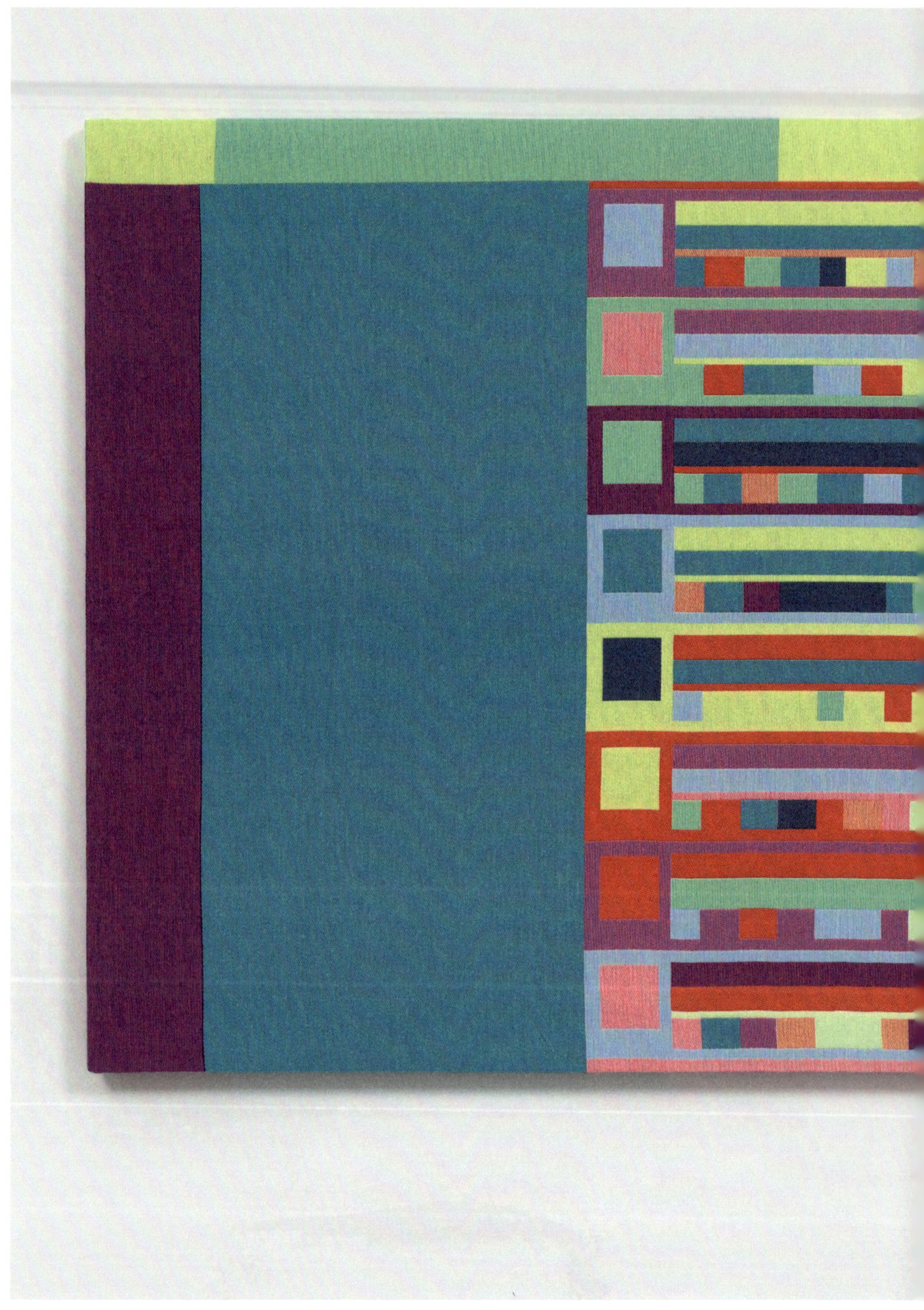

Abstract Browsing 15 05 05 (Twitter), 2015

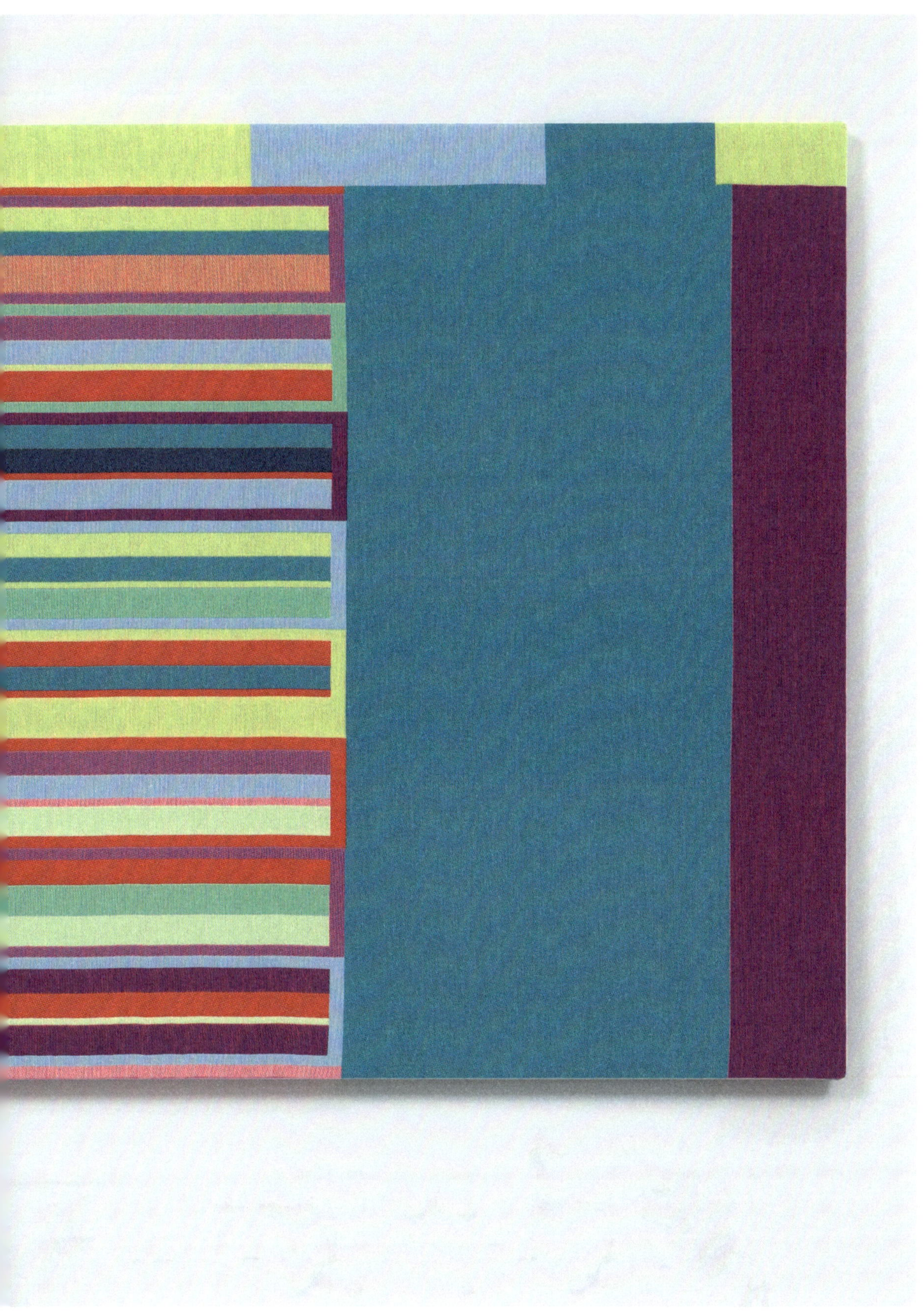

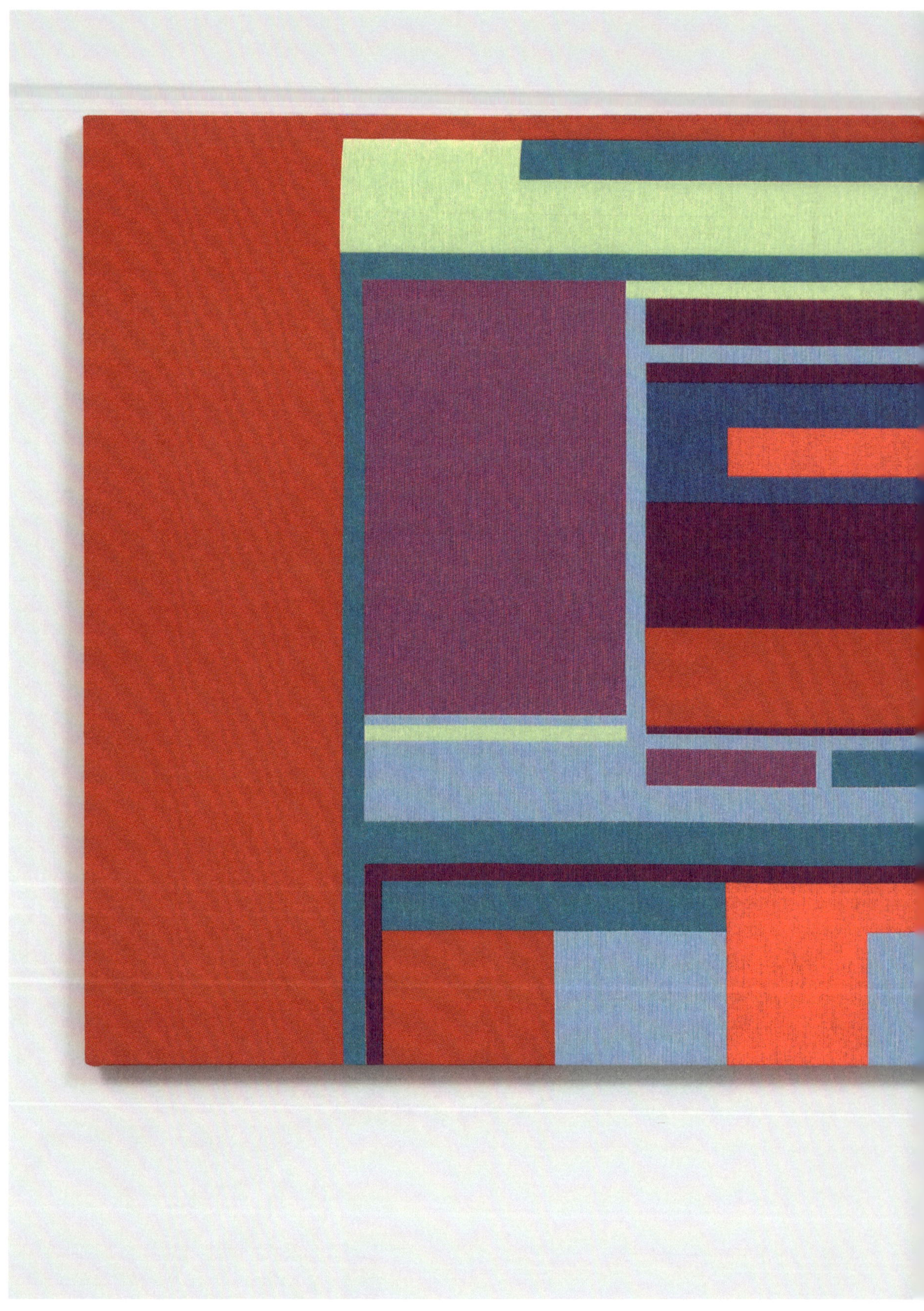

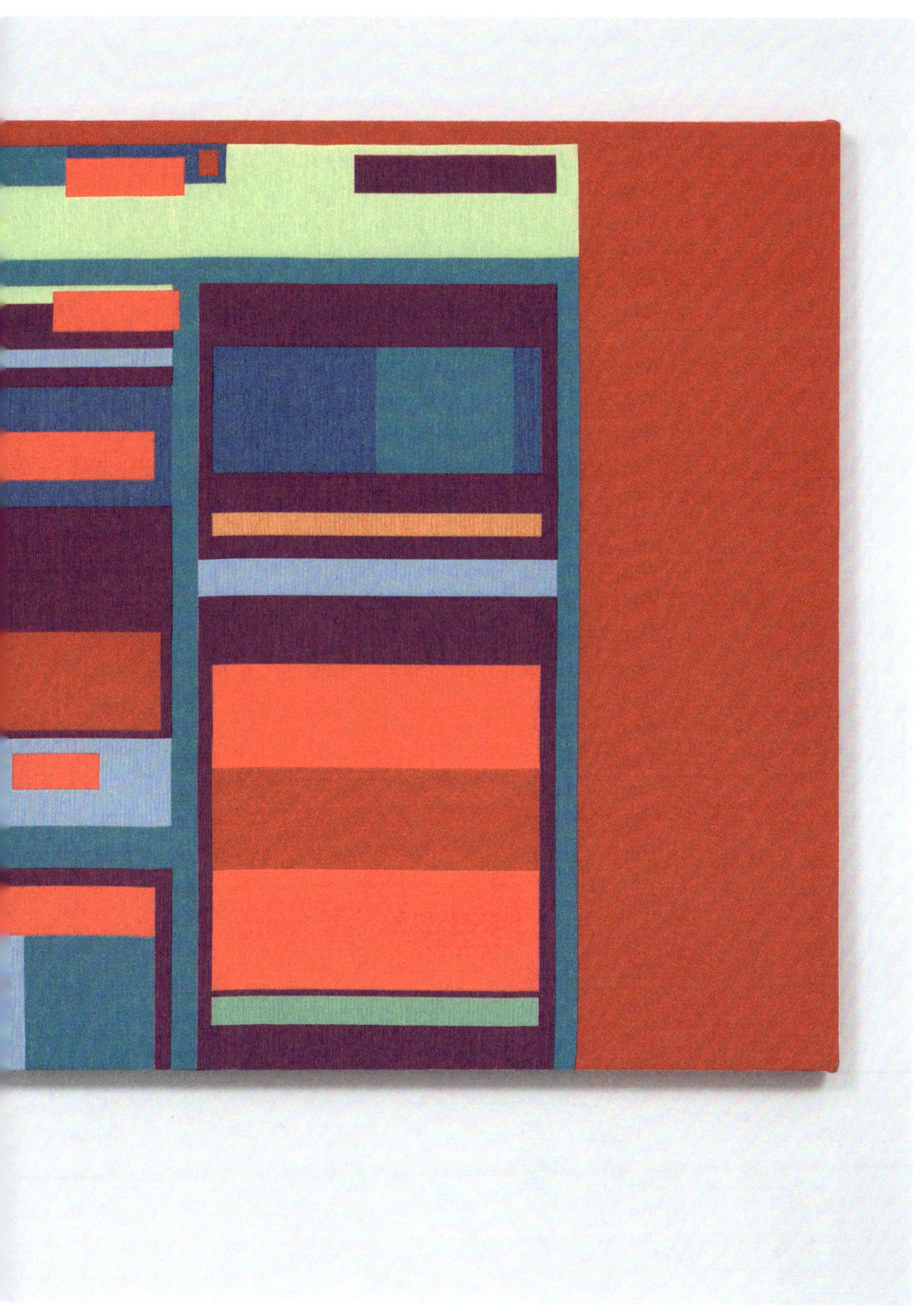

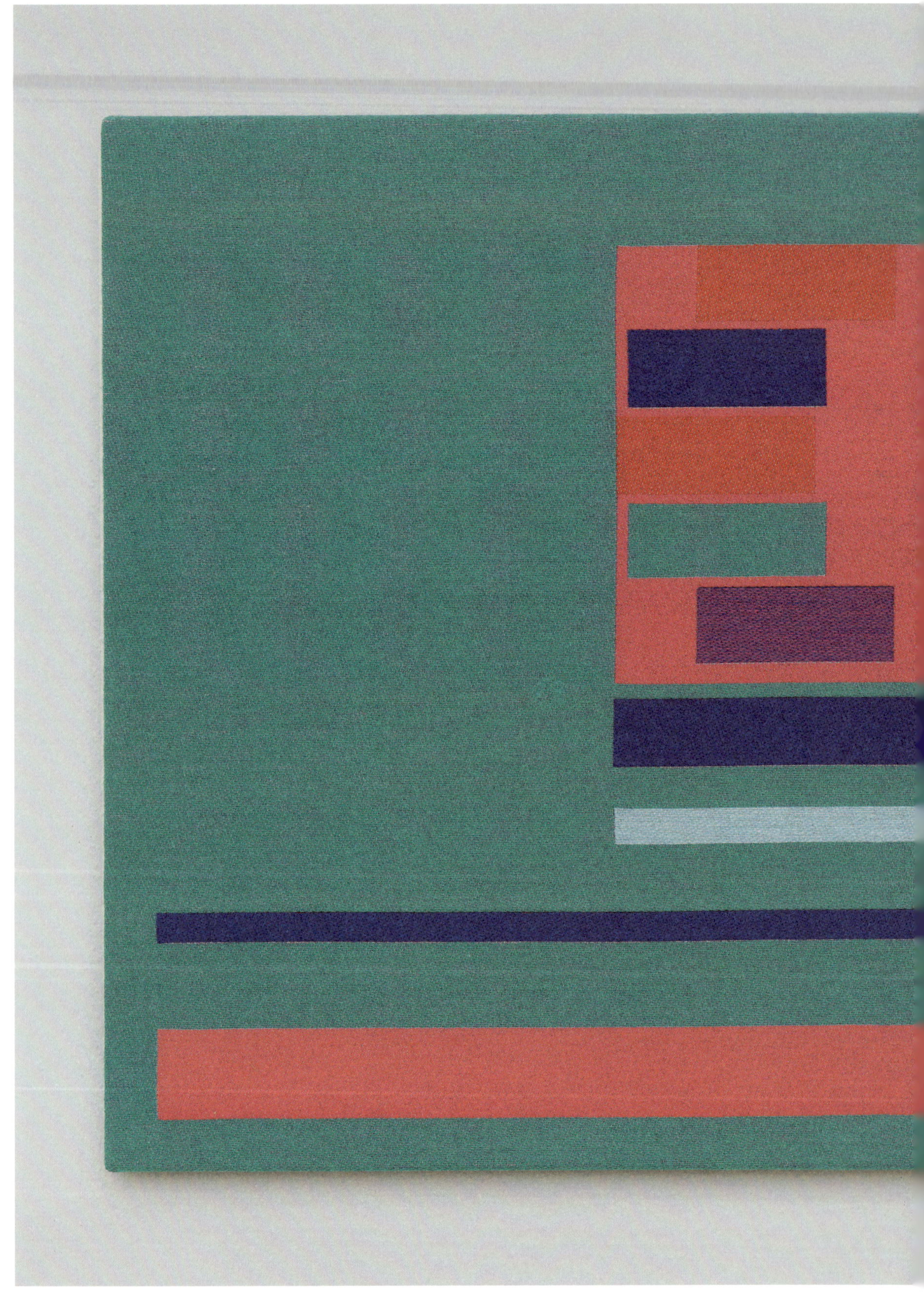

Abstract Browsing 16 03 01 (Wikipedia), 2016

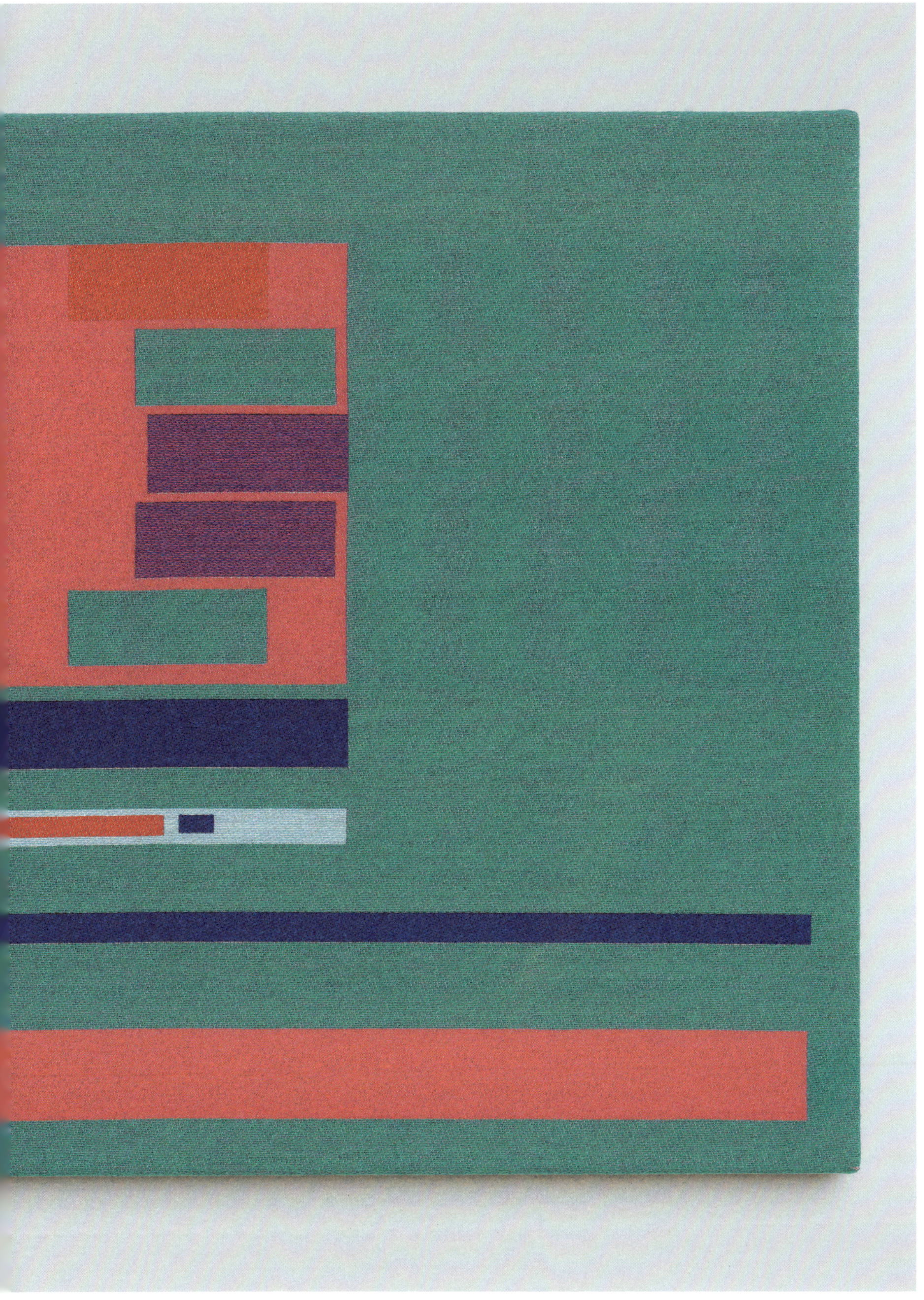

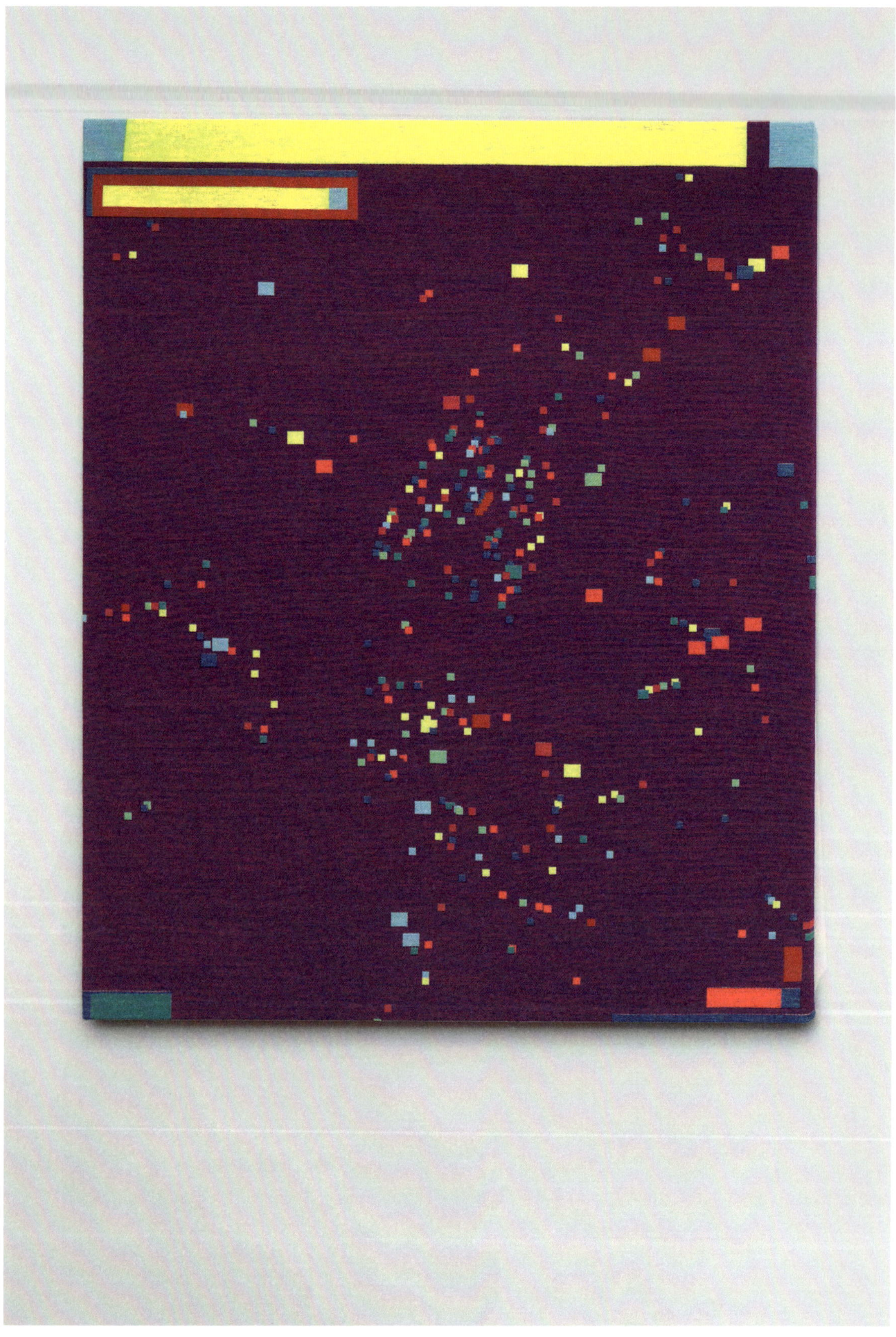

Abstract Browsing 16 03 09 Triptych (Waze), 2016

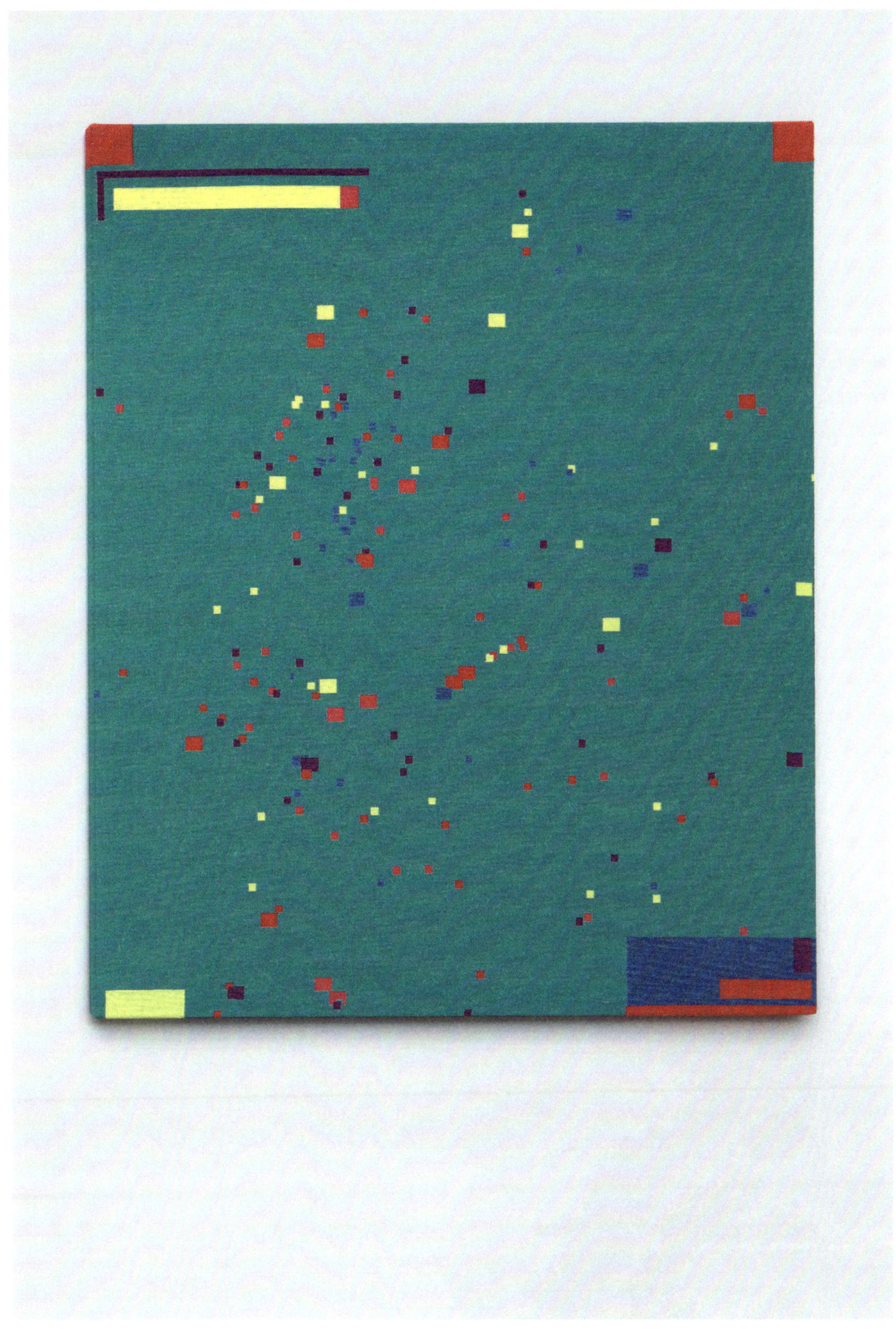

Abstract Browsing 16 03 09 Triptych (Waze), 2016

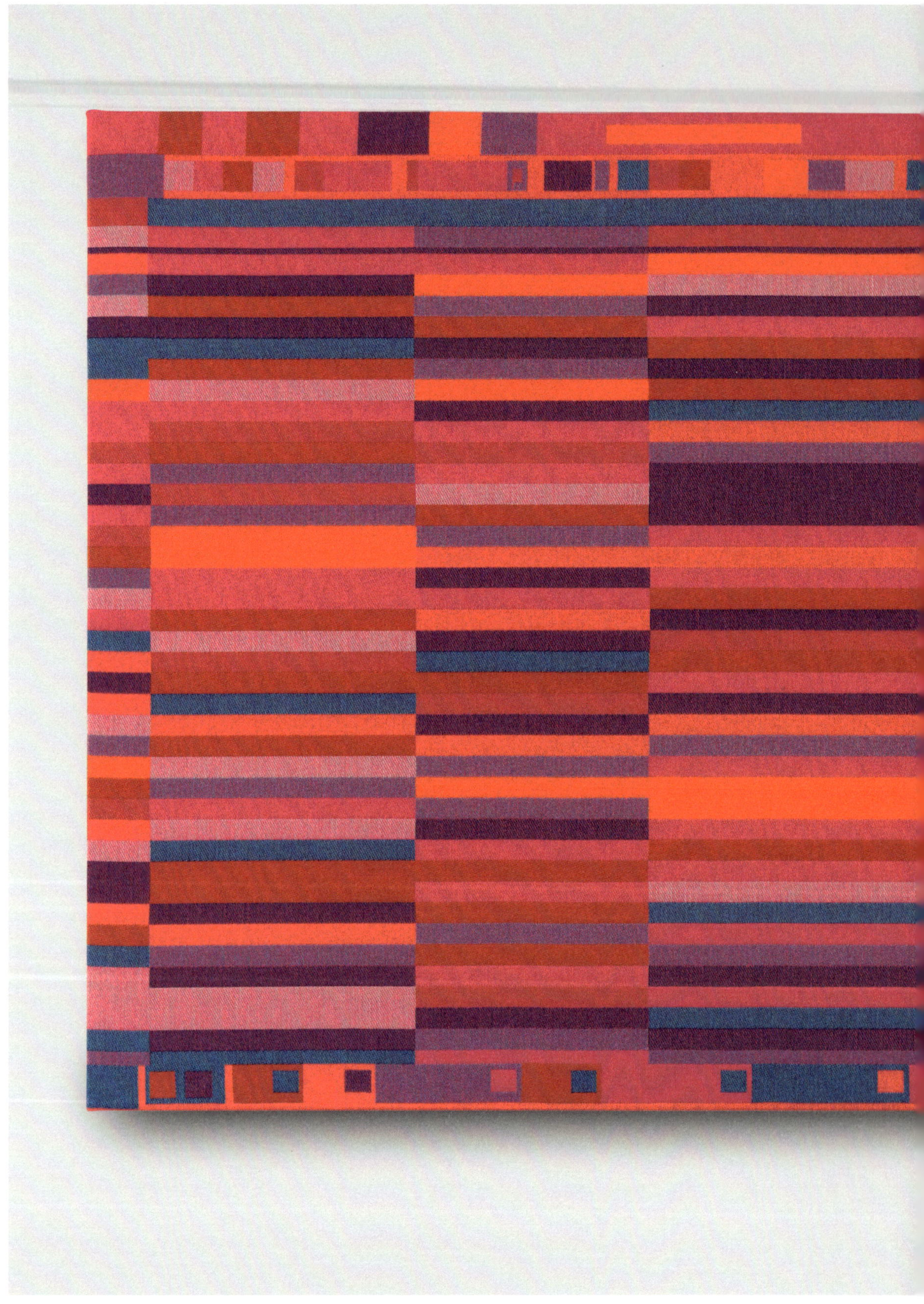

Abstract Browsing 16 10 06 (Google Spreadsheet), 2016

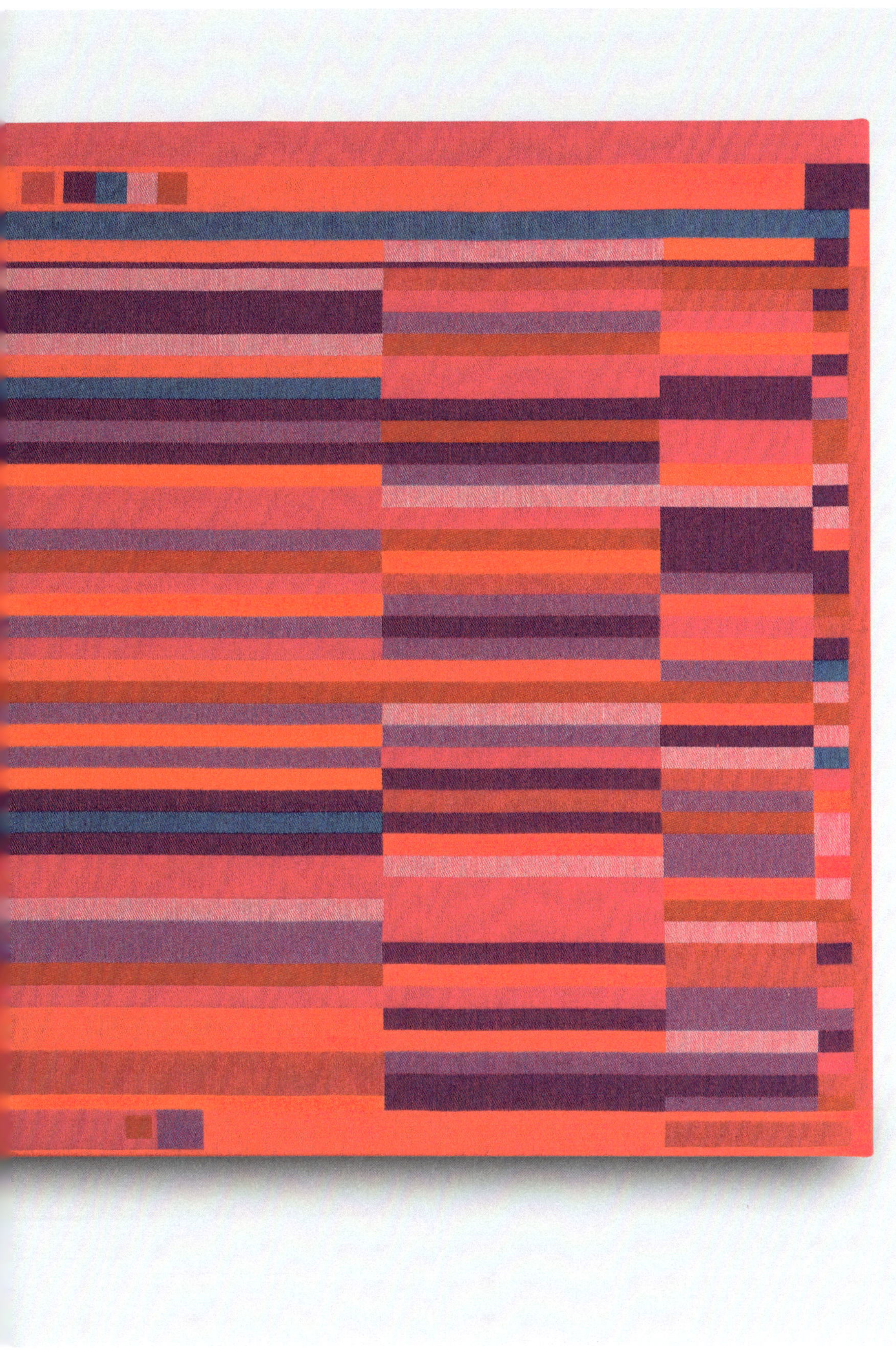

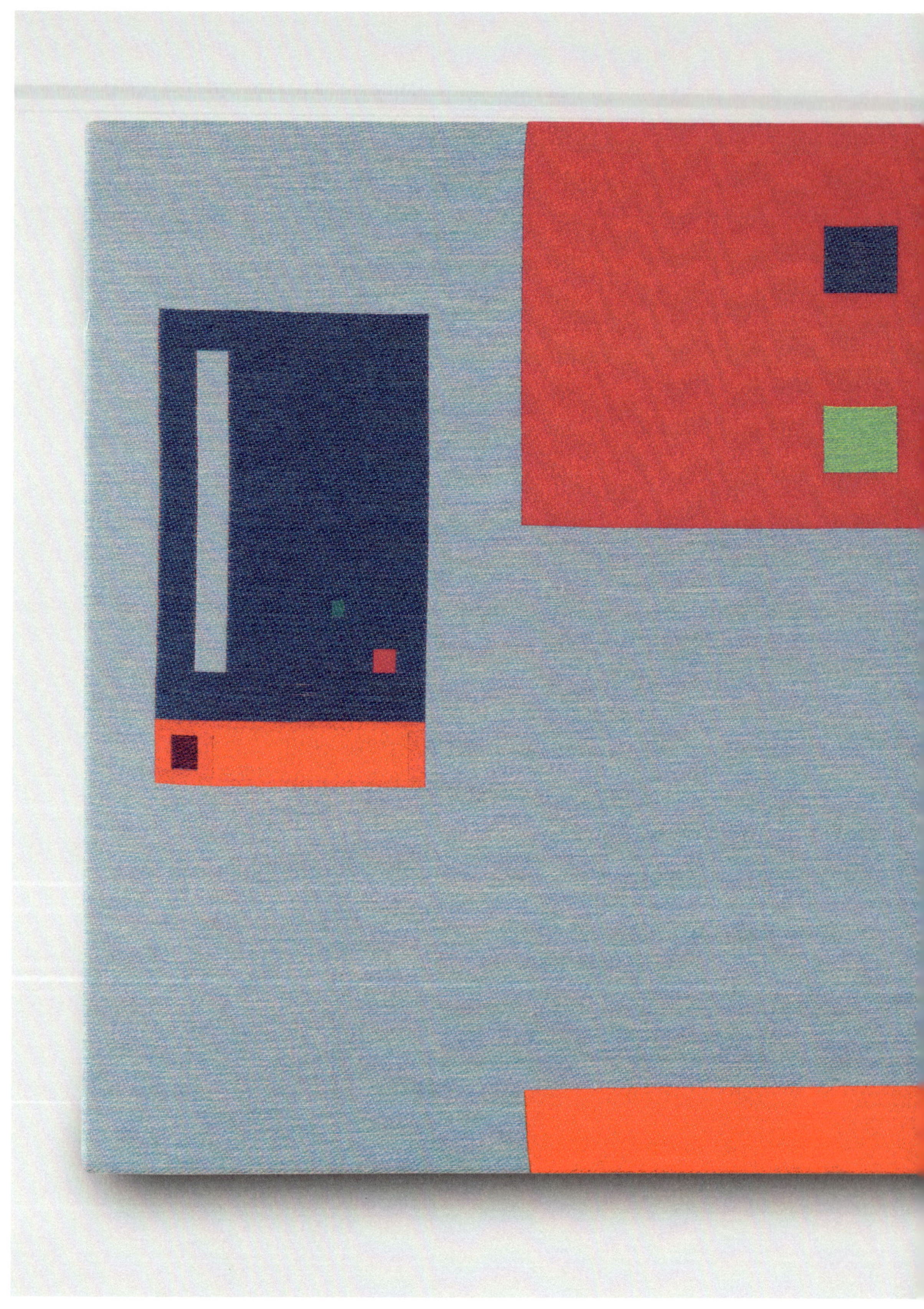

Abstract Browsing 16 10 09 (Guggenheim), 2016

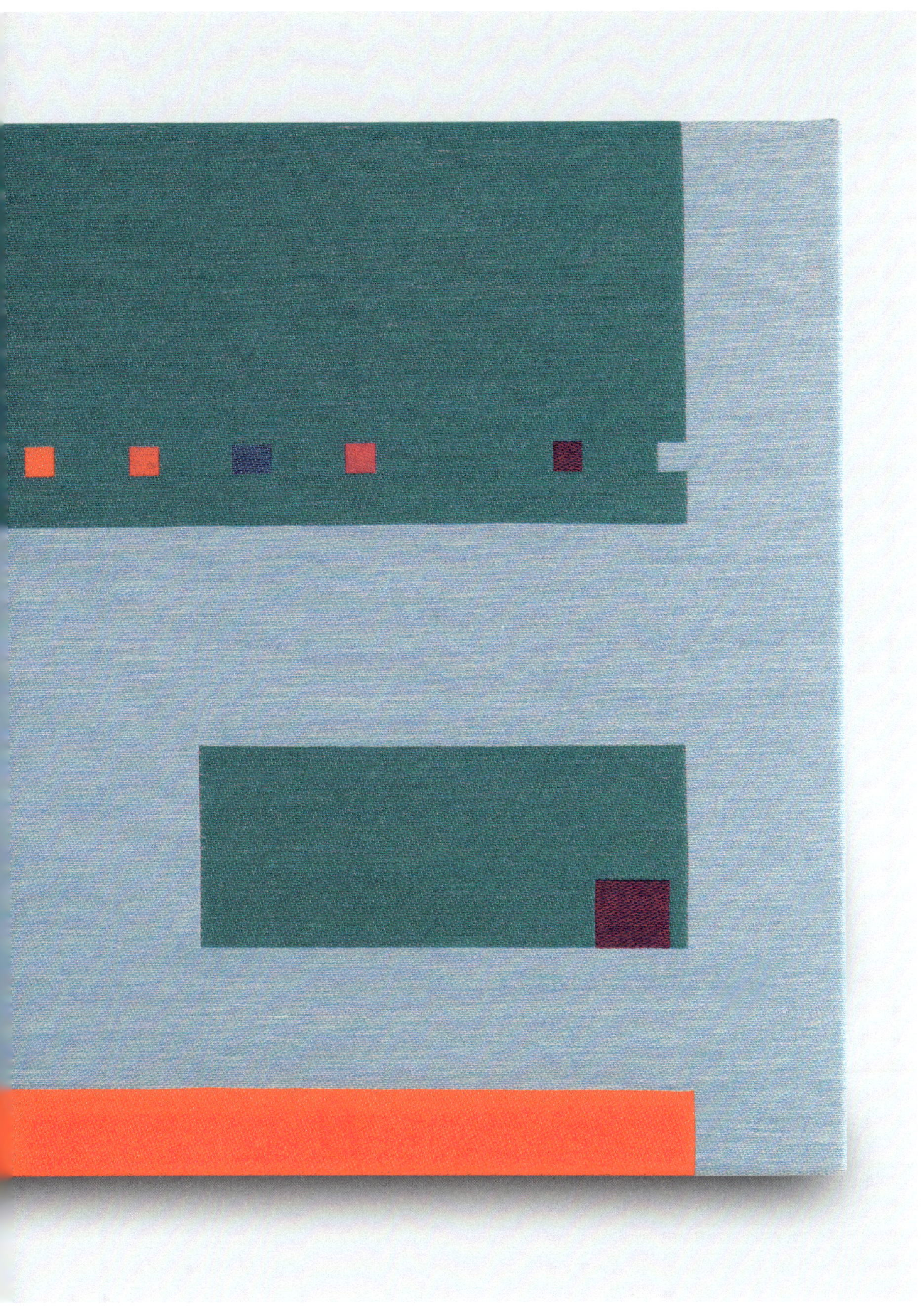

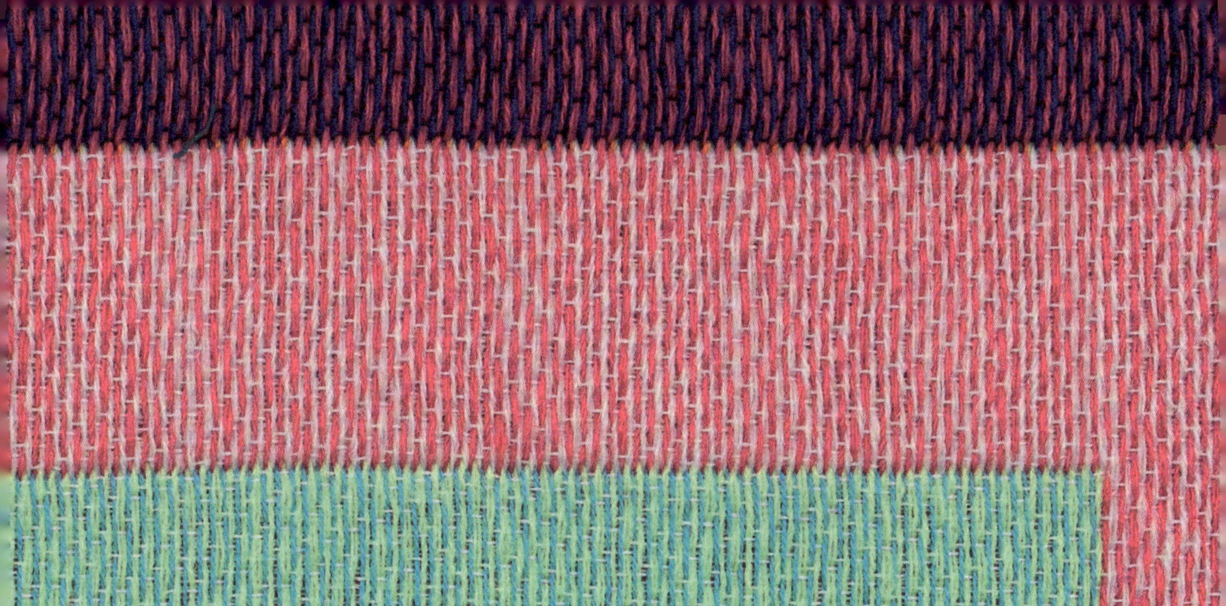

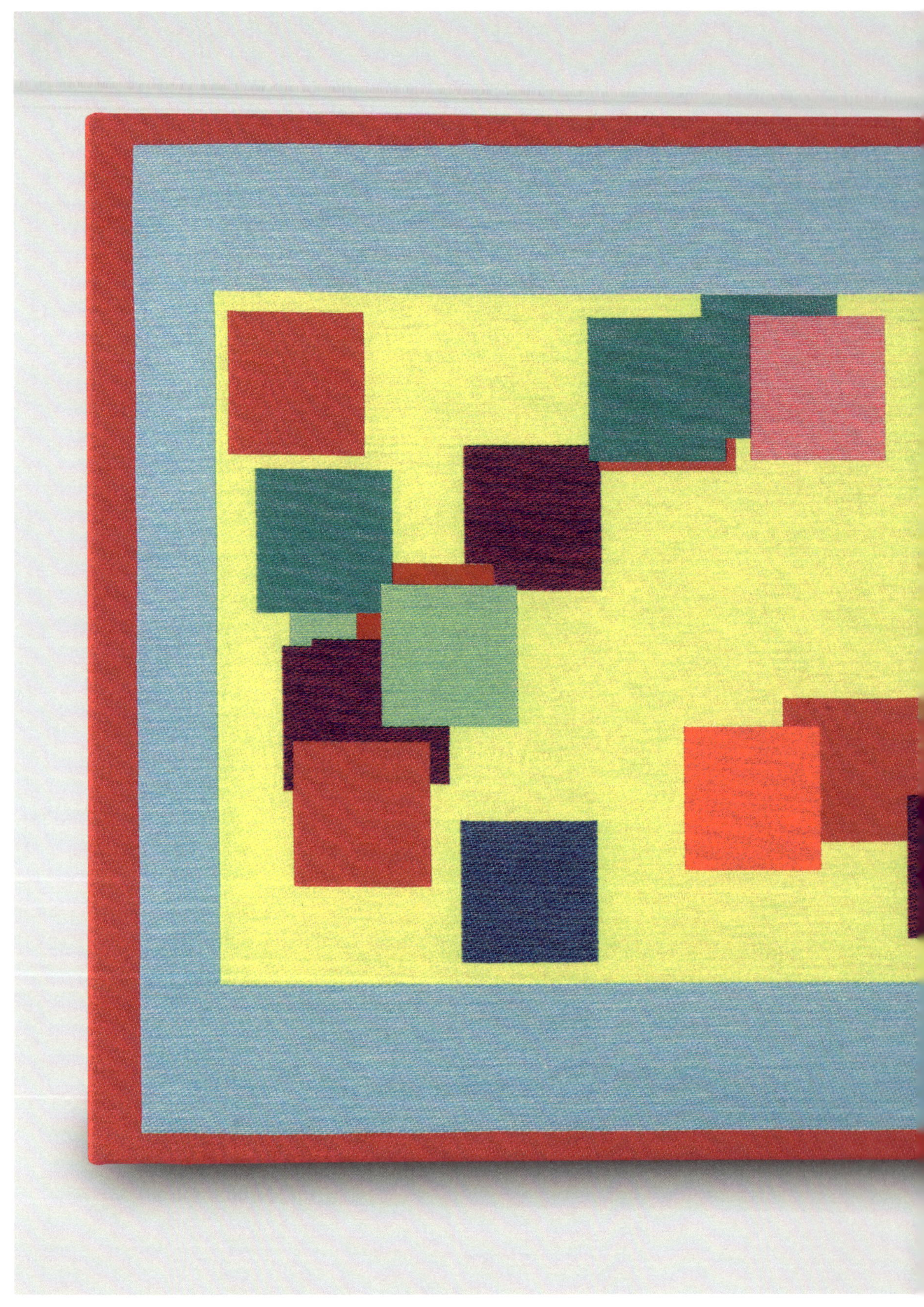

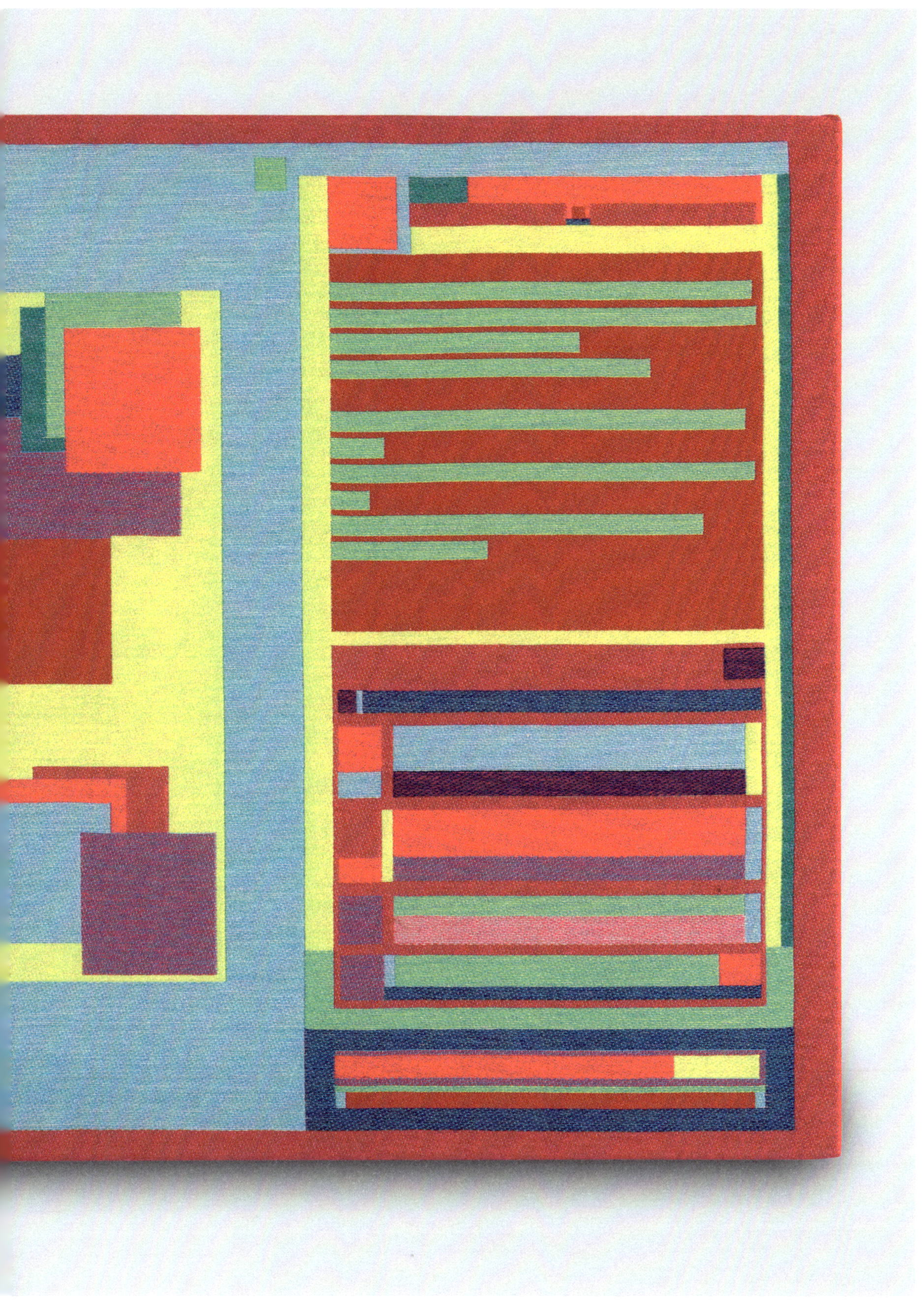

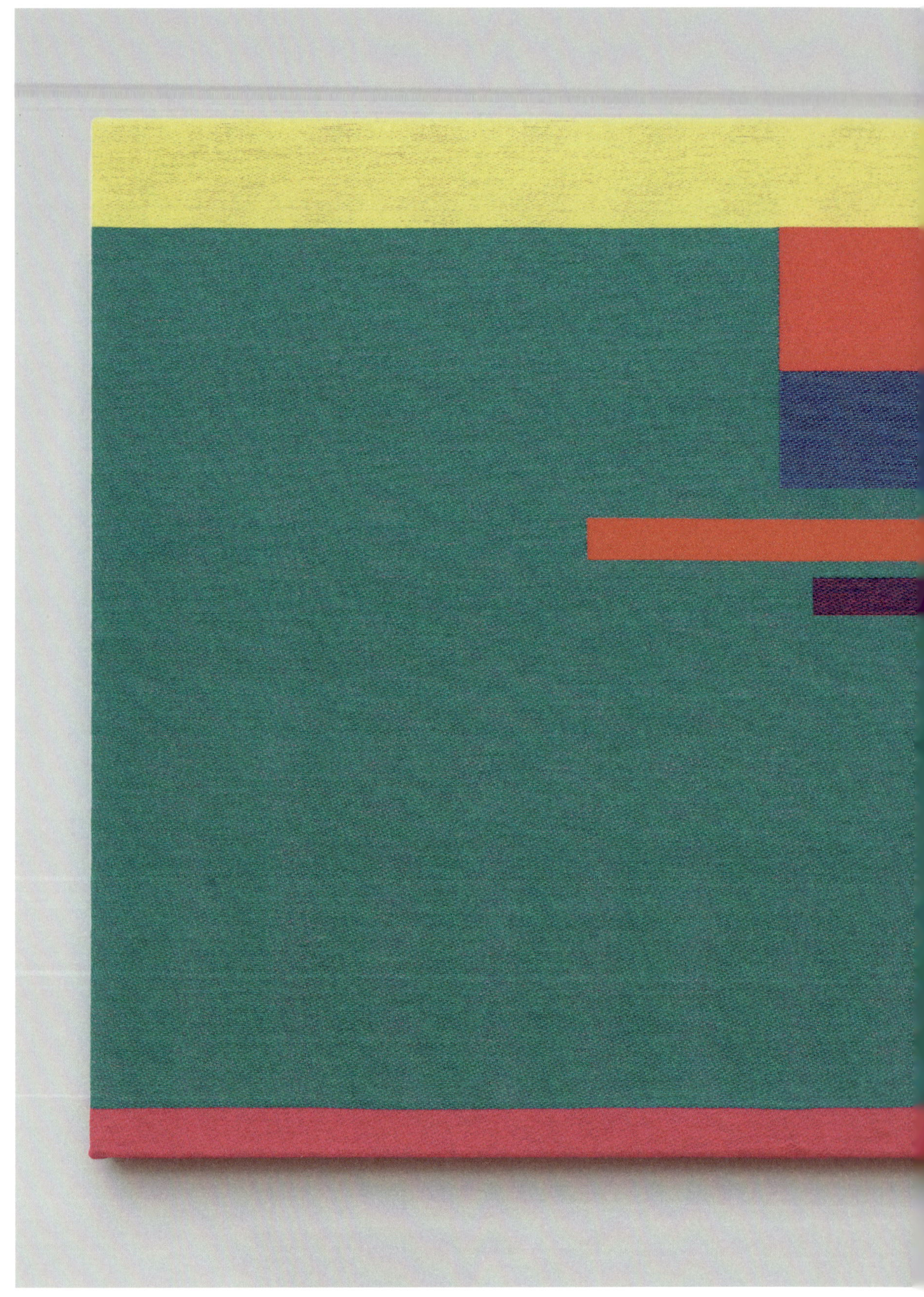

Abstract Browsing 16 03 05 (Google), 2016

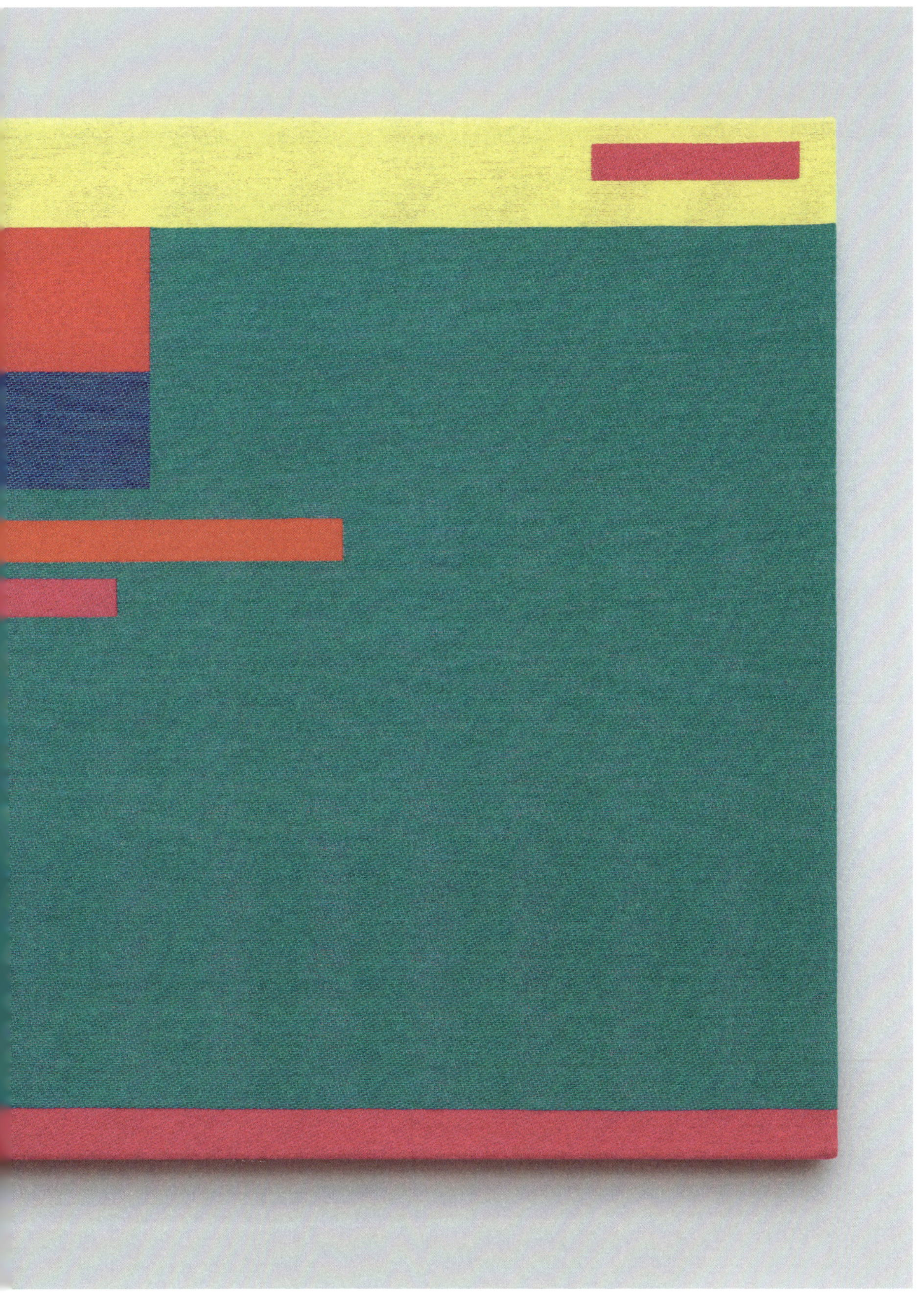

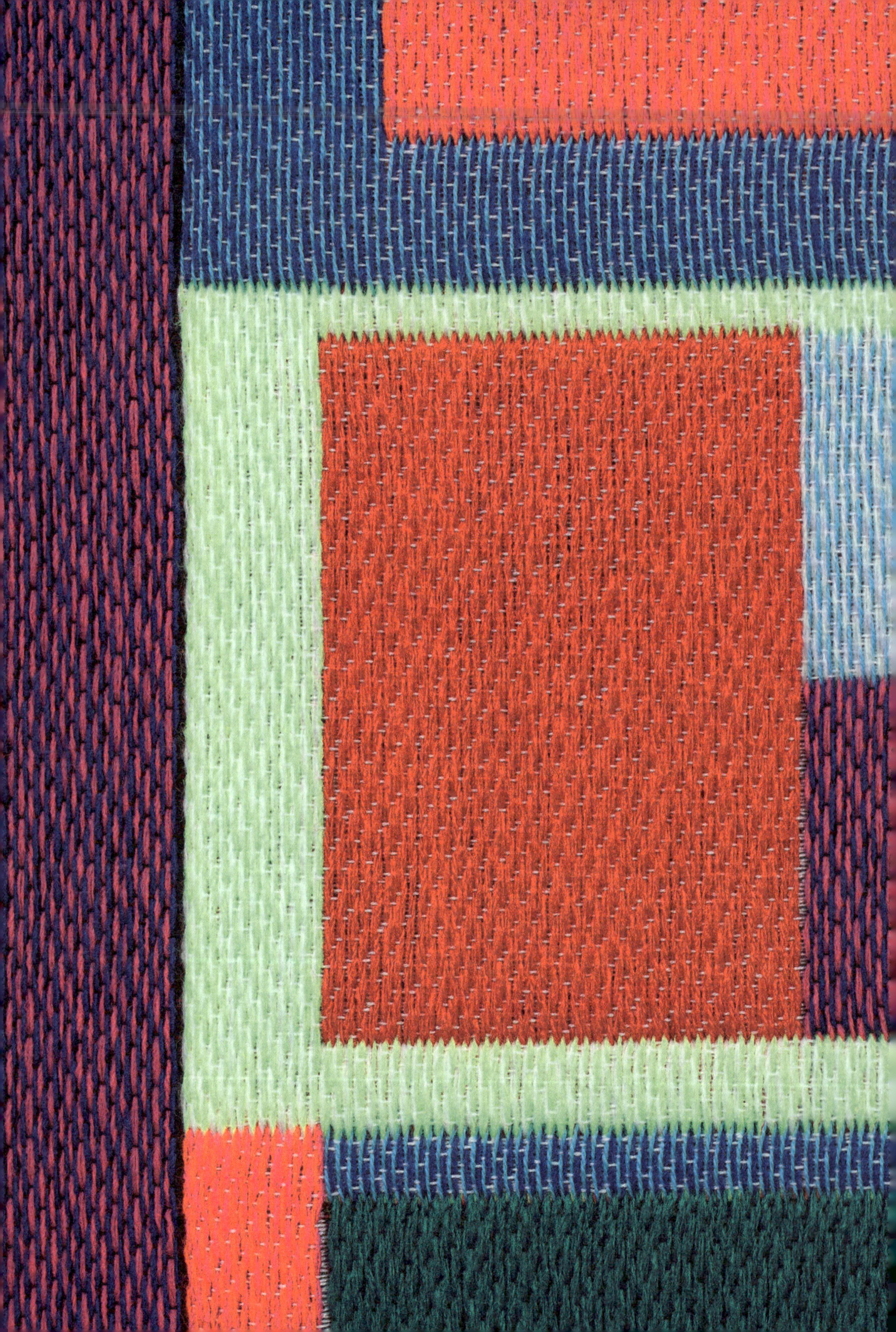

[284] Detail
[294–295] *Abstract Browsing* – Installation view at Steve Turner, Los Angeles

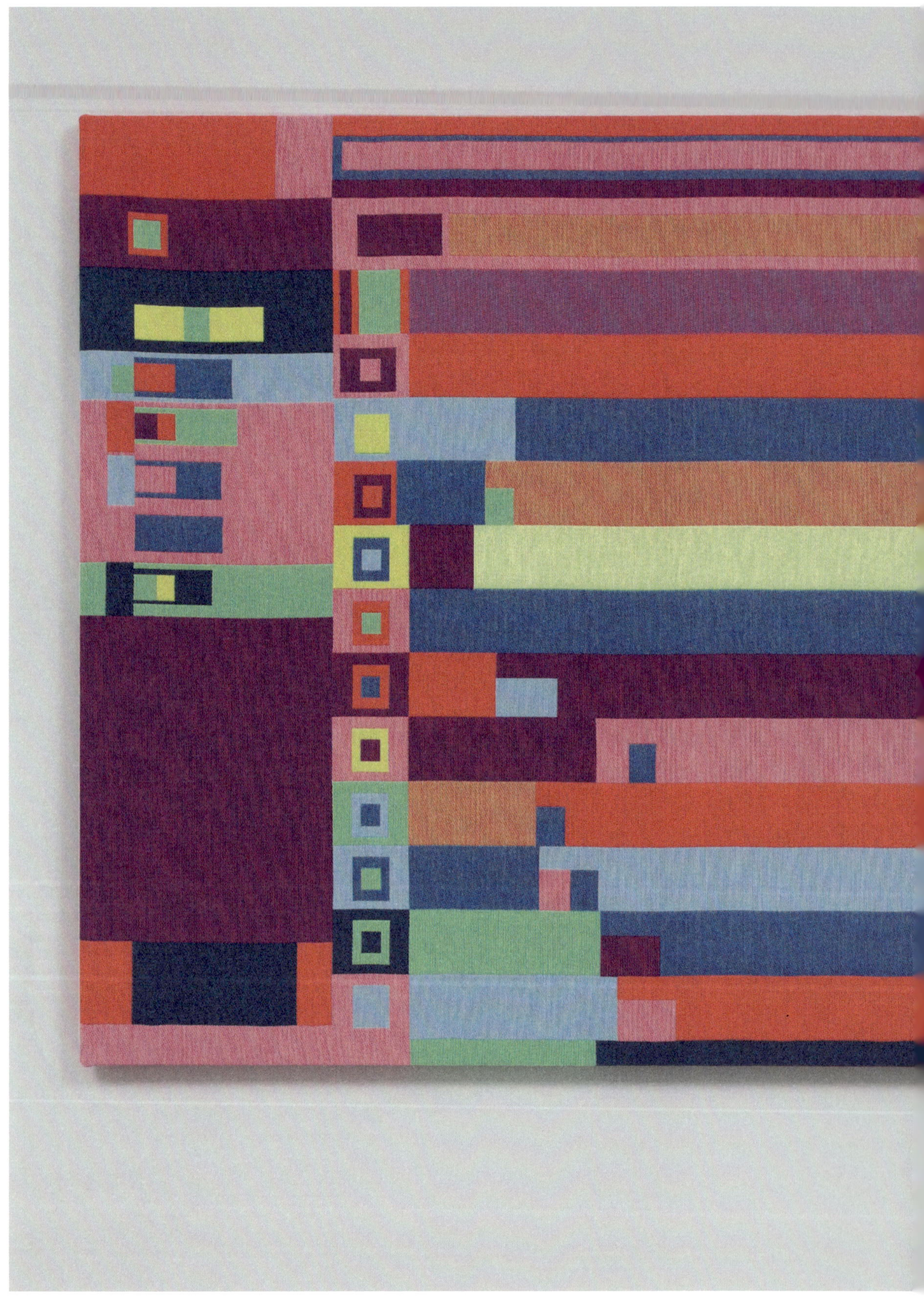

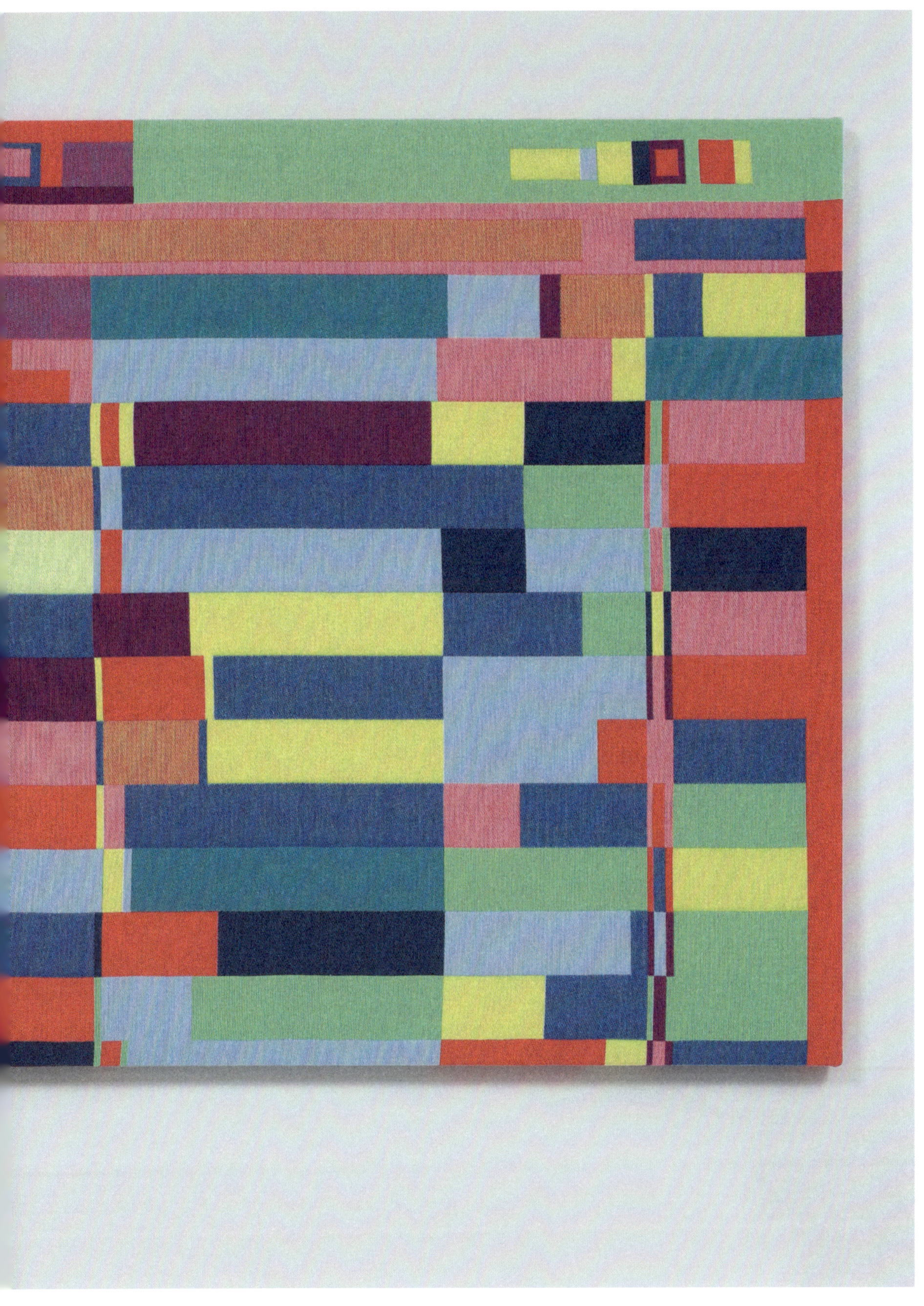

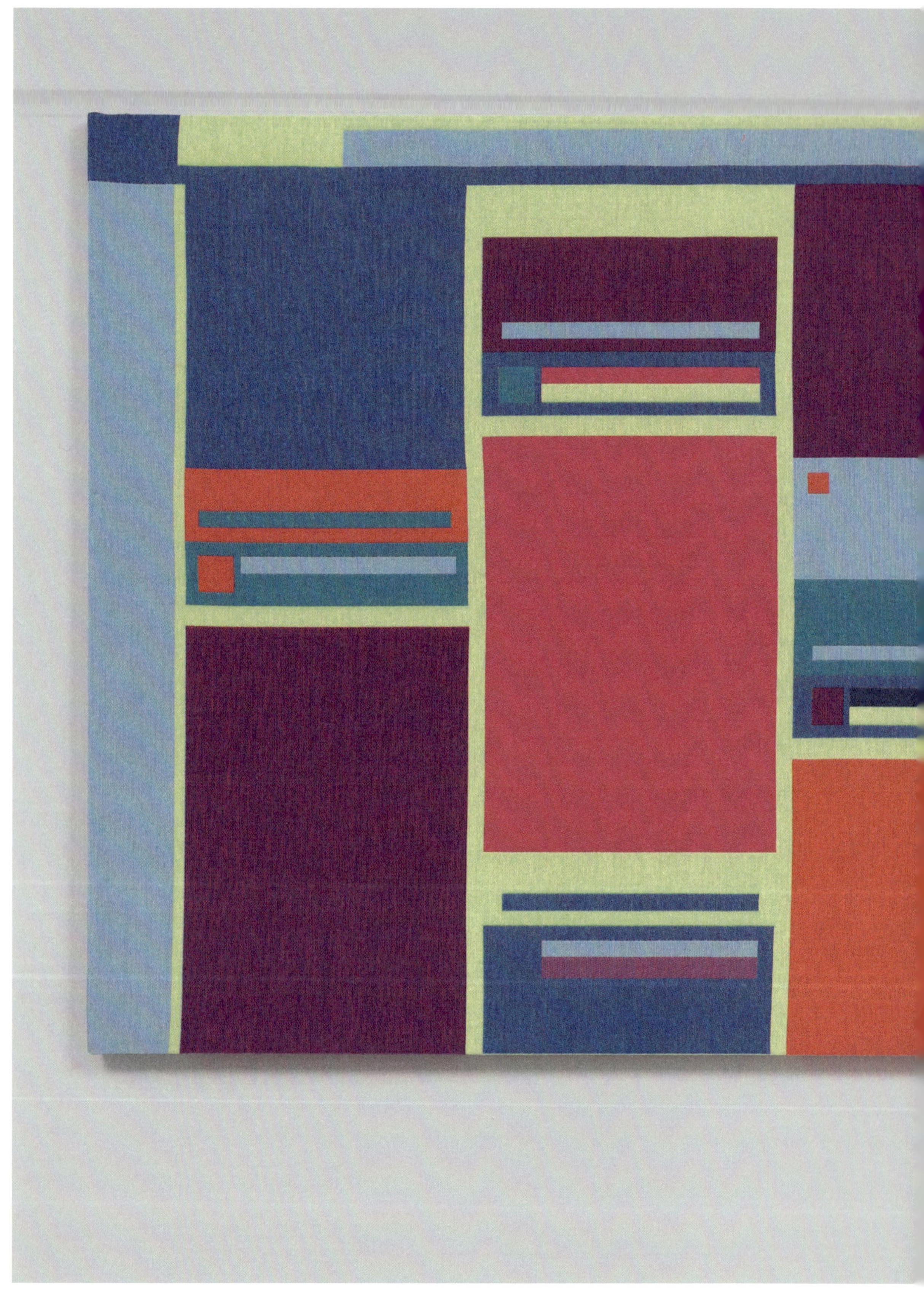

Abstract Browsing 15 05 11 (Pinterest), 2015

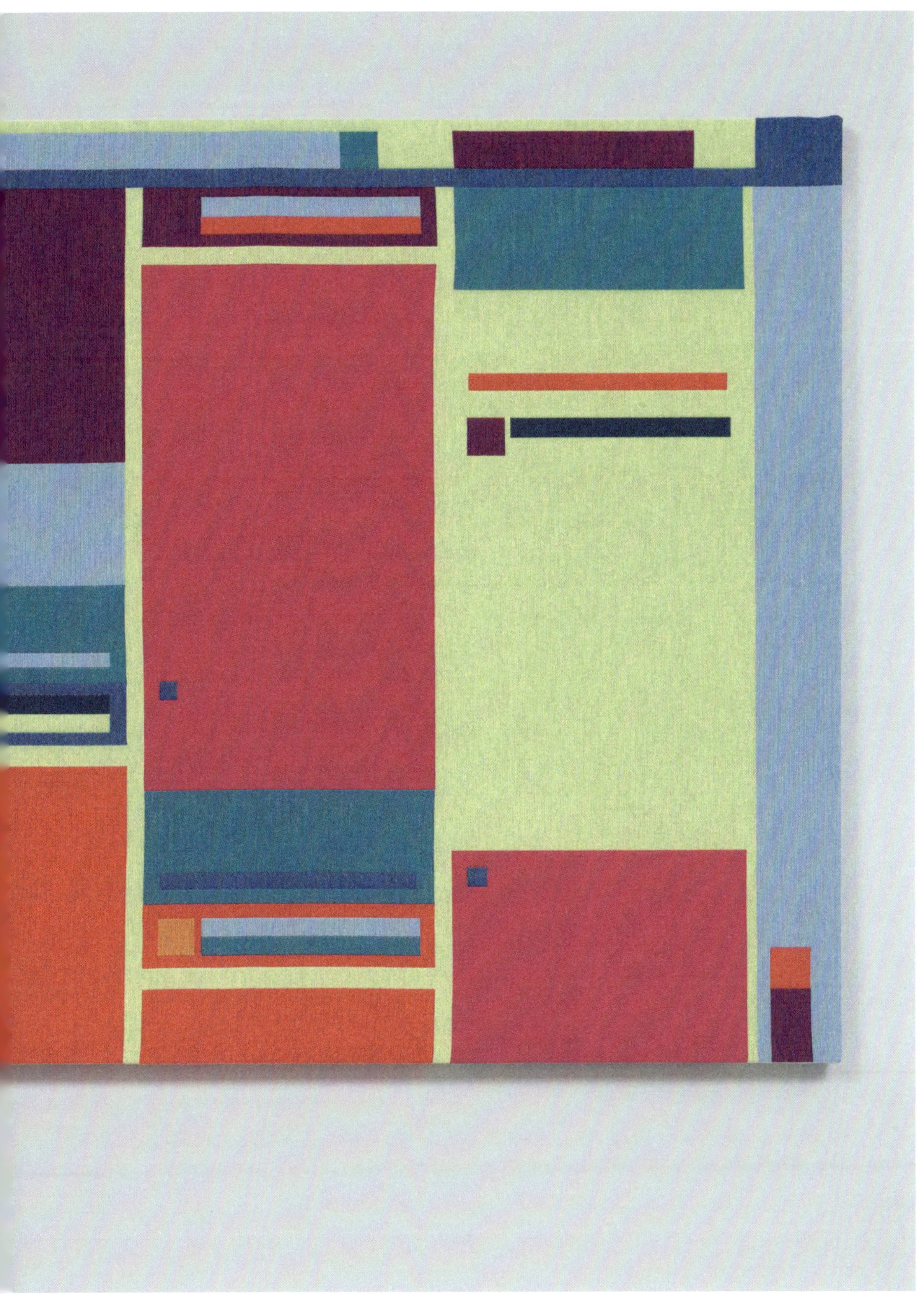

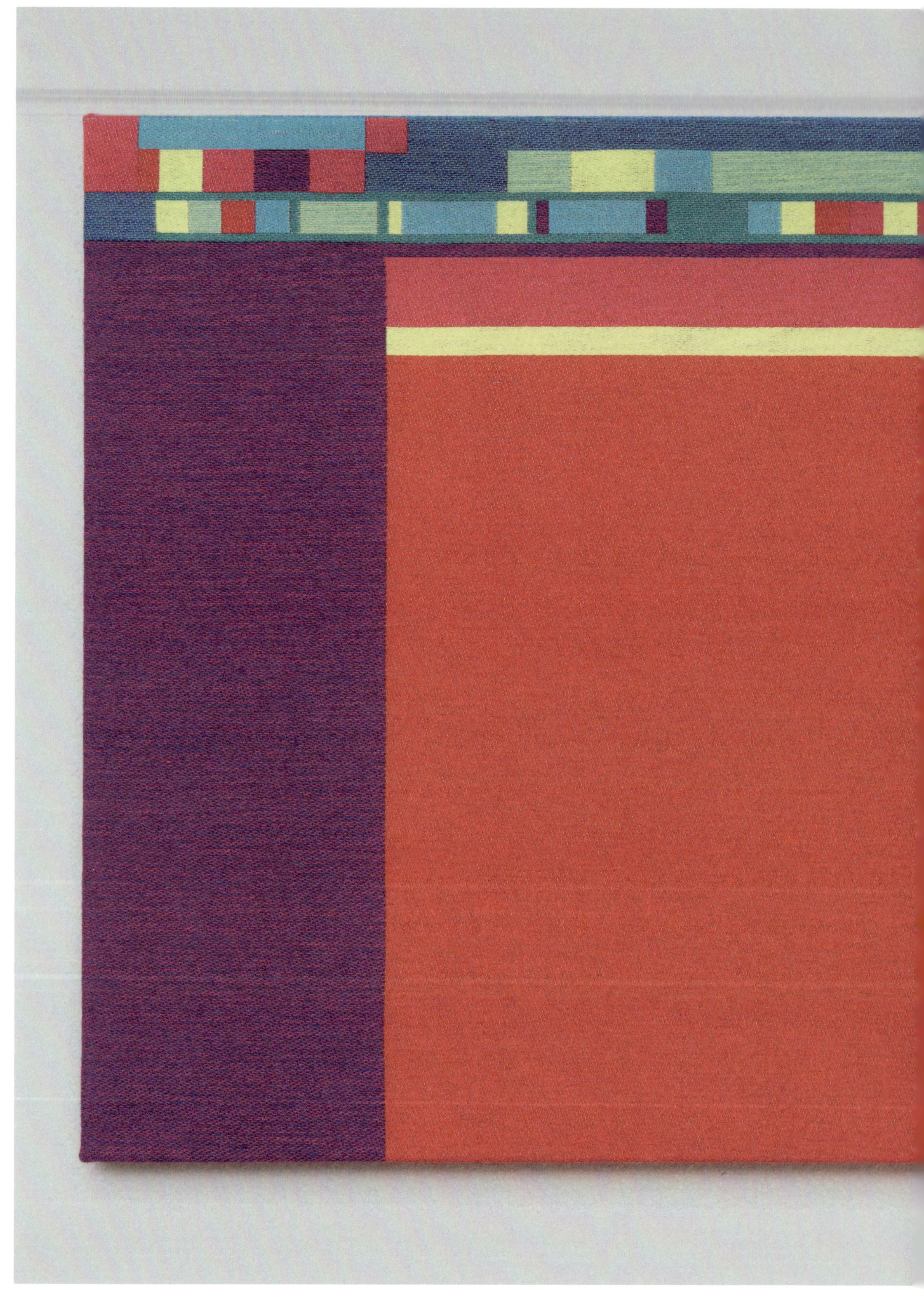

Abstract Browsing 16 03 06 (Google Docs), 2016

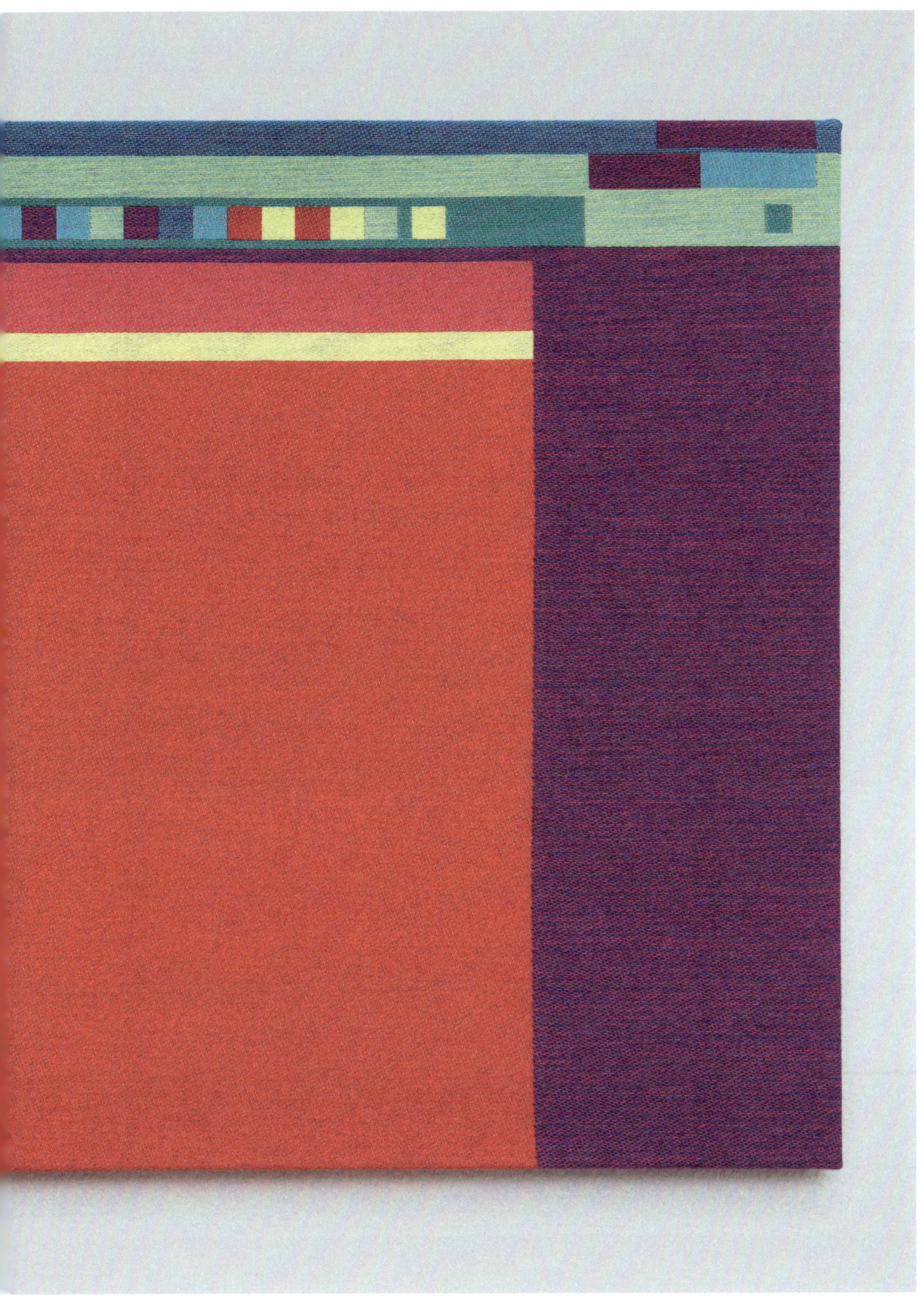

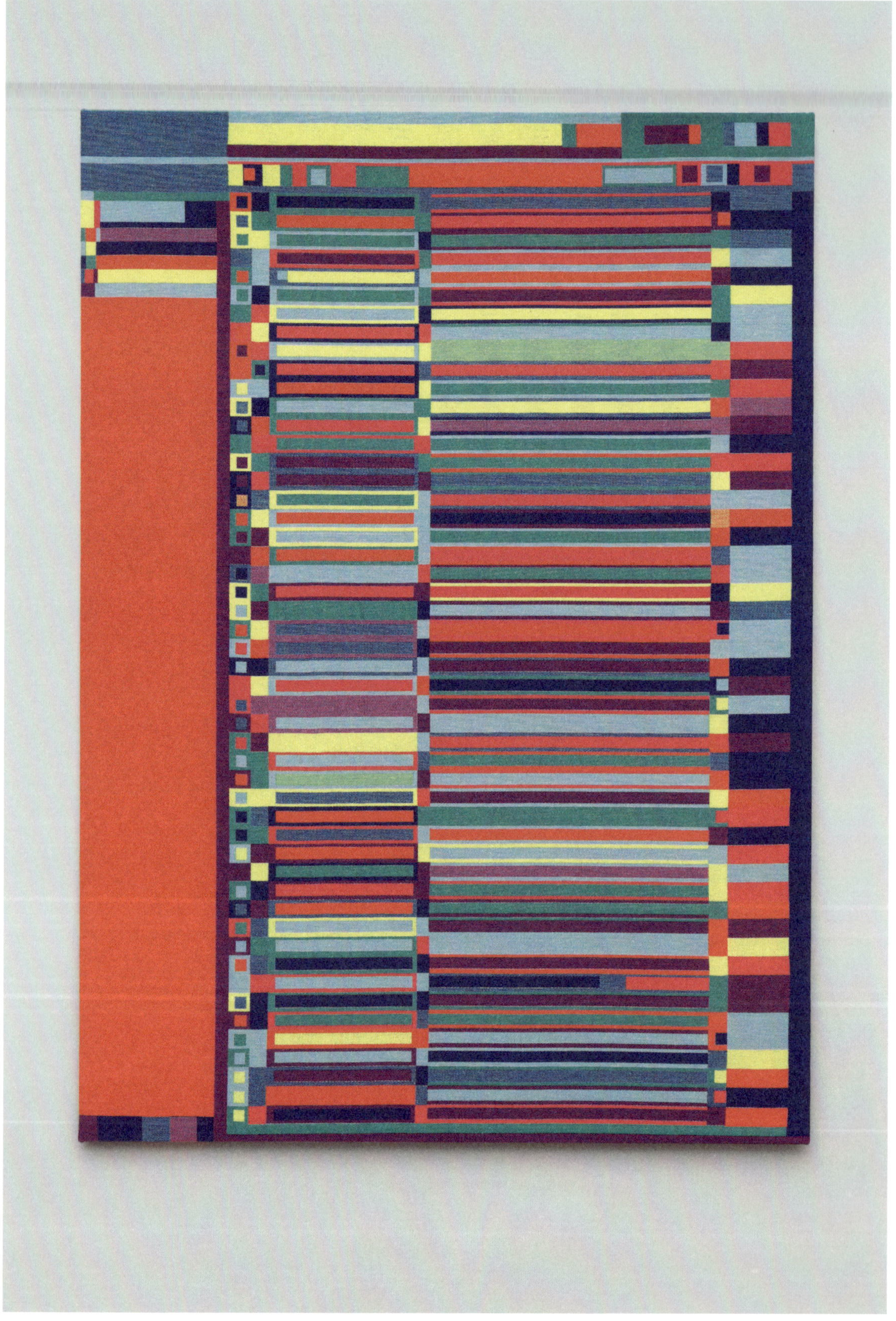

Abstract Browsing 16 03 07 (Gmail), 2016

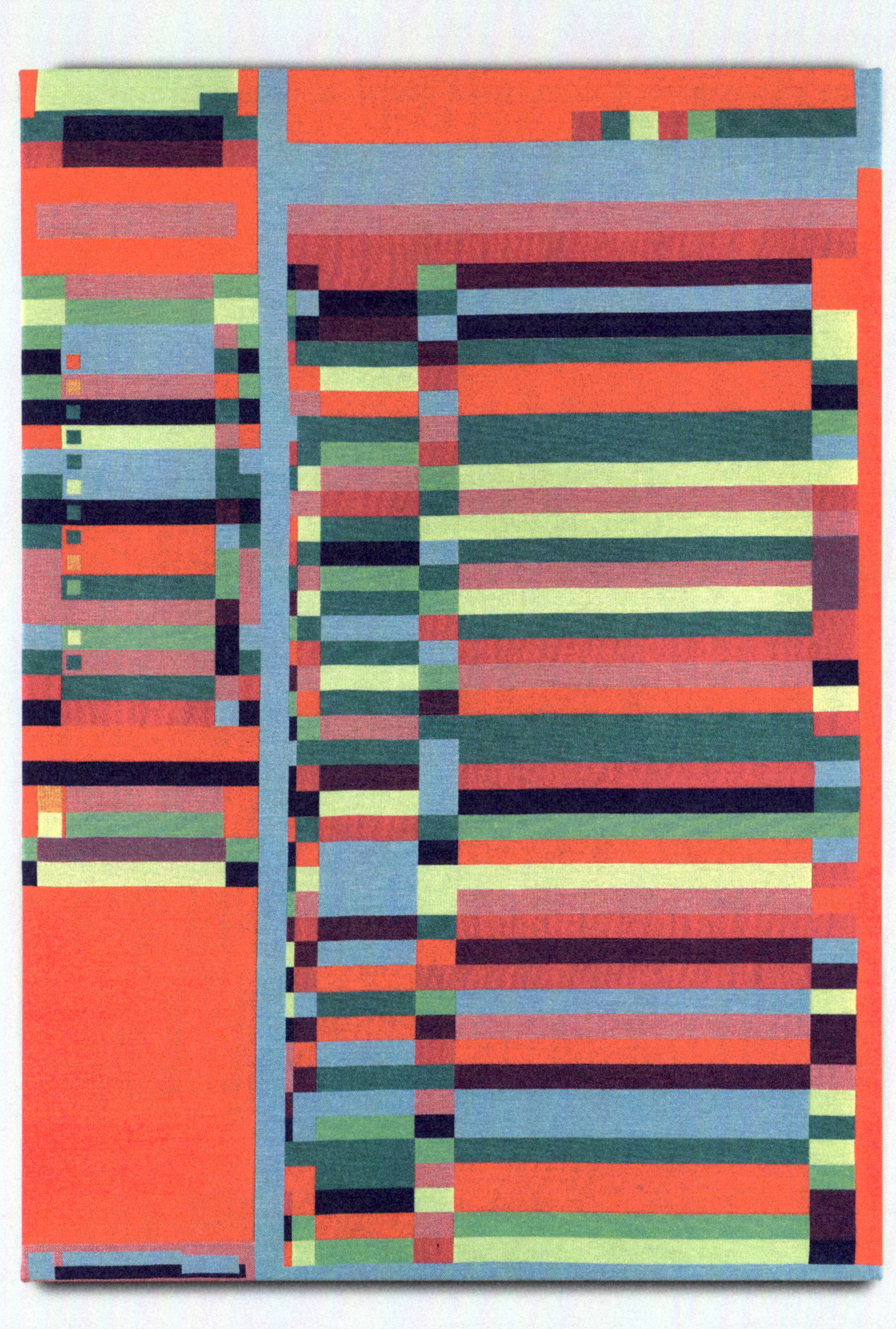

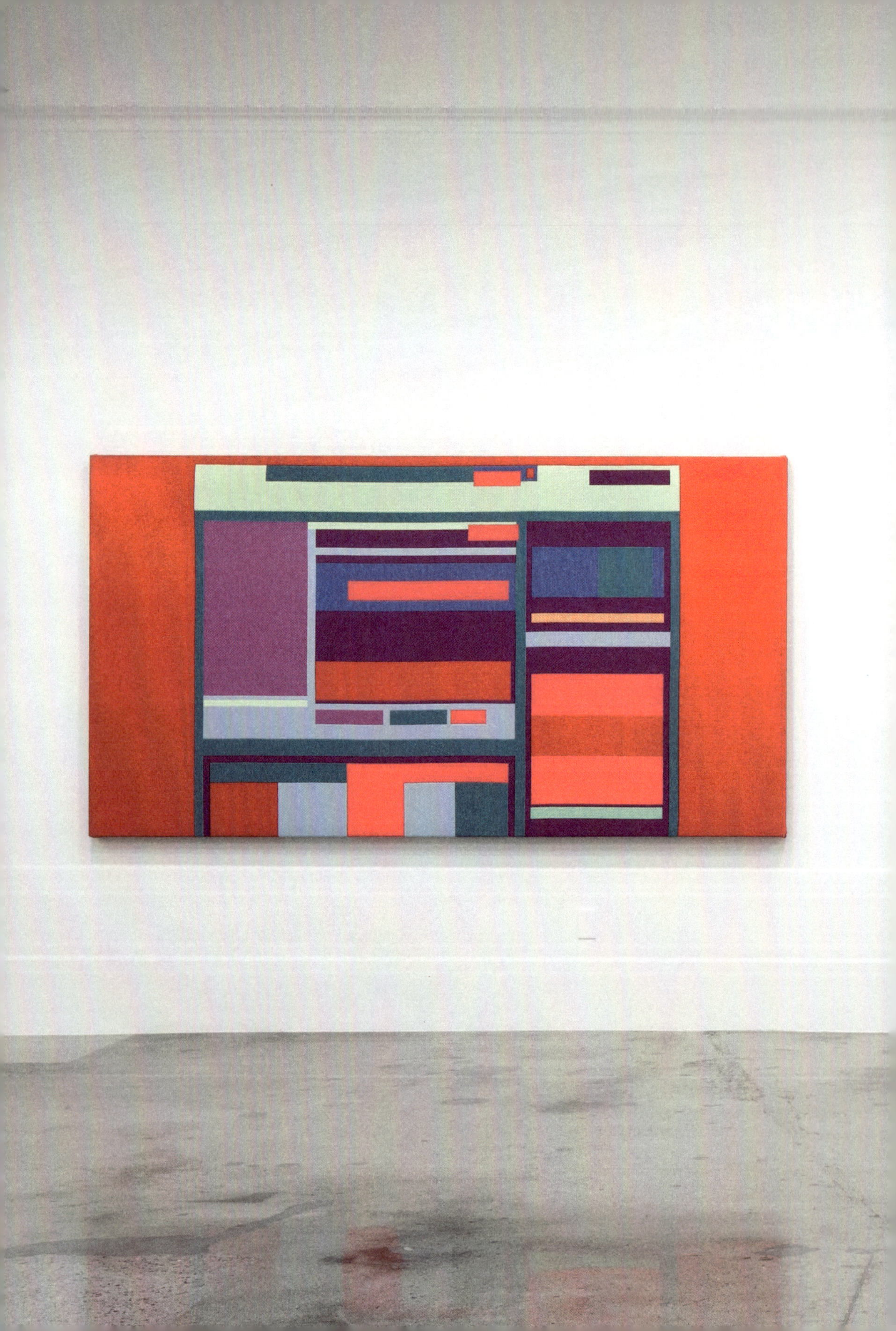

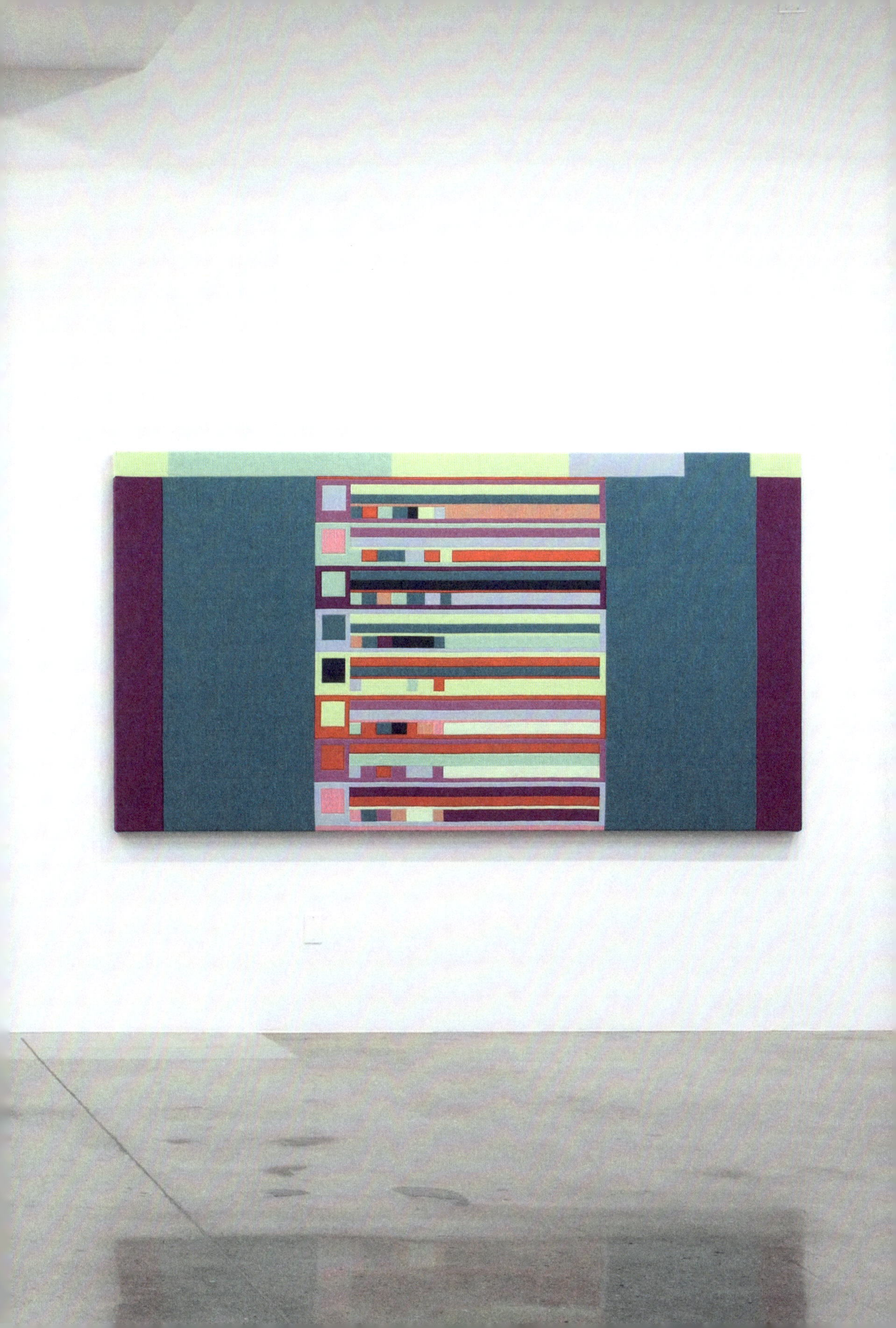

RAFAËL ROZENDAAL
INTERVIEW
Marvin Jordan

Technology asks new questions about composition. I'm looking for unusual compositions. Anti-compositions, unhuman compositions, compositions that humans would not have created on their own.
— Rafaël Rozendaal

MJ   You are widely known as an internet artist, characterized by digital works, domain names and .GIFs—that's the URL Rafaël. But there's also the IRL Rafaël, who makes physical works such as lenticular prints and textiles, which are very much inspired by digital technologies. Is there any overlap or influence between what you do on-screen and off?

RR   Definitely. The lenticulars are my interest in moving images and interactive images—not so much interest in the internet. This is more about programming than about the network. In programming, you know that you have an input, you make a code, and then the machine runs it. And in the case of the internet, it's a different machine every time, it's a slightly different rendering that is always kind of controlled. Whereas in the case of lenticulars, it is much less controlled. You put these four images in, and they are optically mixed by the ridges that are on the material. I see it as analog computation, or a single-purpose computer.

MJ   'Analog computation' is an interesting concept. So instead of thinking about your practice as digital one day, analog another day, you are actually collapsing the lines separating them to reveal underlying techniques common to both. This reminds me of what you have mentioned in the past: that lenticulars and tapestries come from an 'internet mindset.' Can you talk about that?

RR   Yeah, the weavings are definitely related to the internet. When the browsing plug-ins started [referring to the web-based project, Abstract Browsing], I was doing a residency in Turkey. And I came up with the plug-in. But they also asked, 'do you want to do something with local crafts people?' because that was part of the residency. I started thinking about the history of textiles, which is very interesting. We made woven versions of these browser compositions. There's something about pixels and stitches that make sense, there's a relationship between them.

MJ	How do you see that? Like a molecular relationship?

RR	Actually, it's a historical relationship, which I found out later. The first digital information was these musical punch cards. You know those scrolls with the holes in them?

MJ	Yes, like music rolls?

RR	Exactly, which means the paper is either solid or there's a hole.

MJ	Like binary.

RR	Exactly, it is binary. Around the seventeenth century, merchants wanted to wear more elaborate clothing. They wanted patterns on their clothing. And that used to be done only for royalty by hand, embroidered. But to become more efficient, they automated it. These merchants created the same scrolls that they did for music, but for weaving. And the textile industry developed along those lines. That's arguably the first digital image format. Furthermore, that automatic process was then used on Ellis Island to…

MJ	… process immigrants.

RR	Exactly, to process immigrants into these punch cards, and all that was the beginning of the computer. That's the historical context. Now I have all these images, all these screenshots. And then you could make physical versions of them for many reasons. You could paint them, you could print them, et cetera. I thought weaving had a similar limitation as a screen whereby, especially with early computers, there are only so many colors you can use. So I have my color scheme and the weavings are made from combinations and permutations of twelve threads.

MJ	You've mentioned in the past that there is no rule, you go by the rule: 'whatever interests me, I will do.' I was wondering, is this still the case? Or, do you think there's a strategic advantage to doing many different kinds of things?

RR	Oh no, I don't think there's an advantage… I think it's a strategic disadvantage.

MJ	Warhol would be an archetypal example of someone who does everything.

RR	Yeah, there's examples of both scenarios working well. Warhol is the best example. But then there's people like… I really love Peter Halley. He just makes those paintings.

MJ	Right.

RR	So I think it's case by case. Some people are like 'Oh, I'm a favorite artist now, I can also go make a film.' And then it turns out the film sucks but at least they tried it. Or, if you think of Robert Longo, he made *Johnny Mnemonic*, which was kind of a silly movie. I'm sure he had a hard time working with this sort of structure of movie making, but there were a lot of ideas in there that ended up in *The Matrix*.

But for me, I'm just keeping myself busy. I keep coming up with new categories—I started with websites, then lenticulars and haiku, or performance ideas, or lectures. So whenever I come up with a new category, like haiku, I think 'OK, this negates everything that came before.'

MJ   I wanted to get to that. About your haiku writing…

RR   I thought it solved everything. There's no storage, there's no travel cost, there's no technical limitations, there's no problem of conservation. I thought to myself, 'I can create a mental image, and if I just make enough of them there will eventually be one that's brilliant.'

MJ   Do you consider haiku to be an official part of your practice?

RR   Yes. But I do understand that it's confusing when you introduce yourself and people ask, 'Well what do you do? And it's a million things. Then I think to myself, 'Is this answer too negative?' But, it's really true. The fact that I don't feel like I'm particularly tied to one thing means I don't have any reputation to lose. And that makes me feel very safe in the sense that I'm more like a man of the people, and it's an intimate thing and it's very free. So, I don't have that reputation to lose like where there are a lot of critics discussing my work and if I make a different move they'll panic or something.

MJ   The fact that you stick to haiku out of all other kinds of poetry— is there something about its Japanese roots that interests you?

RR   I was always fascinated with Japan. I did a residency there in 2010 and I was there for three months and I visited every museum I could. I immersed myself in the culture. But, I didn't know so much about haiku yet. And I started working with a gallery there so I came back every year. Once or twice a year, I go to Japan. Then I was in a group show and someone in the audience didn't speak English but he wrote a haiku about my work. He taught me this haiku about my format and the domain name and the experience inside and the essence. He had written it in official Japanese, according to the traditional rules.

I thought this was interesting. Then I started reading about haiku, and some of the famous ones were so great that I thought: it's amazing how they don't deteriorate. Because in art you're used to paintings not looking the same way they used to.

MJ Yes, yes. Decay.

RR Yeah, I thought that was amazing, like the famous one about a frog and the water. Every time you read that one, the image is just as fresh as it was then. That's very interesting to me.

MJ Is there something virtual at the core of it? Something analogous to immaterial labor? Or is that just theory?

RR No, no, that aspect is interesting, I think that's a part of it. I like this lightness of being and no luggage. I've done quite a few shows with haiku where I just send them a template in .PDF and that's really nice.

MJ But this is a recurring theme. Not only in your work, but in your life as well. Traveling, light luggage, nomadism… it's like your modus operandi. These themes of course are associated with the internet, so it's not so accidental that you have gravitated towards the haiku, right?

RR Yes, yes. The domain names are also haikus in a way that there are only so many characters you can use. And you also have to play with what's available. There's a kind of game, where you find creativity through limitation.

MJ Now that we've touched on these recent crossover elements in your work—moving between on-screen and off—I'd like to know your thoughts about social media. Is it part of your practice?

RR Well, I come from the pre-social media internet. So I feel like with social media, everything is very temporary. To use it in a primary stage, you're putting your work in the hands of another company. There are many degrees of how deeply embedded social media are.
If you make Instagram works, you're reliant on that company to exist; if you make domain works, you're still reliant on computers to exist, but there's a higher likelihood they will continue. When you do things on the domain level, you have root access. When you're doing things on Instagram, you're using somebody else's frame.

MJ For sure.

RR That's kind of the weaker position. On the other hand, for a lot of people, making domains and programming is way too difficult and using social media is powerful because it's so convenient. Open standards—things like podcasting, and the web, and email—I love all that stuff. But for most people, open standards feel like a to-do list.

MJ   I see.

RR   I like social media in the sense that I see them as my open studio. And I really think that's valuable. A lot of people are kind of cynical about it being a cheap way to get attention, or whatever. I think there's a really great opportunity for the internet and social media to expose people to art. And the reason you want to expose people to art is to show people outside of big cities that something like this exists and that it's possible to live a life with a lot of art in it. I really deeply believe that's important.

That was the internet for me to begin with. Social media then are kind of a secondary gateway to get people to the websites or to work with, and kind of a look over someone's shoulder as things are being made.

MJ   Kind of like a behind-the-scenes.

RR   The downside of Instagram is that it's a big envy machine. Everybody of course makes their life look better than it actually is. You don't make movies of yourself when you can't sleep. Or when you're stressed, or when you can't get your Green Card. But then you go to the beach and everyone's like, oh, why is he at the beach? I wish I was there. I really think social media would be a lot better without the rating system. But, it would drop… it wouldn't be as addictive.

MJ   So going more specific on this topic, have any of your works been overtly influenced by social media?

RR   The abstract browsing works are also about social media. I take screenshots of my browsing behavior—I'm interested in how these compositions can be made for efficiency rather than for beauty. A painter will look at the canvas and think: 'This thing has this…' you're composing, just like a musician. In other words, you're arranging elements in a two-dimensional space for harmony, the same way a composer arranges notes on a timeline. Similarly, when they are building a social platform, they think: 'OK, we're gonna put the chat over here, we're gonna put the ads over here… let's make the ads a little bigger… actually no, then people will go away… let's make them a little smaller… et cetera.' And they constantly AB test it, they test it everywhere, and machines are learning as you are behaving.

These are compositions based on manipulation and efficiency, instead of inner beauty. That's what interests me
in these compositions: the fact that they were started by
humans, but the machines start listening to the users and
start making decisions or recommending things based on
human behavior. 'Hey, Zuckerberg, we tried everything.
Let's put the timeline over there' or whatever. It's interesting how those compositions were made to grab your
attention and be as sticky as possible.

MJ And there's a subtle, undercover critique to it too, where you're
covering up the boring, corporate elements of the web with art.
How do you feel about the question of self-promotion in general?
Is it a necessity?

RR Well, yeah, that's funny. Because I'm very uncomfortable
at openings and when talking to new people. So, it's my
survival strategy. But 'self-promotion' is already a value
judgement. If you make a new work and you're excited
about it, and you use the internet term 'sharing', it sounds
very positive. It's genuine, like when I first made a lenticular and I made a test, I was really excited that I found
this thing… that I could make a moving image without
a computer. I was super excited. I made a little movie on
YouTube, moving my camera around because I'm excited
and I want to show this to my friends. I want to show it to
my audience. Is that self-promotion or is that open studio?

MJ It's both.

RR Exactly, it's excitement. Then, what happened was, a col-
lector who owns a website of mine saw the new version
of it on Instagram, and it was a postcard. And he was like,
oh wow, I love it. I'll support you and pay for the first one
to be produced.

MJ Wow.

RR So, we made the first one and after that a whole series
happened. That's a perfect example of Instagram being
very powerful for me.

MJ Have there been other incidents of social-media-based commerce
for you?

RR Originally, I had the intent with my websites to monetize
them democratically instead of the art-collector model. So,
to have little ads and all this stuff. It just didn't work and
it was way easier to sell to collectors. And then I thought
oh, I can sell merchandise. I tried Tshirts and all this
stuff. It didn't work for me. There's a lot of people, more

'popular' artists, street artists, who I admire for their way of connecting to a broader audience. Ideologically, to me that's more noble than selling to bankers and arms dealers or whatever. Because you know that if you're selling your work for $30,000, that money... Often, it's tricky. But the funny thing is whatever comes out of this more popular model of lots of T-shirts and things for small price, the culture... the visuals, the art that comes out of it is not that interesting. That's the tricky thing. I believe in distribution. But distribution somehow dictates the content. And someone like Agnes Martin doesn't work in the T-shirt brand kind of way. But, of course, she would love it if her work were more broadly available. It just happens that it's in storage everywhere and gets seen once every ten years. But, that's the reality of art objects.

MJ   Most of them are unseen.

RR   And this is one thing that's strongly connected to my work, to the websites: the fact that you create a body of work over the course of your whole life, and the chances that those works are displayed are very small. There's no Mondrian museum, there's no Rembrandt museum, they don't have their own building. You can never see their whole body of work together. And these are pretty famous artists.

MJ   There's no Mondrian museum?

RR   No! There are a number of museums in the Netherlands that have five to ten of his works. They are never shown together. That happens maybe once every ten years, because insuring them is so expensive. Rembrandt doesn't have his own museum. He's in the Rijksmuseum with a few key works. Vermeer doesn't have his own museum. I don't know if there's a Goya museum.
For example, if you're into David Bowie, you can go and look at concert videos, you can listen to his albums, which I don't consider to be documentation—those are works on their own. You can really experience his whole process from the beginning of his career to the end. And that's pretty common for musicians. But, if you're really into Agnes Martin… I was lucky to have seen the retrospective. That happens once every twenty years.

MJ   This is where your internet practice comes in—the format is intrinsically archival. There's no distinction between the archive and the work itself. They're one and the same.

RR   That's why that question will always remain—the question of whether I'm known as a web artist or not. If you're going by the fact that my works are so easily available, that they're much more visible than paintings, then of course...

MJ   But on the other hand, as of recently, you're engaging in a nascent practice, something that I think is embryonic in your oeuvre. Something for which there's no word yet… kind of like 'physicalizing' the internet.

RR   Yes. With the websites, I am creating my own museum. At the end of my life you'll be able to experience everything.

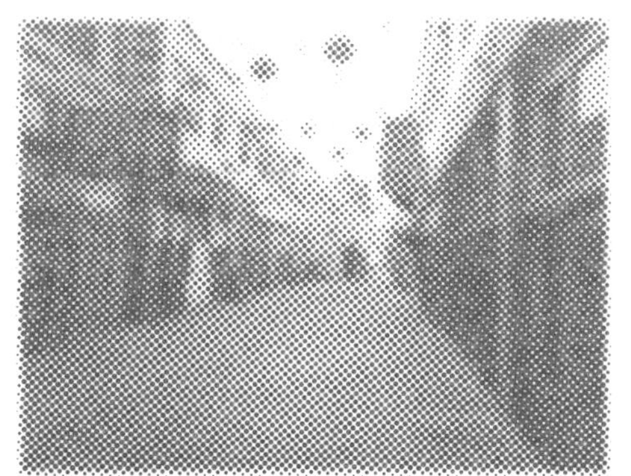
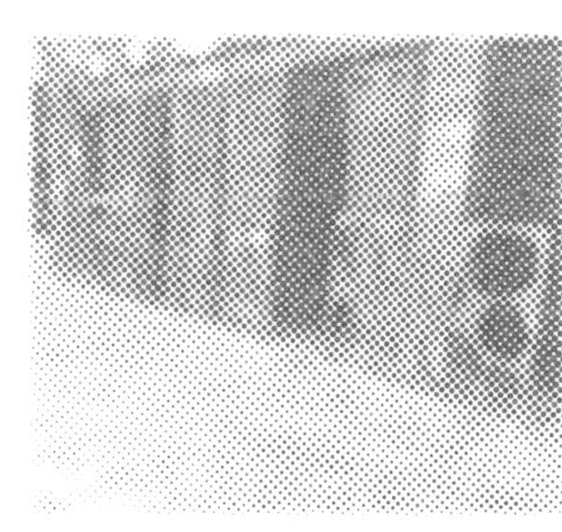
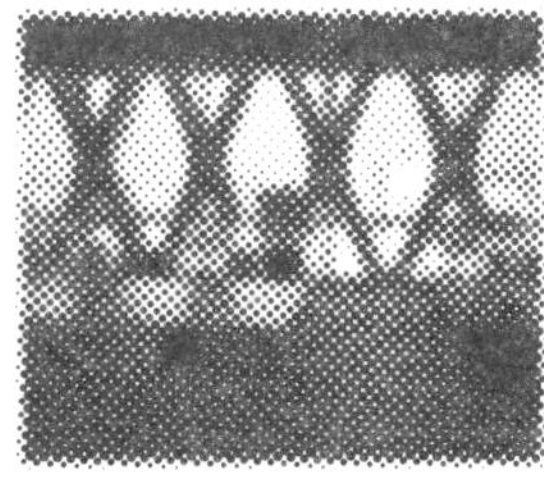
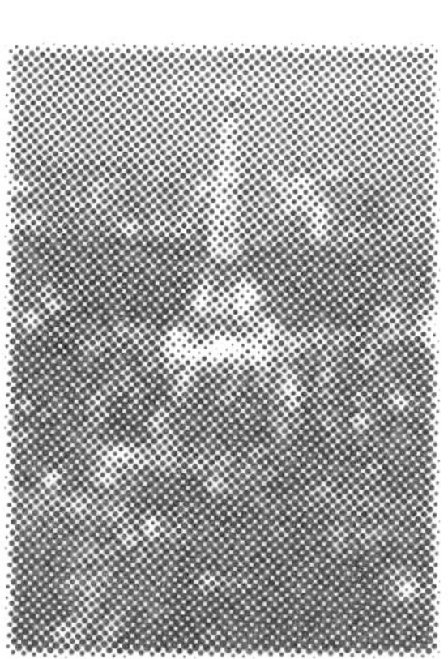
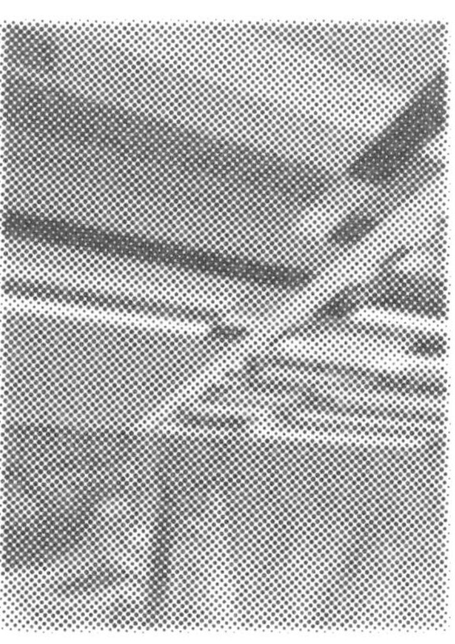
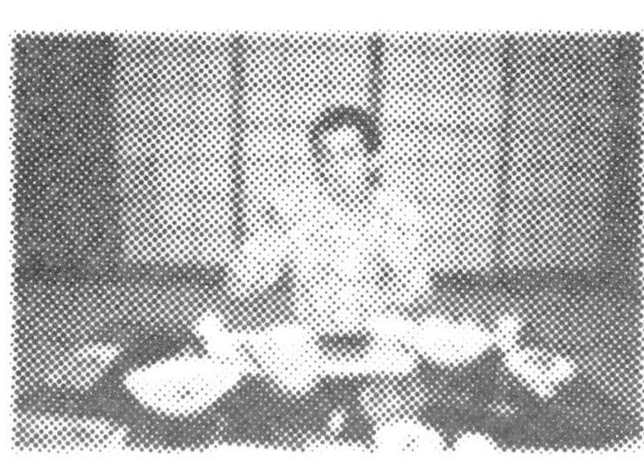
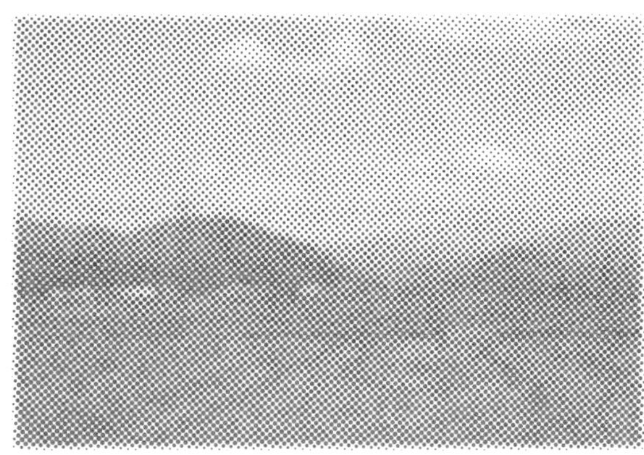
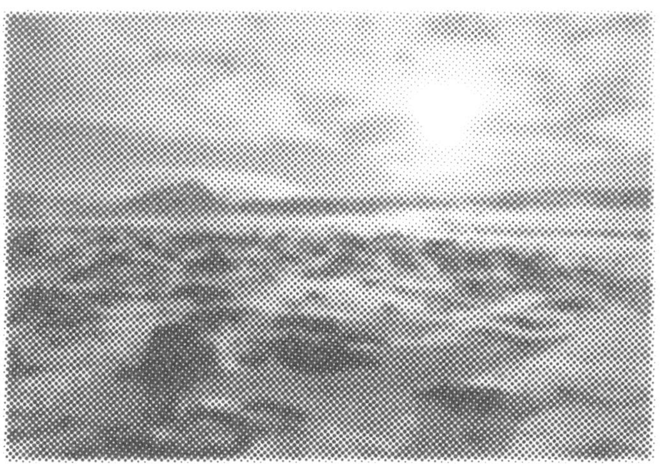
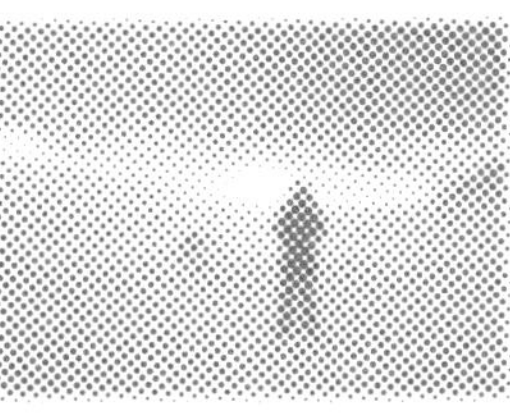
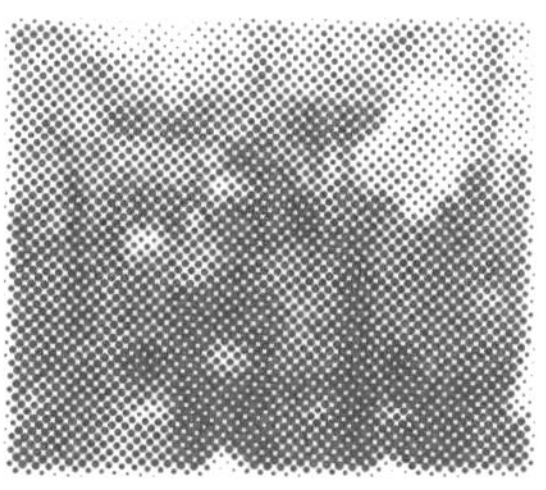

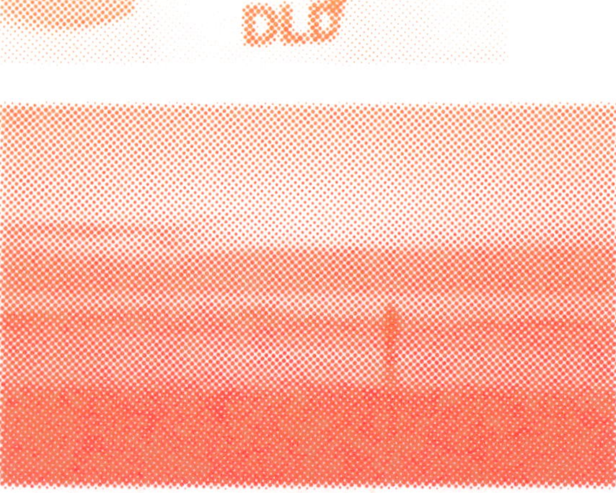
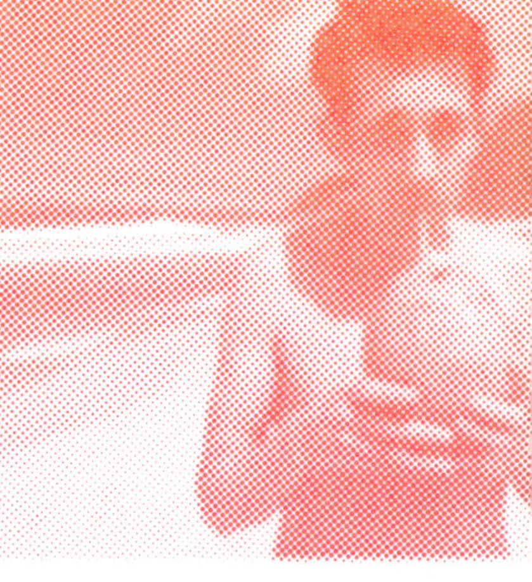
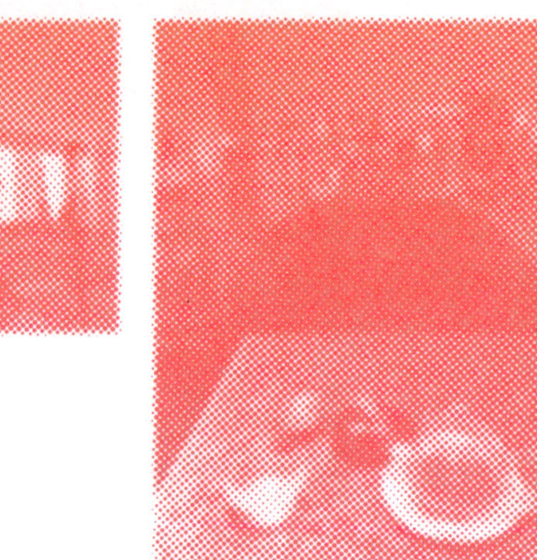

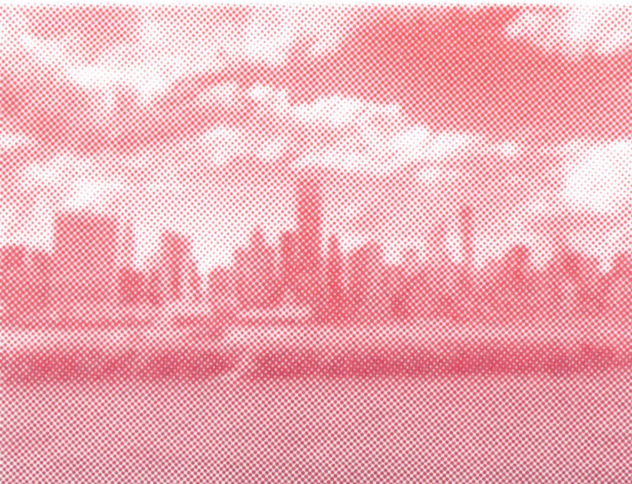

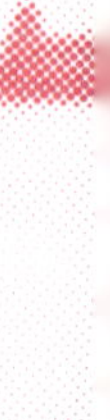

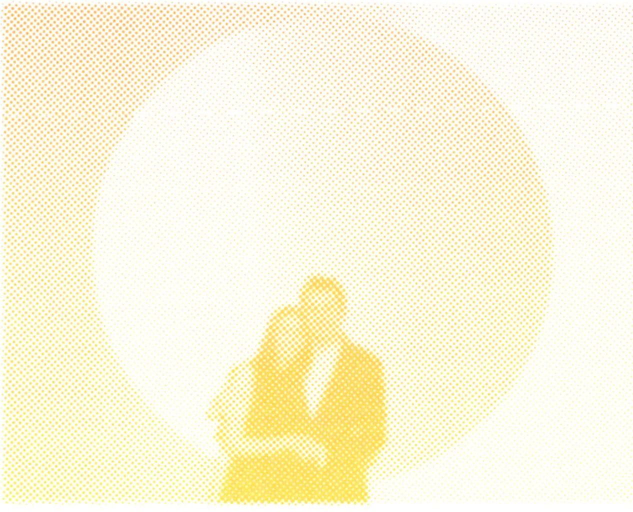
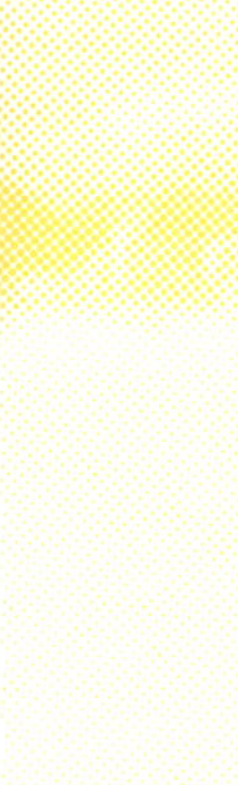

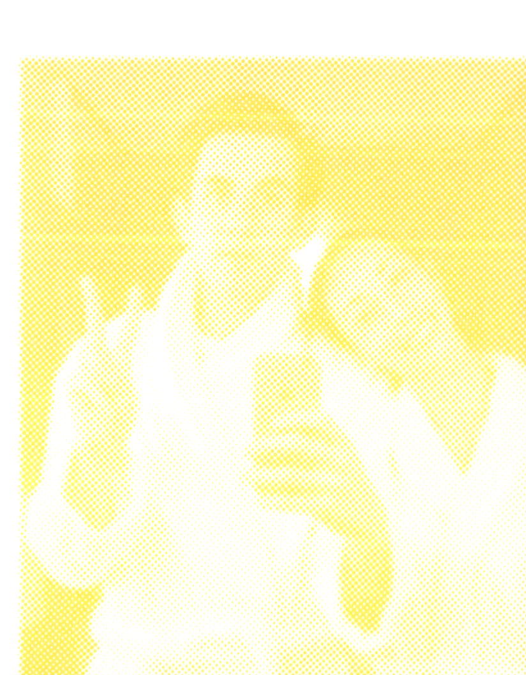

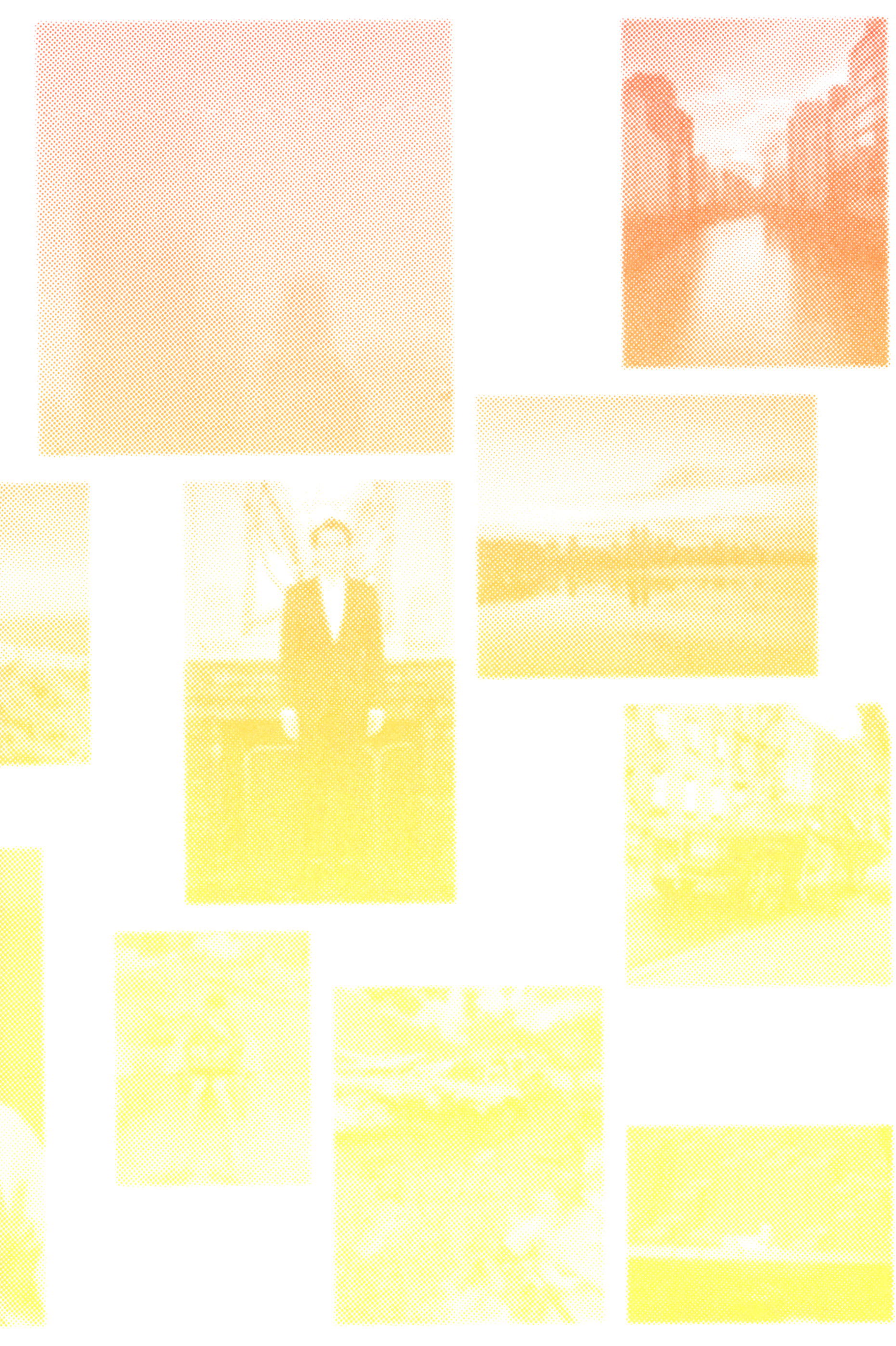

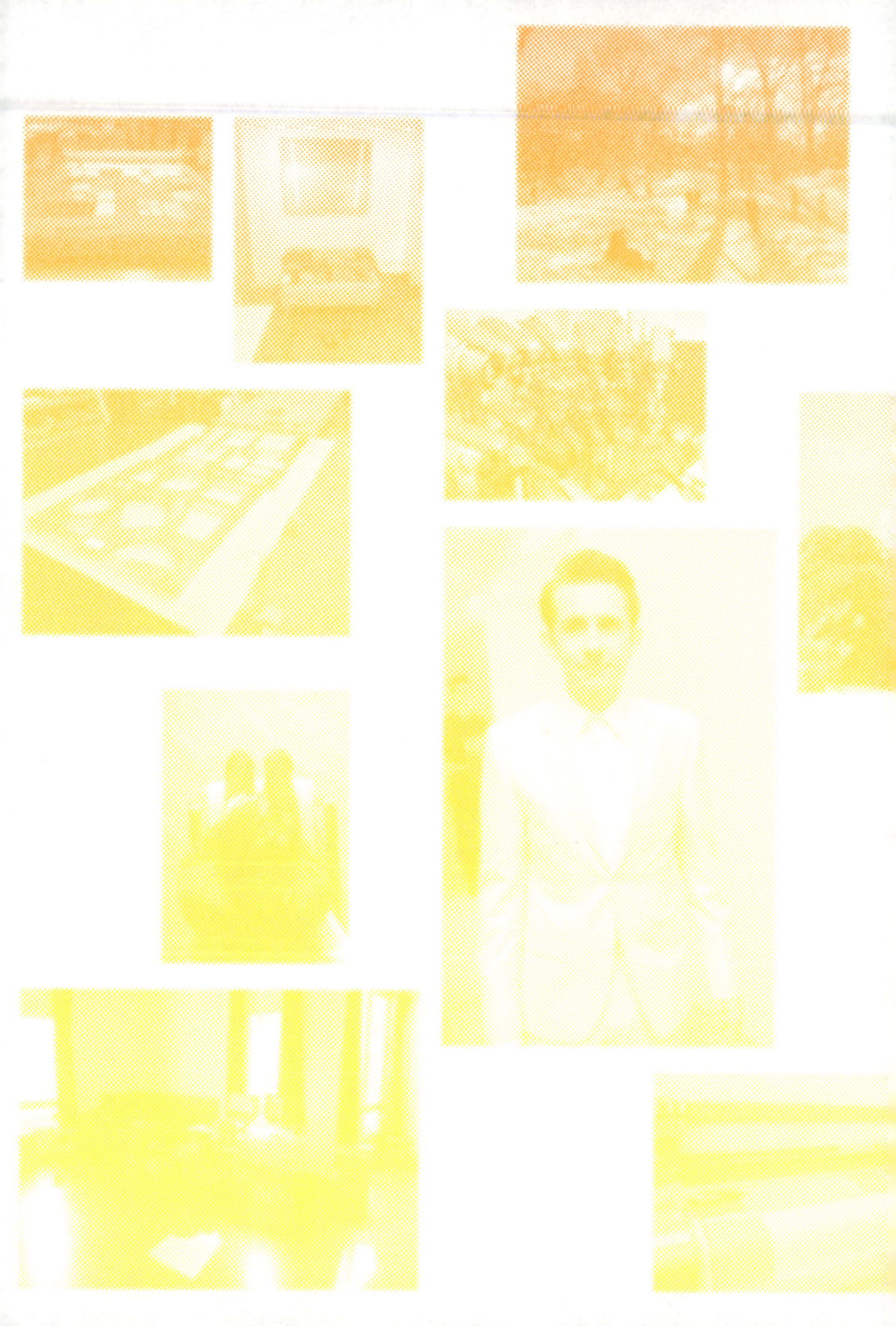

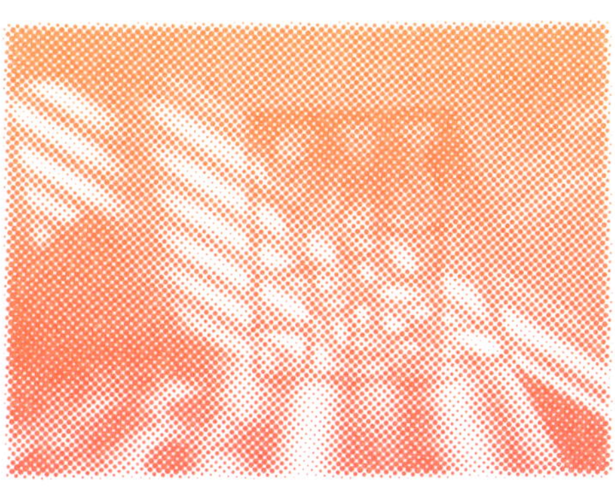

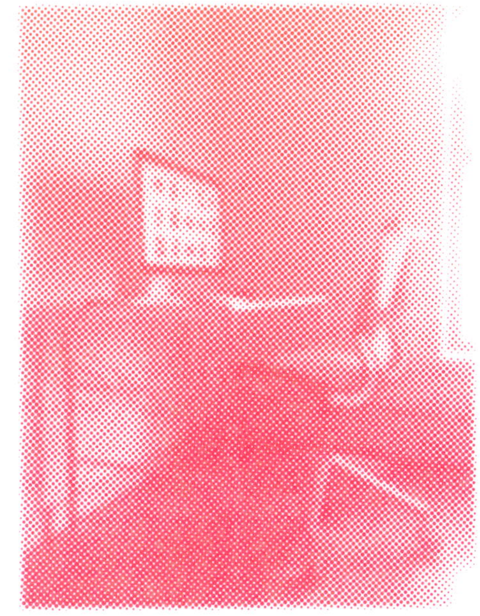
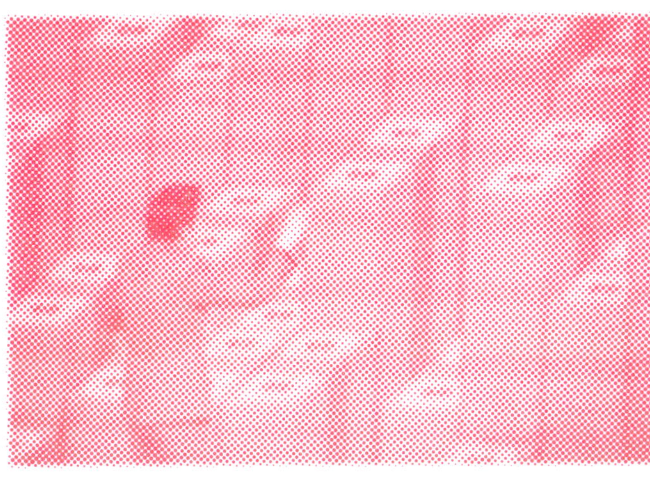
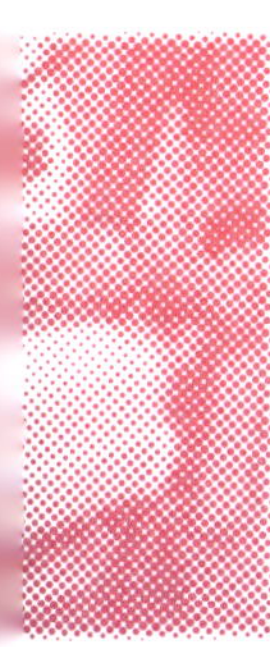

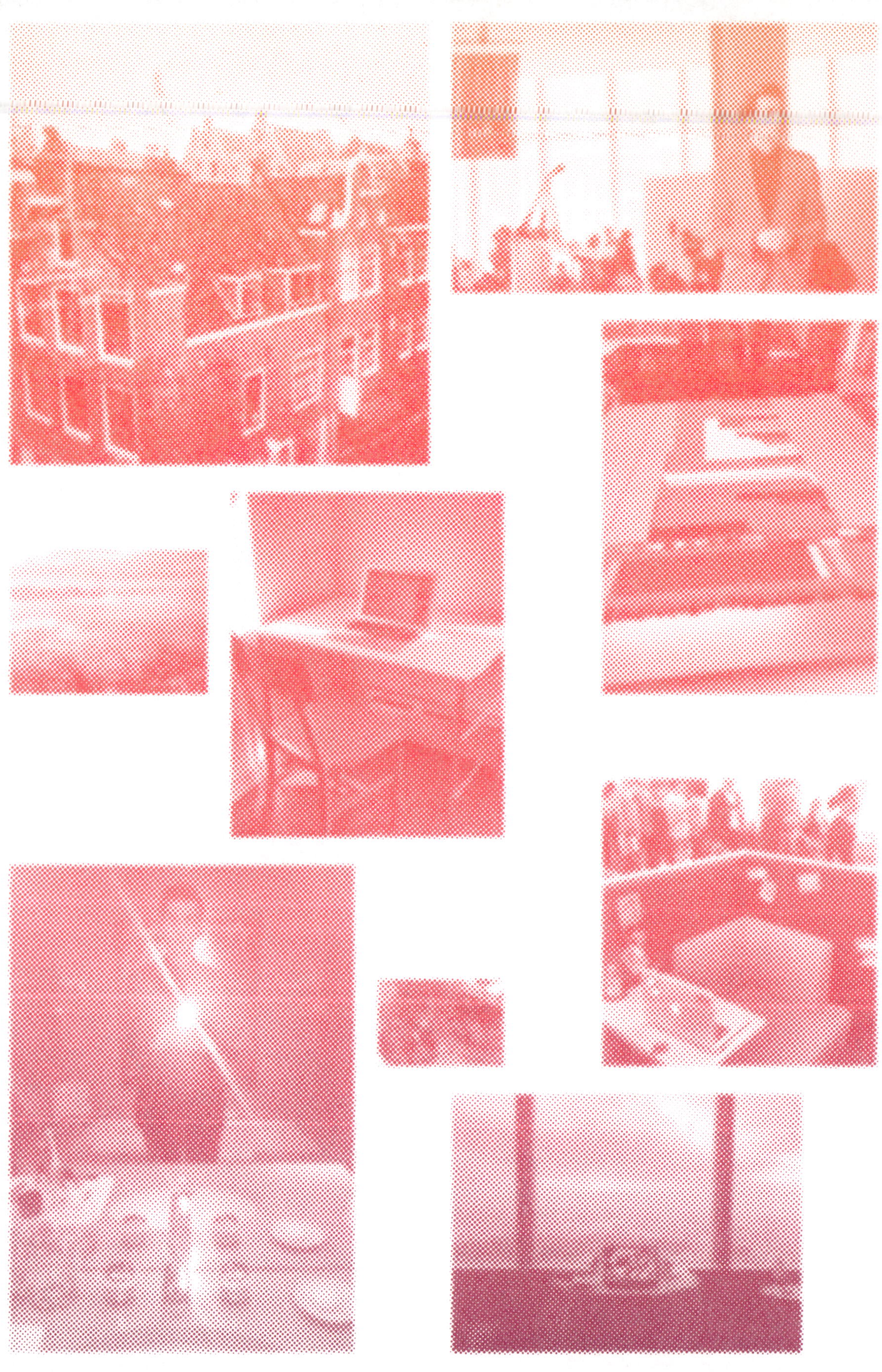

^{09–11} *Almost Calm .com*, 2012
Website, dimensions variable,
duration infinite
Collection MW
Courtesy Upstream Gallery,
Amsterdam

^{13–19} *Into Time .us*, 2012
Website, dimensions variable,
duration infinite
Collection Cobra to
Contemporary

^{21–23} *Never Nowhere .com*, 2014
Website, dimensions variable,
duration infinite
Collection MW
Courtesy Upstream Gallery,
Amsterdam

^{25–29} *Random Fear .com*, 2013
Website, dimensions variable,
duration infinite

^{31–37} *Falling Falling .com*, 2011
Website, dimensions variable,
duration infinite
Collection Hampus Lindwall

^{39–43} *Float Bounce .com*, 2016
Website, dimensions variable,
duration infinite
Takuma Collection
Courtesy Takuro Someya
Contemporary Art, Tokyo

^{45–47} *Hex Attack .com*, 2013
Website, dimensions variable,
duration infinite
Collection MW
Courtesy Upstream Gallery,
Amsterdam

^{49–51} *Pink Yellow Blue .com*, 2014
Website, dimensions variable,
duration infinite

^{53–57} *Yes No If .com*, 2014
Website, dimensions variable,
duration infinite

^{59–61} *Ooze Move .com*, 2014
Website, dimensions variable,
duration infinite

^{63–65} *Blank Windows .com*, 2016
Website, dimensions variable,
duration infinite
Collection Klinkhamer Family
Courtesy Upstream Gallery,
Amsterdam

^{67–69} *Everything Always
Everywhere .com*, 2013
Website, dimensions variable,
duration infinite
Collection Annette Doms

^{71–73} *If Yes No .com*, 2013
Website, dimensions variable,
duration infinite

^{75–77} *Here That .com*, 2015
Website, dimensions variable,
duration infinite

^{79–81} *Inner Doubts .com*, 2012
Website, dimensions variable,
duration infinite
The Ekard Collection
Courtesy Upstream Gallery,
Amsterdam

^{83–87} *Into Time .com*, 2010
Website, dimensions variable,
duration infinite
Collection Nur Abbas

^{89–91} *Looking At Something .com*,
2013
Website, dimensions variable,
duration infinite
Collection Motoi Sadakane
and Copilot Inc.
Courtesy Takuro Someya
Contemporary Art, Tokyo

^{93–95} *Neo Geo City .com*, 2014
Website, dimensions variable,
duration infinite
Collection Jeremy Bailey

^{97–101} *No If Yes .com*, 2014
Website, dimensions variable,
duration infinite
Collection Pontus Lindwall
Courtesy Upstream Gallery,
Amsterdam

^{103–105} *Silent Silence .com*, 2014
Website, dimensions variable,
duration infinite
Collection Museum of
The Image, Breda
Courtesy Upstream Gallery,
Amsterdam

^{107–109} *Slow Empty .com*, 2013
Website, dimensions variable,
duration infinite
Collection Servais Family
Courtesy Postmasters Gallery,
New York

^{111–113} *This Empty Room .com*, 2015
Website, dimensions variable,
duration infinite
Collection Museum
Voorlinden, Wassenaar
Courtesy Upstream Gallery,
Amsterdam

^{115–117} *Color Flip .com*, 2008
Website, dimensions variable,
duration infinite
Collection Sébastien De Ganay

^{139–142} *Deep Sadness .com*, 2014
Website, dimensions variable,
duration infinite
Installation view at the exhibition
'External Memory' at Upstream
Gallery, Amsterdam, 2014
Collection Anne & Many Ameri
Courtesy Upstream Gallery,
Amsterdam
Photo: Gert Jan van Rooij

^{144–145} *Into Time 14 01 17*, 2014
Lenticular print, 90 x 120 cm
Private collection
Courtesy Upstream Gallery,
Amsterdam
Photo: Gert Jan van Rooij

^{146–149} *Silent Silence .com*, 2014
Website, dimensions variable,
duration infinite
Installation view at the exhibition
'Insomnia' at Bonniers Konsthall,
Stockholm, 2016
Collection Museum of
The Image, Breda
Photo: Petter Cohen

^{150–151} *Into Time .us*, 2012
Website, dimensions variable,
duration infinite
Installation view at the exhibition
'Liquid Crystal' at Honor Fraser
Gallery, Los Angeles, 2015
Collection Cobra to Contemporary
Courtesy Honor Fraser Gallery,
Los Angeles
Photo: Joshua White/
JWPictures.com

¹⁵² *Soft Focus*, 2015
Installation (sand, projections,
stretched fabric, audio) at MU
art space, Eindhoven
33 x 33 x 4 m
Photo: Boudewijn Bollmann

¹⁵³ *On and On*, 2015
Installation (broken mirrors,
projection) at Carl Kostyál,
Stockholm
5 x 10 x 4 m
Photo: Carl Henrik Tillberg

¹⁵⁴⁻¹⁵⁵ *On and On*, 2015
Installation (broken mirrors,
projection) at Carl Kostyál,
Stockholm
5 x 10 x 4 m
Photo: Carl Henrik Tillberg

¹⁵⁶⁻¹⁵⁷ *Ooze Move .com*, 2014
Website, dimensions variable,
duration infinite
Installation view at Steve Turner,
Los Angeles
Photo: Don Lewis

^{158–161} *Much Better Than This .com*,
2015
Installation at Times Square,
New York, dimensions variable,
duration 3:00
Collection Almar Van Der Krogt
Photo: Michael Wells

^{162–163} *Yes For Sure .com*, 2010
Installation, projection, mirrors,
audio, at NIMK, Amsterdam
10 x 20 x 3 m
Photo: Sander Tiedema

¹⁶⁴ *On and On*, 2015
Installation (broken mirrors,
projection) at Carl Kostyál,
Stockholm
5 x 10 x 4 m
Photo: Carl Henrik Tillberg

^{165–167} *Soft Focus*, 2015
Installation (sand, projections,
stretched fabric, audio) at MU
art space, Eindhoven
33 x 33 x 4 m
Photo: Boudewijn Bollmann

^{186–187} *Shadow Object 16 07 05*, 2016
Powder coated steel,
105 x 145 x 5 cm
Courtesy Upstream Gallery,
Amsterdam
Photo: Gert Jan van Rooij

¹⁸⁹ *Shadow Object 16 07 06*, 2016
Powder coated steel,
105 x 145 x 5 cm
Courtesy Upstream Gallery,
Amsterdam
Photo: Gert Jan van Rooij

190 *Shadow Object 16 07 08*, 2016
Powder coated steel,
105 x 145 x 5 cm
Private collection
Courtesy Upstream Gallery,
Amsterdam
Photo: Gert Jan van Rooij

193–195 *Popular Screen Sizes
(60", 55", 46", 40", 32", 27",
24", 21", 19", 17", 15", 13",
11", 9.7", 7", 4", 3.5")*, 2011
Mirror, 1400 x 75 cm
Courtesy Nordin Gallery,
Stockholm

197–199 *Popular Screen Sizes
(60", 55", 46", 40", 32", 27",
24", 21", 17", 15", 13", 9.7",
7", 3.5")*, 2016
Mirror, 133 x 20 x 75 cm
Courtesy Upstream Gallery,
Amsterdam
Photo: Gert Jan van Rooij

218–221 *Into Time 13 08 23*, 2013
Lenticular print, 90 x 120 cm
Collection Mattias Berntsson
Courtesy Steve Turner,
Los Angeles
Photo: Don Lewis

223–225 *Into Time 14 09 16*, 2014
Lenticular print, 120 x 160 cm
Private collection
Courtesy Carl Kostyál,
Stockholm
Photo: Carl Henrik Tillberg

226 *Into Time 14 05 24*, 2014
Lenticular print, 90 x 120 cm
Private collection
Courtesy Steve Turner,
Los Angeles
Photo: Don Lewis

227–229 *Into Time 14 09 10*, 2014
Lenticular Print, 120 x 160 cm
Collection of Carl Kostyál
Courtesy Carl Kostyál,
Stockholm
Photo: Carl Henrik Tillberg

230–233 *Into Time 14 09 14*, 2014
Lenticular Print, 120 x 160 cm
Private collection
Courtesy Carl Kostyál, Stockholm
Photo: Carl Henrik Tillberg

234–235 *Into Time 16 04 01*, 2016
Lenticular print, 120 x 160 cm
Private collection
Courtesy Steve Turner,
Los Angeles
Photo: Don Lewis

237–238 *Into Time 14 05 08*, 2014
Lenticular print, 90 x 120 cm
Private collection
Courtesy Upstream Gallery,
Amsterdam
Photo: Gert Jan van Rooij

241–243 *Into Time 15 06 02*, 2015
Lenticular print, 120 x 160 cm
Collection Cobra to Contemporary
Courtesy Upstream Gallery,
Amsterdam
Photo: Gert Jan van Rooij

245–247 *Into Time 14 06 01*, 2014
Lenticular print, 90 x 120 cm
Courtesy Steve Turner,
Los Angeles
Photo: Don Lewis

248–249 Details

251–253 *Into Time 14 06 03*, 2014
Lenticular print, 90 x 120 cm
Private collection
Courtesy Steve Turner,
Los Angeles
Photo: Don Lewis

255–256 *Into Time 14 07 01*, 2014
Lenticular print, 120 x 160 cm
Private collection
Courtesy Steve Turner,
Los Angeles
Photo: Don Lewis

258–259 Details

260–261 *Into Time 14 07 02*, 2014
Lenticular print, 90 x 120 cm
Private collection
Courtesy Steve Turner,
Los Angeles
Photo: Don Lewis

262–263 *Everything Always
Everywhere*, 2014
Installation view at Steve
Turner, Los Angeles, 2014
Photo: Don Lewis

265 *Abstract Browsing 16 03 08
(Reddit)*, 2016
Jacquard weaving, 200 x 144 cm
Collection Stedelijk Museum
Amsterdam
Courtesy Upstream Gallery,
Amsterdam
Photo: Gert Jan van Rooij

266–267 *Abstract Browsing 15 05 05
(Twitter)*, 2015
Jacquard weaving, 266 x 144 cm
Private collection
Courtesy Steve Turner,
Los Angeles
Photo: Don Lewis

268–269 *Abstract Browsing 15 05 10
(IMDb)*, 2015
Jacquard weaving, 266 x 144 cm
Private collection
Courtesy Steve Turner,
Los Angeles
Photo: Don Lewis

270–271 *Abstract Browsing 16 03 01
(Wikipedia)*, 2016
Jacquard weaving, 144 x 86 cm
Collection Jemma Land &
Frank van der Gelt
Courtesy Upstream Gallery,
Amsterdam
Photo: Gert Jan van Rooij

272–273 *Abstract Browsing 16 03 09
Triptych (Waze)*, 2016
Jacquard weaving, 460 x 175 cm
Collection Cobra to Contemporary
Courtesy Upstream Gallery,
Amsterdam
Photo: Gert Jan van Rooij

274–275 *Abstract Browsing 16 10 06
(Google Spreadsheet)*, 2016
Jacquard weaving, 254 x 144 cm
Private collection
Courtesy Upstream Gallery,
Amsterdam
Photo: Gert Jan van Rooij

276–277 *Abstract Browsing 16 10 09
(Guggenheim)*, 2016
Jacquard weaving, 144 x 86 cm
Collection Klinkhamer Family
Courtesy Upstream Gallery,
Amsterdam
Photo: Gert Jan van Rooij

279 Detail

280–281 *Abstract Browsing 16 10 10
(Facebook Photos)*, 2016
Jacquard weaving, 144 x 86 cm
Collection TextielMuseum, Tilburg
Courtesy Upstream Gallery,
Amsterdam
Photo: Gert Jan van Rooij

282–283 *Abstract Browsing 16 03 05
(Google)*, 2016
Jacquard weaving, 144 x 86 cm
Collection Rob Verjans &
Rozemarijn Bloemendal
Courtesy Upstream Gallery,
Amsterdam
Photo: Gert Jan van Rooij

284 Detail

286–287 *Abstract Browsing 15 05 01
(Google Drive)*, 2015
Jacquard weaving, 266 x 144 cm
Private Collection
Courtesy Steve Turner, Los Angeles
Photo: Don Lewis

288–289 *Abstract Browsing 15 05 11
(Pinterest)*, 2015
Jacquard weaving, 266 x 144 cm
Private collection
Courtesy Steve Turner, Los Angeles
Photo: Don Lewis

290–291 *Abstract Browsing 16 03 06
(Google Docs)*, 2016
Jacquard weaving, 144 x 86 cm
Collection Akzo Nobel Art
Foundation
Courtesy Upstream Gallery,
Amsterdam
Photo: Gert Jan van Rooij

292 *Abstract Browsing 16 03 07 (Gmail)*,
2016
Jacquard weaving, 144 x 200 cm
Collection Akzo Nobel Art
Foundation
Courtesy Upstream Gallery,
Amsterdam
Photo: Gert Jan van Rooij

293 *Abstract Browsing 16 10 04
(Feedly)*, 2016
Jacquard weaving, 144 x 200 cm
Private collection
Courtesy Upstream Gallery,
Amsterdam
Photo: Gert Jan van Rooij

294–295 *Abstract Browsing*
Installation view at Steve Turner,
Los Angeles
Photo: Don Lewis

SOLO EXHIBITIONS

2016
'Complex Computational
Composition's', Upstream
Gallery, Amsterdam
'Abstract Browsing', Steve
Turner, Los Angeles
'Somewhere', Takuro Someya
Contemporary Art, Tokyo

2015
'Soft Focus', MU, Eindhoven (NL)
'Haiku', Postmasters, New York
'Times Square Midnight
Moment', New York
'On And On, Carl Kostyál',
Isbrytaren, Stockholm

2014
'Almost Nothing, Hardly
Anything', Steve Turner,
Los Angeles
'External Memory', Upstream
Gallery, Amsterdam
'Seoul Art Square', Seoul, Korea
'Looking at Something:
Selected Work by Rafaël
Rozendaal', Telfair Museum,
Savannah (US)

2013
'Everything You See Is
In The Past', Postmasters
Gallery, New York
'Seoul Art Square', Seoul

2012
'Everything Always
Everywhere', Steve Turner
Contemporary, Los Angeles
'Everything Dies', curated by
Vlado Velkov, Kunstverein
Arnsberg (DE)
'In and Out', Tetem,
Enschede (NL)

2011
'New Information', Nordin
Gallery, Stockholm
'In Motion', curated by
Jiminie Ha, With Projects
Space, New York
'The Shift', curated by
Tim Voss, W139, Amsterdam
'To Walk The Night', Gloria
Maria Gallery, Milan

2010
'Thank You Very Much',
Future Gallery, Berlin
'Perfect Vacuum', curated by
Johanna Bergmark, Galeri
Pictura, Lund (SE)
'Yes For Sure', curated by
Petra Heck, NIMk, Amsterdam
'Broken Self', Spencer
Brownstone Gallery, New York
'Volta Art Fair', New York
'I'm good', TSCA, Tokyo

2007
'Flaming Log', Carmelitas
Gallery, Barcelona
'Piece by Piece', curated by
Martí Peran, Galería dels
Angels, Barcelona

2006
'SMCS op 11', curated by Jelle
Bouwhuis, Amsterdam

2005
'Neen Season', Sketch, London

2004
'It Will Never be the Same',
Quarantine, Amsterdam
'New Rafael', M+R Gallery,
London

2002
'White Trash', Electronic
Orphanage, Los Angeles

GROUP EXHIBITIONS

2017
'Digital Art from the
Hugo Brown Family Collection',
Kunsthal, Rotterdam
'Sleepmode: The Art of the
Screensaver', Het Nieuwe
Instituut, Rotterdam

2016
'Insomnia', Bonniers Konsthall,
Stockholm
Kenpoku Festival, Ibaraki (JP)
'BYOB', Stedelijk Museum,
Amsterdam (curator)
'DOings&kNOTs', Tallinn
Art Hall, Estonia
'Dialogue with Something
Invisible', Artium, Fukuoka (JP)
'New Gameplay', Nam June
Paik Art Center, Seoul
Digital Abstraction', HeK, Basel
'Unknown Landscape',
Upstream Gallery, Amsterdam

2015
STRP Biënnniale, Eindhoven (NL)
'L'Art et le numérique en
résonance', Maison Populaire,
Montreuil (FR)
'Mankind/Machinekind',
Krinzinger Projekte, Vienna

2014
'Born Digital', Museum of
the Image, Breda
'The Moving Museum', Istanbul
'Selected Websites', Hammer
Museum, Los Angeles
'Liquid Crystal', curated by
Michael Connor, Honor Fraser
Gallery, Los Angeles
'Illumination Graphics',
G8 Gallery, Tokyo

2013
'Paddles On!', curated by
Lindsay Howard, Phillips,
New York
'BYOB Mobile', Printed Matter,
New York
'Being in the Wired World',
Kawasaki City Museum (JP)
'Cold Void', KK Outlet,
Los Angeles
'6 websites', arranged by
Mark Brown, Salon 94
Bowery, New York
'Book Machine', Centre
Pompidou, Paris
NODE Festival, Kunstverein
Frankfurt
'#FutureMyth', 319 Scholes,
New York
'Brand Innovations',
Carroll/Fletcher, London
'Notes on a New Nature',
Arti et Amicitiae, Amsterdam

2012
'Mythology Online', Science Museum,
Moscow
'Without Hesitation', Tokyo
'Bright Lights After
Armageddon', curated by Mark
Brown, New York
AND Festival, curated by Ruth
McCullough (UK)
'Seoul Square', curated by
Lauren Cornell and the
New Museum, Seoul
'BYOB MOCA LA', curated by
Mike D, MOCA Geffen,
Los Angeles
'Richteriana', Postmasters
Gallery, New York
'Dotcom', Centre d'Art
Bastille, Grenoble (FR)
'Nova', Museu da Imagem
e do Som de São Paulo
DLD Conference, curated by
Johannes Fricke & Hans Ulrich
Obrist, Munich

2011
'BYOB: Games', curated by
Paul Slocum, Postmasters
Gallery, New York
'Extimacy', curated by Pier
Giorgio De Pinto, CACT,
Lugano (CH)
'BYOB Amsterdam', W139
'BYOB Tokyo', curated by
Yosuke Kurita, Tokyo
'BYOB Venezia', Venice
Biennale, Venice (curator)
File Festival, Rio de Janeiro
'Rhizome at the Armory',
curated by Lauren Cornell,
New York
'BYOB Paris', curated by
Nicolas Maigret, Paris
'BYOB London', curated by
Kernel, London
Rojo Nova Festival, curated by
David Quiles Guilló,
Rio de Janeiro
DLD Conference, curated by
Johannes Fricke, Munich

2010
'Speedshow/PeepShow', curated
by Hitomi Hasegawa, Hong Kong
'BYOB NYC', Spencer Brownstone
Gallery, New York (curator)
'Bal Jaune Ricard', curated by
Claire Staebler, Paris
'BYOB Athens', curated by
Angelo Plessas, Kunsthalle
Athena, Athens
'Speed Show', curated by
Aram Bartholl, Amsterdam
'Happy is a Place', curated by Violeta
Solis Horcasitas,
Mexico City
Taipei Art Fair with TSCA, Taiwan
'BYOB', curated by Anne
de Vries, Berlin
'Binary Code View',
The Agency Gallery, London
Kunsthalle Athena, curated by
Marina Fokidis, Athens
'Multiplex', curated by
vvork, Munich
'Preferiria (si) Hacerlo', Bogota
'Texture Maps', curated by
Eelco van der Lingen, Nest,
The Hague
Circa Art Fair, Preteen Gallery,
Puerto Rico
'Better Brain: Projected
Manifestations of Futurity',
Future Gallery, Berlin

'Don't Worry, Be Happy!',
curated by Gerben Willers,
Mama, Rotterdam

2009
The Last Session, curated by
Jan van Woensel, Amsterdam
*AFK Sculpture Park (away
from keyboard)*, curated by
aids-3D, Berlin
Afficha Festival, curated by
Roman Mazurenko, Moscow
*Biennale di Venezia, Padiglione
Internet,* curated by Miltos
Manetas and Jan Aman, Venice
The New Easy', curated by
Lars Eijssen, Art News, Berlin
Are You Sure You Are You?',
Spencer Brownstone Gallery,
New York
101 Art Fair Project Room',
curated by Kosuke Fujitaka,
Tokyo
Straylight Cavern', Cell
Project Space, London
The Real Thing', MU art
foundation, curated by
vvork, Eindhoven (NL)

2008
Love Delirium', Kunstraum
Niederoesterreich, Vienna
FILE', São Paulo
Rhizome Commissions',
New Museum, New York
Point of no Return', curated
by Caroline Hancock, Rubicon
Gallery, Dublin
The Long Cigarette', 11,
Amsterdam
Webcra.sh', curated by
Jodi, Pictura, Dordrecht (NL)

2007
Dazed & Confused vs. Andy Warhol',
curated by Jerome
Sans, Baltic Mill (GB)
Existential Computing',
Hayward Gallery, London
Much Better Than This',
Horsecross, Perth (AU)

2006
Neen Evening', Amsterdam
Unlike the Rest', Liquid
Room, Tokyo
Neen Demo', curated by
Angelo Plessas, Benaki
Museum, Athens
RAI Art Fair, GMVZ,
Amsterdam
Superneen', Galleria Pack, Milan
ARCO with Galeria Dels
Angels, Madrid
Inside Out', Fonds bkvb, Amsterdam

2005
Loop of Neen', Loop Fair,
Barcelona
Bienal de Valencia, curated
by Franck Gautherot and
Seung-duk Kim, Valencia
Sonar Festival, Barcelona
It Will Never be the Same',
curated by Claude Closky,
le Magasin, Grenoble (FR)

2004
Neen Porn', Galeria dels
Angels, Barcelona
New Masters of Universe',
curated by Wonil Rhee, Moca
Taipei, Taiwan

NeenToday', MU art foundation,
Eindhoven (NL) (curator)
I am Very Very Sorry', gallery
mvz, Amsterdam

2002
Afterneen', casco, Utrecht (NL)
Neen World', Villette
Numérique, Paris
WhitneyBiennial.com,
New York

2001
Biennale.net, Deitch Projects,
New York
Tirana Biennial, Tirana

Rafaël Rozendaal
Rafaël Rozendaal is a Dutch-Brazilian visual
artist who 'uses the internet as his canvas.'
His websites attract an audience of 60 million
unique visits per year. He is best known for
these websites, but also creates drawings,
installations, tapestries, haiku, lectures on
a variety of subjects, and collaborates on a
podcast. He is one of the first visual artists
to sell websites as art objects. Rozendaal
lives and works in New York.
www.newrafael.com

Marvin Jordan
Marvin Jordan is an editorial assistant and
researcher at *DIS Magazine* and a co-founder
of Black Market. His editorial interests range
from the political economy of big data to
the culture of technological unemployment.
Black Market is a program highlighting the
practices of mostly under-recognized, young
artists of color that focuses on deconstructing
and reinventing current themes central to hip
hop—such as finance, determination, and cele-
bration—in the context of contemporary art.

Kodama Kanazawa
Kodama Kanazawa (金澤 韻) is a Japanese in-
dependent curator currently based in Shanghai,
China. Her interest lies in re-reading contemporary art from Japan and around the world using
a perspective that connects Asian modernization
history to the current period of globalization.
www.kodama.snack.ws

Christiane Paul
Christiane Paul is Associate Professor at
the School of Media Studies, New School
and Adjunct Curator of New Media art at
the Whitney Museum of American Art in
New York. She also publishes frequently on
new-media art and the combination of art and
technology. Her recent publications include:
*Context Providers—Conditions of Meaning
in Media Arts* (Intellect, 2011), co-edited with
Margot Lovejoy and Victoria Vesna; *New
Media in the White Cube and Beyond* (UC
Press, 2008); and *Digital Art* (Thames and
Hudson, 2003; 2008; 2015)

Margriet Schavemaker
Margriet Schavemaker studied Art History and
Philosophy at the University of Amsterdam.
She is currently Manager Education, Interpre-
tation and Publications at the Stedelijk Museum
Amsterdam. Schavemaker has published
articles on art and theory and has organized
discursive events at various locations.

Authors: Marvin Jordan, Kodama Kanazawa,
Christiane Paul, Margriet Schavemaker
Graphic design: Studio Remco van Bladel
(Remco van Bladel, Beau Bertens, Quentin Creuzet)
Website programming: Reinier Feijen
Translation: Akebono Translation Service
Copy-editing: Els Brinkman, Leo Reijnen
Editorial advice: Astrid Vorstermans,
Sarah van Binsbergen
Publisher: Pia Pol, Valiz, Amsterdam

Paper inside: Maxi Script, 80 gr/m2,
Munken Polar, 120 gr/m2 and
Munken Polar Rough, 90 gr/m2
Paper cover: Munken Polar, 300 gr/m2
Typefaces: Times New Roman, Akzidenz
Grotesk Medium, Ryumin Pro M–KL
Lithography: Die Keure, Brugge
Printing: Die Keure, Brugge

This publication *Rafaël Rozendaal, Everything,
Always, Everywhere* was made possible through
the generous support of
Postmasters Gallery, New York
Steve Turner, Los Angeles
Takuro Someya Contemporary Art, Tokyo
Upstream Gallery, Amsterdam
Mondriaan Fund, Amsterdam
Stichting Jaap Harten Fonds, Den Haag

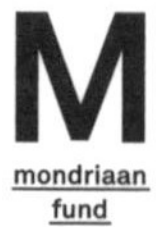

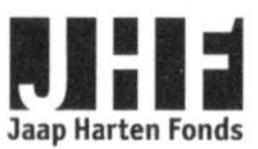

© 2017 Rafaël Rozendaal; Valiz, book and
cultural projects, Amsterdam; authors; artists
All rights reserved. No part of this publication
may be reproduced, stored in a retrieval
system, or transmitted in any form or by any
means, electronic, mechanical, photocopying,
recording or otherwise, without the prior written
permission of the publisher.

The publisher has made every effort to secure
permission to reproduce the listed material,
illustrations and photographs. We apologize
for any inadvertent errors or omissions.
Parties who nevertheless believe they can
claim specific legal rights are invited to contact
the publisher.

Distribution:
BE/NL/LU: Coen Sligting,
www.coensligtingbookimport.nl;
Centraal Boekhuis,
www.centraal.boekhuis.nl
GB/IE: Anagram Books,
www.anagrambooks.com
Europe/Asia: Idea Books,
www.ideabooks.nl
Australia: Perimeter,
www.perimeterdistribution.com
USA /Canada/Latin America: D.A.P.,
www.artbook.com
Individual orders:
www.valiz.nl; info@valiz.nl

ISBN 978 94 92095 30 5
Printed and bound in the EU

Here Hear is an iPhone app that accompanies
this book. When you point your camera at
these pages, the app looks for contrast and
rhythm in the images. A busy image will result
in a busy melody, an empty page produces
calm sounds. The app was developed by
Rafaël Rozendaal and Tibor Udvari.

To download Here Hear, please visit
www.newrafael.com/herehear.